Radosław Palonka

# Defensive Architecture and the Depopulation of the Mesa Verde Region, Utah-Colorado in the Thirteenth Century A.D.

**Prace Archeologiczne z. 64**
**Monografie**

Prace Archeologiczne No. 64
Monographs

Radosław Palonka

# Defensive Architecture and the Depopulation of the Mesa Verde Region, Utah-Colorado in the Thirteenth Century A.D.

Jagiellonian University Press

The publication of this volume was supported by the Department of History and the Institute of Archaeology of the Jagiellonian University

REVIEWER

*Prof. dr hab. Janusz K. Kozłowski*

COVER DESIGN

*Agnieszka Dobosz*

Photograph on the cover: Sunny Alcove site (photograph by the author)

TECHNICAL EDITOR

*Jadwiga Makowiec*

PROOFREADERS

*Jerzy Hrycyk*
*Małgorzata Szul*

TYPESETTING

*Wojciech Wojewoda*


First edition, Cracow 2011



ISBN 978-83-233-3184-1

ISSN 0083-4300

WYDAWNICTWO UNIWERSYTETU JAGIELLOŃSKIEGO

www.wuj.pl

Jagiellonian University Press
Editorial Offices: ul. Michałowskiego 9/2, 31-126 Kraków
Phone +48 12 631 18 81, Phone/Fax +48 12 631 18 83
Distribution: tel. +48 12 631 01 97, Phone/Fax +48 12 631 01 98
Cell Phone +48 506 006 674, e-mail: sprzedaz@wuj.pl
Bank: PEKAO SA, IBAN PL 80 1240 4722 1111 0000 4856 3325

*For my Family*

# CONTENTS

# LIST OF FIGURES

# ACKNOWLEDGMENTS

I would like to express my gratitude to all those who made it possible to prepare this book which is based on my doctoral dissertation, *Defensive Architecture and the Depopulation of the Mesa Verde Region, Utah-Colorado, USA in the Thirteenth Century A.D.* I am very thankful to my supervisor and mentor, Professor Janusz Krzysztof Kozłowski from the Jagiellonian University for his guidance, comments, and help both before and during the preparation of the dissertation. I am extremely grateful to Professor William D. Lipe, Washington State University for his constructive comments, solid advice, and instructive criticism as well as for the academic and moral support he has provided throughout the gathering of data and the writing of the dissertation and the book. I would also like to express my gratitude to Dr. Mark D. Varien, Crow Canyon Archaeological Center, Colorado, for insightful comments and remarks and his invaluable help and assistance in obtaining necessary data and accessing unpublished manuscripts. I am also very thankful to Prof. Aleksander Posern-Zieliński from Adam Mickiewicz University for his help, comments and remarks during the preparation of this dissertation, especially in terms of the anthropological issues.

My research in the United States was made possible by the financial support of numerous institutions to which I am very thankful, especially the Fulbright Commission, the Kosciuszko Foundation, the Sasakawa Young Leaders Fellowship Fund (the Tokyo Foundation), and the Polish-American Ethnological Society in Memory of Bronislaw Malinowski. I also thank the former Dean of the History Faculty, Professor Piotr Kaczanowski; the current Dean of the History Faculty, Professor Andrzej Banach, as well as the former Director of the Institute of Archaeology of the Jagiellonian University, Professor Jan Chochorowski. Without the support and financial aid of these individuals my participation in archaeological research in the United States would not have been possible.

I would like to express my gratitude to many people at the Crow Canyon Archaeological Center (CCAC), Colorado who I met during several stays there. I am very thankful for the opportunity to participate in their excavations and conduct research there as well as to become familiar with methods of conducting archaeological research with public involvement and in collaboration with American Indians. I would like to express my gratitude to Kristin A. Kuckelman, director of the Goodman Point Archaeological Project, for her factual supervision, assistance, and introduction to the archaeology of the Mesa Verde region and for the many conversations we had on archaeology. Thanks also to Scott Ortman for his suggestions and his invaluable help in obtaining electronic site data and survey reports. I would like to thank Grant Coffey, Erin Baxter, and Steve Copeland – my colleagues during excavations – for the great time we spent at Goodman Point Pueblo and at the Crow Canyon campus. I would also like to thank the CCAC staff and friends for their help, support, interest, and insight. Thanks Margie, Susan, Jamie,

Jonathan, Fumi, Karen, Paul, Lew, Becky, Mary, and so many more. Special thanks also to Jim Martin and the kitchen staff for feeding me during my several visits to Crow Canyon.

I am extremely thankful to Professor William I. Woods, University of Kansas (formerly of Southern Illinois University, Edwardsville), for his generous help during my two first visits to the United States. Professor Woods introduced me to the fieldwork of North American archaeology during field schools at Cahokia Mounds in Illinois.

I am very thankful to Dr. Aleksandra Ziółkowska-Boehm for her encouragement, friendship, and help during the preparation of the dissertation and stay in the United States.

For their factual and gratuitous help, I owe inexpressible gratitude to numerous people at various American institutions where I conducted research for the dissertation. I am very thankful to professors Ezra Zubrow and Doug Perrelli, University of Buffalo, Professor Timothy Kohler and Dr. Brian Kemp, Washington State University, Professor Michelle Hegmon, Arizona State University, and professors Barbara Mills, Daniela Triadan, and Steven Kuhn, University of Arizona. I am particularly grateful to Professor Paul R. Fish, University of Arizona, for his invaluable help and support while I spent two great springs finishing the dissertation. I am very grateful to Professor Jeffrey Dean, Laboratory of Tree-Ring Research, University of Arizona, for his suggestions concerning the defensive aspects of settlements in the Kayenta and Mesa Verde regions and for his generosity in allowing me to use the Laboratory's electronic First Choice Data Files of tree-ring dates for the Mesa Verde region.

I wish to also thank Vince Lee for his guidance in the Sand Canyon area and for sharing his opinions on the archaeology of the Mesa Verde region. Individual thanks to Linda Farnsworth, Anasazi Heritage Center, Dolores, Colorado, for her invaluable help in obtaining the necessary survey reports for sites located in the Lower Sand Canyon area. I would also like to thank to Julie Bell, National Park Service, for help in obtaining site plans of some sites analyzed in the book.

During my several visits to the United States I was fortunate to stay with friends who were very helpful and interested and supported me in my dissertation research. I am especially thankful to Chris and Teresa Włodyka and Susan and Chuck Giannone of Cortez, Colorado, and to Wendy Weston, Navajo and her family and Frank and Maria Kobylarczyk of Phoenix, Arizona.

I was also fortunate to meet and engage in long conversations with American Indians of various tribes and nations who provided me with the opportunity to learn Native points of view on different aspects of archaeology and anthropology and allowed me to spend time on different Indian reservations. I am especially grateful to Becky Hammond (Ute), Wendy Weston (Navajo), and Kevin Shendo from Jemez (Walatowa) Pueblo.

I owe inexpressible gratitude again to Kristin A. Kuckelman for her suggestions concerning this book and for her invaluable help in preparing this manuscript in English. I wish to also thank Colleen Sunderland for her help in preparing the English version of this paper.

Last, but not least, I would like to express my deepest gratitude to my family for their love, understanding, and indulgence during the preparation of this book and always.

# Chapter I

# INTRODUCTION

This book is a shortened and updated version of the doctoral dissertation that was completed and defended by the author in 2009. The main objective of the book is to examine cultural situation in the thirteenth century A.D. in the central portion of the Mesa Verde region, located in southwestern Colorado and southeastern Utah, and analyze selected sites from the area in terms of location and architectural features that may suggest that these settlements were constructed for defensive purposes. The central Mesa Verde region is well known to archaeologists and many tourists because of the famous cliff dwellings in the alcoves of the sandstone canyons of Mesa Verde National Park. These ancient Puebloan villages were constructed and inhabited mostly during the late Pueblo III period (ca. 1225–1300 A.D.); however, Ancestral Puebloan occupation of the area began many centuries before, in the first millennium B.C. (Charles 2006; Cordell 1997; Lipe 1999b). The late Pueblo III period was a time of many changes and reorganization in the ancient Pueblo world that are apparent in both the remaining architecture and the artifact assemblages in the Mesa Verde region. Socio-cultural changes probably occurred as well. The late Pueblo III period was a time of peak population in the region and, near the end of the thirteenth century A.D., of final depopulation and emigrations from the area.

This book consists of six chapters. The first is an introductory chapter that presents the objectives and scope of the book. Chapter II describes the natural and cultural boundaries of the Mesa Verde region. It also provides information on the natural environment of the region, as well as on the history and methodology of archaeological research conducted in the area from the middle of the nineteenth century until the present. In addition, the chapter presents introductory information on Pueblo culture both within the region and beyond.

The third chapter defines the term "defensive architecture" and examines how such architecture can be manifested in the archaeological record, especially in non-state societies. The theory of defensive architecture is supported with analogies to, and examples of, sites considered defensive in terms of their architecture and location on the landscape in different areas of the American Southwest, in other parts of North America, and in other areas of the world, primarily central-eastern and southern European sites dating from the Neolithic, Bronze Age-Iron Age and Early Medieval periods. These data can lend insight into the nature of the development and functioning of defensive architecture in the central Mesa Verde region, and comparisons with other areas and cultures could contribute to a deeper understanding of the changes in Pueblo society that occurred in the thirteenth century A.D. and the circumstances that motivated migration from the region.

In Chapter IV, information is presented regarding defensive architecture, site location, and evidence of conflict and migration of Pueblo people during different time periods. Included are examples from ethnohistoric chronicles and notes made by the first Europeans in the American Southwest, mainly Spanish conquistadors, missionaries, and travelers penetrating the area beginning in the first half of the sixteenth century. I also utilized a huge ethnographic database of nineteenth and early twentieth century Pueblo societies as well as extensive information derived from oral traditions of American Indians in the Southwest, especially contemporary Pueblo groups.

Chapter V is the main chapter of the book that focuses on the analysis of ancient Puebloan sites in the central Mesa Verde region. I examine these sites on both macro- and micro-regional scales to highlight characteristics of their locations and architectural features that might be interpreted as defensive:

– Examination at the macro-regional scale includes a study of 15 selected large sites – most are categorized as community centers – in the central Mesa Verde region, which includes also area of Mesa Verde National Park.

– Study at the micro-regional scale includes examination of a total of about 40 small sites, mostly cliff dwellings that are in the general vicinity of one of the large sites, Castle Rock Pueblo. This cluster of settlements and structures could have functioned as a community (Ortman 2008; Varien 1999; Varien et al. 2000: 52–56).

Each site is described and analyzed along several parameters: location; access; distance to and availability of domestic water; distance to nearby sites; line-of-sight contact; and presence of apparently defensive architectural features, e.g., village-enclosing/retaining walls, towers, loopholes, underground tunnels, structure access (ground level vs. upper story), and any other feature that could have been designed for the protection or defense of the inhabitants.

The final chapter, Chapter VI, consists of a summary and the conclusions drawn from this research, drawing analogies from sources of information in chapters III and IV. The last chapter also includes a discussion of factors that probably contributed to the final migrations and depopulation of the Mesa Verde region during the A.D. 1270s/1280s, and it focuses on increasing conflict in the region as reflected in the architecture, settlement location, and village layout during the final few decades of the Puebloan occupation of the area.

The 15 large sites or community centers analyzed in this book were chosen from the more than 50 community centers that existed in the central Mesa Verde region in the thirteenth century because of the quality and abundance of published information, including excavation and survey reports, available for these particular sites. Some sites at Mesa Verde National Park were examined archaeologically at the turn of the twentieth century, and the resulting archaeological reports and amateur descriptions are the primary sources of information concerning these sites even today. Examples include reports of archaeological excavations by Gustaf Nordenskiöld and Jesse W. Fewkes. Only a few of the large cliff dwellings in the area of the park have been studied recently; such research consists primarily of the documentation of architecture and of stabilization work conducted by Larry V. Nordby and Kathleen Fiero, for example (see chapters II and V).

In the second half of the twentieth century, large-scale archaeological excavations occurred at only a few sites such as Long House (Site 5MV1200) and Mug House (Site 5MV1229). This research was part of a larger project, the *Wetherill Mesa Archaeological Project* (Cattanach 1980; Hayes 1964; Rohn 1971), which was conducted between the late 1950s and the early 1960s.

However, the earliest scientific research in the Mesa Verde area was associated with military and scientific expeditions to the Southwest beginning in the 1850s (the Hayden Expedition of 1874–1876, for example), and the first archaeological and ethnographic works occurred at the end of the nineteenth and during the early part of the twentieth century. Archaeological excavations conducted by Gustaf Nordenskiöld, the Wetherill family, Jesse Fewkes, or Jesse Nusbaum during this early period of research in the region focused primarily on the spectacular cliff dwellings in what is today Mesa Verde National Park. The park itself was established in 1906 to protect archaeological sites in the area, although the first archaeological site in the Mesa Verde region set aside for protection by the federal government was the Goodman Point Unit, in 1889. Few community centers in the central Mesa Verde region outside the park area were excavated during this initial period of archaeological research; Cannonball Ruin (Site 5MT338) is one exception (Morley 1908). Invaluable descriptions and photographs from the second half the nineteenth century and the first decades of the twentieth century are available for some sites outside the park area. However, the primary source of information for such sites resulted from fieldwork conducted in the past few decades by the Crow Canyon Archaeological Center, a research and education institution located near Cortez in southwestern Colorado. Some of these reports are available in print, and others can be accessed through Crow Canyon's web site.

The main sources of information for small sites located within the Castle Rock community (Lower Sand Canyon locality) are reports from surveys conducted by different institutions in that area since the 1960s. A few such sites examined through archaeological excavations by Crow Canyon archaeologists have been published on the Internet. Nearly all sites in the Lower Sand Canyon locality and the central Mesa Verde region analyzed in the book were surveyed by the author between 2005 and 2009.

More than a century of research in the Mesa Verde region has yielded abundant data from archaeological excavations and surveys as well as other scientific study. However, since the first archaeological research in the region, during the second half of the nineteenth century, some aspects of ancient Pueblo culture remain poorly understood. Still unresolved are the causes of the migration of Pueblo people from the Mesa Verde region to the south and southeast into what are now northern and central Arizona and New Mexico.

However, ever-increasing data have enabled archaeologists to formulate several possible explanations for that migration. The theories most cited and most supported by scientific data include environmental changes, increasing conflict and violence, social changes, and the attraction of a new cult or ideologies from the south (see for example Adler et al. 1996; Cameron 1995, 2006; Lipe 1995a). However, it seems that none of these theories can fully explain the total depopulation of the region. It is probable that no single factor was responsible, but presumably some combination of these and other factors contributed to the depopulation.

One reason often cited for the depopulation of the area – increasing conflict and violence – refers to conflicts between Puebloan groups or between Pueblo and non-Pueblo people. Evidence of conflict is clearly visible archaeologically: sites located in places difficult to access; defensive buildings, architectural features, and settlement layouts; the presence of burned structures; human remains with evidence of violent death; and rock art depicting violent interactions. During the thirteenth century A.D. many types of defensive architecture – including towers, underground tunnels connecting two or more structures in a settlement, loopholes, and massive stone walls that partly or fully enclosed villages – were constructed in the Mesa Verde region (Kenzle 1993, 1997; Lipe and Varien 1999a, 1999b; Thompson et al. 1997; Varien et al. 1996). Some such architectural features were built in the twelfth century A.D. as well; however, far more were constructed during the thirteenth century. These architectural changes were associated with population aggregation and relocation; during the thirteenth century, most people lived in large settlements situated such that they were difficult to access and easy to defend. In many villages, water sources were secured within the boundary of the settlement or were at least nearby.

As mentioned above, defensive aspects of ancient Pueblo sites were noted as early as the nineteenth century in records of the first military and scientific expeditions and in initial archaeological records. Although many scholars pointed out that at least some characteristics of the architecture were defensive, there have been only sporadic attempts to study this topic more thoroughly. An early attempt to classify and systematize possibly defensive architecture was undertaken by Malcolm F. Farmer in his article, *A Suggested Typology of Defensive Systems of the Southwest*, published in the *Southwestern Journal of Anthropology* in 1957 or Albert Schulman in his studies on the towers in Mesa Verde and Gallina regions (Schulman 1950). Later studies include research by Susan C. Kenzle on enclosing walls at selected sites in the Mesa Verde region (Kenzle 1993, 1997) or LeBlanc studies on defensive sites (LeBlanc 1999).

When considering the depopulation of the Mesa Verde region we should also remember that Euro-Americans and Indians perceive ancient Pueblo habitations differently (Naranjo 1995). According to contemporary Pueblo Indians, these places were not abandoned. Instead, they are still inhabited by spirits of their ancestors. These ancient sites are respected by modern American Indians, and some are mentioned in oral traditions.

Chapter II

# MESA VERDE REGION – DEFINITION, NATURAL ENVIRONMENT, HISTORY AND METHODOLOGY OF RESEARCH

## II.1. DEFINITION AND BORDERS OF THE CENTRAL MESA VERDE REGION

The Mesa Verde region is part of a larger area called the North American Southwest (Fig. 1). Archaeologically, the North American Southwest covers the approximate area of what is today Utah, Colorado, Arizona, New Mexico, southern California, southeastern Nevada, and western Texas in the U.S., and northern portions of the states of Sonora and Chihuahua in Mexico (Cordell 1997; Plog 1997). This area includes diverse geography and climatic conditions, though dry semi-desert plains prevail; these plains are interrupted by plateaus and mountain ranges with many pine and spruce woodlands.

Archaeologically, the Mesa Verde region includes adjacent parts of what are presently southeastern Utah, southwestern Colorado, northeastern Arizona, and northwestern New Mexico. These four states meet at what is known as the Four Corners, and that general area is referred to as the Four Corners area of the U.S. The Mesa Verde region is also known as the Northern San Juan region, and these two terms are often used interchangeably (Lipe 1995a: 143–144; Rohn 1989: 149–150; Varien 2000: 6). San Juan River begins in southern Colorado (in the San Juan Mountains), passes through the northwestern part of New Mexico, and feeds into Colorado River in Utah; this river might have been treated as a natural boundary in ancient times, and it roughly serves as a cultural boundary between the Mesa Verde region and areas to the south, including the Chaco region in northwestern New Mexico and the Kayenta region in northeastern Arizona. Even today it is considered the natural northern border of the land of the Navajo Indian nation (Glowacki 2006: 12, refer there for further literature).

However, these two regional terms – Mesa Verde and Northern San Juan – are not synonymous, because the latter region is commonly defined as the geographic area encompassed by the northern drainage of the San Juan River (Varien 2000: 6) and as being surrounded by the La Plata, San Juan, Abajo, LaSal, and Carrizo mountains, whereas the Mesa Verde region is more a cultural designation, the boundaries of which varied through time. Nevertheless, for the time under consideration in this book – the thirteenth century

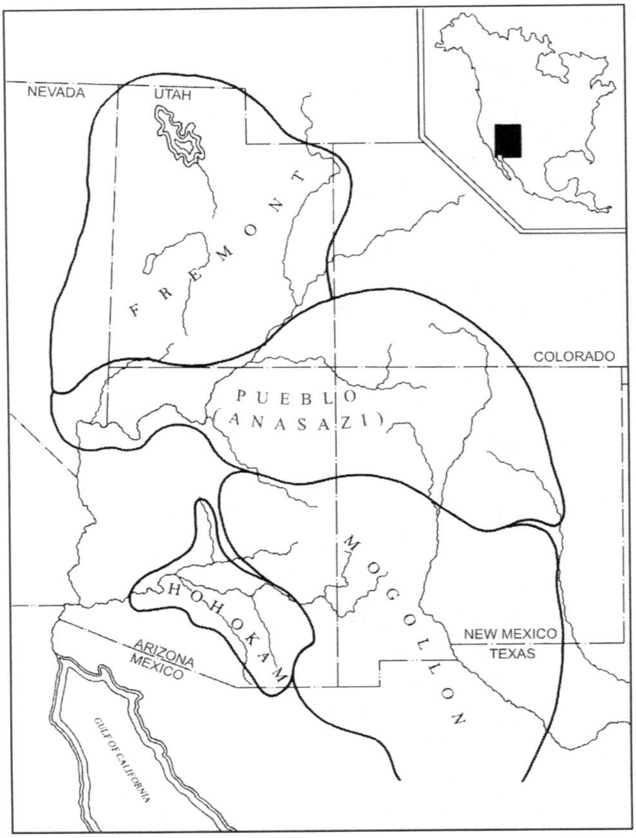


Fig. 1. Location of the North American Southwest (after Cordell 1997: Fig. 1.1 modified by M. and M. Przybyła)

A.D. and the entire Pueblo III period (A.D. 1150–1300) – these two terms are nearly synonymous.

For some purposes, the Mesa Verde region is divided into smaller parts or sub-regions. One of the proposed divisions is, from east to west: Totah, Mesa Verde Proper, McElmo-Monument, West Mesa Verde, and Lower San Juan (Glowacki 2006: 6–7). In this scheme, the central Mesa Verde, the region on which this book focuses, comprises three sub-regions: Mesa Verde Proper, McElmo-Monument, and West Mesa Verde.

The central Mesa Verde region was originally defined as the area between Mesa Verde National Park in southwestern Colorado and the Utah-Colorado border (Lipe 1995a: 143), but this definition was recently extended to include the area from the Mancos River and Mesa Verde National Park in Colorado to Cottonwood Wash in southeastern Utah (Varien 2000: 6–7, Fig. 2). In other words, the central Mesa Verde region is located in the area of the northern tributaries that drain into the middle part of the San Juan River and is bounded by the Mancos River on the east and by Cottonwood Wash on the west. The total area of the central Mesa Verde region is approximately 8742 km$^2$ (Glowacki 2006: 17–18).

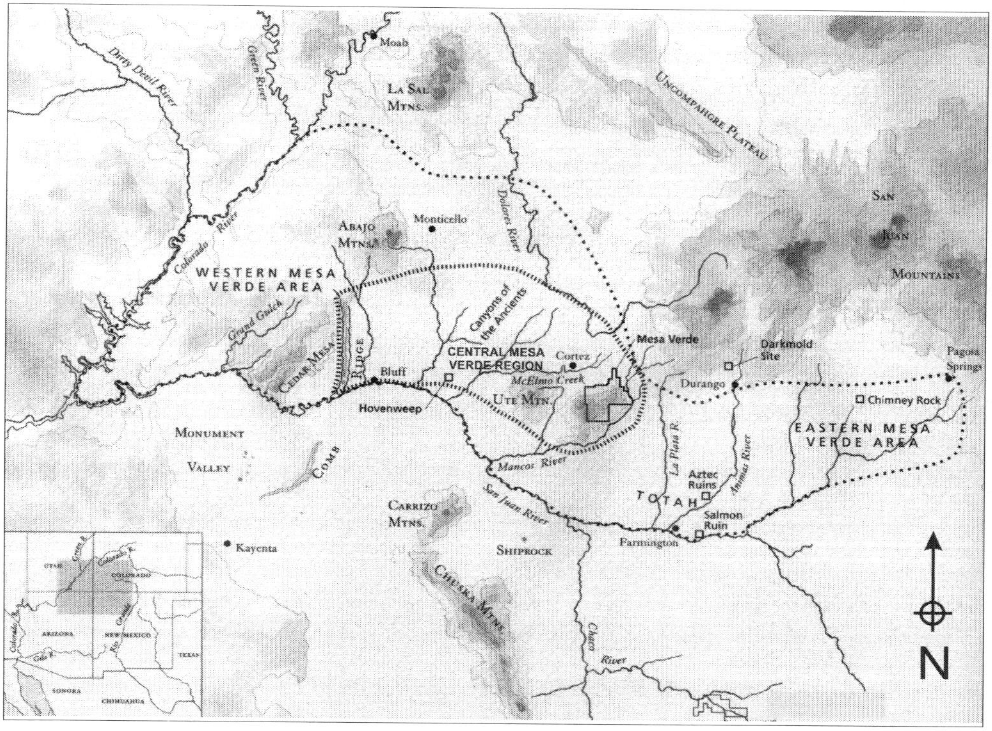


Fig. 2. Location of the Mesa Verde region in North American Southwest (after Noble, ed. by 2006: Map.1 modified by A. Danecki)

## II.2. NATURAL ENVIRONMENT

On the basis of the consistency of Pueblo cultural remains and settlement patterns and of the environment across the area, the entire Mesa Verde region is often treated as a culturally and geographically homogeneous unit. This approach is useful for many considerations of different aspects of prehistoric Pueblo culture in the region, but in some ways this is an over-simplification, because there were differences in human habitation (like settlement patterns and population density) of the area and even more environmental variation.

The study and reconstruction of the prehistoric natural environment of the central Mesa Verde region involves interdisciplinary research. Dendrochronology (tree-ring studies), for example, provides a large amount of crucial information regarding the ancient environment of the North American Southwest and particularly the Mesa Verde region (e.g., Dean 1996; Van West and Dean 2000; Dean and Van West 2002) as well as data essential for establishing a fine-grained chronology of the Southwest.

Elevational differences across the region are significant today, and probably were even more important in the past, which suggests that in the process of reconstructing ancient Pueblo culture one must remember that the Mesa Verde region as a whole is similar but not exactly a coherent geographic area, and it is highly probable that this variability affected the existence of prehistoric Pueblo societies living there (Glowacki 2006: 15). However, there are some general tendencies in the natural environment that are represented by, for example, similar flora and fauna, geology, and geomorphology. Of course, the distribution of these features does vary across the region (Glowacki 2006). Generally, the Mesa Verde region is not as dry as the other areas of the Southwest, primarily because it lies at a relatively high elevation and is farther north than the rest of the Southwest (Cordell 1997). The Mesa Verde region is located in "a cold, middle latitude, semiarid climate, in which potential atmospheric evaporation regularly exceeds the amounts of precipitation available" (Adams and Petersen 1999: 23; see also Van West and Dean 2000: 20–21 after Trewartha 1954: 267).

Geologically, the Mesa Verde region includes mainly Dakota Sandstone, Mancos Shale, Summerville, Dolores, Entrada, and Morrison formations, although there is variability within the region in terms of the distribution and exposure of those formations. Dakota Sandstone was a good source of building stone used commonly for the construction of dwellings by ancient Pueblo people, and the Morrison Formation provided raw material for making stone tools (Adams and Petersen 1999: 21).

Within the more restricted area that constitutes the central Mesa Verde region, the natural environment is generally homogeneous, although there are some important variations. Differences in elevation affected precipitation, angle and availability of sunlight, length of the growing and harvesting seasons, distribution of flora and fauna, and other characteristics of the environment. This region has a relatively high elevation, roughly from 1500 to 3200 m (4500–9600 ft.) above sea level. The highest elevations occur in the western part of the region and also in the eastern part in Mesa Verde proper (approximately the area of Mesa Verde National Park and Ute Mountain Ute Tribal Park). Most of the prehistoric human habitation in the central Mesa Verde region occurred below 2500 m; maize agriculture would not have been possible at higher elevations (Adams and Petersen 1999; Erdman et al. 1969: 57).

In many places in the central Mesa Verde region there are canyons with steep talus slopes. Many rock overhangs or alcoves are present in the sandstone cliff faces of the canyons. Long-term erosional processes created unique geographic features such as canyons and *mesas* (Griffitts 1990). Alcoves were chosen for dwelling by ancient Puebloans over a vast period of time but especially during the thirteenth century A.D. (Varien et al. 1996: 98). Cliff dwellings are located in Mesa Verde National Park as well as in other areas of the central Mesa Verde region, for example, in the Sand Canyon locality and in Johnson Canyon on the Ute Mountain Ute Reservation.

The distribution of soils that have potential for agriculture also varies across the area. Their suitability of a particular soil for agriculture depends on factors such as topography, elevation, aspect, precipitation, availability of water, temperature, and length of the growing season (Van West and Dean 2000: 22). The loamy soils offering the best potential for the cultivation of maize and other crops, as well as for foraging, are concentrated in, but not limited to, the McElmo-Monument and the Mesa Verde proper areas (Adams and Petersen 1999: 33). Evidence indicates that dry-land farming would be favored between 1824/1829 and 2195 m (6000–7200 ft.) elevation, whereas below about 1829 m (ca. 6000 ft.) there is a need for artificial water management (Adams and Petersen 1999: 33). Also, floodplain agriculture would have been possible, mostly in drainage bottoms

(Adams and Petersen 1999: 32) but often also depends on level of water table and runoff after storms ("runoff farming" includes also "akchin" farms on fans). However, the distribution of good soils differs even within small areas such as the Sand Canyon locality and often varied with physiography (Adams and Bowyer 2002: 123–124; Lipe and Varien 2003: 3). Also, the distribution of productive lands would have changed through time as climatic conditions varied. Many parts of the central Mesa Verde region including Lower Sand Canyon is covered by deep deposits of eolian-derived silty loam soils (Mesa Verde Loess) that often covers uplands and mesa tops and sometimes occurs in lower portions of the canyons for example on relatively level benches; also farming was at least occasionally possible in canyons bottom (Lipe and Varien 2003: 3).

The potential for agriculture in the Mesa Verde region is associated with the amount of precipitation and the number of frost-free days. The annual precipitation ranges from 18 to 48 cm across the area, with the greatest levels in higher elevations, for example in Mesa Verde Proper (Mesa Verde National Park), and it seems that at elevations higher than 1800–1830 m (ca. 6000 ft.) there was adequate rainfall for maize agriculture in terms of dry-farming (Adams and Petersen 1999: 23, 33). Precipitation in the central Mesa Verde region correlates strongly with elevation, aspect, topography, and distance from the mountains (Van West and Dean 2000: 21).

Most varieties of maize require a minimum of 120 frost-free days to reach maturity; this requirement is usually met at elevations below 2195 m (ca. 7200 ft.). Above this elevation there were also many locations where maize could have been grown, given a favorable aspect (Adams, Petersen 1999: 26–28).

Besides the San Juan River, the only major permanent water sources in the area were the Mancos River (a tributary of the San Juan River) at the eastern edge of the central Mesa Verde region and the Dolores River (a tributary of the Colorado River) in the northern part of the region. There are also seasonal creeks and many seeps and springs. Numerous cliff alcoves contain seeps as well, seeps or springs occur also at the base of the alcove walls. There is evidence of water management by the ancient Puebloans, for instance, the construction of check-dams, reservoirs, and farming terraces (Erdman et al. 1969: 57–58; Rohn 1963b; Wilshusen et al. 1997).

The flora of the central Mesa Verde region (Adams and Petersen 1999: 14–21, 29–30; Erdman et al. 1969; Smith 2002: 31–32) varies by elevation but includes mainly piñon pine (*Pinus edulis*) and Utah juniper (*Juniperus osteosperma*) woodlands located particularly on mesas and uplands, and sagebrush (*Artemisia tridentata*) and a variety of other shrubs on more level areas of the landscape. Other trees, less common and usually found at higher elevations, include Douglas fir (*Pseudotsuga menziesii*), Ponderosa pine (*Pinus ponderosa*), aspen (*Populus tremuloides*), Rocky Mountain juniper (*Juniperus scopulorum*), and spruce (*Picea*). In numerous parts of the central Mesa Verde region there are many shrubs besides sagebrush including, for example, serviceberry (*Amelanchier utahensis*), mountain mahogany (*Cercocarpus montanus*), broad-leaf yucca (*Yucca baccata*), prickly pear cactus (*Opuntia sp.*) and bitterbrush (*Purshia tridentata*). Lower and drier elevations host grasslands.

Piñon-juniper woodlands, grasslands, and sagebrush-saltbush areas were good places for foraging for juniper berries, piñon nuts, cacti, yucca, and a variety of grasses, as well as for hunting mule deer and cottontail rabbits.

The juniper and piñon trees were an important resource for ancient Puebloans in the Mesa Verde region, especially as sources of beams for building material (Adams and Petersen 1999: 22–23). These trees were especially important after resources became depleted in some parts of the region as a result of human activity (Adams and Bowyer 2002; Kohler et al. 2005). Roofing beams were salvaged when structures were abandoned; people reused good beams when constructing new buildings (important issue in terms of chronology based on the tree rings). Trees and shrubs also provided fuel and material for tools.

The most common wild fauna (Driver 2002: 143–160; Smith 2002: 32–33) important to ancient Pueblo people in the Mesa Verde area include cottontails (*Sylvilagus*), jackrabbits (*Lepus*), mule deer (*Odocoileus hemionus*), bighorn sheep (*Ovis canadensis*), antelope (*Antilocapra americana*) and, less commonly, elk (*Cervus elaphus*). Turkey (*Meleagris gallopavo*) was also very important in the diet of Ancestral Puebloans, but during the thirteenth century A.D. most turkey consumed was from domesticated rather than wild turkeys (Driver 2002: 151). Other species of mammals and birds that were used relatively less include such species as bobcat (*Lynx rufus*), coyote (*Canis latrans*), grey fox (*Urocyon cineroargenteus*), and rarely, especially in Mesa Verde proper, black bear (*Ursus americanus*) and mountain lion (*Felis concolor*) (Smith 2002: 32–33).

During the 2,000 years of Puebloan occupation of the Mesa Verde region there were changes in the natural environment. Some changes led to shifts in settlement patterning and even migrations and depopulation of the area (Dean and Van West 2002; Kohler et al. 2005; Van West and Dean 2000). Significant climate change (especially a series of cold and dry years) that probably coincided resource depletion (for example, deforestation near settlements), occurred about 900 A.D. or during the early Pueblo II period. These conditions probably caused a partial depopulation of the region (Kohler et al. 2005; Lipe and Varien 1999a: 253, 265).

Climatic perturbations and variability in the thirteenth century A.D. were brought about by the Great Drought (A.D. 1276–1299) in the northern San Juan region and episodes colder-than-normal temperatures (sometimes connected with the beginning of the Little Ice Age – ca. 1200 A.D. in many parts of the world including North America). These factors are considered by many researchers to be the primary reasons that Puebloan societies migrated south and southeast out of the Mesa Verde region, leaving the region depopulated by the end of thirteenth century A.D. The high elevation of the central Mesa Verde region makes it susceptible to changes in temperature, and thus these variations might have affected ancient societies living in this region more than those living at lower elevations (Kohler at al. 2005). It is also probable that the region was depleted of wood both for fuel and for buildings by the late thirteenth century A.D. (Kohler and Matthews 1998; Kohler et al. 2005), but it doesn't seem that was one of the contributing factors of migration from Mesa Verde region in this period (Varien et al. 2007: 291–292). However, deforestation is often considered one of the main causes of collapse or migration in different ancient societies around the world, for example in terms of Maya culture (Źrałka 2008 after Shaw 2003) or other parts of the world including ancient Mesopotamia. A reduction in the number of animals that Puebloans in the Mesa Verde area hunted, such as mule deer connected with other factors, might also have contributed to decisions to migrate (Kohler et al. 2005; Varien et al. 2007).

However, recent data (Dean and Van West 2002; Kohler et al. 2005; Van West and Dean 2000; Varien et al. 2007) show that even though depletion of natural resources, climatic variability and the Great Drought were probably serious problems for the ancient Pueblo farmers in the Mesa Verde region, environmental conditions would have allowed some people to remain. There were still some places or areas with enough water and adequate conditions for farming and human habitation, moreover, the Great Drought was neither the longest nor the most severe drought that occurred in the region during the several hundred years of Puebloan occupation of the area (Dean and Van West 2002: 87; Kohler et al. 2005; Van West and Dean 2000: 26–27). Also, it is necessary to remember that before the thirteenth century A.D. there had occurred at least similar or even more serious environmental and climatic perturbations including severe droughts that didn't effected the depopulation of the whole region (Van West and Dean 2000).

## II.3. HISTORY AND METHODOLOGY OF RESEARCH

The term "Mesa Verde" derives from the Spanish language and means "Green Table" or "Green Tableland." It was probably used for the first time by the Spanish friars or travelers who were sent in the 1700s by the Spanish colonies in New Mexico to explore the Four Corners region and to try to find a route that could connect Santa Fe in New Mexico with the Spanish colonies in California (Lipe 1999a: 51–52). One of the first such explorers was Juan Maria Rivera who traveled through the Mesa Verde area in 1765, and it was probably he who first used the name "Mesa Verde" (Smith 2002: 5). Another Spanish expedition mentioned in written sources and that was important for collecting information about Mesa Verde was the so-called Domínguez-Escalante or Escalante expedition that took place in 1776 (Lipe 1999a: 52). The route of that expedition was through present-day northwestern New Mexico, southwestern Colorado, and Utah. Even though the references from that expedition didn't say much about the archaeological sites or ruins, some sites in southwestern Colorado (for example Escalante Ruin) were referred to as Puebloan. Probably the same route taken by Domínguez-Escalante was later used, at least in part, as a trade route linking Santa Fe and California (Los Angeles) during the period 1829–1848.

After 1848, when the United States took control of the Southwest from Mexico, there were several American parties, both civil and military expeditions that surveyed southwestern Colorado and southeastern Utah, partly following the Spanish Trail established decades earlier. Both the Spanish and American explorers linked the ruins they encountered in Utah and Colorado with ruins and historic pueblos in Arizona and New Mexico (Downum 1993: 4). In 1859 one of the U.S. government surveys, led by Captain John N. Macomb, encountered many Pueblo sites described later by a member of that expedition, geologist J.S. Newberry (Smith 2002: 5; Lipe 1999a: 52–53).

Between 1867 and 1878 a scientific survey, the United States Geological and Geographical Survey of the Territories, was conducted and was called the Hayden Survey or Hayden Expedition after its leader (Jackson and Holmes 1981; Lipe 1999a: 53). Important information about the Mesa Verde region and the Pueblo III period were published in reports prepared by two members of that expedition, William H. Holmes and

William H. Jackson (Holmes 1876, 1878; Jackson 1876a, 1876b; Jackson and Holmes 1981). From 1874 to 1876 they explored, described, and drew sketches of many sites, some of which they also photographed (for example, Castle Rock Pueblo). This information is crucial today, because at the time of the Hayden Survey most sites were in a much better state of preservation than they are today (due to natural deterioration or to pothunting or other destructive human activity).

However, in none of the records from these early expeditions is there reference to cliff dwellings in the area of what is presently Mesa Verde National Park, although Jackson and Holmes documented some cliff dwellings for the lower Mancos River Canyon, and small dwellings in McElmo and Sand canyons were briefly described as well.

The first published reports of surveys such as those of Holmes and Jackson attracted many people who wanted to explore the Mesa Verde region. One of these was Lewis Henry Morgan who in 1870s surveyed, mapped, and described some of the sites in the Mesa Verde area (Lipe 1999a: 54–55). In 1886 Virginia Donaghe McClurg (Wenger 1980: 66), a correspondent of New York Graphic, with hired people from Colorado, located and described a few pueblos, mainly small cliff dwellings. Later, at the turn of the century, McClurg put a lot of effort into protecting and preserving the cliff dwellings of Mesa Verde (Smith 2002).

The first discovery of the Mesa Verde cliff dwellings is attributed to members of Wetherill family, ranchers who lived near the town of Mancos in southwestern Colorado. In December 1888 Richard Wetherill and his brother-in-law Charles Mason discovered Cliff Palace while searching for stray cattle and later discovered Spruce Tree House and Square Tower House (Smith 2002: 7–8, 18–21; Wenger 1980: 66–67). Before "discovering" Cliff Palace, the Wetherill brothers had found some smaller cliff dwellings in Mancos Canyon, following stories told by Acowitz, a Ute man who shared stories about "many houses of the old people-ancient ones" (Wenger 1980). Over the following months members of the Wetherill family discovered many more cliff dwellings in what is today Mesa Verde National Park. They also began nonprofessional excavations of some of the ruins and collected many artifacts. Fortunately, they soon began to create records where artifacts came from; most of these artifacts were later sold (to the Colorado State Historical Society and to the University of Pennsylvania, for example).

It is probable that some residents of the towns of Cortez or Mancos (among them Mr. James Frink) saw some of the cliff dwellings at Mesa Verde before the Wetherills and Mason did (Fewkes 1911: 13). Also, in 1883–1884, S.E. Osborn visited some of the cliff dwellings in Mesa Verde and published a newspaper article about the exploration, but this article did not attract much public attention at the time (Smith 2002: 16–17).

Later, the Wetherills worked as guides for visitors who wanted to explore Mesa Verde ruins, which had become famous. They also accompanied a Swedish archaeologist, Gustaf A. Nordenskiöld, in his exploration and excavation of some ruins in Wetherill and Chapin mesas of Mesa Verde. Gustaf Nordenskiöld, although not trained in archaeology, knew scientific methods well because he had studied geology, botany, and chemistry. In 1891 he conducted excavations in some cliff dwellings with considerable thoroughness; he also took measurements, high quality photographs, and prepared maps and plans of the ruins (Smith 2002: 27–32). Two years later, in 1893, one of the most important books about the archaeology of Mesa Verde was published by Nordenskiöld, *The Cliff Dwellers of Mesa Verde*; this work remains an important record to this day.

After the discovery of Cliff Palace and other large cliff dwellings, Mesa Verde attracted more people. Unfortunately, many were treasure- or pot-hunters, but there were also visitors wanting to admire the ruins, as well as scientists wanting to study them. At the end of the nineteenth century and in the early part of the twentieth century many ruins were looted, vandalized, and at least partly destroyed by treasure-hunters. Cliff Palace, the largest of the cliff dwellings, was one of the sites that was most heavily looted and damaged (Fewkes 1911: 11–12, 24–25).

At the same time, more detailed descriptions (books as well as articles, some of which appeared in professional journals) of Mesa Verde cliff dwellings and other Pueblo ruins outside the area of the present park were published, including articles by T. Mitchell Prudden, F.H. Chapin, W.R. Birdsall, and Stephen D. Peet. These men visited, explored, and wrote descriptions of ruins located not only where Mesa Verde National Park exists today, but elsewhere across the Mesa Verde region as well. They also conducted some excavations. Early publications such as these about the cliff dwellings and other archaeological sites in the region called national attention to the ruins (Smith 2002: 27). These first explorers contributed more than just descriptions of the ruins; for example, T. Mitchell Prudden (Prudden 1903) classified the sites he examined and recognized as a "unit-type pueblo," that is, a kiva with associated rooms and a trash midden (Lipe 1999a: 58) and he recognized that the unit pueblo was the basic building block for large villages.

Other archaeological expeditions to the Mesa Verde area were also organized, such as a party in 1907–1908 led by Professor Edgar L. Hewett, Director of American Archaeology at the Archaeological Institute of America (Downum 1993: 6; Torres-Reyes 1970). Among others recruited by Hewett were Alfred V. Kidder, Jesse L. Nusbaum, and Sylvanus G. Morley, who later became prominent Southwestern archaeologists (see for example Morley 1908, 1917).

In 1906, the Antiquities Act was passed by Congress. In the same year, due to the efforts of many people, Mesa Verde National Park was established[1] with the aim of protecting archaeological sites in the area, especially the famous cliff dwellings. Also, Virginia McClurg successfully arranged an agreement with the Ute Mountain Ute tribe regarding the protection of cliff dwellings located on their reservation, which is adjacent to Mesa Verde National Park (Lipe 1999a: 57; Wegner 1980: 73).

William D. Leonard, the first superintendent of the Mesa Verde National Park in charge of the Southern Ute Agency, was responsible for the protection of the park's ruins. In 1906, he called for better and quicker protection and stabilization of the sites within the park (Torres-Reyes 1970). Two years later, in 1907/8, the first official and professional excavation, repair and stabilization project began. It was led by Dr. Jesse Walter Fewkes from the Bureau of American Ethnology at the Smithsonian Institution. He was recommended by Professor Edgar L. Hewett who was also engaged in the protection of the Mesa Verde ruins. Fewkes, besides conducting excavations and stabilization, was also willing to adapt the ruins for visitors. He continued his archaeological work in Mesa Verde National Park until 1922 (Torres-Reyes 1970).

Even though the first official excavations at the turn of the century in the Mesa Verde region as well as in other parts of the Southwest did not always meet today's norms and

[1] However, the first archaeological area in the Mesa Verde region set aside for protection by the federal government was the Goodman Point Unit, in 1889, which today is a part of Hovenweep National Monument (Kuckelman et al. 2004).

standards and sometimes focused on collecting artifacts, some notable archaeologists conducted responsible research, by the standards of that time, and attempted to protect sites from further destruction and vandalism. Also, the reports published about these initial excavations are the only or the main sources of information for many archaeological sites.

These pioneering years of archaeology of the Mesa Verde region were heavily influenced by ethnographic analogy. Many archaeological interpretations were based more on ethnography and direct analogy with living Pueblo societies than on archaeological data (Downum 1993). There was also a tendency to equate Pueblo people from the nineteenth and twentieth centuries with prehistoric Pueblo culture and infer many aspects of ancient culture through ethnographic analogy. Research was conducted without systematic methods and necessary critique. This situation occurred partly because many archaeologists of that time, like Fewkes and Cushing, had ad also worked extensively for a long time among Pueblo societies in Arizona and New Mexico (Downum 1993: 4–5; Lipe 1999a: 59–60; Spielmann 2005: 195).

Intermittently, from 1921 until the late 1940s, archaeologist Jesse L. Nusbaum worked as the superintendent of Mesa Verde National Park. He began to develop the park by initiating many new archaeological projects, developing park facilities, and employing many American Indian workers, such as Navajos, in the park (Smith 2002). He later served as senior archaeologist of the National Park Service and began one of the first salvage archaeology projects in the Mesa Verde area.

In 1916, the National Park Service was created, which was a great help in terms of protection, controlling, and coordinating archaeological sites both within the park boundaries and outside the park. When the Historic Sites Act was created in 1935, the National Park Service assumed more responsibility for the identification and protection of the most important historic sites (Smith, ed. by 2005).

In the early decades the twentieth century, the first aerial photographs of some areas of Mesa Verde were taken that later aided archaeological investigations of the area. The earliest of these were photographs taken by Charles Lindbergh in the 1930s of the Goodman Point vicinity (Kuckelman et al. 2004).

During the second and the third decades of the twentieth century stratigraphic methods were gradually added to Southwestern field methodology, particularly in the Mesa Verde region. This study and documentation helped to establish the first chronological sequencing for the area by such researchers as Alfred V. Kidder and Earl Morris (Lipe 1999a: 61–63). At the Pecos Conference in 1927, Kidder presented a chronology of Pueblo culture and the Southwest (Kidder 1927; Lipe 1999a: 65–66).

Development of a chronology of the Mesa Verde region and the entire North American Southwest was greatly facilitated by the dendrochronology, which was a new method of dating archaeological sites. This method is especially applicable in the hot and dry climate of the U.S. Southwest. The use of this dating method began in the 1920s (by Dr. A.E. Douglass, leader of the National Geographic tree-ring expeditions) and in the 1930s when the first tree-ring samples from different sites at Chapin Mesa in Mesa Verde National Park were collected and the dates published (Rohn 1977: 3–4).

Between 1927 and 1957 there were numerous archaeological activities and published reports focusing more on work in different areas of the Mesa Verde region and establishing a better and more accurate chronology of particular areas (Lipe 1999a: 69–72, Torres-Reyes 1970; Rohn 1977). Also, this work was supervised by professional institutions such as universities, museums, local associations, and private research foundations (Downum 1993: 6–7). During this time, excavations and surveys were conducted both in Mesa Verde National Park and outside the park. In Mesa Verde National Park, several projects were conducted: some sites were surveyed in 1934 by Stanley Morse, Robert Burgh and Gilbert Perkins; also in 1934, there was extensive stabilization work in different cliff dwellings by Earl Morris, Robert F. Burgh, James A. Lancaster; lastly, excavations were conducted by Dr. Deric O'Bryan, Assistant Director of Gila Pueblo Archeological Foundation in 1947–1948 and in 1950 – his work also contributed a great deal in terms of introducing and familiarizing visitors with different periods of Pueblo culture. Outside the park significant excavation projects were also carried out, such as several years of archaeological work in the Monument-McElmo drainage unit by Paul Martin for the Field Museum of Natural History in Chicago; in the La Plata region by Earl Morris between 1915 and 1930; and by Erik Reed in Mancos Canyon (Lipe 1999a; Torres-Reyes 1970).

During the 1950s and 1960s, new archaeological and anthropological concepts, theories, and interpretations were introduced to Southwestern archaeology, as well as to the archaeology of many other areas of the world: "cultural ecology" and "new archaeology" focused more on environmental studies, settlement pattern analysis, and social organization than before (Lipe 1999a: 73, 77). This resulted in new influence on many interpretations of Pueblo culture in the Mesa Verde region.

From the 1950s through the 1970s there were many more archaeological surveys and excavations conducted in the Mesa Verde region. Between 1956 and 1958 a few important, large-scale archaeological projects began. The first of these was a salvage archaeology project associated with the construction of the Navajo Dam (Navajo Reservoir Archaeological Salvage Project) that began in 1956 and ended in 1964. Another salvage project took place in southeastern Utah, just on the western edge of the Mesa Verde region.

In Mesa Verde National Park a large project, *The Wetherill Mesa Archaeological Project*, which began in 1958 and lasted till 1963, involved excavating some archaeological sites and cliff dwellings located at Wetherill Mesa; these sites were to be opened and made accessible to the public (Hayes 1964; Lipe 1999a: 72–76). There were also significant surveys in the Mesa Verde region, such as a survey of the Bureau of Land Management lands in the Sand Canyon Locality, Yellow Jacket vicinity, McElmo-Monument drainages, as well as surveys in Mesa Verde National Park that were conducted in the 1960s and 1970s first by the Department of Anthropology and later the Mesa Verde Archaeological Research Center at the University of Colorado.

There were important published reports and syntheses of these projects. These large projects and publications of their results allowed a better understanding of the nature of Puebloan occupation of the Mesa Verde area, especially as they were conducted with more modern scientific standards than previous research in the area. An example of one of the better known syntheses of the Puebloan occupation of Mesa Verde from this time is Arthur C. Rohn's dissertation published in 1977, *Cultural Change and Continuity on Chapin Mesa*. This and other research and publications devoted to Mesa Verde archaeology contributed significantly to its development (Lipe 1999a, Torres-Reyes 1970).

In the 1970s, and especially after 1974, there was an increase in the number of surveys and salvage projects in the area in response to economic development activities on public lands. One of the largest salvage archaeology projects was the Dolores Archaeological Program (DAP), which was carried out from 1978 to the 1985. It was also one of the largest archaeological projects in United States (Lipe 1999: 79–83). From 1974 to 1977 a large-scale survey project was conducted on Cajon Mesa and Hovenweep National Monument on the Utah-Colorado border (Lipe 1999a: 91; Winter 1975, 1976, 1977). More recent projects include surveys and excavations, for example, in the Chimney Rock area, at Escalante Ruin in the Dolores drainage, the Animas-LaPlata Project in the Animas drainage, and the Four Corners Archaeological Program (FCAP); the last was carried out from 1983 through 1997 (Lipe 1999a: 83–85).

As the needs of archaeological research began to coincide with increasing public involvement in archaeology, new professional institutions were established. For example, in 1988 the Anasazi Heritage Center was constructed near Dolores, Colorado, and in 1983 the Crow Canyon Archaeological Center (CCAC) in Cortez, Colorado was founded in. CCAC is located near the town of Cortez, Colorado, and is today one of the leading non-profit archaeological institutions in the Southwest and the entire U.S. CCAC successfully responds both to the need for a high standard of archaeological research (with long-term excavations and survey projects, such as the Sand Canyon and Goodman Point projects conducted in the 1980s, 1990s, and 2000s) as well as the need to educate the public about ancient and modern American Indian cultures of the Southwest.

The collaboration of archaeologists and anthropologists with Native American tribes is also one of the main approaches of modern archaeology in the Mesa Verde region. For example at Mesa Verde National Park American Indians are involved in consultations and in the Park's public interpretive programs (Varien et al. 1999: 393). CCAC has also initiated many programs of such cooperation (Lipe 1999a; Varien and Wilshusen 2002; http://www.crowcanyon.org). In 1995, CCAC established a Native American Advisory Group (NAAG) composed of several members who are from various Indian tribes. They serve as consultants who review educational curricula and provide feedback on research designs and publications, among other activities and duties (Thompson 2002; Kuckelman et al. 2004; Varien and Wilshusen 2002). Members of NAAG were also consulted during the drafting of CCAC's policy on the treatment of human remains found during excavations (Crow Canyon Field Manual). Cooperation between archaeologists at CCAC (and other institutions) with modern Pueblo people and other American Indian societies to reconstruct the Mesa Verde past is also focusing on examining Native American oral tradition regarding such issues as traditional agriculture, the native view of the landscape, ancient sites, migrations, and changes in past societies.

Numerous projects are conducted now by various institutions, mostly in cooperation with the National Park Service (NPS) or the Bureau of Land Management (BLM) which manage most of the public lands. However, on private lands, archaeological excavations today are conducted both by academic and non-profit institutions and organizations. Also, a significant amount of archaeological work is carried out by privately owned companies and since the 1970s, the great majority of archaeological projects in the area have been done by contract archaeologists under the mandates of federal historic preservation law (William D. Lipe, personal communication 2009).

There is also important activity of the Archaeological Conservancy for the protection of archaeological sites in the Mesa Verde region and the entire United States (Renfrew and Bahn 2002: 530), which has acquired a number of important sites on private land (for example Albert Porter Pueblo and most of Yellow Jacket in the Mesa Verde region).

In recent decades, new methodological and theoretical orientations have been applied to archaeological research in the area; moreover, field and laboratory methods have been improved as well. This has resulted in new directions for research such as the study of environment-human interaction and community social organization as well as the study of sociopolitical, ideological, and symbolic aspects of the ancient peoples of the Mesa Verde region and other areas of the Southwest. Some changes have also been introduced by "postprocessual and postmodern archaeology" (Lipe 1999a: 77–78).

Many archaeological projects are now designed around so-called "conservation archaeology" that focuses on gaining the maximum amount of information with the least amount of physical invasion and destruction of the site (Lipe 1974). Also, new themes have been introduced to archaeological studies and interpretations, such as the study of ancient migrations and conflicts. More collaboration with other disciplines and interdisciplinarity of research, as well as the application of new technologies have widely become the new standard of archaeological investigations. This includes, for example, better developed dendrochronological methods, paleoenvironmental and settlement studies and computer simulations. Examples of computer simulation include studies by Linda Cordell in 1970s and 1980s (Lipe 1999a: 91) or more recent computer modeling (agent-based modeling) by the Village Ecodynamics Project, a new interdisciplinary project focusing on examining settlement patterns of sites from the Mesa Verde region in the period A.D. 600–1300, conducted primarily by scientists and researchers from Washington State University-Pullman and Crow Canyon Archaeological Center (e.g., Kohler et al. 2005; Varien et al. 2007). Recent years have also seen new anthropological and biological studies of ancient DNA from the northern Southwest (e.g. Kemp 2006).

In the 1990s, several sites were nominated to the National Register of Historic Places and aerial photographs (that helped with preparation of topographic maps) were taken of some sites as part of Montezuma County Regional Survey and Preservation Program conducted by Rocky Mountain Aerial Surveys of Englewood, Colorado, in cooperation with CCAC under the grant of Colorado Historical Society (Lipe 1995b: 8).

Stabilization, detailed documentation, hi-tech mapping, and architectural analysis of archaeological sites are frequently conducted by the National Park Service in cooperation with other institutions in Mesa Verde National Park in such cliff dwellings as Cliff Palace, Spruce Tree House, and Balcony House (Fiero 1998; Lipe 1999a: 93). In the 1990s, new architectural studies of cliff dwellings were conducted during stabilization work (Nordby 2001). In 1994, the National Park Service and the Architectural Conservation Laboratory & Research Center (ACL) of the University of Pennsylvania, with the financial aid of several institutions, initiated a partnership program to document and preserve the earthen finishing and plaster in cliff dwellings at Mesa Verde National Park, including Cliff Palace, Spruce Tree House, and Long House (http://www.nps.gov/meve/historyculture/partnerships.htm).

In 1996, the Archeological Site Conservation Program (ASCP) was established at Mesa Verde National Park and is devoted to preservation and to the collection of data in cliff dwellings. That project is ongoing (www.nps.gov/meve/).

In 2007, a new collaboration program began between CCAC and Mesa Verde National Park. This project will include computer models that simulate natural resources that were available and used by ancient Pueblo people during their occupation of Mesa Verde (http://www.nps.gov/meve/historyculture/partnerships.htm). The collaboration between CCAC and Mesa Verde continues in various ways; for example, in 2008–2009, CCAC analyzed pottery collected at Mesa Verde National Park in the mid-twentieth century.

Most of the recent and more detailed investigations of the sites of the Lower Sand Canyon locality (Chapter V) took place between the 1960s and the 1990s (Gleichman and Gleichman 1989: 9–11; Lipe and Varien 2003: section 7, page 6). These were mostly surveys, but some excavations were also conducted. Before that, in 1957, some sites were surveyed and located on a USGS topographic map. In 1965, the Lower Sand Canyon area was surveyed by archaeologists from the Mesa Verde Research Center (MVRC) of the University of Colorado, Boulder, and the Bureau of Land Management. In 1975 MVRC, under the supervision of Curtis W. Martin, conducted a ruins stabilization inventory of the Sand Canyon area. Also in the early 1970s George Kelly of McElmo Canyon conducted temporary stabilization at six sites in the Lower Sand Canyon area (Gleichman and Gleichman 1989: 10–11).

In 1983 and 1984, the Crow Canyon Archaeological Center began recording and surveying sites in the area. Limited excavations were also conducted at some sites as part of the Sand Canyon Archaeological Project Site Testing Program (Varien, ed. by 1999). Also, in 1986 and 1987 the Sand Canyon Survey Project was conducted; the Sand Canyon Archaeological Project fieldwork began in 1983 and continued through 1993. In October and November 1988, another survey of Lower Sand Canyon was conducted as part of a survey of the larger Sand Canyon area. This survey was conducted by Carol L. Gleichman and Peter J. Gleichman under the Native Cultural Services (NCS) for the Bureau of Land Management (BLM) (Gleichman and Gleichman 1989, 1992). In the 1980s, the Crow Canyon Archaeological Center began test excavations at a few sites within the Lower Sand Canyon area.

One of the most recent surveys of the area, which also recorded some previously unknown sites, occurred in 1998 and 2002. Some of the sites in the area were also monitored by the Bureau of Land Management in 2007. The author of the book also surveyed most of the small sites in Lower Sand Canyon area in May 2009.

## II.4. PUEBLO CULTURE IN THE MESA VERDE REGION AND BEYOND – AN OUTLINE

In the past, the widest territory inhabited by Pueblo Indians[2] was the vast area that today encompasses the southern parts of Utah and Colorado, and the northern and middle parts of Arizona and the northern, middle, and southern parts of New Mexico. The Mesa Verde

[2] The ancient Pueblo culture is also called the Anasazi culture. The latter term has been used by archaeologists since the 1930s. One translation of this Navajo term is "enemy ancestors." Modern Pueblo Indians consider this term inappropriate and call their ancestors either "Hisatsinom" (People of Long Ago) like Hopis, or "Ancestral Pueblo."

region was one area where ancient Puebloans developed their culture to a great extent, so it is puzzling as to why they left their settlements near the end of thirteenth century A.D. and migrated southward.

The origin of the Pueblo culture dates from the period before Christ, about 1000 B.C. (Charles 2006; Cordell 1997; Lipe 1999b). Although local chronologies vary to some extent across the region, they are all based on the traditional chronology – the Pecos Classification – established in 1927 (Kidder 1927; Cordell and Fowler, ed. by 2005). The periods of this classification are as follows (with a little modern modification): Basketmaker II (1000 B.C.–A.D. 500), Basketmaker III (A.D. 500–750), Pueblo I (A.D. 700/750–900), Pueblo II (A.D. 900–1150), Pueblo III (A.D. 1150–1300), and proto-Historic and Historic Pueblo (A.D. 1300–1840) (Lipe et al., ed. by 1999). The Modern Pueblo period continues to the present, represented by 20 contemporary Pueblo Indian societies, for example, the Hopi in Arizona and the Zuni, Acoma, and Jemez in New Mexico. Consequently, Pueblo culture exemplifies cultural continuity from ancient times to the present day.

Results of archaeological research provide clear evidence that the economy of the Pueblo people was based from its origins on farming, dominated by growing maize as well as squash and later beans (Cordell 1997; Matson 1991; Plog 1997). These three crops are known to many North American Indian peoples as the Three Sisters. During later time periods, cotton was also cultivated. To supplement crop foods, ancient Pueblo Indians gathered and consumed wild plant foods and procured meat by hunting local animals such as mule deer, rabbits, and turkeys. Wild turkeys were at least semi-domesticated as early as Basketmaker II period, and domesticated turkeys became the principal source of animal protein for Pueblo Indians by the late Pueblo II period (A.D. 900–1150) (Van West and Dean 2000: 22).

During the Basketmaker period, the ancient Pueblo Indians lived in hamlets or villages of a few or as many as several dozen pithouses (Lipe et al., ed. by 1999; Plog 1997; Wilshusen 1999a). Most pithouses were subrectangular or circular in plan and were excavated 20 cm to 1.00 m into the ground; structures became progressively deeper through time. Superstructures were built of beams, smaller wood limbs, and brush or juniper bark, all covered by a thick layer of soil. Entry was by way of a sloping ramp through an antechamber, which was a small room off the south wall of the pithouse.

During the Pueblo periods, architecture underwent a series of significant changes, and buildings two or more stories tall were eventually constructed (e.g. Lipe et al., ed. by 1999; Plog 1997; Wilshusen 2006). The walls of these buildings were built of shaped sandstone rocks; the roofs were of wooden beams, poles, and brush, topped with a layer of soil. Ordinary-size kivas (especially from Pueblo II or Pueblo III periods) were the primary domiciles that were also used for household rituals, although great kivas were nonresidential structures used for ceremonies and other large gatherings (Lipe and Hegmon, ed. by 1989). The first Europeans in the Southwest used the term "pueblo"[3] for these settlements, a Spanish term meaning "village."

---

[3] The capitalized term "Pueblo" is used to denote Indian culture from the North American Southwest, a stage in the development of this culture, and a proper name for a given archaeological site or a current settlement of the Pueblo Indians. Lowercase, "pueblo" refers in general to the traditional settlements of the Pueblo Indians, usually built of stone.

The settlements in the Pueblo I period generally consisted of above-ground masonry rooms usually located in the north part of the site and pit structures south of the roomblock (Wilshusen 1999b, 2006). In the Pueblo II period, the site layout usually included one or more habitation units (roomblocks and kivas), also at that time other structures such as towers were constructed (Lipe and Varien 1999a: 244, 253). This was also when Chaco-related great houses (sites with architecture similar to the Puebloan architecture in Chaco Canyon, New Mexico) were built in the Mesa Verde region; sites such as these might have served as community centers in Mesa Verde at that time (Lipe and Varien 1999a: 256; Varien 1999; Varien et al. 2000).

The Pueblo III period (1150–1300 A.D.) and especially Late Pueblo III period (1225–1300 A.D.), was a time of many significant changes and disturbances across the entire Mesa Verde region that affected the Puebloan societies living there. Nearly two millenia of Puebloan occupation of this area finally ended at the close of the thirteenth century A.D., probably in the late A.D. 1270s or the early- to mid-1280s, as indicated by tree-ring dates available from many sites (Database of Tree-Ring Dates, LTRR 2007; Dean 2001; Lipe 1995a; Varien 1999; Varien et al. 1996). At that time, surviving Pueblo groups probably migrated south and southeast into present-day Arizona and New Mexico (Fig. 4).

The changes and transformations in the area during this period of time are visible in archaeological data and include changes in the architecture, layout of sites, and shift in site location. In the thirteenth century A.D., and especially in the second half of this century, most habitations in the area were canyon-oriented settlements located on canyon rims, on talus slopes below the rims, as well as in cliff alcoves and other places very difficult to access (Kuckelman 2002, 2006; Lipe and Varien 1999b; Varien et al. 1996;

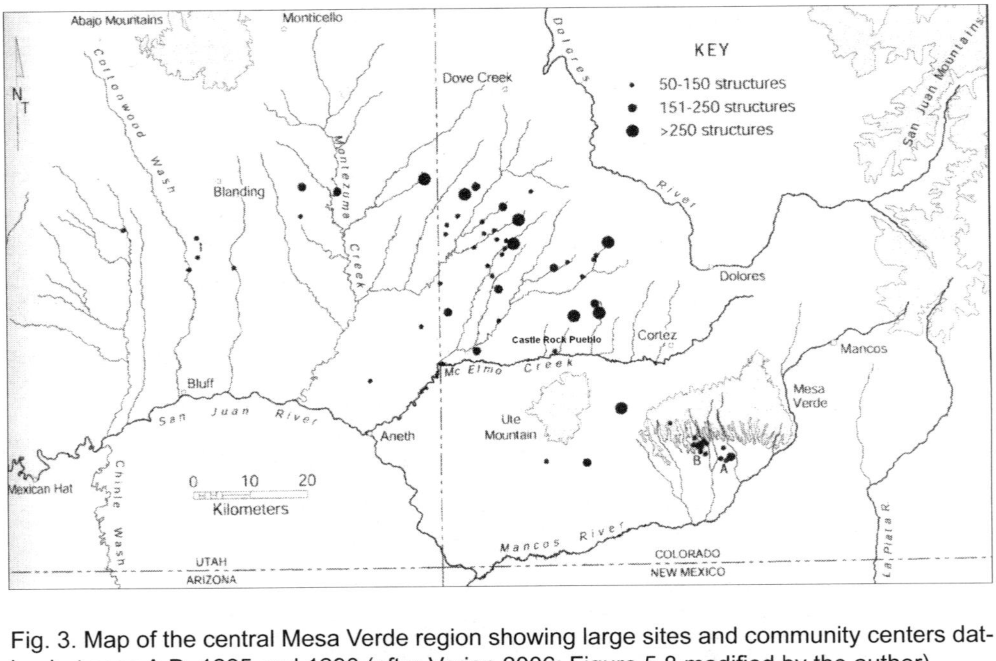


Fig. 3. Map of the central Mesa Verde region showing large sites and community centers dating between A.D. 1225 and 1290 (after Varien 2006: Figure 5.8 modified by the author)

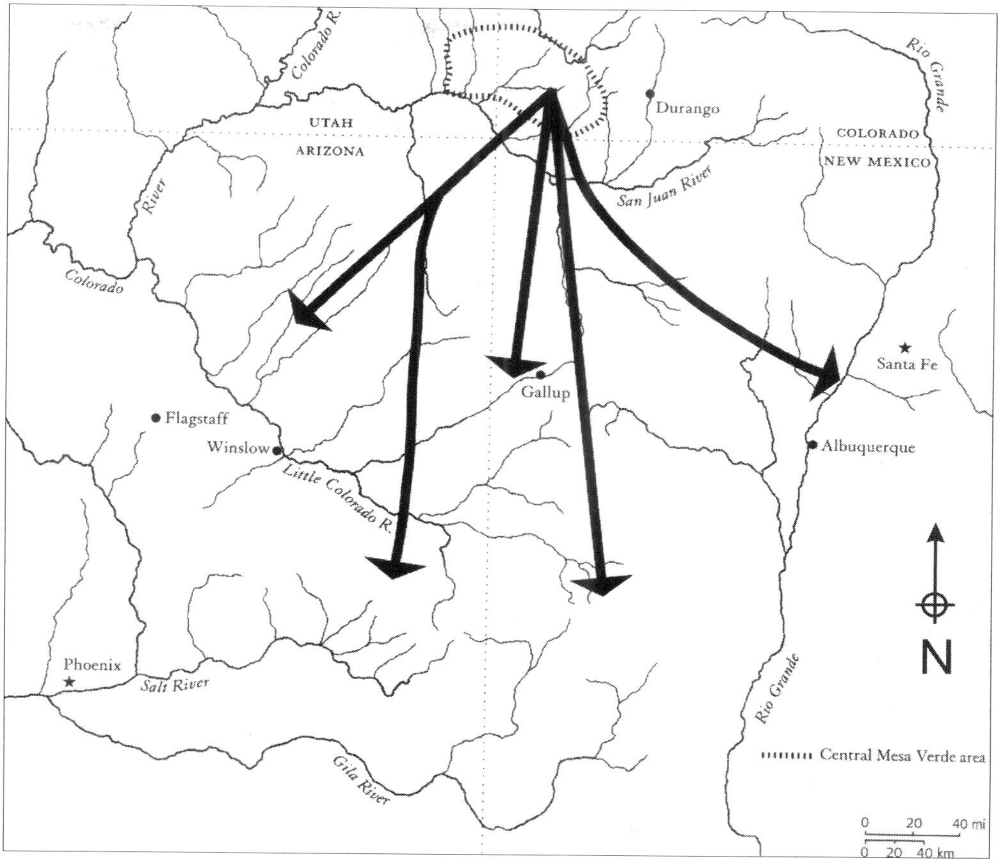


Fig. 4. Possible migration routes of Pueblo people from the central Mesa Verde region to the south and southeast near the end of the thirteenth century A.D. (after Cameron 2006: Fig. 18.5 modified by A. Danecki)

Varien 1999). Many pueblos were located near water sources such as springs (Lipe and Ortman 2000). That shift – from upland and mesa top locations that characterized the Puebloan settlement pattern before the thirteenth century A.D. to canyon rims and cliff alcoves during the A.D. 1200s – probably also increased the distance to the crop fields, at least in the case of the cliff dwellings.

In addition to this change in settlement location, there was also a change in the settlement pattern, for example, aggregation (Lipe and Varien 1999b: 303; Varien et al. 1996: 100–101). The settlements became larger, more populated, and some were well-planned in terms of the layout. The settlement pattern or model that existed during the thirteenth century A.D. in the central Mesa Verde region included communities or clusters of habitations consisting of a community center and about 15–40 smaller settlements near the community center (e.g. Lipe 2002; Rohn 1977; Varien 1999; Varien et al. 1996).

The change in settlement pattern was associated with differentiation in the architecture within the villages. Still, the primary dwelling structures in the villages were rooms and kivas, although kivas were probably also used for household-level rituals. In historic and modern times, kivas were used primarily for ritual and social gatherings and ceremonies (Plog 1997). Roomblocks were created by kiva suites consisting of a kiva, courtyard, and several (usually fewer than 12) rooms for living and storage. Such compact complexes of dwellings and storage rooms were characteristic of the architecture of the Pueblo Indians during the Pueblo III period (A.D. 1150–1300) and were probably inhabited by one or more households (or families or individual clans) (Lipe and Ortman 2000; Nordby 2006).

In the late Pueblo III period, more public architecture and structures that involved the cooperation and labor of many village residents were built, including village-enclosing walls or retaining walls, towers, plazas, D-shaped structures, and great kivas (Glowacki 2006; Lipe 2002: 220–224; Lipe and Ortman 2000; Varien et al. 1996). Some of such structures might have been used for social gatherings and rituals; however, the actual functions of some of these structures remains unknown, and several types of this kind of architecture are sometimes referred to as AWUF (architecture with unknown function) (Thompson et al. 1997; Varien et al. 1996: 90). The presence, within the sites, of structures such as circular, rectangular, or D-shaped towers and walls that enclosed whole villages or parts of villages and features such as loopholes in towers or in enclosing or protecting walls, and underground tunnels that connected two or more buildings that also became more common in this century and may be considered to have served defensive functions (Kenzle 1993; Kuckelman 2006; Lipe and Varien 1999b; Varien et al. 1996).

Population estimates vary for the Mesa Verde region during the thirteenth century A.D. The greatest estimated number of people inhabiting the area at that time is about 30,000 (Rohn 1989: 166), and they would have lived in community centers and small sites near the large sites; however, recent estimates propose that the number of people living in the area was around 10,000 or maximum 10,000 to 15,000 people (Lipe 2002: 213–217; Varien 2006: 44; Varien et al. 2007: 280–284, 288–289; Wilshusen 2002). The peak in population might have occurred early to middle A.D. 1200s (Glowacki 2006: 144; Lipe 2002; Lipe and Varien 1999b) and was at least partly caused by an influx of Puebloan populations coming from the western part of the region and perhaps from the north as well. The western portion of the Mesa Verde region was depopulated first, and the migration from this sub-region to other sub-regions, probably McElmo Monument and Mesa Verde proper, might have begun in the first half of the thirteenth century A.D. and probably ended in the A.D. 1260s (Glowacki 2006).

The thirteenth century A.D. in the central Mesa Verde region was also a time when inter-regional exchange decreased, although intra-regional exchange between the particular areas or sub-regions increased (Glowacki 2006; Varien 2006: 44). Glowacki (2006: 15) suggests that the differences in environment as well as in physiographic and geographic features between Mesa Verde proper and the rest of the central Mesa Verde region might have led to differences in lifestyle, interactions, and social networks between Puebloan communities living in these different areas.

Several possible explanations for migrations and the depopulation of the area have been proposed on the basis of the abundant data generated during the past century of research (e.g., Adler et al. 1996; Cameron 1995, 2006; Glowacki 2006; Lipe 1995a; Varien 2006) including environmental changes such as the Great Drought, resource depletion, or hostile relationships with different native groups (most often cited are ancestors of the present Ute, Navajo, and Apache) or among different Puebloan societies in the Mesa Verde region. Other theories focus on social change and attraction of new cults or ideologies from the south such as the *katchina* cult. It is also possible that social changes resulted from the environmental disturbances.

Whatever the reasons for depopulation and migration, which probably occurred in stages during the late A.D. 1270s and early 1280s, the end of the thirteenth century A.D. witnessed the final stage of Puebloan occupation of the entire Mesa Verde region. The most likely destinations of the emigrants (that is, the survivors of conflict and possible famine) include the northern and central parts of Arizona and New Mexico (Cameron 2006; Cordell 1995; Lipe 1995a; Ortman 2008; Roney 1995).

Chapter III

# DEFINING AND INTERPRETING DEFENSIVE ARCHITECTURE

## III.1. THEORY AND DIFFERENT VIEWS ON DEFENSIVE ARCHITECTURE IN NON-STATE SOCIETIES

Defensive architecture and defensive sites are commonly imagined as the medieval strongholds, castles, and fortifications built across Europe between the fifth or sixth century A.D. and the nineteenth century. The early medieval and later European fortifications exhibited traits characteristic of the architecture of both state and non-state societies; these traits were effective, especially until artillery was incorporated into warfare, but different types of fortifications continued to be used even later (Hacker 1994; Keeley et al. 2007). However, an enormous number of defensible site locations and defensive structures were utilized for defense and protection during different periods in non-state societies worldwide including some on the North American continent.

The simple definition of a "stronghold" or a defensive site is a site that is artificially defended by different kinds of fortifications or structures that protected its entrance (Hensel 1948: 16). However, it is worth mentioning that the presence of a structure that surrounds a site does not always indicate that the site or architectural feature was built for defense (Dulinicz 2000: 85). Also, although the terms "fortification" and "defensive site" are largely self-explanatory, interpreting the functions of particular ancient structures within archaeological sites, communities, or systems of related sites, is often difficult using only architectural remains and artifacts collected during archaeological investigations. The task is much easier with written records concerning specific sites or cultures. The existence of historic records is one reason that large-scale studies on defensive sites and systems of defensive sites are conducted on medieval European strongholds and castles and to some extent on defensive sites dating from earlier periods (such as the Iron Age and Bronze Age). For this reason, archaeologists and anthropologists often use analogy with historically documented defensive architecture for prehistoric societies of different levels of complexity and development.

According to *Encyclopedia Britannica* (http://www.britannica.com/EBchecked/ topic/214241/fortification), fortifications are "Any work erected to strengthen a position against attack. Fortifications are usually of two types: permanent and field. Permanent fortifications include elaborate forts and troop shelters and are most often erected in times of peace or upon threat of war. Field fortifications, which are constructed when in contact with an enemy or when contact is imminent, consist of entrenched positions for personnel and crew-served weapons, cleared fields of fire, and obstacles such as explosive mines, barbed-wire entanglements, felled trees, and antitank ditches;" and in addition, "the main purpose of early field fortifications, particularly among the Greeks, was to secure an advantage by standing on higher ground so that the enemy was forced to attack uphill."

However, defensive architecture and defensible settlement location may be perceived differently from military, civil, and scientific points of view. Representatives of the same discipline may interpret the function of a specific place differently, which occurs in the American Southwest in terms of inferring the function of particular ancient Pueblo sites. Moreover, interpretations regarding specific sites or areas might change through time. For example, Jesuit missionary Eusebio Kino concluded that hill-top sites in southern Arizona were used for religious purposes. Later, settlers in southern and central Arizona perceived such hill-top sites as lookouts or "temples of sun worship." Some modern archaeologists infer that these sites were defensive and could also have been used as lookouts, intervisibility between such sites has been proposed as well (Wilcox et al. 2001b: 142). Another example is southeastern part of North America where the Mississippian people built earthen mounds as platforms for the temples and houses of the chiefs and the elite of the society. Early European explorers of the area in the eighteenth and nineteenth centuries interpreted these mounds as defensive structures built by Spanish conquistadors as fortifications against Indians (Ceram 1977: 216); only later were the true origins of these mounds revealed. These two examples clearly show that site function can be difficult to determine and that interpretations can change through time.

In the Southwest, many ancient Pueblo settlements were constructed in locations difficult to access such as cliff alcoves or isolated mesa tops. These sites were often perceived as defensive by the members of the first U.S. military and scientific expeditions to the area in the A.D. 1850s–1870s and by the first archaeologists and ethnographers who worked in this area near the turn of the twentieth century. The same interpretation can be found in ethnohistoric records from the time of Spanish conquest, colonization and settlement of the Southwest (e.g. Hammond and Rey 1940, 1953). In addition, many contemporary Pueblo people and other American Indian groups in the Southwest believe that ancestral Pueblo sites, especially those located in locations difficult to access, were constructed for defensive purposes (see below and Chapter IV).

Today, archaeologists and anthropologists differ in their interpretations of the nature and function of these sites. However, detailed analyses of the settlement patterns of Pueblo people and other societies across the Southwest, in concert with data on population aggregation, burned structures, human osteology, and rock art, indicate that during specific periods in some areas there was widespread knowledge of the defensibility of particular locations and of the defensiveness of specific architectural constructions that could help protect people from their enemies (e.g., Kuckelman 2002; LeBlanc 1999; Lightfoot and Kuckelman 2001; Wilcox 2001a; 2001b). Some ancient settlements in the Southwest have been judged defensive also from a military point of view, such as those on Perry Mesa studied by David Wilcox and former military serviceman Jerry Robertson (Wilcox et al. 2001b: 143–147).

Defensive or fortified sites, as indicated by archaeological and ethnographic data, were built either across an entire territory inhabited by a society, in just few areas of the territory, or just on the borders (usually the case when the society was large). Fortified sites were constructed on the borders of Mandan and Arikara communities of the Upper Missouri River (Keeley 1996: 56–57) and of some Early Medieval defensive systems (Poleski 2008: 84).

## III.1.1. Defensive architecture as a response to threat

Ember and Ember (1992) conclude, in their study of 186 non-state or pre-industrial societies around the world, that fear of other people and fear of resource scarcity, natural disturbances and disasters "such as droughts, floods, storms, killing frosts, and locust infestation" that can destroy food resources are usually the factors responsible for conflict and warfare. "Both of these factors create fear – fear of nature and fear of others – which may lead people (particularly in non-state societies) to try to protect themselves against future unpredictable disasters by going to war to take resources from enemies" (Ember and Ember 1992: 243, 256). One means of allaying such fears and protecting against possible future danger is architectural, including building houses and villages in response to feeling threatened; thus, a threat – probably real and predictable – was responsible for the construction of defensive architecture.

Herbert Jankuhn (Jankuhn 2004), in his book *Wprowadzenie do archeologii osadnictwa* [*An Introduction to Settlement Archaeology*], originally published as *Einführung in die Siedlungsarchäologie*, Berlin–New York, 1977, describes strongholds and defensive sites from Neolithic, Bronze Age, and Early Medieval times, and also differentiates between types of defensive features: strongholds inhabited permanently; fortified hamlets, villages, and proto-cities; and refuge strongholds. He also distinguishes between these types in terms of their functions: central strongholds as sites of regional local authorities; strongholds as guard villages for the protection of community borders and roads; strongholds as religious centers; and refuges, usually in places difficult to access or in marshes or forested areas (Jankuhn 2004: 30).

Keeley, in his study of ancient warfare, identifies four types of defensive settlements (Keeley 1996: 57–58): fortified settlements, fortified refuges, fortified elite residences, and military fortresses. He states that only the first two of these were constructed in non-state societies, and that fortified settlements were more numerous than refuges; the latter two were very sparse or absent in non-state societies but were common in state-level societies.

LeBlanc (1999: 55–56) points out four major defensive characteristics of settlement patterning in the American Southwest that could also be applied to other areas, including site configuration, location of sites on defensible landforms, site clustering with empty zones between the clusters, and inter-visibility of sites (sites with line-of-sight communication). In Malcolm Farmer's (1957) article, *A Suggested Typology of Defensive Systems of the Southwest*, Farmer used archaeological and ethnographic data to categorize defensive systems in the Southwest as follows: palisades, towers, forts, hill-slope retreats, fortified villages, and guard villages. He also argues that the number and development of defensive sites increased in the thirteenth century A.D. (Farmer 1957: 259).

Many fortifications and defensive sites in the Southwest and beyond are in locations difficult to access; access to some sites requires the use of a ladder, log, or other equipment. Such places often contain defensive architecture including site enclosing walls, rectangular or square openings called loopholes, towers or tower-like structures that are usually taller than the other buildings at the site and would have provided a commanding view of the surrounding area, and in some cases underground tunnels connecting two or more buildings within a site (LeBlanc 1999: 55–73; Keeley et al. 2007). The defensiveness of sites displaying these characteristics may be further evaluated through analyses of site location, intervisibility with other settlements, distance to farm fields and suitable water sources, as well as other factors. These traits are present in many settlements constructed in the thirteenth century A.D. (Late Pueblo III period) in the Mesa Verde region and are analyzed in Chapter V of this book.

Villages that were surrounded by palisades or stone walls or those located in inaccessible places enjoyed particular benefits and advantages. Settlements with defensive architecture are better protected than open settlements with no defensive features; attackers are visible but usually cannot see the number and movements of the defenders. Attackers may be obliged to attack a fortified settlement at one or a few points, especially if the village is located in a place that is difficult to access, and the attackers are thus clustered and clearly visible to the defenders. However, there are some disadvantages to living in a fortified settlement. For example, protected villages could have been more attractive to possible attackers as places where valuables such as food or exotic items might be concentrated and stored. Also, some defensive sites would have been more difficult to live in than open settlements; for example, many cliff dwellings in the Southwest were difficult to access, and some could be reached only with the use of ladders or hand-and-toe holds pecked into the cliff face.

Nonetheless, when times were turbulent, living in defensive structures within defensible locations would have had more advantages and benefits than disadvantages even if this lifestyle entailed more labor and less pleasant living conditions. However, one issue is whether these extensive efforts were sufficient to defend the inhabitants against possible enemies. It appears that, in the thirteenth century A.D. in the Mesa Verde region, even well-protected villages, so costly in terms of the time and labor required for construction, were sometimes inadequate against enemy attack, for example at least parts of Castle Rock Pueblo as well as Sand Canyon Puelbo were defeated and destroyed (Kuckelman et al. 2002; Kuckelman 2010).

Construction of defensive architecture in a society is usually a response to threat on a relatively large scale, because if danger is not constant or repeated it may be overcome without investing the large amount of labor necessary to build structures that are not needed during times of peace (Keeley 1996: 55–56). Thus, the construction of many settlements in defensible locations and containing defensive architectural features in the Mesa Verde region and other parts of the Southwest could have been the result of relatively large-scale and long-term threats and conflict (LeBlanc 1999; Lekson 2002).

Also, various societies around the world built houses and villages similar to those of the ancient Pueblo people in the Mesa Verde region. For example, many Dogon villages in Mali are constructed in defensible locations: on plateaus behind narrow gorges, on mountain scree slopes, on cliff rims, in difficult-to-access shelters, and on benches of sandstone cliffs (Hard and Roney 2007: 38, Appendix 2.1; Rudofsky 2003: 40–41); some of these villages were walled. The primary reason these locations were chosen and this type of architecture was constructed was the need for protection against enemy attacks.

A cross-cultural study by Hard and Roney (2007: 11–52) of 42 cultural groups that use hills, knolls, or other elevated landforms for residential sites indicates that for 15 groups (38 percent), defense was the sole reason for selecting upland residential locations. Seventeen groups gave multiple explanations for the elevation of their settlements. Sixteen societies stated that defense and environmental considerations led to their choice of settlement location (Hard and Roney 2007: 18–20). Three ethnographic groups chose elevated landforms at least partly for symbolic reasons. Symbolic reasons for using hills and other kinds of upland locations are also mentioned by Kelley (1996: 57). Early Slavs used hilltops for conducting rituals, and some of these locations were later used as defensive sites and strongholds (Kurnatowska 2008).

Hard and Roney (2007: 20–22) examined patterns of land use vis-a-vis outbreaks and cessation of warfare. Their study reveals that many sites were wholly or partly relocated to lower elevations after hostile threats ended.

Similar and earlier ethnographic studies concerning possible associations between the frequency of conflicts and warfare and the presence or absence of fortifications and defensive sites among non-centralized societies were conducted by Otterbein (1970), who analyzed 50 societies world-wide and found a strong correlation between site location, fortified villages, and frequent warfare. Otterbein (1970: 84) studied both internal war, or war between political communities within the same cultural unit, and external warfare between cultural units.

## III.1.2. Defensive architecture as evidence of social changes and economic power

The creation of defensive features often involves the labor and cooperation of many people in a society. The existence of long enclosing or protecting walls, moats, palisades, or other structures may indicate that there was a reason (besides threat) for people to come together and work for the whole society. The existence of such structures also may indicate that some kind of power existed there that could legitimate and manage these building activities, and could persuade or force community members to cooperate. In many cases, defensive structures and sites were constructed when a society, or some members of the society such as leaders or elites, accumulated enough economic power to conduct building activity on a large scale even though the group was not directly threatened, such as in some Slavic societies or tribes in early medieval Europe (Buko 2005: 89; Dulinicz 2001: 186–187; Kurnatowska 2008: 313–315; Urbańczyk 2000). Kobyliński (1988: 206) points out that the emergence of strongholds and other defensive sites may be evidence of settlement stability, and such sites are usually built when a territory is worth defending and there is a social group that realizes this difficult task.

These characteristics are often connected with the existence of some kind of social stratification, or at least with the presence of leaders, and usually appear in farming societies. Defensive sites are more characteristic of farming societies than hunter-gatherer societies because the latter are more mobile and invest less time and effort in construction of such structures (Keeley 1996: 55). Not only pre-Hispanic and historic Puebloan farming societies were threatened by nomads living near them, many American Indian groups, both prehistoric and historic, built fortifications against hostile attacks either inside their territories or on their borders (Keeley 1996: 190–192; see also this Chapter below).

Interactions and connections between social changes and conflicts or warfare (evidence of which may be among other things construction of defensive sites) may be also found in neoevolutionism theory. For example, Carneiro (1970) attempts to explain how the constraints of the environment interact with population pressures and warfare. Anthropologists such as T. Earle, M.H. Fried, M.D. Sahlins, and E. Service have suggested a division of societies into several categories (e.g., Earle 2002: 940–961; Renfrew and Bahn 2002: 166–169) that was supplemented and modified by other researchers. Four levels of integration of societies may be distinguished in this division, primarily on the basis of the preferred type of economy, settlement pattern, population, social stratification, and leadership method. The levels of this proposed integration comprise bands, segmentary societies or tribes, chiefdoms, and states[4].

## III.2. DEFINING MESA VERDEAN DEFENSIVE ARCHITECTURE

Although most of the architecture considered defensive in the central Mesa Verde region was constructed during the Pueblo III period, this was not the only time when Ancestral Puebloans built structures to protect their villages. For example, in the Basketmaker III or later in Pueblo periods, centuries before the famous thirteenth century A.D. cliff dwellings were built and inhabited, some settlements in the Mesa Verde region were surrounded by palisades; several sites from this time period include Knobby Knee, and the Gilliland and Payne sites in southwestern Colorado (Wilshusen 1999a: 180).

Also, the famous cliff dwellings in present-day Mesa Verde National Park were not the first large pueblos constructed in sandstone niches and alcoves in the area. For example, relatively large cliff dwellings were built in Johnson Canyon and Lion Canyon south of Mancos Canyon and Mesa Verde National Park (Harrill and Breternitz 1976; Rohn and Ferguson 2006: 129–133). Early occupation of these alcoves began in the late A.D. 1130s and early A.D. 1140s and continued until the A.D. 1160s, and later occupation began in the early A.D. 1200s and lasted through about A.D. 1215, although at least two tree-ring samples from Lion House dated to A.D. 1241 (Harrill and Breternitz 1976). Early dates from cliff dwellings such as Lion House, Hoy House, Fortified House, Site 5

[4] The level or classification of a society does not always indicate the exact level of complexity and does not explain all aspects, and it is often difficult to categorize a society as a tribe, chiefdom, or other level, such division is often useful and could be helpful for some considerations and explanations of different aspects of a society.

(Morris), Tree House, and Eagle Nest House suggests that along the southern periphery of the central Mesa Verde region the "rise and fall" of living in cliff dwellings occurred earlier than farther to the north (Harrill and Breternitz 1976; Lipe and Varien 1999b: 322).

Only a few researchers have attempted systematic or detailed studies of the architecture of the Mesa Verde region in terms of possible defensive function. However, most studies devoted to this topic point out that the function of enclosing walls, towers, loopholes, and other types of architecture was defense. These studies include mainly the above-mentioned studies of defensive architecture by Malcolm Farmer (1957), of enclosing walls by Susan Kenzle (1993, 1997), and of towers in the Mesa Verde and Gallina regions by Albert Schulman (1950); however, a recent study by David Johnson (2003) argues for possible other functions of towers such as visual monitoring of valuable resources or farmland. Other possible explanations of Mesa Verde towers include use for religious or ceremonial purposes, astronomical observation, communication, or food storage (Thompson 2004: 29).

Defense is one of several possible functions of towers and other architectural features (Kenzle 1993; Lipe and Varien 1999a, 1999b; Thompson 2004; Thompson et al. 1997; Varien et al. 1996; Winter 1975, 1976, 1977), and although the main function of these structures might have varied at different sites, towers and other possibly defensive structures should be assessed in the wider context of the architecture of the entire settlement, the village layout, and the surrounding landscape. Most towers were integral to the architecture of the pueblo and shouldn't be analyzed only as free-standing structures; this problem is related to the wider issue of the interpretation of Puebloan architecture by different scholars, among whom there is not a consensus on the nature of the defensiveness of these sites.

Most structures built at late Pueblo III sites in the Mesa Verde region were constructed using the pecked-face McElmo masonry style (Lipe and Varien 1999b: 318–319). However, there were local variations in masonry construction techniques, including dry-laid (stones laid without mortar), dry-laid/daubed (dry-laid walls with daub pressed into the joints), and wet-laid (stones set in wet mortar). Some sites contain evidence of jacal, or wattle-and-daub, construction, which is a wall constructed of a framework of vertical poles, usually tied together with horizontal poles and plastered with mud or covered with daub (CCAC 2001).

The following paragraphs contain definitions of enclosing walls, towers, loopholes, and tunnels, which are features often considered defensive and that might have been constructed for the defense, and that I use in Chapter V (a catalogue of sites from the central Mesa Verde region); these definitions were derived from descriptions of these features contained in several sources (CCAC 2001; Kenzle 1997; Kuckelman, ed. by 2000; Lipe and Varien 1999a, 1999b):

**Enclosing walls** are masonry walls that enclosed all or parts of settlements; some enclosing walls enclosed structures or groups of structures whereas others extend between structures. Some of the enclosing walls in the Mesa Verde region were single-course dry-laid masonry, although some had mortar and were double-stone-with-core in cross section. Probably some walls described as retaining walls could have also been enclosing or protecting walls.

**Towers** are circular, D-shaped, or rectangular; usually two or three stories tall; are single- or multi-roomed; can be isolated or attached to other structures (for example enclosing walls); are usually located on mesa tops, at canyon heads, or in canyon bottoms, but can be in a variety of other locations; can be linked by tunnels to kivas or rooms. Towers in the Mesa Verde region might have served any of numerous possible functions.

**Loopholes** are openings through an exterior or a free-standing wall and are usually smaller than 20 cm in length or width. Many researchers have proposed that loopholes served as a means of sighting or viewing through a wall or possibly as apertures through which arrows were shot.

**Tunnels** are usually enclosed subsurface passage, longer than the thickness of the wall, that connects two or more structures or open spaces. Most tunnels are found in kivas and allowed subsurface access to another kiva, or to a tower or room.

The architectural features and structures described above were not only constructed in the thirteenth century A.D. nor were they built only in the Mesa Verde region. Towers, for example, were constructed as early as the late Pueblo II or early Pueblo III periods in the central Mesa Verde region, although these were smaller and less numerous than the towers built in the late Pueblo III period (Lipe et al., ed. by 1999). These changes may also indicate that their function changed through the time.

## III.3. EXAMPLES OF DEFENSIVE ARCHITECTURE IN DIFFERENT NON-STATE SOCIETIES

### III.3.1. Defensive sites in other parts of the Southwest

Many sites that may be considered defensive can be found across the Southwest dating from the Pueblo III and other time periods. Sites in locations that were difficult to access, often with intervisibility with other sites, as well as incorporation of defensive architectural features in site layouts, have been documented both at Pueblo sites and sites of other cultures in this region. Numerous studies have focused on the conflict and defensive architecture of different cultures in the Southwest (e.g., LeBlanc 1999; Rice and LeBlanc, ed. by 2001; Tkaczuk and Vivian, ed. by 1989; Welch and Bostwick, ed. by 2001; Wilcox and Haas 1994).

#### III.3.1.a. West-Central Colorado

Defensive architecture is present in the west-central part of Colorado, north of Mesa Verde region, including the Paradox Valley in Montrose County (McMahon 2000; McMahon and Bedingfield 2001; personal communication with Todd McMahon 2008). This region was a borderland and interaction sphere between ancestral Pueblo and Fremont peoples. The architecture exhibits strong influence from the Mesa Verde region to the south. Several sites in west-central Colorado may be interpreted as defensive because of the presence of masonry walls in front of the villages and settlement locations on high, prominent points with good visibility of the surrounding landscape. Stone-circle structures (probably towers) fit into this latter category; however, the exact functions of these sites have not yet been determined. Further and detailed study, more data collection, and interpretation of settlement patterns in this area are needed.

### III.3.1.b. Kayenta region, northeastern Arizona

The Kayenta region, located in the northeastern part of present-day Arizona, also contains Pueblo sites that were constructed during the thirteenth century A.D. in difficult-to-access locations such as cliff alcoves or rock shelters and that contain defensive structures (e.g., Dean 1970; Gilpin 2001; Haas and Creamer 1993). Winifred Creamer and Jonathan Haas (Haas and Creamer 1993) studied settlements in the Long House, Kayenta, and Klethla valleys, as well as in Tsegi Canyon, especially sites dating from the Tsegi Phase (ca. A.D. 1250–1300), and they noted that many of these sites were in locations that were difficult to access for intruders and easy to defend for inhabitants. These locations include hilltops, knolls, isolated cliffs, and cliff alcoves or caves, many of which, such as Organ Rock Ruin, Tower House, Fireside Ruin and Long House Ruin, provided commanding views of the surrounding areas and the main access routes to the sites and valleys (Plog 1997: 147). Organ Rock Ruin is located on a high, isolated mesa that is difficult to access and Twoozis Kin (Glass House), is extremely difficult to access. Some sites can be entered only with the aid of hand-and-toe holds. Also, many other defensive settlements were also constructed in this time, mostly in locations difficult to access in the Kayenta region, such as Betatakin and Kiet Siel sites in Navajo National Monument as well as White House, Antelope House, and other cliff dwellings in Canyon de Chelly (e.g., Plog 1997: 151; Rohn and Ferguson 2006: 185–218).

Between some villages there was intervisibility. In Long House Valley, for example, ancestral Puebloans cut deep notches in the escarpment of a mesa to allow intervisibility between Tower House and Fireside sites (Haas and Creamer 1993: 16, 30–31). In addition, from these two sites was possible to see at least three other sites in the valley.

In the thirteenth century A.D. settlement patterns changed with the construction of large settlements (focal sites) that were surrounded with between two and 13 smaller habitations. Four of five large villages in Long House Valley also had reservoirs for collecting water (Haas and Creamer 1993: 16). Similar to the Mesa Verde region, by A.D. 1300 the Kayenta region was also depopulated (Haas and Creamer 1993; Kohler et al. 2005).

### III.3.1.c. Perry Mesa, central Arizona

The settlements patterns of sites on Perry Mesa, a small, isolated plateau in the central part of Arizona, have been studied by several researchers and some of these studies or part of them focused on the evidence and locations of defensive architecture (Ahlstrom and Roberts 1995; Kruse 2007; Wilcox 2005: 24–35; Wilcox et al. 2001a, 2001b). Many of these sites that date from the thirteenth and fourteenth centuries A.D. were located in high, difficult-to-access locations such as hills, mesa tops, or knobs.

According to Ahlstrom and Roberts (1995: 20, Table 1; 22) a minimum of six different site types in the area can be distinguished on the basis of architecture and other factors; defensive sites constitute one type. They distinguish between two varieties or groups of defensive sites (Ahlstrom and Roberts 1995: 28–31). One group is formed of sites with specific characteristics, such as location, that could be related to defense; the sites in the other group are primarily defensive in character. The primary characteristics of defensive sites in this area are location (many sites are located on isolated hills, mesa tops, or knobs), the existence of relatively tall and thick enclosing walls, and the presence of loopholes in walls. However, according to Spoerl and Gumerman (1984: 268–270), not all sites located on hill tops were strictly defensive or served as lookout posts or signaling stations. Some were probably multifunctional; i.e., they were residential and agricultural as well as defensive.

Some sites on Perry Mesa contain little or no evidence of permanent human habitation but show strong evidence of defensive use, like NA13,350 and ARIZ N:16:1(PC) sites (Ahlstrom and Roberts 1995: 28–29). These sites are often located on the mesa tops that have a good view of the surrounding area and are surrounded by walls with loopholes. Some of the loopholes provide a good view of the area outside the site, especially the most accessible entrances to the site (Spoerl and Gumerman, ed. by 1984). The entrances to the sites are sometimes restricted and may be accessible from one or very few directions, cliff faces below the sites also prevent access from other directions. Further study of sites such as these may lend additional support to the theory that some sites were used as defensive retreats or refuges (Ahlstrom and Roberts 1995).

David Wilcox (2005: 27–30) infers that in the twelfth century A.D. and in the first half of the thirteenth century, the residents of Perry Mesa were in conflict with people belonged to Hohoham culture living south of Perry Mesa in the Phoenix Basin of the Salt and Gila river valleys. He suggests that Perry Mesa inhabitants were raiding the flourishing Hohokam settlements in the Phoenix Basin for food and cotton textiles and perhaps also for women and children. War parties of Phoenix Basin Hohokam probably retaliated against these attacks and raids. Wilcox et al. (2001a, 2001b) claim that then the Perry Mesa inhabitants built a system of line-of-sight defensive structures on defensible hilltops.

This situation changed radically after A.D. 1250 when settlements in the Phoenix Basin were reorganized into walled compounds and the population was probably growing (Wilcox 2005: 28). According to Wilcox, at that time the system of defensive hilltop sites was not effective enough to protect the Perry Mesa people from the Phoenix Basin people, and the settlement pattern on Perry Mesa changed again. This new pattern included the distribution of small and large settlements around the perimeter of the mesa. Many structures were built in inaccessible locations on the edges of mesa tops. The sites were in proximity to one another to facilitate better protection (Wilcox 2005: 30).

### III.3.1.d. New Mexico

Research on Puebloan settlements in the area of present-day New Mexico has revealed that during some periods in different areas of the Puebloan world, sites were built in a defensive manner, in defensible locations, or fortified by adding defensive architectural features that could have enhanced the protection of villages and the residents thereof (LeBlanc 1999, 2001; Snead 2008).

LeBlanc's (2001) study of warfare and aggregation in the El Morro Valley in west-central New Mexico indicates that during the Muerto phase, approximately the late

1270s to the early 1280s A.D., some sites, such as Scribe S, were dismantled, burned, and then abandoned, whereas others, including Pueblo de los Muertos, Atsinna, Cienega, and Mirabal, were built in proximity. Many of the Muerto phase sites share traits such as "high exterior walls created by the outer wall of the outermost rooms of the pueblo." These rooms usually enclosed a plaza, and access to the rooms was primarily from the interior of the pueblo. Also, access to most of the structures, or at least the upper stories, necessitated the use of ladders.

Another characteristic trait is locating a settlement such that a water source is either secured within the village, such as at Cienega, Kluckhohn, Atsinna, and Mirabal, or is very near the settlement, such as at Pueblo de los Muertos; intervisibility between particular sites is also characteristic (LeBlanc 2001: 30–34).

Recent archaeological excavations and surveys of ancestral Pueblo landscapes in the northern Rio Grande area of New Mexico by James Snead (2005, 2008) and others, reveal that many sites in this area that date from the late Pueblo III and the Pueblo IV periods were built in defensible locations and incorporate defensive architectural features. For example, the location of Burnt Corn Pueblo of the Galisteo Basin on a ridgetop with steep slopes indicates a concern for defense, and access routes to the site "were blocked by outlying roomblocks, which effectively served as watchposts" (Snead 2008: 92–93). According to Snead, the organization of the entire Burnt Corn Pueblo community reflects "tactical considerations" that include the location of Burnt Corn Pueblo itself and other sites in the community, which are also in locations difficult to access, as well as the possible existence of intervisibility between sites. These settlement and architectural patterns that show a concern for protection of the inhabitants, as seen in defensible locations or the intervisibility of sites, have also been documented at other sites in the area such as those in the Los Aguajes, Tsankawi and T'obimpaenge communities (Snead 2008: 139, 150–151) as well as in other sites and communities in the area.

### III.3.1.e. Sites on the US-Mexico borderland

Most Trincheras sites or *cerro de trincheras*, sometimes called the "trincheras phenomenon," are located in southern Arizona and New Mexico, and northern Mexico (in Sonora and Chihuahua states); they are located on hills, exhibit dry-laid masonry features, and were built sometime during a long span of time that began in the Early Agricultural (called also Late Archaic) about 1300/1250 B.C. and lasted until A.D. 1450 (Fish et al., ed. by 2007). Multiple explanations of the function of these sites have been proferred, one of which is that they served for the defense and protection of people living there or who lived there in turbulent times (Hard and Roney 2007). Hard and Roney (2007: 11–52) analyzed data regarding location, site layout, rapidity of construction, and site intervisibility for many trincheras sites, and also used ethnographic analogy. They concluded that "raiding and warfare are the most likely explanation for residential use of the ceros de trincheras" (Hard and Roney 2007: 33). This conclusion may be supported by artifact assemblages from Cerro Juanaqueña, one of the trincheras sites, which contained several hundred projectile points and biface fragments (Hard and Roney 2007: 32).

However, not all scholars agree that trincheras functioned as defensive sites or refuges, and other explanations include avoidance of flooding, access to agricultural fields and wild resources, as well as symbolic or religious purposes (see Fish et al., ed. by 2007).

### III.3.1.f. Apache breastworks and Navajo Pueblitos of New Mexico

That Apaches were aware of the defensibility of particular site locations is evidenced by the Apache leader, Geronimo, hiding from American soldiers in the area of the Gila Cliff Dwellings (Morgan 1994: 106). Apache breastworks were built primarily by Mescalero Apaches for example on high, defensible ridgetops in the Guadalupe Mounatins of southeastern New Mexico at elevations between 1555 and 1585 m, although some were constructed in canyon bottoms about 100–150 m below the ridgetop sites (Adams et al. 2001). These breastworks were small, constructed of stone, usually a single course wide, and probably provided protection for individuals during a battle (Adams et al. 2001: 98).

The breastworks were probably associated with raiding and warfare between the Apaches and the U.S. Army in the second half of the nineteenth century, and they were most likely used for lookout and as defensive sites, either habitational or as temporary refuges. There is no evidence of long-term habitation of these sites and they were probably occupied for only short periods of time (Adams et al. 2001: 97–98), although many breastworks were located near *rancherías*, or more permanent villages.

Navajo pueblitos appear to have been more numerous than Apache breastworks and are masonry structures built on boulders and mesa rims, and a few were constructed in rock shelters that overlook the surrounding landscape. Many boulder-top structures occupy the entire surface of the boulder. Pueblitos were constructed by Navajos (Diné) during the late 1600s and early 1700s especially in the northwestern part of New Mexico in the Dinétah, or the ancestral homeland of the Navajo people (Towner 1999, 2004; Towner et al. 2001). Pueblitos were used until the mid-1700s, when the Dinétah was abandoned. The archaeological data that indicate a defensive function for these sites are supported by tree-ring dates, Navajo oral tradition, and ethnohistoric records.

It is probable that while Navajos were adopting many other traits from Pueblo people, they also adopted defensive architecture and line-of-sight communication (Towner et al. 2001). Constructing pueblitos was probably a tactic for raiding with Ute and Comanche groups and as defense against Spaniards who had already established permanent settlements in the Southwest. The conflicts between Navajos and Utes in the A.D. 1740s and 1750s were probably larger than those previous. Recent studies have revealed that most pueblitos were built in one of two periods (Towner 1999: 8–9; Towner et al. 2001: 113–116): the first was in the A.D. 1710s and has been linked to Spanish entradas into Navajo country such as that of Roque Madrid in 1705; the second was between A.D. 1725 and 1755, probably a response to Ute and Comanche raiding.

Pueblitos usually consist of one or more masonry rooms, one or several hogans, multiple sweatlodges, and other structures and features (Towner et al. 2001: 117). Pueblitos show some traits that may be interpreted as defensive. They have loopholes or "shooting portals" (Towner et al. 2001: 119), many of which are located near entryways and access points, and the entryways are usually narrow and limited to a single access point. Access to many of these sites was possible only by ladders or logs. The layout was such that movement within the site boundary was, of necessity, rather slow, and structures that might be classified as defensive, such as circular stone towers, can also be present.

Studies conducted in the 1990s and in 2009 tested communication and intervisibility between pueblitos with smoke or fire (Bryan 2009; http://www.blm.gov/nm/st/en.html). As indicated by these studies, many pueblitos had intervisibility, but according to Patrick Hogan "they aren't going to have line of sight to all of them. They're going to be in clusters, and those clusters might give us a basis for then defining larger cooperating groups" (Bryan 2009). For a better analysis of these studies, computer modeling is also conducted.

## III.3.2. Defensive architecture in other parts of North America

Defensive architecture and defensive sites were present in American Indian cultures both in egalitarian societies such as small bands in northern California and the state of Washington and in more complex and developed societies such as the chiefdoms of southeastern North America (e.g., Chacon and Mendoza, ed. by 2007; Keeley 1996; LeBlanc and Register 2003). Of course, types of defensive architecture varied between cultures and areas partly because of the availability of specific building materials, such as wood or stone, and because of diverse warfare strategies.

In northeastern North America palisades were constructed by Pequots (McBride 1990), Nanticoke, and Delaware. Some fortified villages of the Pequots, located on hilltops, are associated with the time of European contact (McBride 1990: 101–102). The Iroquois built multiple lines of palisades and attached bastions to some (Keeley 1996: 191). Many villages of the Middle and Late Owasco culture were "protected by earth rings, palisades, or both" (Snow 2004: 28–29). In the later period of Iroquoian culture many "villages had double or triple palisades, and they were occupied for long periods, perhaps up to a century" (Snow 2004: 36).

People of the Mississippian Tradition in the eastern area of North America constructed many palisades surrounding either whole settlements or only the central part; some palisades were built before contact with Europeans, and others were constructed after the arrival of Spaniards, Frenchmen, and Englishmen (Fowler 1997; Pauketat 1994: 157–159). Numerous palisades were covered by mud or clay, a technique also used in early medieval Europe where many palisades in strongholds were covered by mud or clay to protect them from fire. Palisades with bastions were present in many Mississippian sites, including Cahokia Mounds and the Dickson Site in Illinois and Moundville in Alabama. The height of palisades varied from about 3.0 to 4.5 meters. Some enclosed just the centers of the mound cities, which suggests that they were used as a kind of social barrier between the elite living in the center of the city and the rest of the people in the village or town living outside the boundary of palisade rather than for protection from enemies (Dalan et al. 2003: 104–105). One of the late societies of the Mississippian Tradition, the Natchez, who lived during the seventeenth and eighteenth centuries A.D. in what is now western Mississippi, built palisades with baffle gates and towers to protect their villages.

Also in the Southeast, the Choctaw built palisades, and the Creeks built towers, battlements, and multiple palisades; the Timucua in Florida built moats, baffle gates, and gate houses in addition to palisades (Keeley 1996: 190).

Ancestors of historic Mandan, Arikara, and Hidatsa tribes built villages along the Upper Missouri River and farmed the floodplains. In this type of settlement pattern nearly every village were on the edge of tribal territory, on a "frontier." Archaeological data indicate that between A.D. 1300 and 1500, and especially after 1400, many villages were fortified, which could have been a response to threat, scarcity of resources, and increasing conflict (Keeley 1996: 56–57; Nabokov and Easton 1989: 127–135). Many settlements were then "forced" by adding log palisades or stockades and moats. French notes from the first half of the eighteenth century describe one of the Mandan villages as having very clean streets and "the palisade supported on cross-pieces mortised into posts of fifteen feet" (Nabokov and Easton 1989: 127).

Palisades and other defensive structures were also built on the Northwest Coast and in present-day Alaska by Aleut, Alutiiq, Tlingit, Salish, Chumash, and Kwakiutl Indians. Forts, refuge rocks, and other defensive sites were constructed by these groups, and some of the oldest forts in the Tlingit region date from about A.D. 500 (Moss and Erlandson 1992). Archaeological and ethnographic sources indicate that defensive sites were permanently inhabited, but many were located near villages and probably served as refuges. Most defensive sites were constructed on small islands or on landforms with steep slopes and were protected with defensive architecture such as palisades, trenches, village-enclosing walls, and escape tunnels; some sites were accessible only by ladder (Mitchell 1968; Moss and Erlandson 1992: 74–75). Between A.D. 900 and 1400 there was a "dramatic increase in the number of forts in use" (Moss and Erlandson 1992: 83) that probably reflects an intensification of competition and conflict in the region. The construction and maintenance of defensive sites in this area continued into the time of European contact.

Some Tlingit settlements were only partly surrounded by a palisade; in the Tlingit village of Hoonah in Alaska, for example, a palisade was built just to protect the part of the village where the Raven clan houses stood (Keeley 1996: Plate 5). Numerous summer camps of Copper Inuit were located on hills for "fear of Indian attack, to watch for caribou, and to avoid mosquitoes. Tents were camouflaged for fear of attacks" (Hard and Roney 2007: 37, Appendix 2.1).

## III.3.3. Defensive sites in prehistoric and early historic central-eastern and southern Europe

### III.3.3.a. Neolithic, Bronze Age and Early Iron Age strongholds and defensive sites

One of the earliest examples of possible defensive architecture was found "at Jericho in the Pre-Pottery Neolithic (PPNA and PPNB, 8000–6000 B.C.) layers." These "defenses" consisted of a ditch backed by a massive rock wall nearly 6 m tall and a large circular tower at least 8 m tall that was built later just behind this wall (Keeley et al. 2007: 83–84). During the Neolithic in central-eastern and southern Europe numerous defensive settlements incorporated ditches and earthen or wooden enclosures, and they were built in locations that were easy to defend (Jankuhn 2004: 114–117; Keeley et al. 2007: 84–85; Kozłowski and Kaczanowski 1998: 112–113; Kruk 2008).

Many Neolithic and Bronze Age settlements in Crete, especially in the Cretan Mountains, were constructed in the mountains on mountain peaks or hill tops protected by steep talus slopes and in locations difficult or nearly impossible to access (Alušik 2008). The most common types of defensive architecture at these sites include partial or full enclosing walls, some of which were abutted by tower-like structures, "guard houses" located near a road, pass, spring or other water source, and some of which also safeguarded the entrance paths to the sites (Alušik 2008: 76–78; Nowicki 2000). Caves were also used, but it is difficult to determine whether they were used for defensive purposes or refuges, because no evidence of defensive architecture has been documented; they were also probably used for ritual purposes (Alušik 2008: 79).

Some of these sites were permanent habitations, but others served as refuges for nearby settlements. Refuges could have been used by multiple villages located within several hours' walk. In some cases, only the uppermost portion of a site was walled, and this area probably served as a refuge for the entire settlement (Alušik 2008: 81). Zakros Gorge Ellinika is one example of a settlement that consisted of a "lower town" and "upper town" (Alušik 2008: 76). Avrakontes Kastellon is an example of a defensive site situated "on the southern and western slopes of the mountain ridge of Kastellon in the saddle between two summits" and "the site is well protected by steep slopes from all sides except for the southwestern" (Alušik 2008: 77).

Alušik (2008: 81–82), after analyzing more than 200 defensive sites in this area, concludes that the defensive function of many of these sites, such as Juktas and Kofinas, was doubled because many sites served "for religious (peak sanctuaries) and/or economic/exploitation (so-called guard houses)," and the defensive function was probably a response to the need for protecting people, food, supplies, and access to the natural resources in the area (Alušik 2008: 81).

Many defensive sites, including defensible structures on uplands or hills, were built during the Bronze Age and Early Iron Age by cultural groups in central-eastern and southern Europe such as the Hatvan and Vucedol Zók cultures in the Balkans and Carpathian Basin. In at least some cases, such as the Vatya culture (1900–1800 B.C.), these sites were integrated and organized into larger defensive systems (Chochorowski 1999a: 209–210, 217), probably in response to a threat. In the late phase of the Gava and Kyjatice cultures in the Carpathian Basin, many people fortified existing settlements or relocated to difficult-to-access points that were not convenient – some were very inconvenient – for habitation; the only reasonable explanation for choosing such locations was the threat of attack (Chochorowski 1993: 212). However, Bronze Age strongholds are more complicated and complex in terms of location, construction materials, and chronology, and probably varied in different parts of central-eastern Europe (Gediga, ed. by 1989; Gedl 1989: 153).

Bronze Age settlement systems are characterized by the appearance, presence, and development of defensive sites; some such systems were associated with the threat of nomads such as Scythians or Kimmers from eastern European and the Asian steppes, who, according to archaeological data and written records, troubled farming societies in central-eastern and southern Europe with frequent and well-organized attacks

(Chochorowski 1993: 212–213, 267–272; Chochorowski 1999b; Kozłowski and Kaczanowski 1998: 176–179). Some cultures might have collapsed as a result of such attacks. Data also suggest that, during times of attack, Bronze Age societies used high and nearly inaccessible places such as pinnacles or hilltops, or even caves and shelters; arrowheads of nomadic origin have been found in or near some of these locations, indicating attacks on these sites. Shelters in Rzędkowice and Piaseczno, near Zawiercie in Lesser Poland are examples of nearly inaccessible refuges (Bukowski 1977: 99, 106–109; Kozłowski and Kaczanowski 1998: 178). Many of the bronze, three-sided arrowheads found at those sites are bent, probably as a result of striking rock (Bukowski 1977: 99, 106). Caves and rock shelters located roughly in this area and especially near Kraków were used also later, during the Late Medieval period at the beginning of the fourteenth century A.D. An oral tradition tells of a Polish king, Władysław Łokietek, who, with his knights, used the caves as refuges while Poland was being raided by Czechs (Kołodziejski 1995: 158).

Defensive sites and strongholds were constructed by various groups of the Lusatian culture and by other cultures in the central-eastern Europe. Most of these sites were located in difficult-to-access places and were built using a variety of techniques and materials that depended on available construction material; most common were wooden, stone, and earthen fortifications. Moats and protected gates were also constructed (Chochorowski 1999a: 231). These settlements and strongholds were dwellings, residences of elites that could have controlled the communities, but also as sites for conducting religious ceremonies.

Strongholds were built in response to danger, some were permanent settlements, and others were just refuges. A stronghold in Łubowice in Upper Silesia, in the present territory of Poland, occupied 25 ha and was surrounded by wooden and earthen fortifications (Chochorowski 1999b). The use of this site changed through time, although its primary function was to protect the inhabitants of nearby settlements in case of a threat (Chochorowski 1999b: 390–391).

Another type of Lusatian culture strongholds were so-called Biskupin-type strongholds that were built in the early phase of the Iron Age; tree-ring dates for the founding of Biskupin are 738/737 B.C. (Grossman 2006: 18). Many of these strongholds were constructed near lakes, rivers, or springs, and some were located on west-facing slopes with good sunlight exposure. Settlements such as Biskupin were surrounded by palisades or other fortifications (see Śmigielski 1991 for a detailed description of Lusatian culture strongholds). Within the fortification, houses were neatly laid out, densely packed, and reflected an egalitarian social structure. The presence of such fortified villages is often associated with the influence of urban Greek colonies in northern and central Italy through the Hallstatt culture; however, those sites were constructed with a concern for defense as well. Biskupin-type strongholds were apparently the last stage of the occupation of Lusatian culture in the area, and that settlement pattern included a large site such as a community center that was usually a stronghold and that was surrounded by several or several dozen small sites (Harding and Ostoja-Zagórski 1989: 176). The stronghold, as the political center of the community, was also probably the religious center and served as the "guarantor" of socio-political order (Harding and Ostoja-Zagórski 1989: 180).

The Biskupin site itself was built in the middle of a lake, could be accessed by one road only, and was surrounded by tall fortifications. This road and a gate were constructed in such a manner that attackers were obliged to approach with their right side toward the site; because most warriors held their shields in their left hands, they were thus vulnerable to defenders' arrows approaching from the right (Kozłowski and Kaczanowski 1998: 181–182).

The end of the occupation of the Biskupin stronghold, and the collapse of other defensive sites built in a similar manner in the region of Wielkopolska, was probably the result of a shift toward a colder and wetter climate about 700 B.C. (Chochorowski 1999b: 392; Kozłowski and Kaczanowski 1998: 182) coupled with an inadequate adaptation of the people to these new conditions. These events could have caused big groups to disintegrate into smaller ones and the social system to collapse (Harding and Ostoja-Zagórski 1989: 180).

During the Early Iron Age, the settlement pattern changed in some areas in the Lusatian culture in Małopolska. Settlements were constructed in uplands, and those in Mników, Piekary, and Tyniec were also fortified (Rydzewski 1995: 109).

### III.3.3.b. Early Medieval defensive sites

Early Medieval strongholds differed in location, size, chronology, length of use, construction, and layout; moreover, their function varied in early Slavic societies (Dulinicz 2001: 182; Jaworski 2005: 101–116; Poleski 2004: 92–120, 153–178). Most were probably built to protect the inhabitants and people dispersed in nearby smaller settlements. However, some might have been constructed by local leaders as a manifestation of their power, for military and prestige reasons, and intervisibility with other sites was probably also important. Many of these sites were probably community centers for larger communities or clusters of sites (Dulinicz 2001: 186). Some strongholds in Lesser Poland might have been built for protection against the nomadic Awars (Poleski 2004: 158). Locations of strongholds varied; strongholds in the Carpathian Mountains in southern part of Lesser Poland were built on the edges of a community territory, but in the northern part of the region they were located within the territory as community centers for nearby settlements (Poleski 2008: 84; Wojenka 2008: 282).

However, early Slavs did not build strongholds and defensive sites, but they probably used a variety of defensive strategies; the construction of defensive sites might have begun when leaders achieved a sufficient level of power and were able to accumulate goods for redistribution (Buko 2005: 89; Dulinicz 2001: 186–187; Kurnatowska 2008: 313–315; Urbańczyk 2000). According to detailed studies of strongholds built in central-eastern Europe, including in the present area of Poland (Dulinicz 2001; Jaworski 2005; Poleski 2004), these sites were first constructed at a later stage of Slavic culture.

These strongholds were built in a variety of locations. Some were located in difficult-to-access places on hills or the edges of plateaus, but others were in valleys and on floodplains. Studies of strongholds in the Sudety Mountains (Jaworski 2005) indicate that in some parts of this region defensive settlements were built on headlands or promontories with steep talus slopes on three sides (Jaworski 2005: 101). Some strongholds were easier to enter from a specific direction, but this route was protected by an architectural feature such as a wall or palisade. The existence of only one access route was a common trait in early Medieval strongholds (Dulinicz 2000: 89).

Recent studies have revealed that most of early Medieval strongholds in Lesser Poland (Poleski 2004) were located no farther than 150 m from a water source, and springs or other water sources were located within the boundaries of many sites (Poleski 2004: 93–94). Tribal defensive settlements in the Sudety Mountains and other areas were probably situated similarly (Jaworski 2005: 101–102). However, it is important to note that water sources that existed in the past might not exist today. An oral tradition still repeated by local people tells of water sources on the southern slope of a hill where the stronghold Naszacowice is located; no water sources exist there today (Poleski 2004: 93).

A significant shift in the defense of Wielkopolska (Greater Poland) region occurred in the first half of the tenth century A.D., when many new strongholds were built while many old ones were burned and destroyed. This development is usually interpreted as replacing the old tribal strongholds with new ones, probably under the rule of one leader or "leading family," and involved changing the locations of strongholds, previously clustered in the southern and western parts of Wielkopolska, to the northern and eastern areas of the region (Kurnatowska 2000: 104–105). The primary settlement or center was Gniezno, which became the first capital of Poland a few decades later, and other important strongholds include Giecz, Poznań, and Ostrów Lednicki. Most of these new strongholds were larger and contained different fortifications from the older ones (Kurnatowska 2000: 105). Other strongholds were also fortified; however, they appear to have been real community centers for smaller settlements rather than defensive sites (Dulinicz 2000: 89).

The developments mentioned above, other large strongholds, and suitable economic and military power probably led to the first stage in the creation of the state (Kara and Krąpiec 2000: 320; Kurnatowska 2000: 106). Also, the "defensive" structures in some of the early Medieval strongholds were not necessarily used for defense (Dulinicz 2000: 92–95; Poleski 2008: 81) in contrast to later structures built in "military" fashion. Gniezno was a very important ceremonial site for local societies, but after the Piast dynasty took control of the region, the site was fortified and its function changed (Kurnatowska 2008).

Recent analysis of tree-ring dates indicates that about A.D. 940 the process of building and renovating strongholds in Wielkopolska began. A similar process occurred in the A.D. 970s and 980s just after the beginning of the Polish state. Poland accepted Christianity in A.D. 966, and this is often considered the beginning of the Polish state (during this time Poland was ruled by the first ruler recorded in historic documents, Mieszko I). Building and renovating strongholds also occurred about A.D. 1000, in the late A.D. 1020s, and in the early 1030s during the beginning of the first political and social crisis of the new Polish state (Kara and Krąpiec 2000: 320–321). Many researchers associate the building activity of the A.D. 940s with an escalating threat from the Germans, improvement in the economy of the leaders of local tribes, and an influx of valuable goods and money, such as Arabic dirhems, that would have financed the construction of many strongholds. These developments were dependent upon a level of political thought and organization able to conduct and support such activities.

Building a state was not a necessary stage; nevertheless, it occurred in many territories of Early Medieval central-eastern Europe and probably also was associated with powerful elites and local leaders. Urbańczyk (2000: 63–64) suggests that before a state was created in Lesser Poland there had been a period of consolidating and strengthening the role of elites in forming a base for a more complex and developed society. That process could have taken a long time – in this case about 150–200 years. The process of the consolidation and aggregation of settlements began about the middle of the seventh century A.D. and continued into the eighth and ninth centuries (Buko 2005: 412). At the same time, a new type of tribal or ethnic group structure developed. One of the primary issues of the archaeology of this "tribal" period, and later the creation of the state, concerns the beginning and the stage of development of stronghold construction (Buko 2005: 412).

# Chapter IV

# ETHNOGRAPHY, ETHNOHISTORY, AND NATIVE AMERICAN ORAL TRADITIONS CONCERNING DEFENSIVE ARCHITECTURE AND CONFLICTS IN THE SOUTHWEST

Archaeology, as the study of a past rarely preserved in written form, faces a very difficult task. Having often only 'mute' artifacts at its disposal, archaeology can never reconstruct a particular culture in its entirety. Moreover, it is not always clear which artifacts are indicators of membership in a particular linguistic, religious, ethnic, or social group or how to select those artifacts from the full assemblage (Renfrew and Bahn 2002). Detailed analysis of the material culture left by humans, and accurate reconstruction of societies requires archaeologists to incorporate the work and research results of other disciplines. Thus, it may require cooperation and a multidisciplinary or interdisciplinary approach more than other fields of study.

Southwestern archaeology, including the archaeology of the Mesa Verde region, owes much of its successful progress to its collaboration with researchers in other scientific disciplines, for example, history, cultural anthropology,[5] sociology, linguistics, environmental studies, and dendrochronology, as well as other sciences, and even mathematics and computer sciences (computer modeling of ancient societies) in recent times. Ethnohistoric and ethnographic data, as well as oral traditions of contemporary American Indians, are also very useful to the archaeology of the Southwest. Even though such records usually refer to historic and more recent times, they may help us understand what happened near the end of the thirteenth century A.D. in the Mesa Verde region. Using oral tradition and ethnographic and ethnohistoric records to supplement archaeological data can lead to more comprehensive archaeological views and theories (e.g., Brumfiel 2003).

[1] In many European universities, archaeology is considered a historical discipline, sometimes associated with botanical sciences like in some places in France; however, in so-called Anglo-Saxon archaeology, for example, in Great Britain and the United States, archaeology is linked with social sciences, mainly with cultural anthropology. In those countries, archaeology is considered a branch of anthropology.

These differing perceptions of the correct place of the science of archaeology may lead to misunderstandings between scientists in different countries; however, a willingness to cooperate can lead to broader and more comprehensive explanations and reconstructions of past cultures.

However, the interdisciplinarity of research and the use of ethnographic analogy, as well as the reliance on results of research in other fields, often creates disputes between researchers across both Europe and the U.S. and has occurred in the Southwest. In Central-Eastern Europe and Poland particularly, studies of the ethnogenesis and topogenesis of the Slavs have given rise to disputes involving the disciplines of archaeology, history, genetics, and linguistics (e.g., Tabaczyński 1998), although language in this case includes not only studies of linguistics but also biology and physical anthropology.

Thus, the interdisciplinarity of research involves the use of a specific and appropriate methodology of study (Anyon et al. 1997; Echo-Hawk 1997; Kozłowski 1999: 18–19; Lyons 2003: 82–99; Posern-Zieliński 1997; Renfrew and Bahn 2002). This can be achieved only when different disciplines participating in the process of reconstructing human cultures not only rely on data or widely known information from other sciences, but are vitally interested in learning the methods and treatment of cultures by these different disciplines (Posern-Zieliński and Ostoja-Zagórski 1977). The interdisciplinarity of research means the integration of diverse paths of study and research methods, and the result of interdisciplinary study is not the sum of varying competencies of particular experts, but a product, i.e., something qualitatively and quantitatively different, which satisfies the expectations of the cooperating disciplines (Donato 1986).

In this chapter, information is presented concerning defensive architecture and evidence of conflict among different Pueblo societies as seen in ethnohistoric and ethnographic data as well as in the oral traditions of historic and contemporary American Indians in the Southwest. Sometimes it is difficult to distinguish between oral traditions recorded by early ethnographers and their own interpretations and suggestions, which introduces the possibility that information treated as oral tradition might be mixed with ethnographic data. However, despite the possible duplication of information, the author divided those data into two separate subchapters.

This information is not being offered as a direct analogy to the pre-Hispanic Pueblo world, but rather as data that clearly indicate the existence of defensive architectural features and contain specific site locations that were well known in Pueblo societies and were present not only in prehistory but during times of unrest in the historic period. This information can help us understand the social context and events that occurred in the central Mesa Verde region in the thirteenth century A.D. "The three disciplines (archaeology, history and ethnology) differ in the diversity of their base sources, research methods and contexts for the interpretations, but they should be united by questions formed in a similar way, related issues and parallel study objectives" (Posern-Zieliński 1997: 100).

## IV.1. ETHNOHISTORIC RECORDS

According to Godłowski (2000: 350), "written sources are the starting point and guideline for interpreting data from other disciplines." Many issues and inquiries regarding the functioning of human societies through time can be studied through historical written records of the culture under investigation and by the careful application of ethnohistoric analogy if there is compelling evidence that the comparison is justified. Of course, the frequency of written relics and reports obviously varies both through time and geographically. Available ethnohistoric records made by Spaniards in the Southwest from the beginning of the sixteenth century A.D. are invaluable sources of such information for archaeology. However, as with other historic sources, this ethnohistoric data must be examined using scientific methodology, and the information therein must be approached with due caution.

The first contact between Europeans and American Indians, as well as the later permanent presence of the Europeans in the Southwest, resulted in written (ethnohistoric) records on the population of American Indians, the distribution of particular settlements, and the organization of the societies and their beliefs. The first written records referring to the North American Southwest date from the early half of the sixteenth century A.D., when several expeditions were sent by the Spanish Crown to penetrate and explore the Southwest, which was the area north of Mexico then called New Spain. Some of the expeditions that were led by conquistadors were motivated by lust for new lands, labor, and gold and other precious items. This was similar to actions in Mexico where conquistadors destroyed the Aztec empire and in Peru where they conquered the Inca state. After these conquests Europeans turned toward the North American continent – a region that was then poorly known.

In 1539, Franciscan Fray Marcos de Niza, on the orders of Antonio de Mendoza (the viceroy of New Spain), proceeded from Mexico toward the area that is now New Mexico to search for wealthy mythical cities (the Seven Golden Cities of Cibola). The following year two expeditions set out; one was an overland expedition led by Francisco Vásquez de Coronado (there are at least two chronicles from that expedition, by Pedro Castaneda de Náxera and Juan Jaramillo), the other proceeded by sea along the shoreline under the command of Hernando de Alarcón. These expeditions followed the journey of Álvar Núñez Cabeza de Vaca (1529–1536), one of four members of the Pánfilo de Narváez expedition who survived (Narváez's expedition set out along the southeastern coast of North America). The expeditions also followed the legend of the treasures of the Seven Golden Cities of Cibola brought by Cabeza de Vaca (Bolton 1949; Gąssowski 1996: 127–128; Hammond and Rey 1940; Plog 1997: 181–193; Riley 1987).

Probably the largest expedition was that of Coronado. It lasted two years (from 1540 to 1542) and reached as far as the Hopi pueblos in present-day Arizona as well as the pueblos of the Zuni and those along the Rio Grande in present-day New Mexico. The expedition went as far as today Kansas to northeast and the Grand Canyon to the west. Most of the expeditions in the Southwest mentioned above failed: conquistadors did not find the gold and other valuables they searched for, treasures that had been previously found in Mexico and Peru. Many conquistadors were killed or died from illnesses. Vásquez de Coronado managed to return to Mexico, but according to his chronicler, instead of gold, "he found only corn, beans, and poultry (turkeys) in abundance" (Fagan 2000: 27–28).

However, after their early misfortunes, the Spaniards finally conquered this region and established their permanent settlements. The first permanent Spanish settlement in New Mexico was founded in 1598 by Juan Zaldivar de Oñate, sometimes called "the Last Conquistador". The settlement was named San Juan de los Caballeros and was located near the Chama River, north of present-day Albuquerque. De Oñate served as the first governor of New Mexico for eight years (Riley 1987). The North American Southwest was under Spanish (New Spain) authority until 1821 when Mexico won its independence and took control of the Southwest territory. In 1848, after a war between the U.S. and Mexico, the Southwest was incorporated into U.S. territory. Thus, Spanish documents are the main source of written information on native societies in the Southwest until the middle of the nineteenth century; however, after that time, sources written in English predominated. Some of the Spanish chronicles have now been translated into English, others exist only in Spanish, although various institutions have undertaken English translations (for example it is worth to mention such efforts by Office of Ethnohistorical Research, Arizona State Museum, University of Arizona, Tucson).

As might be expected, a great deal of information about the level of defensiveness of Puebloan architecture and society is contained in ethnohistoric records (Haas and Creamer 1997: 240, 242). This is not surprising, because the Spaniards were intruders in the Southwest, and there was a need for information concerning "military" aspects of encountered societies for later use by other expeditions and parties and for bringing the land under Spanish rule. However, it is worth noting that early Spaniards in the Southwest, like Coronado, were rather disappointed that the societies living there were not as complex, populous, or rich as Indians in Mexico which affected the amount of information collected by Spaniards about the native Southwestern societies they encountered (Lekson 2005: 159). Spaniards often mentioned in their chronicles and reports that many pueblos they encountered were built in a defensive manner and reflected defensive considerations in terms of their location, enclosing walls, or even the construction style of their houses. The Spaniards often called a site they visited (both the ruins and villages still inhabited by Pueblo people) "fortress" or noted that sites were located in places very difficult to access. The defensible locations of sites as well as the presence of defensive architecture attests to the considerable number of conflicts between Pueblo groups as well as between Puebloans and non-Pueblo tribes (most often cited, but especially referring from seventeenth to nineteenth century, are Navajo, Apache, Ute, Paiute, and Comanche), and between Puebloans and Spaniards.

Spanish administrative records from the seventeenth and eighteenth centuries and the first quarter of nineteenth century, the time of New Spain's governing of the area, contains information on Puebloan architecture, warfare, and military potential, as well as on the Pueblo Revolt of 1680, which was a rebellion of allied pueblos, and to some extent other tribes, against Spanish rule in the Southwest. The Pueblo Revolt caused the retreat of the Spaniards from a large part of the Southwest for more than ten years (Knaut 1997; Preucel, ed. by 2002). However, in 1692 Spaniards returned to this area.

### IV.1.1. Location of sites

Some accounts chronicle Pueblo Indians heading to mountains, mesa tops, butte tops, or canyon refuges when threatened by other tribes or Spanish soldiers. This was a common response to threatening situations among historic Pueblo societies across the Southwest and has been documented for many prehistoric and historic societies around the world.

Such defensive measures were described in sixteenth century Spanish chronicles from the time of the first conquistador expeditions. Spanish conquistadors under Vásquez de Coronado heard during their expedition about Indians with fortifications in the mountains and on mesa tops (Winship 1904: 189) that were probably constructed before Spanish incursion into the Southwest. Pedro Castaneda de Náxera, a soldier under Coronado, mentioned in his chronicle that pueblos like Acuco (possibly Acoma) were built "on the very strong rock" where maize fields and water cisterns were also located (Hammond and Rey 1940: 218; Winship 1904: 192, 203). Another village built on a mesa top with difficult access was referred to as "the strongest place that they had ever seen with such a rough ascent that we repented having gone up to the place" (Winship 1904: 242). According to Spaniards, the location of these pueblos resulted directly from a need for defense. Spanish records also describe the time after the Pueblo Revolt of 1680 when many historic Pueblo villages changed their locations from valley bottoms to mesa tops (Preucel, ed. by 2002; Knaut 1997; Haas and Creamer 1996: 206).

The journals of Don Diego de Vargas, written near the end of the seventeenth century, describe the pueblos of Jemez, located on high mesas (above the present Walatowa, or Jemez Pueblo), that were the target of Spanish attacks (Elliot 2002: 45–60) during the Pueblo Revolt. Also during the Pueblo Revolt, Zuni Indians from all six Zuni pueblos established a several-year settlement on top of Dowa Yalanne mesa, which rises approximately 300 meters above the valley bottom; in 1692, after the revolt, the residents moved off the mesa to where the present pueblo of Zuni exists (Ferguson 2002: 36, 41). Dowa Yalanne has steep talus slopes, few trails led to the pueblo on the mesa top, and only one trail could be traversed by horses.

The topography of this mesa and the location of the village there added to the defensiveness of the pueblo; in addition, it was protected by low walls, and piles of stones had been created for bombarding the attackers (Ferguson 2002: 36). The Zuni also built checkdams and reservoirs within the village that provided water for the pueblo; this arrangement would have been especially crucial in the event of a siege (Ferguson 2002: 36–37). Dowa Yalanne served at least once more as a refuge for Zuni people, when some villagers left the pueblo in 1703 after killing three Spaniards who lived in the Zuni Pueblo illegally and who were aggressive to the Zuni residents (Ferguson 2002: 42).

The Hopi relocated many of their villages to mesa tops during the Pueblo Revolt, including Walpi on First Mesa and Shungopavi on Second Mesa. Before the Revolt, most villages were on the valley floor in more accessible locations (T.J. Ferguson, personal communication 2008).

Several years after the Revolt, when the danger of Spanish attack waned, some societies like Zuni and Jemez left the mesa tops and re-established their settlements in the valley bottoms. However, some Pueblo groups, such as those living in Hopi villages on high mesa tops with limited access and that were built before the Pueblo Revolt, continued to live in their mesa-top settlements.

## IV.1.2. Evidence of defensive architecture

Early Spanish records state that many pueblos were built in a very defensive manner as if the residents believed that attacks on their villages were a real danger (LeBlanc 1999: 46, 236–237). The above-mentioned chronicle by de Náxera claims that Acuco (Acoma) people said that the pueblo was protected by a wall "built of large and small stones" (Hammond and Rey 1940: 218), that the people living there could have effectively protected themselves while hiding behind the wall, and that they could have withstood a siege because their fields for growing maize and their cisterns for collecting water were located on the tops of the mesas as well.

Cicuye (Pecos Pueblo) was surrounded by a wall, although the wall was relatively low, and a seep spring was contained within the village (Hammond and Rey 1940: 256–257). The data suggest that the wall was built to protect the people and safeguard the seep spring, and some data suggest that Pecos Pueblo was a very strong settlement in the sixteenth century (Haas and Creamer 1997: 244–245). Caspar Castano de Sosa, a Portugese explorer serving under the Spanish Crown in the sixteenth century, reported in 1590, after his expedition to New Mexico, that Pecos Pueblo was defended and protected by barricades, trenches, and ramparts (Spielmann 1994: 51).

The presence of a stone wall that protected a pueblo "up to six stories high with flat roof and balconies good for defense" is mentioned in Spanish records in reference to the village of Granada or Hawikuh (Winship 1904: 187–189). According to those records, Indians secured themselves within the structures, and it was necessary for the Spanish to surround the pueblo and lay it under siege it in order to gain entry. Winship (1904: 241–242) also mentions several other sites and ruins that were no longer inhabited during the early Spanish expeditions and that were built like fortresses with tall, finely made walls. Spanish chronicles state that some buildings in the Zuni village of Matsaki were "higher than the others and set up above them like towers" with embrasures and loopholes that served for defending the roofs of different stories (Spielmann 1994: 51; Winship 1904: 45).

Visiting the pueblos along the Rio Grande River and farther west, the Spaniards noticed that Puebloans usually did not build doorways on the ground level of a structure and often used exterior ladders to gain access to rooftops, where a lot of daily work took place (Haas and Creamer 1997: 241; Hammond and Rey 1940; Winship 1904: 103–104).

During the historic period, Puebloans reportedly collected rocks and pebbles to be thrown down on enemies. The rocks were stockpiled on the flat roofs of the pueblos, for example. According to Castaneda, Coronado was injured by rocks thrown from a roof at Zuni Pueblo (Haas and Creamer 1997: 241–242; Winship 1904: 189). The presence of a large quantity of stones and stone balls at one pueblo that was destroyed (probably by Plains Indians or other nomadic people) might have been evidence of such rock-throwing at attackers, although the Spaniards supposed that the rocks had been used by attackers "armed with catapults" (Hammond and Rey 1940: 257–258; Winship 1904: 104).

The existence of walls protecting villages is mentioned also in Spanish chronicles written during the time of the Pueblo Revolt. Defensive walls are mentioned, for example, in reference to the Zuni settlement on Dowa Yalanne mesa (Ferguson 2002) and to Jemez sites such as Astialakwa and Boletsakwa, also located on high mesas (Elliot 2002).

Structures were probably built very rapidly, and many of the buildings were situated against relatively high cliffs or boulders (Elliot 2002: 52).

## IV.1.3. Information on conflicts and warfare

A great deal of information in ethnohistoric records refers to evidence of conflicts that occurred both between Pueblo groups and between Pueblo and non-Pueblo tribes such as Ute, Navajo, Apache, Comanche, Paiute, as well as between Pueblo groups and the Spaniards who explored the lands inhabited by Puebloans (Bolton 1949; Hammond and Rey 1940; Haas and Creamer 1997: 240–245; LeBlanc 1999: 44–52; Winship 1904). Records of hostile interactions with nomadic tribes often mention that Navajos, Utes, and other tribes raided pueblos for food and women. It is also possible that hostile relations between Puebloans and other tribes occurred mostly after A.D. 1700, whereas before that time there were more inter-Pueblo conflicts (e.g., LeBlanc 1999: 45), hovewer it is disputable. Some historic accounts refer to Navajo raids (e.g., Minge 1976: 49) but later expeditions against Puebloans were led by Spaniards or Mexicans, for example, with the help of other pueblos like Laguna, Ysleta, or Acoma (Minge 1976: 50–51; Dozier 1970: 79).

Many Spanish parties were supported by native warriors who accompanied the Spaniards on their expeditions. For example, on Coronado's expedition to pueblos located in what are today the states of Arizona and New Mexico, the party was composed of about 300 Spaniards but as many as 1300 native warriors from Mexico, mostly from Tenochtitlan, Tlaleloco, Coyoacán, Acámbaro, Zapotlán, Culiacán, and Pátzcuaro (Flint 2005: 205). Recent studies show also that Spaniards were armed more like Indians than Europeans in "military fashion," and only 45 percent wore metal helmets (Flint 2005: 206).

Perhaps surprisingly, there is abundant information regarding inter-Pueblo conflicts. One example cited is a "large village destroyed in their wars" (Winship 1904: 193). There are also well-known examples of Hopi-Zuni and Zuni-Acoma conflicts that occurred in historic times (Bolton 1949; Hammond and Rey 1940); however, better relationships existed between the Hopi and the pueblos along the northern Rio Grande, such as the Tewa and Tano (LeBlanc 1999: 51). The lack of significant similarities between Zuni and Hopi pottery designs in historic times could be inferred to reflect non-peaceful relations between these groups. Spanish records describe some pueblos as large, relatively powerful, and sometimes built defensively, whereas others were smaller and partly depopulated. For example, Pecos Pueblo is described several times as one of the most powerful villages during the time of early Spanish domination in the Southwest, and the residents of this pueblo claimed that they could conquer any other "pueblos or different tribes" (Spielmann 1994: 51).

However, despite conflicts between pueblos, ethnohistoric sources clearly indicate that pueblos also made alliances and confederacies (Upham et al. 1994; Wilcox 1991). Such pacts might have might have provided better protection for their villages and lands from intruders like Spaniards and other native tribes, both Puebloan and non-Puebloan, than did defensive architecture. This possibility has recently been supported by archaeological data; alliances were an effective means of defense even between pueblos that were widely separated on the landscape (LeBlanc 1999: 287, 318; Spielmann 1994; Minge 1976: 49–51). Alliances between pueblos might have been more common after the mid-1600s, when Athapascan raids and attacks became more frequent (Holt 1983: 595; LeBlanc 1999: 45).

Historic accounts relate how warfare or particular battles were conducted (LeBlanc 1999: 236–237; Bolton 1949). War chiefs or leaders were important for warfare activity and leadership during that time and important even after the warfare ended. The death of a war leader sometimes led to the collapse of resistance; this occurred in native Mexico during its conquest by Hernán Cortés.

Also, with sufficient cause, Puebloans did not wait for the enemy in their villages, but went forth to fight in a well-organized fashion and try to steer the battle away from the village. If they were defeated, they usually went to the edge of the village and continued the resistance there. When the Spanish attacked Hawikuh, most of the villagers, mainly women, children, and elders, left the pueblo and hid in cliffs while the men protected the village (Bolton 1949: 119). Some old men remained in the village to direct the defense and advise and instruct the warriors about tactics.

## IV.2. ETHNOGRAPHY

In addition to the written ethnohistoric sources, photographs of households, villages, farm fields, traditional dances, and customs of the second half of the nineteenth century and the beginning of the twentieth century are also of historical value (see, for example, Plog 1997: 17–23). The most important photographs for this book are those depicting pueblos at the turn of twentieth century that were taken by archaeologists, ethnographers, photographers, and travelers. Some nineteenth century photographs and drawings of particular sites in the Mesa Verde region were produced during the first U.S. survey of the area as well as during early archaeological explorations (e.g., Jackson and Holmes 1981; Nordenskiöld 1990 [1893]). It was also at this time that ethnographers and archaeologists began recording oral traditions among different native groups in the Southwest, a process that continues today (Bandelier 1890, 1892; Cushing 1981; Bernardini 2005; Ferguson and Colwell-Chanthaphonh 2006).

American archaeologists recognized quite early the need for cooperation with researchers in other disciplines (cultural anthropology and ethnology in particular). Thus, American archaeologists and ethnographers have cooperated closely almost from the advent of archaeological research in the Southwest. Most archaeologists from the turn of the twentieth century were also ethnographers; they conducted excavations in ancient ruins and also collected objects from living Pueblo societies and recorded their customs, beliefs, and oral traditions. Applying ethnographic knowledge to the archaeological reconstruction of past societies was common then but was often done without modern systematic methodology (Downum 1993: 4–5). For example, some archaeologists from that time, like Frank H. Cushing and Jesse W. Fewkes, claimed that ancestral Pueblo sites were almost the same as modern settlements. Fewkes pointed out that Spruce Tree House in Mesa Verde National Park was nearly identical to the village of Walpi on the

Hopi First Mesa (Fewkes 1911; Spielmann 2005: 195 after Fewkes 1909: 53). The earliest use of ethnographic analogy in the northern Southwest derived from living Pueblo societies and concerned, among other things, architecture and its role in Pueblo life. One of the first comprehensive and detailed studies of the nineteenth century Puebloan architecture was a report prepared for the Bureau of Ethnology of the Smithsonian Institution (Mindeleff 1989 [1891]).

Later, archaeologists were more careful in their use of ethnographic analogy, and comparative methods were gradually developed (Cordell 1997) by such researchers as Alfred V. Kidder and others. Franz Boas' methods were developed on the basis of a wider approach that reached beyond cultural anthropology and that were continued by his students and followers, researchers such as Ruth Benedict and Alfred L. Kroeber, whose research also encompassed the Puebloan communities of that time. Some of these theories no longer hold sway or have been refuted. For example, Benedict's characterization of "the peaceful Pueblos" is now regarded as inaccurate (Dozier 1970: 78–82), because archaeological data clearly indicate that conflict and warfare were common among prehistoric as well historic Pueblo societies (see, for example, LeBlanc 1999; Rice and LeBlanc, ed. by 2001). However, both ethnohistoric and ethnographic records contain a considerable amount of such questionable information.

Kidder enlisted the aid and cooperation of researchers from numerous disciplines in his work. His research focused in particular on the pueblos of New Mexico, and he generated a great deal of valuable information that contributed significantly to the understanding of Southwestern archaeology and built up the classics of North American archaeology (Renfrew and Bahn 2002: 33).

Today, ethnographic and ethnohistoric records are still invaluable sources of information, some of which are very helpful for archaeological interpretation and reconstruction of past societies in the Southwest. However, archaeologists nevertheless question the utility and the appropriate use of these data for archaeology (Dozier 1970; Spielmann 2005: 194–197). Also, there is still a need to develop new and appropriate methods for applying these types of information to archaeology in the most valid and appropriate ways possible.

## IV.2.1. Location of sites

Defensive architectural elements, defensible locations of particular sites, and a history of conflict between different native groups have been noted by many ethnographers and archaeologists studying Puebloans and other native societies in the Southwest (Bandelier 1890; Cushing 1981; Fewkes 1919; Mindeleff 1989 [1891]). Victor Mindeleff (1989 [1891]: 77) points out that even though defensive locations on mesas or butte tops were inconvenient in many ways, Puebloans like the Zuni and Hopi used these places in the past in times of danger, when they would move their settlements from the valley bottoms to these more inaccessible locations of refuge. Mindeleff mentioned ruins and ancient pueblos near Tusayan (Hopi) and Zuni; villages that were located on high mesas were difficult to access, and showed evidence of defensive architecture (Mindeleff 1989

[1891]: 55–61, 76–77, 91). He also points out traits in nineteenth century Hopi architecture that are indicative of defensiveness as well as defensible, mesa-top village locations.

Many access trails to pueblos even at the turn of the twentieth century passed through narrow and tightly controlled passageways such as those described in ethnographic accounts and depicted in historic drawings. Photographs from that time include William H. Jackson's photographs of First Trail leading to Acoma Pueblo (Minge 1976: Ill. 5). Even where more than one trail led to a village, most routes exhibited evidence that access was controlled by the residents.

Bandelier suggested that water was the main consideration when Puebloans chose a place for settlement, and the second consideration was the need for a location where the people could feel reasonably safe from enemies (Bandelier 1890: 30, 32, 56). Also, when necessary, such as in times of danger, Pueblo people would leave their settlements and usually settle on mesa tops. They usually returned from these mesas or plateaus when the danger abated, but it was common under those circumstances to then shift the village to a different location (Bandelier 1890: 155). Some of the settlements described by Bandelier were located in defensible places that also featured good access to fields and water (Mindeleff 1989 [1891]: 52–53).

## IV.2.2. Evidence of defensive architecture

Well-known from the historic and ethnographic data was the manner of building room-blocks where particular rooms were tied together and created line of rooms without spaces among them that may have allowed the entrance to the site. Ladders were usually used to access the upper stories of the buildings, and there were relatively few exterior doorways in the ground-level stories, as described for the historic pueblos of Acoma, Santa Ana and Hopi (LeBlanc 2001: 31; White 1942: 38; Mindeleff 1989 [1891]: 77). White (1942: 303) states that different Pueblos in the Southwest were concerned about warfare and defense and the "necessity of defense was reflected at almost every point;" also, some Puebloan names of prehistoric and historic villages reflect the locations of those sites as high up with difficult access.

V. Mindeleff points out numerous times, in his study of the late nineteenth century Pueblo architecture, that many structures were built with a consideration for defensiveness, and sometimes it was necessary to build a structure quickly (Mindeleff 1989 [1891]). When he discusses conflicts between the Hopi pueblos of Walpi and Sikyátki, he mentions the construction of a defensive wall, although he also states that such a wall was uncommon in Hopi settlements (Mindeleff 1989 [1891]: 25–26, 52). Mindeleff distinguishes different defensive techniques; he concludes, for example, that the use of many defensive architectural features at Zuni can be explained by the fact that Zuni Pueblo is not located in an easily defensible location, whereas fewer defensive architectural components were constructed in Hopi pueblos because they are located on high, defensible mesas (Mindeleff 1989 [1891]: 76–77). Significant changes occurred between the earlier Pueblo architecture and that of the nineteenth century, namely that the former incorporated more defensive features such as narrower and more protected access routes both to a village as well as within it and also the paucity of doorways on the ground level referred to earlier (Mindeleff 1989 [1891]: 181–195).

Mindeleff offers the following as evidence of defensive architecture: the layout and arrangement of the domestic architecture, the use of roof hatchways for access, small wall openings, multistoried and terraced buildings requiring the use of a ladder to access upper-story rooms, and the common absence of ground-level doorways or large windows. Zuni ladders were constructed with very loose rungs so that the uprights could be pulled apart to render the ladder useless if the village was attacked and there was insufficient time to pull the ladders to the roof (T.J. Ferguson, personal communication 2009).

The layout and architecture of Zuni Pueblo also exhibited evidence of defense: massive, multistoried structures; enclosed extramural spaces such as plazas; and restricted access to the pueblo (a plan from 1881 shows that entry into the pueblo was possible through only three controlled gates or entrances). Ferguson (1996: 121–122) suggests that incorporating defensive features into the architecture and village configuration might have been why Zuni Pueblo was rarely attacked. When conflicts became infrequent, architecture and village configuration began to change (Ferguson 1996).

Photographs and descriptions from the end of nineteenth century show remnants of walls that had probably been village-enclosing walls built from very large rocks (Mindeleff 1989 [1891]: 85–86; Powell 1961 [1895]) and that might corroborate descriptions from the first conquistadors' expeditions of walls enclosing some pueblos.

## IV.2.3. Information on conflicts and warfare

At the end of the nineteenth century and the beginning of the twentieth century, most overt conflict between tribes ended as the U.S. government exerted its influence. White (1942: 303–318, 321) points out that in the early twentieth century only a few people who still knew how to treat battle wounds remained in Santa Ana Pueblo. However, abundant evidence of warfare and conflict between different Pueblos and between Pueblos and non-Pueblo tribes still existed in the memory of Pueblo people, and there were still many witnesses and direct participants of such events, which was noted by numerous ethnographers and archaeologists working among different Pueblos (e.g., Bandelier 1890, 1892, 1916; Cushing 1981). Bandelier (1890: 176) stated that during nearly every year in the past there were periods of fighting between Navajos and Pueblos.

The oral traditions of different Pueblo societies contain references to warfare. War dances, war or warrior societies, war leaders or caciques, and ceremonialism associated with warfare, such as scalp dances, were also frequently noted by ethnographers. Such observations were made at Cochiti (Lange 1959), Santo Domingo and Santa Ana (White 1935: 38–41; White 1942: 303–318, 321) pueblos, and at other pueblos in New Mexico, as well as at Hopi villages in Arizona (Bandelier 1890: 153; Cushing 1981). At San Ildefonso Pueblo, a War Captain was elected for one year, or longer if there wasn't another qualified candidate. His duties were both religious and civil. He was accompanied by assistants, the Warriors, also appointed for one year or longer (Whitman 1969 [1947]: 18–19). The subject of war was present in oral traditions, such as the well-known myth of the twin war gods or warrior twins that is related in numerous pueblos like Zuni,

Cochiti, Santo Domingo, and others (Cushing 1981: 90–94; Eggan 1950; Ellis 1951: 185; Lange 1959: 199–200, 276–277; Parson 1929: 136–138; White 1935: 182–191).

Warfare equipment has been described by some researchers: bows, quivers, spears, and war-clubs, as well as shields and helmets made of buffalo skin for protection (Bandelier 1890: 153–154; 1916: 230; Cushing 1981: 201–202). Some tactics and methods of warfare were similar to those of other Southwestern peoples (Bandelier 1890: 153–154; 1916: 328, 378), including hide-and-seek tactics, sending a messenger to other villages for help when the enemy party was too large, and going forth to fight the enemy away from the village.

## IV.3. ORAL TRADITIONS

The first Europeans who settled in North America were probably aware of the abundant information that existed in the oral traditions of American Indians. Because no writing systems had been developed, knowledge that was passed orally from generation to generation was the only source of information about ancestors, traditions, and religion. Some of this knowledge was recorded by Europeans, and some survived in the ethnohistoric sources described briefly above.

More scientific use and application of oral tradition in the archaeology and anthropology of the Southwest began near the end of the nineteenth century and at the beginning of the twentieth century, and then it was frequently used by researchers to link modern and ancient Pueblo societies (Dongoske et al. 1997: 602; Downum 1993: 5). Oral tradition, along with ethnographic analogy, was widely used without necessary critique and sometimes inappropriately, and many aspects of ancient Pueblo societies were explained and reconstructed directly from the Pueblo people and cultures that still existed in Arizona and New Mexico (Cameron 1995: 106; Dongoske et al. 1997: 601–602; Downum 1993: 4–5). However, not all archeologists of the late nineteenth or early twentieth centuries (Alfred V. Kidder is one example) considered oral traditions of living Pueblo people to have useful application in archaeological interpretations (Spielmann 2005: 197); nonetheless, many did use such information in their explanations of the ancient Pueblo world.

This inappropriate use of oral tradition was probably one reason that, for many years in the twentieth century, traditional knowledge of American Indian societies was largely ignored, and scientists relied primarily on data from archaeological excavations or ethnologies of historic and contemporary Indian societies. As a result, the existing traditional native knowledge was rarely incorporated into the process of archaeological explanations of prehistoric Pueblo societies of the Mesa Verde region and across the great Southwest. However, in the past two or three decades, there has been significant change in the treatment of traditional knowledge (e.g., Varien et al. 1999: 380–389).

Archaeologists and anthropologists realized at last that oral tradition, used appropriately, was an invaluable source of information for scientists interpreting, explaining, and understanding the world of the past. Use of oral tradition can also foster better and closer cooperation between archaeologists/anthropologists and American Indians both for the development of knowledge and for maintaining native identities and a rich heritage for the future (Ferguson and Colwell-Chanthaphonh 2006; Deloria 1992: 598; Echo-Hawk 1997: 96–100, 102; Lekson and Cameron 1995). However, the incorporation of traditional native knowledge (like study of ethnohistoric and ethnographic sources) must be preceded by detailed studies using appropriate methods (Anyon et al. 1997; Dongoske et al. 1997: 605; Varien et al. 1999: 388–389; Lyons 2003: 82–99; Trimble et al. 2008; Vansina 1985).

Scientists must realize that the point of view of American Indians on different aspects of their history is often contrary to the Euro-American perception of history. For example, oral traditions of American Indians often include multiple levels of meaning within one story; moreover, there is not just one "native" perspective or viewpoint (Dongoske et al. 1997: 603; Ferguson and Colwell-Chanthaphonh 2006; Naranjo 1995). In Hopi and Zuni societies each clan or religious group has its own history, and each clan can tell the same history in a slightly different way, where the main part or core of the story is similar, but there are many differences in specific details (Dongoske et al. 1997: 603).

Differing perceptions are clearly evident on the subject of migration. Euro-Americans and Indians perceive the depopulation of ancient Pueblo settlements and regions differently. According to contemporary Pueblo Indians these places were not abandoned (see for example Lekson and Cameron 1995: 195; Thompson 2002: 260); instead, they are still inhabited by spirits of their ancestors. These ancient sites are respected by modern American Indians, some are still mentioned in oral traditions, and some are even the object of pilgrimages (Thompson 2002; Snead 2008: 147–148).

## IV.3.1. Location of sites

The location of sites on high mesas or other places not easily accessible to attackers is mentioned in many historic accounts and Pueblo oral traditions. For example, Zuni oral history refers to a site located on the high mesa named Dowa Yallane (the village was moved from a lower elevation to the mesa top during the Pueblo Revolt) and to barrier walls built for protection against Spaniards. That oral account, from nineteenth and twentieth century Zunis, also mentions stockpiles of stones for use in the event of Spanish attack (Ferguson 2002: 36). The site on Dowa Yallane is also known archaeologically and from ethnohistoric records (see above).

Ferguson and Colwell-Chanthaphonh, in their study of the prehistory of the San Pedro Valley and the associated traditional American Indian knowledge, noted that the Hopi believed that Reeve Ruin and other sites located on mesa tops had been built in those locations for defense and protection (Ferguson and Colwell-Chanthaphonh 2006: 116). A similar view was expressed by a Zuni member of the same project, who also described how, in the past, their people often built their villages in such locations to avoid floods, for protection against enemies, and to gain better views of the surrounding area (Ferguson and Colwell-Chanthaphonh 2006: 163).

The oral history of Jemez refers to similar sites located on mesa tops in the Jemez Mountains above present-day Jemez Pueblo (Walatowa); these villages were built during the time of the Spanish presence in the Southwest and the Pueblo Revolt. Many of these sites are still important and sacred for contemporary Jemez people (Kevin Shendo, personal communication 2006). One traditional story tells of a mesa-top pueblo that was not conquered because, for several months, the Spaniards could not find the trail that led to the pueblo. After a few months of unsuccessful attempts to reach the village, they nearly left it unconquered. But finally early one morning a soldier saw a woman descending from the pueblo following a secret trail to fetch water in a vessel. The Spaniards then discovered the trail and ascended the mesa.

An oral account of conflict between ancestors of Santa Ana and Zia pueblos relates that the ancestors of Santa Ana sought shelter on a mesa top (and probably later lived there) to escape an attack by Zia (Haas and Creamer 1997: 253).

## IV.3.2. Evidence of defensive architecture

Information contained in oral traditions indicates that Pueblo people were aware of different features and details of building construction that could help protect their homes and villages. One traditional story tells of a conflict between Acoma people and the k'a'tsina spirits in which people built a "barricade" made of poles and skins (Haas and Creamer 1997: 252).

Mindeleff (1989 [1891]: 85–86) quoted a nineteenth century Pueblo oral tradition that told of creating a kind of wall described as a "number of stones imbedded in the ground" against Apache raids. Hopi participants of the aforementioned Ferguson and Colwell-Chanthaphonh project interpreted the wall that separates Reeve Ruin from open space on the mesa top as a structure built for the defense of villagers (Ferguson and Colwell-Chanthaphonh 2006: 116).

In a Zuni traditional story, a village called Kia'makia was surrounded by a tall thick wall that protected the village. This site is thought to be south of Zuni and near a trail that leads to the Zuni salt lake. The story tells of a battle between Zunis and Kia'nakwe (inhabitants of Kia'makia) that lasted three days. In the end, the Zunis won the battle (Haas and Creamer 1997: 250–251).

## IV.3.3. Information on conflicts and warfare

A considerable volume of traditional information refers to conflicts that occurred between Pueblo groups or between Pueblo groups and other tribes. Some accounts refer to specific places or areas. One story about the northern Rio Grande area recorded by Adolph Bandelier near the end of the nineteenth century (Bandelier 1892: 166) describes attacks on the village of Kua-pa by "hostile tribes." In consequence, the village was devastated and the survivors abandoned it. Archaeological data available now confirms that the site described to Bandelier by Pueblo Indians as Kua-pa was depopulated in the sixteenth century A.D. (Haas and Creamer 1997: 235). Also, there are histories of conflicts and warfare among different Pueblos, like Cochiti and other pueblos, or battles between Santa Ana and Zia pueblos, in the last of which Navajo warriors were recruited in an attempt to attack Santa Ana (Haas and Creamer 1997: 253).

The most frequently mentioned traditional stories of battles that took place in the past between different Hopi pueblos are accounts of the destruction of Sikyátki and Awat'ovi (Haas and Creamer 1997: 253–255; Lomatuway'ma et al. 1993: 145–147, 391–392; Malotki 1993). The most commonly cited reasons for the destruction of these villages by their close neighbors are immoral behavior or wife stealing; the reason cited most often for the destruction of Sikyatki was rivalry between witches and the Coyote clan, and the prevalent reason for destroying Awat'ovi was the presence of Spanish priests and conversions to Christianity (Haas and Creamer 1997: 255).

Some traditional stories refer to migrations associated with conflict between ancestral Pueblo people living in Mesa Verde region and other native societies in the past such as the ancestors of the Utes; one such story was told by the Greasewood Clan at Hopi about conflicts with the Utes and migration out of the Mesa Verde region (Thompson 2002: 261–262). The migration of Pueblo people is often connected with ancestral Ute or other invaders who were Numic speakers.

Many histories among Pueblo people refer to conflicts with other tribes such as Navajos, Apaches, Comanches, and Paiutes (e.g., Haas and Creamer 1997: 237; White 1942: 316–318; Mindeleff 1989 [1891]). Moreover, oral traditions of other tribes also tell of hostile interactions with Pueblo people, such as Navajo legends and ceremonies associated with tales of raids on Pueblos; in addition, the Navajo term "Anasazi" (the name for ancient Pueblo culture) means "enemy ancestors" (Holt 1983: 595). The Navajos also had hostile relations with the Utes when the Utes raided Navajos and Pueblos for slaves who were later sold to the Spaniards[6] (Towner 1999: 8–9).

A specific account of a conflict that led to migration of ancient Pueblo people from the Mesa Verde region, and that could be connected with the depopulation of the region in the thirteenth century A.D., is a well-known oral tradition recorded in 1874 by a member of the Hayden expedition and that describes an ancient battle which could have taken place at Battle Rock (Castle Rock Pueblo) between the Pueblo residents and their enemies (Ingersoll 2006; Kuckelman, ed. by 2000; Kuckelman 2002: 234, 242). Castle Rock Pueblo was a community center (so called by archaeologists), and it was the largest village in the Lower Sand Canyon area in the thirteenth century A.D. Archaeological evidence from excavations conducted at the site in 1990s suggests that the Castle Rock Pueblo legend had been passed down from generation to generation (Kuckelman, ed. by 2000).

This oral tradition referring to Castle Rock Pueblo was told by John Moss to members of the Hayden Expedition in 1874. Moss, who had been, from 1864 to 1868, the first Indian agent for the Hopi and who spoke the Hopi language, stated that he heard this story from a Hopi man. Ernest Ingersoll, a member of that expedition, published the story in the *New York Tribune* on November 3, 1874. It tells about the last battle that oc-

[6] However, it is necessary to remember that these accounts of hostile interactions refer mostly to historic times of the sixteenth century A.D. and later; there is no archaeological evidence of an Athapascans (Navajo and Apache) presence in the Southwest before the fifteenth century A.D. Thus, they probably could not have been a factor in the abandonment of Mesa Verde region by Pueblo people in the thirteenth century A.D.

It is also worth mentioning that interactions between these tribes were peaceful at times, and other tribes traded with Pueblos. Intermarriage also occurred but was not always considered desirable (personal observation and talks in the Hopi village of Oraibi, 2006).

curred between Pueblo people who lived there and (as told by Moss) the ancestors of the Ute Indians, which led to the evacuation of the pueblo by the survivors, who went south:

> Formerly, the aborigines inhabited all this country we had been over as far west as the headwaters of the San Juan, as far north as the Rio Dolores, west some distance into Utah, and south and southwest throughout Arizona and on down into Mexico. They had lived there from time immemorial – since the earth was a small island, which augmented as its inhabitants multiplied. They cultivated the valley, fashioned whatever utensils and tools they needed very neatly and handsomely out of clay and wood and stone, not knowing any of the useful metals; built their homes and kept their flocks and herds in the fertile river-bottoms, and worshiped the sun. They were an eminently peaceful and prosperous people, living by agriculture rather than by the chase. About a thousand years ago, however, they were visited by savage strangers from the North, whom they treated hospitably. Soon these visits became more frequent and annoying. Then their troublesome neighbors – ancestors of the present Utes – began to forage upon them, and, at last, to massacre them and devastate their farms; so, to save their lives at least, they built houses high upon the cliffs, where they could store food and hide away till the raiders left. But one summer the invaders did not go back to their mountains as the people expected, but brought their families with them and settled down. So, driven from their homes and lands, starving in their little niches on the high cliffs, they could only steal away during the night, and wander across the cheerless uplands. To one who has traveled these steppes, such a flight seems terrible, and the mind hesitates to picture the suffering of the sad fugitives.
>
> At the *cristone* [a volcanic dike, according to Ingersoll] they halted, and probably found friends, for the rocks and caves are full of the nests of these human wrens and swallows. Here they collected, erected stone fortifications and watch-towers, dug reservoirs in the rocks to hold a supply of water, which in all cases is precarious in this latitude, and once more stood at bay. Their foes came, and for one long month fought and were beaten back, and returned day after day to the attack as merciless and inevitable as the tide. Meanwhile, the families of the defenders were evacuating and moving south, and bravely did their protectors shield them till they were all safely a hundred miles away. The besiegers were beaten back and went away. But the narrative tells us that the hollows of the rocks were filled to the brim with the mingled blood of conquerors and conquered, and red veins of it ran down into the cañon. It was such a victory as they could not afford to gain again, and they were glad, when the long fight was over, to follow their wives and little ones to the south. There, in the deserts of Arizona, on well-nigh unapproachable isolated bluffs, they built new towns, and their few descendants, the Moquis [Hopi], live in them to this day, preserving more carefully and purely the history and veneration of their forefathers than their skill or wisdom. It was from one of their old men that this traditional sketch was obtained (Kuckelman, ed. by 2000; Lightfoot and Kuckelman 2001: 55–56 after Jackson and Holmes 1981: 380).

Archaeological excavations conducted by archaeologists from the Crow Canyon Archeological Center from 1990 through 1994 revealed that the village had been attacked during its final stage of occupation, and the bodies of many people had been left there (Kuckelman et al. 2000; Lightfoot and Kuckelman 2001). A rock art panel at the site depicts three anthropomorphic figures fighting; two figures armed with bow-and-arrow are standing back-to-back as though protecting each other, and a third appears to be holding up a shield in defense (Kuckelman, ed. by 2000). For a detailed description of Castle Rock Pueblo, see Chapter V of this book (V.2.1.).

## IV.3.4. Migrations and depopulation of the Mesa Verde region

Archaeological explanations of the depopulation of the Mesa Verde region near the end of the thirteenth century A.D. include speculation about areas where Pueblo emigrants settled; theories include areas in Arizona as well as the Rio Grande valley in New Mexico (Cameron 2006; Cordell 1995; Lekson and Cameron 1995; Kuckelman et al. 2004; Lipe 1995a; Ortman 2008; Thompson 2002). The work of the first archaeologist-ethnographers from the end of the nineteenth and beginning of the twentieth centuries, such as Frank H. Cushing and Jesse W. Fewkes, contributed much to our knowledge of the traditional migration histories of particular clans (Spielmann 2005: 195). The latest research and linking of archaeology with oral tradition that of the Hopi Indians concerning migration, for example, has also contributed significantly to our understanding of migrations in the past (e.g., Anyon et al. 1997; Bernardini 2005; Ferguson and Colwell-Chanthaphonh 2006; Kuckelman et al. 2000; Naranjo 1995, 2006).

Traditional knowledge of many contemporary Puebloan societies (and other native non-Puebloan groups in the Southwest) contains descriptions of migrations that occurred in the past, because migrations were an integral part of life of Puebloan ancestors. Many tribal histories of contemporary Puebloan groups, such as Hopi and Zuni, include migration stories that tell about the ancestors of their clans who migrated from different places seeking the "Center Place" or "Middle Place" (Plog 1997: 122). Many include accounts of the origins of their ancestors in the underworld and their journey to Fourth World (Dongoske et al. 1997: 603; Thompson 2002: 257–258; Ortiz 1969).

Tessie Naranjo, a member of Santa Clara Pueblo, states that for Santa Clara people, the exact dates of migrations, or locations where their ancestors migrated from, or the reasons they migrated, are not important (Naranjo 1995: 247–250). Although elders from Santa Clara Pueblo refer to some places from where their ancestors could have come many years ago, the names and locations of those places are not precise enough to pinpoint their locations today (Naranjo 1995: 248–249; 2006). People from Santa Clara are more interested in the movement itself, because it is an essential part of the life of Pueblo people and "movement is one of the big ideological concepts of Pueblo thought because it is necessary for the perpetuation of life" (Naranjo 1995: 248). Despite the fact that movement and the concept of place are important and central in Pueblo oral traditions, much traditional knowledge refers to regions or areas rather than to specific places. Although information about particular places is not abundant, there are some examples of quite detailed descriptions of sites (see this chapter above).

Even though precise locations of specific villages or migration routes can be difficult to distinguish in oral traditions, some traditional knowledge provides important information in reference to larger regions or areas such as the Grand Canyon, Chaco Canyon, or Mesa Verde (Lekson and Cameron 1995: 194–195). It is obvious from archaeological data that those areas were occupied by Pueblo people in the past. Many contemporary Pueblo groups (as well as some archaeologists) identify the so-called White House or White City mentioned in their traditions, which is one of the places from which their ancestors migrated, as the Mesa Verde region. However, there is some doubt as to whether Mesa Verde could have served as the "house" for so many different groups at one time in prehistory (Lekson and Cameron 1995: 194–195, 202). Keres Pueblo people in the

Rio Grande Valley point out that as conditions in White House deteriorated, people migrated from that area and finally reached the Rio Grande Valley (Snead 2008: 29).

Oral traditions of the Tewa Pueblo group in New Mexico identify one site in the Mesa Verde region, Yucca House (Site 5MT5006), and other sites in the area as places connected with their migration histories and where their ancestors lived (Ortman 2008: 139–140). The name Yucca House is after the Tewa name of the site.

There is also oral tradition in Zia Pueblo concerning migration from the Mesa Verde region (Zia Pueblo lies about 250 km/150 miles southeast of Mesa Verde):

> Every December 29, in our council meeting, our migration story gets told and retold. It takes four or five hours to tell. There are more than a hundred names of places our ancestors passed on their way to Zia. One of the places they name is this place here (Cliff Palace and Mesa Verde). We call it Ka-cha-ka-tru-ti-the Vast Area with Many Houses (Roberts 1999).

In 1994, the Crow Canyon Archaeological Center invited Pueblo people from Hopi villages in Arizona as well as from Taos, San Juan, Santa Clara, Zia, Acoma, and Zuni pueblos in New Mexico to visit and consult on particular archaeological sites in the Mesa Verde region such as Sand Canyon Pueblo and to learn the traditional knowledge of contemporary Pueblo people about these sites (Thompson 2002: 257–279). All of those pueblos are within about five days' walking distance south and southeast of Sand Canyon Pueblo and the Mesa Verde region, and they could be places where thirteenth century emigrants from the Mesa Verde later settled (see Ortman 2009 for study of relationship between ancestral Tewa communities of north-central New Mexico and earlier communities of the Mesa Verde region). The oral traditions of every Pueblo represented state that some of their ancestors' clans came from the Mesa Verde area and its vicinity, but few contain references to particular archaeological sites in the Mesa Verde region (Thompson 2002: 257).

Many oral histories of the Zuni refer to migration especially in reference to different routes that particular groups of their ancestors followed (Dongoske et al. 1997: 603–604; Lekson and Cameron 1995: 194). Conflicts were often an integral part of the migration process; at the end of the route taken by a group of Zuni ancestors, at the Middle Place, a battle ensued between the ancestors and the people who were already there. Also, many Pueblo stories and myths tell of conflict and warfare such as the Zuni myth involving the "first people" in such battles (Haas and Creamer 1997: 249–250).

For the Hopi people in Arizona, it is obvious that in the past different groups joined their villages, and it was a method of growth for Hopi society (Bernardini 2005; Colwell-Chanthaphonh and Ferguson 2006; Plog 1997: 122). Some accounts tell how new clans that arrived were welcomed by the residents; it was common to ask for permission to settle near the existing villages. Often, specific clans were allowed to stay and settle near the existing ones because they possessed specific skills or were able to conduct ceremonies that would be useful for those already living there. An example of this is the founding of the Hopi-Tewa village of Hano on First Mesa; chiefs of the Hopi village Walpi invited these Tewa to settle beside them after the Pueblo Revolt of A.D. 1680 (Stanislawski 1979: 600).

Chapter V

# ANALYSIS OF THE CENTRAL MESA VERDE REGION ARCHITECTURE IN THE THIRTEENTH CENTURY A.D.

This chapter presents an analysis of fifteen large sites from the central Mesa Verde region dated to the thirteen century A.D. that probably were community centers and forty one small sites located in Lower Sand Canyon area around one of community centers, Castle Rock Pueblo. Castle Rock Pueblo and nearby small sites probably created a community of allied sites (e.g., Ortman 2008: 129; Varien 1999). The analysis of particulars sites is focusing on defensive aspects of them. This includes analysis of site location, availability of water, access to the site, site layout, and presence or not architectural features and structures that may inform us of defensive character of particular structure or the whole site (this mainly includes investigations of towers, enclosing and protecting walls, loopholes, and underground tunnels). This is completed by presenting the chronology of these sites and conclusions.

## V.1. ANALYSIS OF LARGE SITES AND COMMUNITY CENTERS IN THE CENTRAL MESA VERDE REGION

I use the term "community" to refer to "social organization that defines access to necessary natural resources, provides a level of social identity for its constituent households, and serves as a significant decision-making entity above the level of the primary household unit 'that can play' several roles, including the definition of both land use territories and associated resource access rights for local populations within the broader regional system" (Varien et al. 1996: 100; see also Adler 2002; Varien 1999: 19–23). From the neo-evolutionary point of view the community may be perceived as an "important social element in formative agricultural societies, particularly in terms of suprafamily economic and social integration" where integration is perceived "as important for reasons that include defense, risk aversion, capital investment in technology, and trade" (Kolb and Snead 1997: 610, after Johnson and Earle 1984: 131).

A community center in the central Mesa Verde region is considered as a settlement with nine or more pitstructures with more than 50 structures total that included rooms for living and storage, kivas, and other buildings, including the public architecture (Lipe 2002: 211; Varien et al. 1996: 86). About 50 (or little more) community centers existed in the central Mesa Verde region in the late Pueblo III period (A.D. 1225–1300) (Lipe 2002; Lipe and Varien 1999b: 303–310; Varien 1999) that were the longest occupied sites in the region and served as centers for social, political, religious, and economic activities that did not occur on smaller sites. The analyzed data is divided into two categories that allow examination defensive settlements and conflicts at two scales:

– the regional scale is investigated by examining community centers located throughout the region (Fig. 5),

– the community scale: the Castle Rock Community is examined to assess the defensive nature of a community where violence was known to occur at least in Castle Rock Pueblo, the community center (Figs. 24, 25).

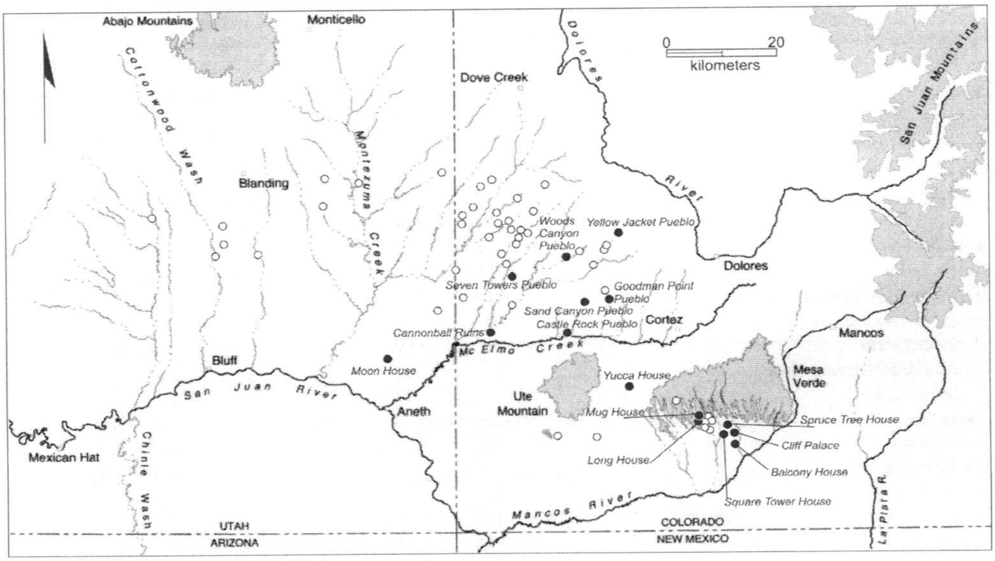


Fig. 5. Location of sites in the central Mesa Verde region dating between A.D. 1225 and 1290 analyzed in this dissertation (after Lipe 2002: Fig. 10.2 modified by the author)

I analyze in the book fifteen large sites and community centers from the central Mesa Verde region that are dated to the thirteenth century A.D. (Late Pueblo III period). These sites are located in different parts of the region from Mesa Verde National Park in southwestern Colorado to Cedar Mesa in southeastern Utah. They are ones of the largest and best known sites in the region (considering relatively large amount of published and unpublished information available about them) as well as are well dated (mostly on the basis of the dendrochronology, pottery typology, and architecture styles) and these dates indicate they were occupied in the period immediately before the regional depopulation. The architecture in those sites exhibits exceptional preservation which allows examine the defensive characteristics of these settlements like site-enclosing or protecting walls, towers, underground tunnels, loopholes (see description of these elements in Chapter III). Also, the location of these sites in the landscape is analyzed in terms of their defensiveness.

The examination on regional scale includes analysis of sites in Lower Sand Canyon locality (so-called Castle Rock Community) with the community center in this area, Castle Rock Pueblo, where there is the best documented case of warfare in the region that allows examine the defensive aspects of the settlement system in a community where violence and conflicts (or warfare) occurred. There has been full-coverage survey in the area around Castle Rock Pueblo helping define the associated small site community. Many sites in this small site community are cliff dwellings that are well dated to the period right before regional depopulation (especially on the basis of pottery and architecture styles, there are only few tree-ring dates from these sites). Also, the sites in Castle Rock Community have relatively good architectural preservation allowing assess the defensive character of the community.

## V.1.1. Mesa Verde Proper (Mesa Verde National Park): Chapin Mesa

### V.1.1.a. Site 5MV615 (Balcony House)

#### Location

Site type: cliff dwelling. The site (Fig. 6) is located in a large alcove in the upper Cliff House Formation on the west side of Soda Canyon on Chapin Mesa (Griffitts 1990: 25). It is situated at an elevation of about 2000 m (6700 ft.) and sits approximately 180 m (600 ft.) above the floor of Soda Canyon (Balcony House Trail Guide). This alcove is a maximum of ca. 80 m (250 ft.) long, ca. 15 m (50 ft.) deep, and about 10 m (35 ft.) high. The site faces east and northeast (Fiero 1998: 11–12).

Balcony House and an additional 11 sites nearby are interpreted as a cluster of sites or a community (Ferguson 1996: 43). Balcony House was the largest Puebloan settlement in this proposed Soda Canyon Community in the thirteenth century A.D. Together, these 12 pueblos contain 81 rooms and six kivas (Ferguson 1996: 43; Fiero 1998: 17). Besides Balcony House, this community included Site 5MV515 with 11 rooms and three kivas, Site 5MV617 with a relatively well preserved retaining wall, Site 5MV516, and at least six smaller sites (5MV613, 5MV614, 5MV616, 5MV618, 5MV622, and 5MV1063). These smaller sites were probably used mainly for storage (Fiero 1998: 17). Below the southern part of the site at the top of the talus, evidence is visible of two small rooms probably used for storage; rubble below the northern part of the site indicates the presence of a structure (Fiero 1998: App. E-21). Rohn (1977: 86) suggested that turkey pens were built in the vicinity of Balcony House.

#### History of investigation

The site was first discovered and described in 1884 by prospector S.E. Osborn and W.H. Hayes. Probably at least one of these men explored the site, and two years later Osborn described Balcony House, along with several other sites in Soda Canyon, in a newspaper

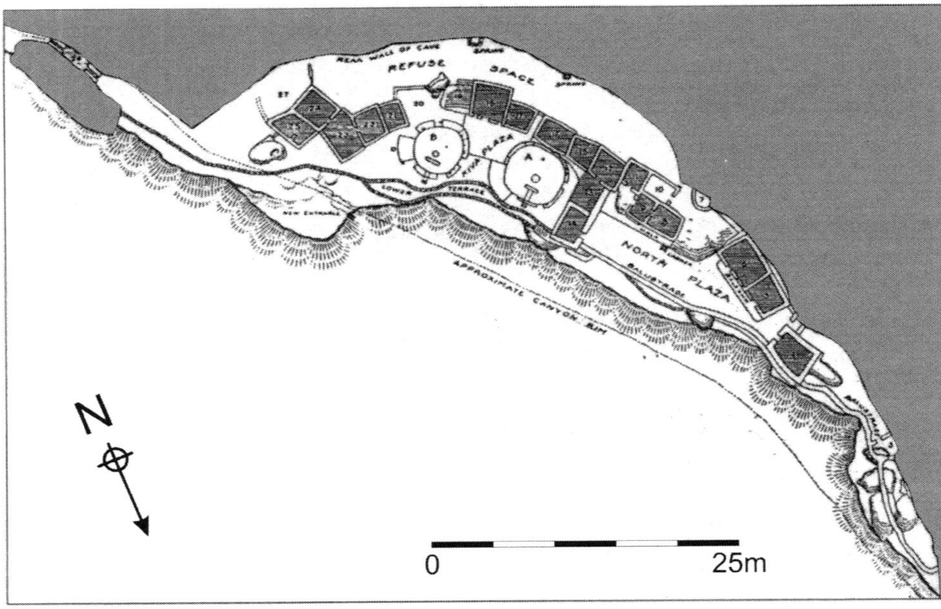


Fig. 6. Plan of the Site 5MV615, Balcony House (after Fiero 1998: Fig. 2.6 on the basis of 1910 Ground Plan Map by Adams and Chapman modified by A. Danecki)

article.[7] Soon after this, the site was visited by others, including Virginia Donaghe McClurg in 1886, and Frederick Chapin who, with Wetherill brothers and Charlie Mason as guides, explored the site in 1889 (Fiero 1998: 17–18; Smith 2002). At that time the site was called "Brownstone Front." Its present name, Balcony House, was bestowed by Gustaf Nordenskiöld (Balcony House Guide). The name "Balcony House" comes from one well-preserved balcony in the North Plaza of the site and a few other preserved remnants of balconies.

Gustaf Nordenskiöld was the first to describe Balcony House in detail. According to him, Balcony House was the best preserved of all the cliff dwellings in the area of today's park. He pointed out the very good masonry and building techniques at Balcony House as compared to those at Cliff Palace (Nordenskiöld 1990 [1893]: 66), although not all parts of Balcony House were built using the same techniques and are in the same good state of preservation today (Fiero 1998).

In 1907 William D. Leonard, superintendent of the Southern Ute Agency, described Balcony House as a site that showed traces of destruction and needed masonry repairs (Torres-Reyes 1970). Initial excavations and stabilization were conducted over the course of six weeks in 1910 by Jesse L. Nusbaum under the direction of Edgar L. Hewett and the School of American Archaeology (Fiero 1998; Nusbaum 1998a, 1998b). The project was financed by Colorado Cliff Dwellings Association. Unfortunately the report

[7] The article was published in the *Denver Tribune-Republican* on December 15, 1886 (Fiero 1998: 18).

from this work is still unpublished. The site was stabilized and restored only where necessary to prevent further destruction of the site (Torres-Reyes 1970). A short unpublished report and letters written by Nusbaum describing some work done in Balcony House have been annotated (Fiero 1998).

Sometime between 1916 and 1919 a kiva in Balcony House that was threatened with destruction by water damage was repaired (Torres-Reyes 1970). Several stabilization projects in 1958, 1977–1978, and 1988 included work in Balcony House (Fiero 1998: 1, 40). The most recent research included surveys and detailed documentation of Balcony House in 1993–1994 by the Historic American Buildings Survey/Historic American Engineering Record (HABS/HAER) of the National Park Service (Fiero 1998: App. C-1).

## History of the occupation of the site

The chronology of this cliff dwelling was established primarily on the basis of dendrochronology, pottery types, and architectural styles. The earliest tree-ring dates are from the A.D. 1190s, and the latest date, A.D. 1280, comes from Room 4 (Database-LTRR 2007; Fiero 1998: 14, Parks and Dean 1998). The earliest dates, A.D. 1190–1210, reflect the first stage of occupation or, more likely, beam reuse, a common practice among the Ancestral Pueblo people (Fiero 1998: 14). The latest tree-ring dates, those in the late A.D. 1270s and in A.D. 1280, come from southern and northern parts of the settlement near village-entry locations and from a room in the central part of the site.

The latest tree-ring dates from the North Plaza of Balcony House are A.D. 1280 from Room 4 and A.D. 1279 from the north or east passage. Relatively late dates also come from rooms 4–6 (A.D. 1275–1279) and the wall that supports Room 4 (A.D. 1271 and A.D. 1274). At the south end of the site, in the South Entry/Passageway or Room 29, the latest tree-ring dates are A.D. 1273 and A.D. 1278–1279; Room 21 yielded a date of A.D. 1273. The latest dates (A.D. 1273–1279) come also from the central part of the site, Room 15, and from a loose log in Room 4 (A.D. 1280) that is some associate with the central or northern part of the site (Database-LTRR 2007; Parks and Dean 1998: 13).

Tree-ring dates indicate that most building activity occurred in the A.D. 1240s and 1270s, which probably represent the two major episodes of village construction. There are two periods of relatively less building activity, the first between A.D. 1224 and 1239, and the second between A.D. 1249 and 1268. Parks and Dean (1998: 12) assume that population fluctuation caused these periods of diminished building activity.

The central part of the village appears to have been built early in the occupation, mostly in the A.D. 1240s, and the northern and southern parts were built, or remodeled, in the A.D. 1270s. Also, in the last stage of occupation, features that further restricted access to the village were constructed, such as a tunnel at the south entrance and the so-called Big Wall or Main Dividing Wall, which restricted access from one part of the pueblo to the other (Fiero 1998: App. C-1).

## Description of the site

### Site layout

Balcony House consists of 38 rooms and two kivas in addition to three main plazas and a refuse area in the back of the alcove (Fiero 1998: App. C-1). Ferguson (1996: 43) gives the number of rooms as 44. A retaining wall or balustrade protected the village from the edge of the cliff. Many of the structures in the pueblo were two stories tall.

Residents divided the village into two parts or sections with a wall now called the Big Wall or Main Dividing Wall which separates the northern part of the site from the southern part (Ferguson 1996: 43). Archaeologists divide the site into even more smaller parts or districts on the basis of architecture (Fiero 1998: 19–22, App. E). The northernmost part of the site is called Lower Plaza and it includes North Passageway and rooms 1–3. A modern entrance to the site, created by the National Park Service, is provided through this part of the site. The central area is North Plaza or North Quarter and includes rooms 4–14, and the southern end of the site is called Kiva Plaza, South Plaza, or Tower Quarter, and includes rooms 15–29, a refuse area, and kivas A and B. The southernmost end of the site, where the ancient entrance to the village was located, is called the Southern Passageway or Room 29.

### Access to the site

During the occupation of the site, probably the only entrance into the village led through the south end of the alcove (Fiero 1998: 21, 35; Ferguson 1996: 43). This was a very narrow passage between a huge boulder and the cliff face. Later, near the end of the occupation, the passage was modified into an even smaller entryway: a thick masonry wall containing a narrow tunnel was built across the passage. Tree-ring dates indicate that the tunnel was probably built in the 1270s (Fiero 1998: 35; Parks and Dean 1998: 11–12). The tunnel measures 0.47 m wide and 0.95 m tall at the south end (outside the site) and 0.40 m wide and 0.70 m high at the north end (Fiero 1998: App. E-21). This tunnel was then probably the sole entry into the village used by the Ancestral Puebloans (Fiero 1998: 21; Nordenskiöld 1990 [1893]: 66–67).

Two routes led to this entrance (Balcony House Trail Guide; Ferguson 1996: 43; Fiero 1998: 35). One route proceeds from the top of the mesa down the cliff face and consisted at least partly of hand-and-toe holds that, because the canyon wall is very steep in this area, might have been supplemented with a rope. This route leads to the south edge of the site near the aforementioned tunnel. Another route, more convenient but longer, begins at the top of the canyon and proceeds along a hand-and-toe-hold route to the far end of the same cliff-face ledge where Balcony House is located, which is 152 m (500 ft.), south of the site. The route then follows the ledge northward to the tunnel entry. Along this route, about 91 m (300 ft.) south Balcony House, is a small site, Site 5MV617, with a relatively well-preserved retaining wall (Fiero 1998: 35; Nusbaum 1998b: 20–21).

Today, the main entrance to Balcony House, used both by tourists and Park rangers, is in the north part of the site and was built by the National Park Service in the twentieth century (Balcony House Trail Guide). It is necessary to climb a ladder 9 m (30 ft.) tall to enter the site at this location (space called the Lower Plaza).

### *Availability of water*

The alcove where Balcony House is located probably contained at least two springs at the back of the alcove in the center of the village near Kiva Plaza (Fiero 1998: 21; Rohn 1963b: 453). The main spring is so productive today that the National Park Service built a cistern to catch and direct water away from the buildings to prevent further destruction (Balcony House Trail Guide). A third spring, just below the north end of Balcony House (Lower Plaza), is not easily accessible from the site (Fiero 1998: 21, 35). The presence of multiple springs in Balcony House itself and in the surrounding area results from a transition from massive sandstone to shaly sandstone and sandy shale that is more resistant to water in this location (Griffitts 1990: 24–25).

### *Evidence of defensive architecture*

A wall built along the front edge of the alcove in Balcony House is called a 'retaining wall,' 'balustrade,' or 'parapet wall.' This wall extends the full length of the alcove. Nordenskiöld (1990 [1893]) mentioned that at least part of the wall was built up to the top of the alcove. According to Nusbaum (1998b: 4), the wall had been mostly destroyed when he started his work in Balcony House in 1910, and the resulting rubble was lying below the site on the talus slope. An early version of the wall was associated with the construction of a "tower" where Room 17 was later built. This first wall was smaller and built farther back into alcove than a later one, which was built at the edge of alcove (Parks and Dean 1998: 10). During the final sequence of building and remodeling at Balcony House, which occurred in the A.D. 1270s, the earlier and smaller retaining wall was replaced by a larger one – this was a major change in the layout of the village, because it facilitated extending construction in the alcove both forward and laterally (Parks and Dean 1998: 10). Nusbaum inferred that the retaining wall in North Plaza near rooms 4 and 5 was built from the floor of the alcove up to the roof of the alcove and might have been about 6.7 m (22 ft.) tall, an unusual feature in cliff dwellings in Mesa Verde (Fiero 1998: 26; Parks and Dean 1998: 11). The height of this wall suggests that it was built not only to prevent children from falling down the cliff face or to prevent erosion in the pueblo but was also for defense.

A four-room two-story tower called "shadow tower" is in the central part of the site and is associated with at least one kiva that was probably built sometime between A.D. 1190 and the 1220s. In the A.D. 1240s, the tower was probably replaced by Room 17 (Parks and Dean 1998: 9–10). In his notes, Nusbaum calls the southern part of the site "Tower Quarter," and describes the tower as a "free-standing two-story roomblock" (Fiero 1998: 19; Parks and Dean 1998: 10). Nusbaum also calls other structures "towers," but that does not indicate that they were used in any specific way. In sum, because the "shadow tower" is poorly preserved, we cannot be certain that it actually was a tower, but perhaps at least one structure at the south end of the site might have been a tower (Fiero 1998: 51). Nordenskiöld described this structure as a "strong tower" (Nordenskiöld 1990 [1893]: 67).

Loopholes in the south wall of Room 29b, the ancient entrance to the cliff dwelling, angle down to the south and provide a view along the route to the site. Fiero (1998: 48, App. E-21) suggests that an associated structure might have been used as a lookout platform allowing observation of anyone approaching the village entry (the platform was built over the tunnel). Nusbaum also noticed loopholes in Room 9 (Room 12, according to Fiero) (Nusbaum 1998b: 9).

Residents restricted access between parts of the village (Fiero 1998: 33–34). A doorway in Room 16 that probably allowed access between Kiva Plaza and North Plaza early in the occupation of the pueblo was later sealed. After this change, the only means of passing from Kiva Plaza to North Plaza was a convoluted route along the back of the alcove behind rooms 13, 14, 17, 18, and 19, and across a boulder to steps into the North Plaza. This route went through a spring, a refuse area, and the Middle Passageway. Nusbaum noted during his work in 1910 that there were fragments of the passageway between the back of the alcove and the wall of Room 13 (Fiero 1998: 33) that are not preserved today. Access between North Plaza and Lower Plaza was also restricted. The access between these two plazas goes through a passage behind rooms 4 and 5, between the rooms and the back of the alcove, then through a hatchway and a T-shaped doorway. All of these modifications to restrict access between different areas of the village were constructed late in the occupation of the pueblo, probably about A.D. 1278–1279 (Fiero 1998: 34; Parks and Dean 1998).

## Conclusions

Balcony House was built in a cliff alcove in Soda Canyon at a location very difficult to access. The village contained two-story structures, about 40 rooms, and just two kivas, which results in a high room-to-kiva ratio (20 rooms per kiva). Compared to other Puebloan sites in the region during the thirteenth century A.D., this is quite unusual (Ferguson 1996: 52). The typical room-to-kiva ratio for the Pueblo III period in the Mesa Verde region is between five and seven rooms per kiva (Lipe and Hegmon, ed. by 1989; Lipe and Ortman 2000: 113).

The alcove in which Balcony House was constructed was apparently selected for habitation primarily for defensive reasons. The presence of multiple springs also might have been an important factor in selecting the alcove for habitation (Fiero 1998: 21). It is worth noting, however, that life for the inhabitants of the pueblo was probably not easy, especially for the children and elderly, or for those with disabilities. Traveling to and from the alcove and communicating with the residents of other villages, especially during the winter, would have been particularly challenging.

The cliff dwelling was inhabited during most of the thirteenth century A.D. (Database-LTRR 2007; Fiero 1998; Parks and Dean 1998); the span of tree-ring dates indicates that construction first occurred in the A.D. 1190s or 1200s. Two periods of building intensification occurred, one in the A.D. 1240s and one in the A.D. 1270s, which probably represent the two major episodes of construction of the pueblo (Fiero 1998: 14; Parks and Dean 1998). The latest tree-ring dates, A.D. 1279 and 1280 (Parks and Dean 1998: 10–12), reflect the final construction in the cliff dwelling and correlate with final migration of Ancestral Puebloans from the Mesa Verde region to the south and southeast. These latest dates come from the southern end of the site where the narrow tunnel entry was built, from the northern end of the site, and from the central part. The retaining or protecting wall was also rebuilt late, during the A.D. 1270s.

Numerous scientists, among them the first explorers of Balcony House, such as Nordenskiöld and Nusbaum, described Balcony House as a very defensive site (Nordenskiöld 1990 [1893]: 66–67; Nusbaum 1998a, 1998b; Torres-Reyes 1970). They especially noticed the defensible location and restricted access to the cliff dwelling. Only one entrance allowed access into the village, and during the final years of occupation this entrance was reduced by the construction of a small tunnel. The tunnel could have been traversed only on hands and knees. The defensiveness of this tunnel might have been further enhanced by the construction of loopholes in a wall above this tunnel that allowed protected viewing of the route leading to the alcove (Fiero 1998: 48, App. E-21). Nusbaum (1998b: 20–21) also interprets the small site along the route to Balcony House as defensive; he was probably referring to Site 5MV617, which boasts a relatively well preserved retaining wall (Fiero 1998: 35).

Near the end of the occupation of Balcony House, the cliff dwelling was divided into northern and southern sections by the so-called Big Wall or Main Dividing Wall. The construction of this wall is interpreted by some researchers as evidence of social change, because the wall might have reflected a social barrier between two groups of people living in Balcony House (Parks and Dean 1998: 11–12) or at least two different kinds of activities that were conducted in those two parts of the pueblo (Fiero 1998). Rohn compares this physical division in the architecture to duality in community similar to the duality (moieties) noted in some modern Pueblos (for example in Tewa pueblos) represented by Winter People and Summer People (Ferguson 1996: 43–45; Ortiz 1969; Rohn 1977). A recent study at Balcony House (Malville and Munson 1998) discovered possible astronomical features of the architecture that may be also connected with defensive features (however, this issue needs further detailed studies).

## V.1.1.b. Site 5MV625 (Cliff Palace)

### Location

Site type: cliff dwelling. Cliff Palace (Fig. 7) is contained within an alcove on the west side of the central part of Chapin Mesa in a canyon overlooking Cliff Canyon. This canyon drains into Soda Canyon, a major drainage of the Mesa Verde escarpment. The canyon where Cliff Palace is situated is deep, approximately 60 m (ca. 200 ft.) below the alcove where Cliff Palace is located (Fewkes 1911: 20; Watson 1950b: 19). The mesa top lies approximately 20–30 m (65–98 ft.) above the alcove.

Cliff Palace is the largest cliff dwelling in Mesa Verde National Park and probably in the entire Southwest. The alcove that houses the site is also large as compared to the other cliff overhangs and alcoves in the park that were inhabited by ancient Puebloans. The alcove measures approximately 99 m (324 ft.) wide, 27 m (89 ft.) deep, and 18 m (59 ft.) tall (Morgan 1994: 139). The elevation of the site is 2270 m or 6790 ft. (Fiero 2002). The site faces mostly west and southwest, and toward the south in the northern part of the site.

Cliff Palace is inferred to have been part of a large community of settlements in Cliff and Fewkes canyons (Ferguson and Rohn 1987; Fiero 2002; Morgan 1994: 139). In the vicinity of Cliff Palace are at least 20 ruins, mostly large and small cliff dwellings (Fewkes 1911: 22). The entire Cliff Palace community could have, however, consisted of about 33 cliff dwellings where about 600 to 800 people lived during the thirteenth century A.D. (Rohn 1977: 284), but other estimates are lower. The communication between those settlements would have been mostly along the top of the steeply sloping talus adjacent to the cliff, because this route was probably easier than climbing to the mesa top and walking there (Rohn 1977: 282). One large structure, Kiva W, sits at the base of the cliff approximately 20 m west of the alcove, but this structure is considered part of the site (Fewkes 1911: Plate 8). This kiva is surrounded by high walls; perhaps the kiva was within a tower (Fiero 2002).

The vegetation near alcove is not as abundant as it is near other large cliff dwellings in the Park, including primarily pinyon pine, juniper, and oak, as well as shrubs (Fewkes 1911: 20; Fiero 2002).

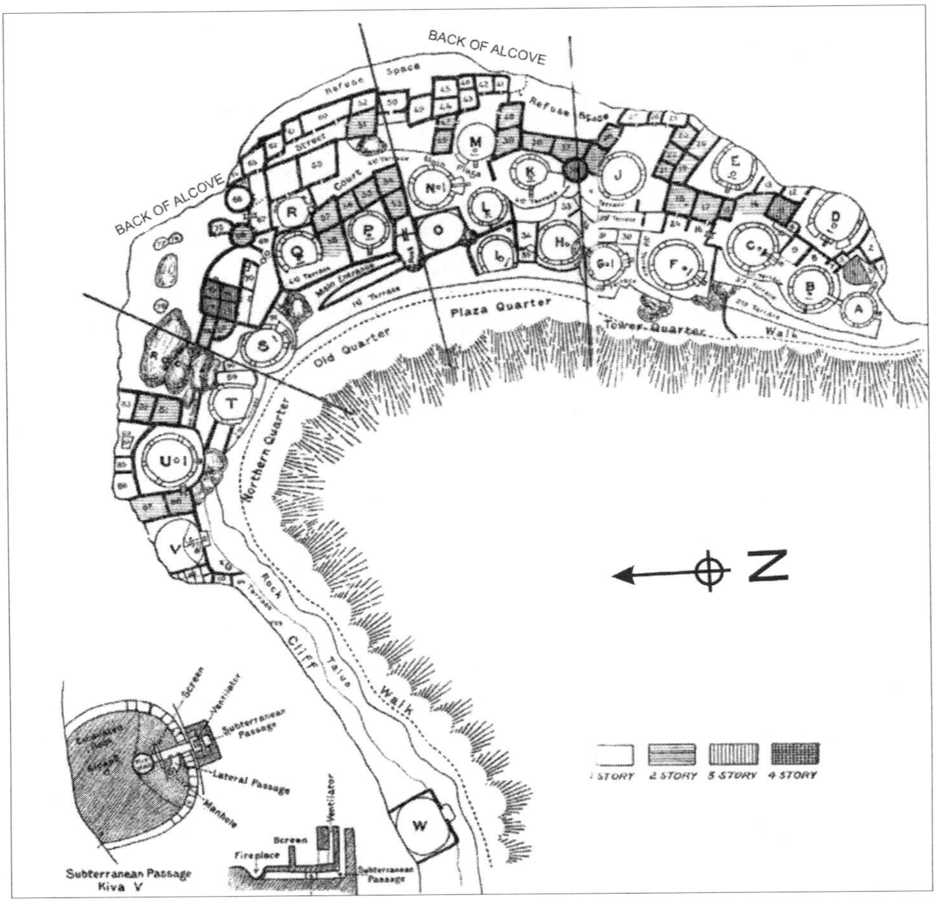


Fig. 7. Plan of the Site 5MV625, Cliff Palace (after Fewkes 1911: 22, Plate 8 modified by A. Danecki)

## History of investigation

Cliff Palace was discovered by Richard Wetherill and his brother-in-law Charlie Mason on December 18, 1888, during a search for lost cattle (Smith 2002). Before this, they had seen smaller cliff dwellings in Mancos Canyon. They heard stories from Acowitz, a Ute Indian, about the largest cliff ruin in the area of Mesa Verde, far larger than the sites in Mancos Canyon that they had already explored. The name "Cliff Palace" was probably bestowed by Richard Wetherill.

Later, after discovering other cliff dwellings in Mesa Verde, Wetherill family members began their exploration of ruins that included non-professional excavations and collection of artifacts in Cliff Palace and other sites. The site quickly became well known to the public partly as a result of published articles about the site that were written by early explorers and visitors such as F.H. Chapin, W.R. Birdsall, or S.D. Peet (Chapin 1892; Birdsall 1891, 1898; Peet 1899).

Unfortunately, Cliff Palace suffered greatly from early pot-hunting and vandalism and was one of the cliff dwellings vandalized on the largest scale (Fewkes 1911: 11–12, 24–25). Also, roofing beams were commonly used as firewood, and a great many roofs were destroyed. Also destructive were wind-and-water erosion; the northern and southern parts of the site were especially affected because they were not protected from the elements by the roof of the alcove.

In 1891, Gustaf Nordenskiöld, during his work in the area of today's Mesa Verde National Park, also excavated and described Cliff Palace. Members of the Wetherill family assisted in this fieldwork. Nordenskiöld published the results of his work in 1893 in *The Cliff Dwellers of the Mesa Verde, Southwestern Colorado. Their Pottery and Implements,* which remains one of the main sources of information about the site.

By 1906, Mesa Verde National Park had been created and embraced by the national park system, which launched a vigorous campaign to restore and stabilize Cliff Palace. Jesse W. Fewkes conducted an excavation and stabilization project at Cliff Palace in 1909 (Fewkes 1911; Smith 2002; Torres-Reyes 1970), and Cliff Palace was the second cliff dwelling excavated and stabilized after the Park was created. As well, spring water was diverted away from the structures to prevent further erosion and destruction, and reconstruction of some structures was undertaken (Fewkes 1911: 25). Fewkes' report and publication of his work at Cliff Palace includes a plan of the site that was probably partly drawn from a map by Kidder, Morley, and Nusbaum in 1907 and a description of Cliff Palace architecture. This report, along with Nordenskiöld's publication of his work there, and recent architectural studies by Nordby (2001), are the primary sources of published information about the site. Although Cliff Palace had been vandalized thoroughly before Fewkes' work, he obtained a fairly representative collection of artifacts (Fiero 2002; Fewkes 1911) and also noted that the cave roof was broken (Fewkes 1911: 22).

In 1933, Public Works Administration (PWA) funds were allocated for the mapping, documentation, and repair of Cliff Palace and other cliff dwellings in the park. In 1934, Earl Morris, Robert F. Burgh, and James A. Lancaster carried out extensive and high quality stabilization and reconstruction works and mapped the northern part of the site, although there are no publications from this work (Fiero 2002; Rohn 1977: 3; Torres-Reyes 1970).

The problem with water in the alcove has been constant during modern times. In 1961, a tunnel was constructed in the cliff face behind the alcove; this tunnel intercepts groundwater at the bedding plane of the shale/sandstone layers before it can reach the alcove and directs the water away from the site to the cliff face south of the site (Fiero 2002).

Little additional work was conducted at Cliff Palace in the second half of the twentieth century until the 1990s, which is surprising considering the fame and size of this cliff dwelling and its importance in understanding Pueblo societies in the Mesa Verde area. In the 1990s, however, additional research, including architectural analysis, was conducted (Nordby 2001; Roberts 1999). In 1994, the National Park Service and the Architectural Conservation Laboratory and Research Center (ACL) of the University of Pennsylvania, with financial aid from several institutions, initiated a partnership program of documenting and preserving the earthen finishing and plasters in some cliff dwellings at Mesa Verde National Park, including Cliff Palace (http://www.nps.gov/meve/historyculture/partnerships.htm). Also, between 1995 and 1998 the National Park Service conducted architectural documentation of Cliff Palace partly as a result of the increasing danger of water damage in many areas of the alcove. This work also helped to develop new methods of controlling the impact of water on the site (Nordby 2001: 1).

## History of the occupation of the site

The occupational chronology of this settlement derives primarily from tree-ring dating, but architectural styles and pottery types are also considered. Few tree-ring dates are available for Cliff Palace, and they have not been systematically studied. However, these dates indicate that the pueblo was inhabited during nearly the entire thirteenth century A.D., probably primarily during between A.D. 1209 and the 1270s (Database-LTRR 2007; Getty 1935a: 22; Morgan 1994: 139; Nordby 2001; Rohn 1977: 245; Schulman 1946: 20). Although Cliff Palace saw at least 60 years of building activity in the thirteenth century A.D., it is reasonable to suppose, on the basis of available tree-ring and architectural data, that building activity increased especially between A.D. 1264 and the 1270s (most likely A.D. 1268–1270s/1280) when many structures were built or existing buildings were remodeled, and some of the biggest and probably the most important structures in the village were built during this time (Database-LTRR 2007; Fiero 2002; Roberts 1999; Rohn 1977: 245).

Many buildings in Cliff Palace, including Courtyard Complex J (in Nordby terminology – Nordby 2001) and part of the Tower Quarter (in Fewkes terminology – Fewkes 1911) were built between A.D. 1260 and 1278, and construction there occurred most intensively between A.D. 1271 and 1278 (Nordby 2001: 19, 46). Other structures were built in the 1270s, for example Room 21 (Roberts 1999). Courtyard Complex M, part of the Plaza Quarter on Fewkes' map, was built between A.D. 1206 and 1280, but most of the tree-ring dates are between A.D. 1268 and 1280 (Nordby 2001: 49).

One of the most impressive structures at the site is the so-called Speaker Chief's House and The Speaker Chief Complex; it is assumed that some important buildings there were constructed before A.D. 1264 (Nordby 2001: 109). Some structures reflecting the proposed dual division of the village were built in the very late A.D. 1270s (Nordby

2001: 107–109). This includes kivas O and R (Database-LTRR 2007) and probably also rooms 59 and 64 (Roberts 1999).

## Description of the site

### *Site layout*

Cliff Palace is the largest cliff dwelling in Mesa Verde National Park and houses at least 220 rooms and 23 kivas or a total number of about 245 structures (Morgan 1994: 139; Lipe 2002: Table 10.2). The pueblo could have been inhabited by a population of around 200–250 people (Cliff Palace Guide); however, Nordby's most accurate estimates of the Cliff Palace population are much lower, or about 100 people (Roberts 1999), especially considering his counts of a total of 150 rooms, 75 other architectural spaces (courtyard areas above kivas, other open areas, slab structures), and 22 kivas (Nordby 2001: 1). In general, the masonry of the architecture at Cliff Palace is considered among the finest of all ancient sites in the Southwest (e.g., Fewkes 1911: 29). The structures within the alcove reached various heights; however, many were two or three stories, and some were four stories tall.

The structures in Cliff Palace are situated in almost every area of the rock shelter. The central part of the pueblo is covered entirely by the roof of the alcove, but structures at the southern and northern ends of the site, such as Kiva V at the northwest end of the site, are partly exposed (Fewkes 1911: 23). Large fallen rocks and boulders were incorporated into the architecture in some places, and several structures were built on boulders.

The site is situated on four terraces or levels that were at least partly created by the inhabitants of the pueblo (Fewkes 1911: 21–22). Fewkes (1911: 27) concluded that the village was terraced, with smaller buildings in the front and taller ones at the back of the alcove similar to the cliff dwellings in Canyon de Chelly. The residents leveled the floor of the cave, which was covered in some places with large stones and boulders, by filling low areas and building retaining walls near the steep talus slope (Cliff Palace Guide, Fewkes 1911: 22). Part of the village was constructed on the upper level of the alcove, a ledge approximately 6 m (20 ft.) above the bedrock floor. At least ten structures were situated there, among them the biggest rooms in the village, which could have served as storage rooms according to Nordby (Roberts 1999). The front or western walls of these structures created one long wall facing west (Fewkes 1991: 40; Nordby 2001: Fig. 6.1).

During his excavation and stabilization work at Cliff Palace, Fewkes distinguished four parts of the pueblo: the tower, plaza, old, and northern quarters (Fewkes 1911: 27–29). This division was, according to Fewkes, mainly for convenience when describing the site. Tower quarter encompassed the entire southern and the southeasternmost part of the site and contained a tower. The plaza in plaza quarter contained evidence of many fireplaces. Old quarter contained the densest concentration of buildings, the highest diversity of structures, and the best quality architecture. Northern quarter, in the northern- and northwesternmost parts of the pueblo, also contained structures of good-quality masonry. The old quarter, which contained the Speaker Chief's House has, according to Fewkes, signs of being the best protected part of the village, the most difficult to access by possible attackers, and contains a "high castle-like cluster of rooms" (Fewkes 1911: 28).

Nordby, in his recent research on the architecture of Cliff Palace, claims, however, that Cliff Palace was divided by ancient Puebloans into two "complete separate parts," northern and southern, by a stone wall that, in a zigzagging manner, begins at the back of the alcove north of Room 62 against the exterior southwest corner of Room 63 and goes between rooms 64 and 59, then proceeds south of the Speaker Chief's House to the north wall of Room 58 (Fiero 2002; Nordby 2001: 107–108; Roberts 1999). The same division is seen in the upper ledge of the alcove where there are three rooms; two rooms in the part of the site marked by the wall below the ledge and one room on the opposite side. This symbolic division is also visible in Kiva Q, a structure in the middle of Cliff Palace, where plaster still divides the kiva into symmetrical halves (Roberts 1999). This dual division is probably associated with the latest part of the occupation of the village, in building episodes that occurred A.D. 1278 to 1280 (Nordby 2001: 109).

Most of the structures in Courtyard Complex J (Nordby 2001) were built during the latest part of the occupation. Room 36, a circular tower, has no openings facing west (the outer part of the complex) other than two or three small orifices, possibly loopholes, located high in the wall. A large plaza within this complex is surrounded on three sides by well preserved rooms, some of which are two stories tall, and on the fourth (west) side by a free-standing wall called Miscellaneous Structure 1 by Nordby. The wall was built at the edge of the upper level or terrace (Nordby 2001: 19–48). The entry to this complex was restricted and led through Miscellaneous Structure 1. Courtyard Complex M consists of 19 architectural spaces and structures toward the back of the alcove on the fourth level or terrace in a manner similar to Complex J. Miscellaneous Structure 4, a wall, separated an open area in this complex from Open Area K, and was probably built about A.D. 1271 (Nordby 2001: 50).

### *Access to the site*

Though there were probably several routes to Cliff Palace, the two main ones appear to have been near the northern and southern ends of the alcove, and these routes led to the mesa top and canyon bottom (Nordenskiöld 1990 [1983]: 58, 60). One could also reach this cliff dwelling from a trail on the opposite side of the canyon, and there was a difficult route leading to the bottom of the canyon (Fewkes 1911: 22; Morgan 1994: 139). There were also some routes leading to other settlements near Cliff Palace.

The two main routes to Cliff Palace that lead along the northern and southern ends of the village are at least partly formed of hand-and-toe holds cut into the sheer cliff face; one-half of one of the routes is formed of these precarious holds. Early explorers at the site, such as Chapin and Fewkes, emphasized the difficulties of entering the pueblo (Fewkes 1911: 14); for example, half of one route (probably the southern one) was formed of hand-and-toe holds, and the other half had to be traversed on a ladder. Ladders might have been easy to hide by inhabitants of the pueblo. This route is called the "Ladder Trail" today and runs partly through a very narrow passage between two cliff walls (Fewkes 1911: 23). Both of these routes are often coated with ice during the winter. Fewkes claims that the main route and the entrance to the pueblo went from the northwestern end of the village to the plaza (Fewkes 1911: 27–28, Plate 9). One of the modern routes to the site was constructed near the ancient hand-and-toe trail made by ancient

Puebloans and goes south of the site. Part of the route today must be traversed by climbing multiple ladders.

Nordby (2001: 107; Roberts 1999) suggests that also communication between the two parts of the pueblo might have been difficult, at least in some places, because the dividing wall was about 2.5 m (8 ft.) tall and 1.5 m wide (5 ft.), and it was probably necessary to go along the front of the alcove to pass from one part of the pueblo to the other. Access to the upper ledge of the village was possible only by ladders resting on the bedrock floor or on the roofs of specific buildings on the lower level of the alcove. Inhabitants of the pueblo might have accessed the upper ledge by, for example, resting a ladder on the roof of a tower (Roberts 1999). Also, some upper-story rooms could only be accessed by ladder. There is some evidence of balconies on the upper stories; however, some rooms probably had roof hatchways (Fewkes 1911: 34).

### *Availability of water*

No large, permanent water source was available within or near the alcove. A small seep is present near the entrance to the pueblo, but this would not have produced enough water to supply the entire village. Several potential water sources, some natural and others created by the residents (for example checkdams), existed nearby and the inhabitants of Cliff Palace could have obtained water from these sources (Morgan 1994: 139; Rohn 1977: 284). One spring exists at the base of the cliff on the opposite side of the canyon, another is available in Fewkes Canyon below Sun Temple, and seeps are located at the top of the talus slope both north and south of Cliff Palace (Fiero 2002).

At a greater distance was the spring at Balcony House, approximately 1.6 km (1 mi) southwest of Cliff Palace, and that at Spruce Tree House more than 3 km (2 mi) northwest of the village (Fewkes 1911: 12; Torres-Reyes 1970). Even so, the most practical and nearest water source, even though not easy to access, was the spring at the bottom of the canyon where Cliff Palace is located.

Fewkes points out that some holes or potholes dug at the back of the alcove might have served as containers for water seeping through the alcove walls. These depressions are located along a path where water runs during rainfall. This runoff might have caused some of the destruction and erosion that has occurred within the alcove (Fewkes 1911: 24). As a result of a tunnel built through the cliff face behind the alcove in 1961, some parts of Cliff Palace, especially the northern part, have become drier than others, and a nearly steady stream of water flows through this tunnel (Fiero 2002). This abundance of water may indicate that, during the Puebloan occupation of the alcove, it was possible to collect water, especially at the back of the alcove. However, it is necessary to remember that the situation might have been different 700 years ago, and the presence of water today could be a result of modern water management and activity (Fiero 2002).

### *Evidence of defensive architecture*

Several retaining walls are visible that were probably used to level the surface and protect the village from the erosion of materials out of the alcove (Fewkes 1911). Other walls enclosed different spaces within the cliff dwelling. Miscellaneous Structure 5 is a 19.5 m (65 ft.) wall that extends along the outer part of the ledge and encloses the front of the ledge. This structure is above Room 68 and has only one entry; the wall now exists on only part of the ledge, but evidence indicates that it was built the entire length of the ledge (Nordby 2001: 86–87). In the Speaker Chief Complex, walls enclosed or defined the open areas (Nordby 2001: 109). Kiva W, an isolated structure west of the alcove, was enclosed by a high wall (Fewkes 1911: Plate 8; Nordby 2001), although some researchers infer that this wall was built to prevent sediment from eroding.

Several structures in Cliff Palace are labeled "towers." Room 11, the so-called square tower, is the only building in Cliff Palace with walls four stories tall; this structure extends from the floor to the roof of the alcove (Fewkes 1911: 41). The entrance to the building was probably on the lowermost story. This structure might have actually been a four-story roomblock (Fiero 2002), although the label we apply to the building does not explain the function it served.

Room 36, a circular structure, is also inferred to have been a tower and is situated on a high rock above kivas G and H (Fewkes 1911: 44). This building was probably two stories tall, had an entrance in the lowest story, similar to Room 11, and contains peepholes or loopholes high in the western wall of the building (Fewkes 1911: 44). Nearly the entire site, as well as the canyon below Cliff Palace, is easily viewed from this structure. Fewkes claims that it was one of the best constructed towers in the region in terms of the masonry and finishing of the walls. Nordby suggests that "the tower was a freestanding unit to which other rooms in the area of Cliff Palace were added" (2001: 46). The area near this tower, and probably the tower itself, was constructed or remodeled relatively late in the occupation of the village, sometime between A.D. 1260 and 1278, but most of the structures in this section of the settlement were built between A.D. 1271 and 1278 (Nordby 2001: 19, 46).

I also suggest that one of the functions of the three-story, partly circular Room 4, located at the southern end of the site and containing no doorways or windows (Fewkes 1911: 41), might have been as a watchtower or other defensive use. A loose log in Room 4 was tree-ring dated to A.D. 1268 or later (Database-LTRR 2007). Kiva W is enclosed by tall walls that might have been tower walls (Fiero 2002) even though the structure is not architecturally typical of Pueblo towers. Many kivas were enclosed by walls, but those walls were usually not tall, so one of the functions of this complex might have been defense.

Additional research is needed for kivas O, R, and W. These kivas were mentioned by Nordenskiöld and Fewkes and were described as "unique" (Nordenskiöld 1990 [1893]; Fewkes 1911). These kivas did not have pilasters and there was no evidence that they were ever roofed (Fiero 2002). According to Nordby (2001: 107), kivas O and R, and probably Kiva W, do not appear to have hearths. All three were enclosed by large and tall walls.

Interestingly, kivas A, B, and D, at the southernmost end of the site, are interconnected, and one kiva is connected by tunnel with a room. All of these structures are associated with massive, two- or even three-story buildings (Nordby 2001: 108–109). That group of structures is near the southern end of the site.

There are not many peepholes or loopholes in Cliff Palace (Fewkes 1911: 35). Although Nordby rejects the possibility of a defensive purpose for architectural features at the site, he notes the presence of loopholes such as those in Room 104 on the upper ledge. The loophole in the central part of this room affords a direct view of the Speaker Chief Complex. The southernmost loophole was probably covered or sealed after it was built, whereas the northern one, remodeled to reduce its dimensions, provides a view of the northwestern entry into Cliff Palace and the Kiva W area north of the alcove (Nordby 2001: 85).

The structures on the upper ledge, such as Room 109 and Miscellaneous Structure 5, contain many additional openings that could have been loopholes. The latter structure contains at least six loopholes that would have enabled unobserved viewing of most of the lower part of Cliff Palace. These loopholes "are placed at unusual angles, suggesting that they were used for something beyond simple light and ventilation" (Nordby 2001: 86). Light and fresh air was necessary in such a place as this, but the angles of these openings strongly suggest use for lookout purposes.

The Speaker-Chief's House is a three-story complex with two plazas, a grinding room, Kiva Q, and a circular tower. This complex probably had been at least partly constructed by A.D. 1264 (Nordby 2001: 109). The complex was large, as tall as three stories, and probably controlled access to the rooms on the upper ledge. Its architecture suggests that defense was at least one of its functions. At the southern end of the site the three kivas A, B, and D are linked to each other; one of these kivas is connected by tunnel to a room, and the kivas are associated with massive buildings two to three stories tall (Nordby 2001: 108–109).

## Conclusions

Cliff Palace is the largest of all cliff dwellings in the Mesa Verde region and in the greater Southwest. In the thirteenth century A.D., 200–250 people might have lived there (Morgan 1994: 139–140); however, Nordby (2001; Roberts 1999) proposes that the cliff dwelling was occupied by a relatively small population most of the time and that this number increased only during part of the year. Tree-ring dates indicate that most construction occurred in A.D. 1260s and 1270s (Fiero 2002; Database of Tree-Ring Dates, LTRR 2007; Roberts 1999; Rohn 1977: 245). Cliff Palace was the largest settlement within a community that probably included at least 33 habitations (Rohn 1977: 282–285).

The latest dates (A.D. 1270s–1280) come from structures that created architectural dual division of the settlement (Database-LTRR 2007; Nordby 2001). Nordby proposes that this division correlates with the Winter People and Summer People social organization (e.g., Ortiz 1969) that exists today in some pueblos along the Rio Grande. This division, similar to division in Balcony House, was also mentioned by other researchers such as Rohn (1965). The dual division may reflect a kind of social organization noted ethnographically in the nineteenth century A.D. and modern pueblos along the Rio Grande.

Defensive architectural features at the site include at least two structures (rooms 11 and 36, and possibly a tower-like structure in Kiva W) that might have been towers, the presence of openings or loopholes in the walls of buildings on the ground level as well as on the ledge, possible walls enclosing the fronts of particular households units (in Courtyard Complex J, for example), and the location of the village in an alcove difficult to access above a steep talus slope. The loopholes associated with ledge structures are angled in strategic directions such as toward the entrance of the village or different areas of the settlement.

Although the function of the towers in Cliff Palace remains unknown, much evidence suggests that they functioned at least partly in a defensive capacity. Other tall structures might have also been built for protection or for some kind of supervising or leadership post, such as the three-story complex of the "Speaker-Chief's House." Also, many buildings have now lost their uppermost stories and their original height and appearance is difficult to reconstruct.

Many structures associated with Cliff Palace that may be considered defensive were built or remodeled late in the occupation of the village. This includes, for example, some structures near Room 36, the circular tower. Also, two complexes of buildings described by Nordby (2001), courtyard complexes J and M, were built or remodeled in the A.D. 1260s and 1270s.

Chapin reported that fragments of disarticulated human remains and one complete skeleton were found on a wall at this site (Fewkes 1911:15) but it is not possible to determine whether the remains were left there when the village was abandoned or if they had been removed from graves by pothunters and placed there in the late nineteenth century or early twentieth century.

Despite of the size and fame of Cliff Palace, little modern archaeological research, apart from architectural studies conducted in the 1990s, has been devoted to the site. Also, not all reports from the research conducted there have been published.

## V.1.1.c. Site 5MV640 (Spruce Tree House)

### Location

Site type: cliff dwelling. The site (Fig. 8) is the third largest cliff dwelling in Mesa Verde National Park. Spruce Tree House is on Chapin Mesa, on the eastern side of Spruce Tree Canyon, a spur of Navajo Canyon (Fewkes 1999: 1; Nordenskiöld 1990 [1893]: 50). The site is situated approximately 45 m (150 ft.) above the bottom of Spruce Tree Canyon, and the slopes of the canyon are steep. The alcove where Spruce Tree House was built is in the geologic formation called Cliff House Formation (Griffitts 1990: 20–21). Within the sandstone are layers or breaks of shale visible as dark lines in the rock walls.

The alcove is approximately 66 m (216 ft.) wide and 27 m (89 ft.) at its greatest depth (Nordenskiöld 1990 [1893]; Spruce Tree House Guide). The alcove roof is low compared to its depth and the back of the alcove is rather dark (Nordenskiöld 1990 [1893]: 51). The elevation of the site is 2097 m (6880 ft.). Most of the site faces west, although northern part faces southwest.

Other small sites consisting of one or a few structures are present nearby; these are mostly in difficult-to-access rock shelters. Spruce Tree House and 13 smaller sites nearby are inferred to have been a cluster of settlements, the Spruce Tree House Community, in which Spruce Tree House was the largest and most centrally-located habitation (Rohn 1977: 285). At least some of these small sites could have served as storage rooms (Nordenskiöld 1990 [1893]) or defensive refuges. Each of these smaller sites could have been home to no more than one family (Nordenskiöld 1990 [1893], Fewkes 1999: 24–25).

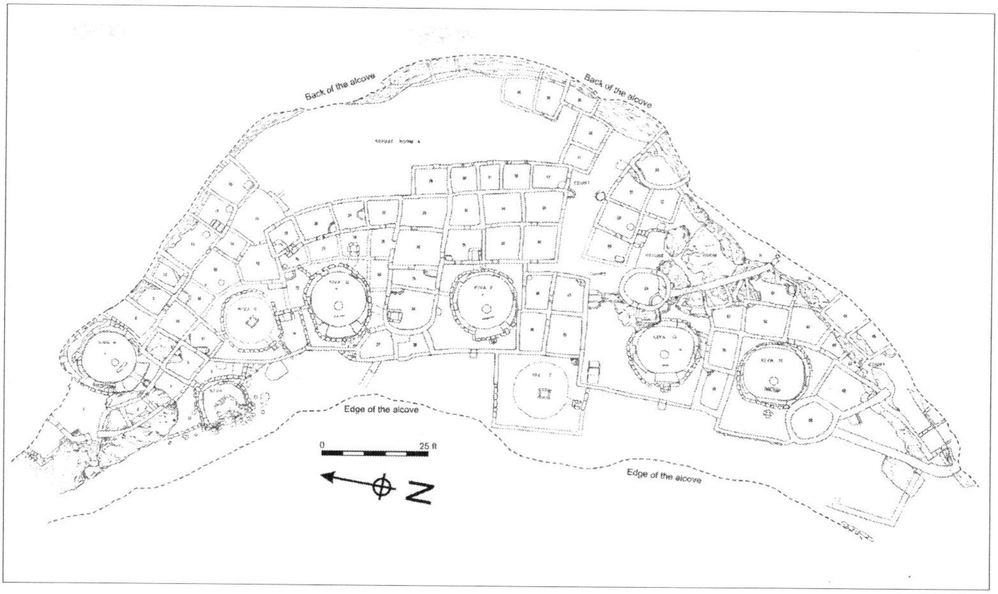


Fig. 8. Plan of the Site 5MV640, Spruce Tree House (Mesa Verde National Park modified by A. Danecki)

From the time of Euro-Americans' discovery of the site at the end of the nineteenth century until the present day there has been abundant plant and tree growth within the vicinity of the site, mainly juniper, pinyon pine, Gamble oak, and other plants and shrubs such as yucca, prickly pear, and Utah serviceberry (Nordenskiöld 1990 [1893]; Spruce Tree House Guide). Above the site on the mesa top was an area of potentially good farmland (Rohn 1977: 286).

## History of investigation

Spruce Tree House and other cliff dwellings were discovered by Richard Wetherill and Charlie Mason during their search for stray cattle in the winter of 1888. According to their account, they reached the site for the first time by way of a tall Douglas fir tree growing from the floor of the alcove to the mesa top above the site. Then began a period of uncontrolled visiting, artifact collecting, and pothunting, similar to events at many other ruins in what is now Mesa Verde National Park.

Short-term excavations were conducted at Spruce Tree House by Gustaf Nordenskiöld in 1891 (Nordenskiöld 1990 [1893]: 50–55). These were the first excavations conducted at the site using scientific methods, and they yielded the first detailed description of the site. Nordenskiöld also mapped the site and described the artifacts he found during excavations.

Spruce Tree House, like some other spectacular cliff dwellings, was singled out for immediate protection and stabilization by William D. Leonard, superintendent in charge of the Southern Ute Agency in 1906 or 1907 (Torres-Reyes 1970). The site, under the direction of George Randolph of the Colorado National Guard who was the first permanent superintendent of Mesa Verde National Park, was cleaned of trash left by visitors, and in 1908 archaeological excavations and stabilization of the ruins were carried out by Jesse Fewkes (Torres-Reyes 1970). Authorities were interested in this cliff dwelling because of its large size, excellent architectural preservation, and the presence of a good water source, which made the site much more convenient for tourists than any other cliff ruins on Chapin Mesa. In 1911–13 guards were introduced to watch several ruins on Chapin Mesa, including Spruce Tree House (Torres-Reyes 1970).

Excavations in May and June of 1908 were conducted by Dr. Jesse W. Fewkes from the Smithsonian Institution (Fewkes 1909). These excavations were associated with stabilization and conservation work associated with the architecture and the alcove itself. Another objective of this work was to adapt the ruin for tourists. In order to preserve the original character and look of the cliff dwelling as much as possible, Fewkes wanted to stabilize and conserve the site only where necessary. According to Fewkes "walls that were found to be in dangerous condition were properly repaired and strengthened, and such restoration was done as seemed necessary for the protection of the buildings" (Fewkes 1909; Spruce Tree House Guide). As a result of these efforts, about 90 percent of the architecture at this site remained as it was when discovered by Wetherill and Mason at the end of the nineteenth century (Spruce Tree House Guide).

The first tree-ring samples from the site were collected in the 1920s, probably by Dr. A.E. Douglass during the National Geographic tree-ring expeditions (Torres-Reyes 1970). In 1934, several sites in Mesa Verde National Park, including Spruce Tree House, were surveyed by Al Lancaster, Earl Morris, and Stanley Morse. Morse prepared a more detailed map of the site; however, he continued the numeric system used in Fewkes' map (Fewkes 1999: vi–vii; Torres-Reyes 1970).

More recent archaeological works include a collaboration begun in 1994 between Mesa Verde National Park and the Architectural Conservation Laboratory and Research Center (ACL) of the University of Pennsylvania. This work resulted in the documentation of architecture and surface finishes and also included detailed drawings or scaled digital photographs of Spruce Tree House and several other sites in the Park area, along with analyses and interpretations (http://www.nps.gov/meve/historyculture/partnerships.htm).

Spruce Tree House is relatively well preserved owing to its location under an overhanging cliff and to early twentieth century stabilization efforts conducted by Fewkes and Mesa Verde National Park. However, some damage to the site was caused by rock slabs falling from the cave roof. Fewkes and Nordenskiöld also mentioned this in their publications (Fewkes 1909: 1; Nordenskiöld 1990 [1893]: 49, 51). The first serious accident of this type was noted in 1923, followed by others in 1960 and 1964; these incidents might have been stimulated by wet weather followed by a heavy frost. After the accident in 1964 part of the site was temporarily closed to visitors (Torres-Reyes 1970).

## History of the occupation of the site

The first tree-ring samples were collected from Spruce Tree House during the National Geographic Beam Expedition of 1923. The first analysis of tree-ring dates from the site (Getty 1935b) yielded dates mostly between A.D. 1230 and 1274 and the earliest date for the site were found in the following locations: the oldest part of the site might be its north-central section, while one of the oldest dates came from the southern and northern ends of the site, for example Rooms 1 (third story), 6 (first story), and 63 (first story) (Database-LTRR 2007; Getty 1935b: 28–29).

More recent studies of tree-ring dates show that the earliest dates, from initial building activity in the village, fall between A.D. 1200 and 1210, which may reflect building activity at that time or reuse of beams from an earlier settlement. The latest tree-ring dates are in the A.D. 1270s, primarily A.D. 1277–1278, and most are associated with structures in the northern and southern ends of the site (Database-LTRR 2007).

Tree-ring dates indicate that most construction occurred between the A.D. 1230s and 1259 (Fiero 1998: 16). Two periods of relatively less building activity occurred – one before the A.D. 1230s and the other after A.D. 1260 – and continuing until the end of village occupation. However, the less active periods of construction as reflected in the tree-ring dates might have been when upper story rooms that now are fallen were built or when beams were used that didn't survive (Getty 1935b: 28). Fewer very late tree-ring dates from the late A.D. 1270s are available for Spruce Tree House than for other large cliff dwellings at Mesa Verde National Park.

## Description of the site

### *Site layout*

The shelter or alcove where Spruce Tree House is located is oriented roughly north-south, and the orientation of structure walls was determined to a large extent by the walls of the alcove (Nordenskiöld 1990 [1893]). Spruce Tree House is, unlike the many other cliff dwellings in Mesa Verde National Park, largely concealed behind trees. The village included structures that were two and three stories tall, and the roofs of many of these buildings were created by the roof of the alcove. The site consists of 114–130 rooms that were used for domestic and storage purposes, and eight kivas (Fewkes 1909: 7; Glowacki 2006: 186; Nordenskiöld 1990 [1893]; Lipe 2002: Table 10.2). The floor of the cave is relatively level. At the front of the shelter, residents built a masonry wall oriented generally north-south along the line of the alcove and cliff. At the back of the pueblo was a trash area containing guano and turkey bones, which indicates that turkeys were kept there (Fewkes 1909: 7, 25). Human burials were located there as well.

The structures in the village were divided into north and south parts by a wide passageway or "street" that trends generally east-west (Fewkes 1909: 7–8, Nordenskiöld 1990 [1893]). The "street" continues the entire width of the pueblo from Kiva G to the back of the alcove. The division is also distinctive for its midden at the back of the alcove (Fewkes 1909: 7, 25). According to Fewkes, the northern part is older and contains masonry that is of better quality and was more carefully constructed than that in the southern part (Fewkes 1909: 7–8). Nordenskiöld (1990 [1893]) suspected that the layout of the village was not pre-planned, and that only a few structures were built when the village was founded; more structures were built in response to a growing population.

### Access to the site

Although Wetherill and Mason, the modern discoverers of this site, first entered the alcove by means of a tall evergreen tree that rose from the alcove floor to the mesa top, at least three ancient trails led to the pueblo. Two were traversed partly by hand-and-toe holds in the cliff face. One of these trails is on the west side of the canyon, near a modern trail to a spring and the site, and the other trail is on the east side of the canyon, very near the north end of the pueblo. A third route went south of the site and along the east canyon wall (Fewkes 1909: 25).

Today the site is one of the most accessible for tourists at Mesa Verde National Park (Torres-Reyes 1970), but this does not reflect the difficulty of access when the village was inhabited. Because Spruce Tree House is easily accessible and because of it relatively big dimensions it is one of the most visited sites at Mesa Verde National Park.

### Availability of water

North of the site, at the head of Spruce Tree Canyon, is a good spring that today is marked by an abundance of flora (Fewkes 1909: 1; Nordenskiöld 1990 [1893]; Rohn 1977: 285). This spring might have been productive enough to support a population of 100 people (Guidebook Spruce Tree House). Rohn suspected that ancient Puebloans built a reservoir above this spring (Rohn 1977: 285–286). The rear of the alcove in which Spruce Tree House is located might have also contained one or more seeps, a situation common to many cliff dwellings in Mesa Verde National Park. The spring at the head of Spruce Tree Canyon is so productive today that a mesa-top location nearby was chosen by park authorities for quarters for the Park's rangers. In the 1920s a cistern for the spring water was also built there for tourists (Torres-Reyes 1970).

### Evidence of defensive architecture

A wall that Fewkes interpreted as a retaining wall was along the outside edge of the alcove. This wall could have prevented erosion of both the talus slope and the sediment from the alcove (Fewkes 1909: 9; Plates 4, 5).

A second, inner wall, behind the retaining wall, extended nearly through the entire outer or western part of the pueblo near the edge of the alcove and talus slope (Fewkes 1909: 8, Nordenskiöld 1990 [1893]). This inner wall began at Room 5 in the northern part of the site and continued to the southern part of the site. Some of the western walls of the rooms along this wall were incorporated into it. The tall west walls of the northernmost structures facing the outer part of the pueblo, e.g., rooms 1–5, formed the extension of this wall in the northernmost part of the site (Fewkes 1909: 11, Plate 1).

The inner wall encompassed most of the buildings and plazas in the village. Only two structures were outside this wall: kivas B and F. Also, between the inner wall and the retaining wall near the talus slope, residents might have been able to communicate between different parts of the pueblo. Before Fewkes conducted excavations at the site, the inner wall was covered by stone debris, and he estimates that it might have originally extended several feet above the level of the plazas "as high as the head" (Fewkes 1909: 9).

Two oval or circular structures, rooms 54 and 69, which Feweks inferred to be towers, are in the southernmost and central part of the pueblo (Fewkes 1909: 14, 23). Room

69, situated near Kiva H, is one of the southernmost buildings in the pueblo, and now only the foundation of its walls remains today. One of the walls of this structure is incorporated into the village inner wall described above and steps at the outer part of the village inner wall were built by residents to access Room 69. Room 54 is behind Kiva G in the south-central part of the site south of the main plaza and the passageway that divides the pueblo.

I propose that two additional structures be called towers. These structures, rooms 1 and 2, share one wall which is the southern wall of Room 1 and northern wall of Room 2 (Fewkes 1909: 11, Plates 1, 8). Room 1 is the northernmost building in Spruce Tree House. It rests on a large boulder, and entry is by means of steps outside the western (outer) part of the room, very similar to the access to Room 69, a tower at the southern end of the site. The location of this room on a boulder caused the floor of Room 1 to be at a high elevation and at the same level as the floors of other second-story rooms. Room 2, which was probably three stories tall originally, still has one wall that stands as much as 6 m (20 ft.) tall (Fewkes 1999: 11; Nordenskiöld 1973 [1893]: 54).

The original entryway into Room 2 was probably by means of a balcony that no longer exists; later, access was through a T-shaped doorway in the southern wall (Fewkes 1909: 11). Balconies were observed in different parts of the pueblo, for example above rooms 20–22, and probably aided communication between neighboring rooms as well as providing access to second- and third-story rooms (Fewkes 1909: 15). However, some rooms had hatchways in their roofs that served as entrances (Fewkes 1911: 34). Rooms 2–4, in the northern part of the pueblo, appear to have been built later than Kiva A behind them at the back of the alcove (Fewkes 1909: 11). Therefore, they may represent a late construction event in the settlement.

Small openings or holes mentioned by both Nordenskiöld and Fewkes could have been loopholes rather than windows (Fewkes 1909: 16; Nordenskiöld 1990 [1893]: 54). Some of these openings, which were square or rectangular and sloped downward toward the exterior of the walls, were considered by Fewkes to be for lookout rather than just for fresh air. Fewkes (1909: 9) also left brief and imprecise information concerning the small rectangular openings through the inner wall of the village.

## Conclusions

Spruce Tree House is the third largest cliff dwelling in the Mesa Verde National Park – only Cliff Palace and Long House are larger – and the largest site in Navajo Canyon. This village might have been inhabited by 70–100 people (Spruce Tree House Guide). Tree-ring dates indicate that the cliff dwelling was inhabited during most of thirteenth century A.D., especially between A.D. 1210 and 1278. The latest tree-ring dates come from the southern and northernmost parts of the site (Database-LTRR 2007; Getty 1935b). Spruce Tree House was the largest settlement in the Spruce Tree House Community that also included other structures this site. Most of these sites are very small and in locations difficult to access. They are inferred to have been storage rooms or structures that were also used for protection and defense (Nordenskiöld 1990 [1893]: 55–56).

Some evidence indicates that the location of the village in an alcove that was difficult to access (unlike today situation) and possibly defensive architectural features were at least partly for the purpose of defense and protection. Architectural features within the site include loopholes and circular or oval buildings that may be identified as towers such as rooms 54, 69, and possibly rooms 1 and 2, which are connected. Access to the settlement was apparently controlled by the villagers. I suggest that Room 1, situated on a large boulder and attached to Room 2 (another high structure), created a building that could have been used for viewing down the canyon and other areas outside Spruce Tree House, for controlling access to the village, and for protection in case of an attack.

The location of structures that might be called towers at the extreme ends of the Spruce Tree House (rooms 1, 2, and 69) is similar to that of other large cliff dwellings in present-day Mesa Verde National Park including Cliff Palace and Long House. Fewkes (1909: 9) concluded that the inner wall at the front of the pueblo could have been also built for defensive purposes. Room 54, considered by Fewkes to have been a ceremonial tower, and Room 69, "the bastion," were included in the line of that front wall (Fewkes 1909: 23).

## V.1.1.d. Site 5MV650 (Square Tower House)

### Location

The site (Fig. 9) sits in a shallow and very tall alcove at the head of a spur of Navajo Canyon in the west wall of Chapin Mesa in Mesa Verde National Park (Nordenskiöld 1990 [1893]; Rohn and Ferguson 2006: 113). The elevation of the site is 2073 m (6800 ft.). The dimensions of the alcove, as shown on the site map by Fewkes and reprinted by Munson (2008), are roughly 45 m (ca. 140 ft.) long and 12–16.5 m (35–50 ft.) deep; the dimensions vary slightly between Fewkes' map of the site and a CyArk map (Munson 2008, http://archive.cyark.org). The site faces south and southwest (Rohn and Ferguson 2006: 112).

Square Tower House and nearby sites are inferred to have been a cluster or a community. Square Tower House was the largest of these settlements. Rohn (1977: 285) estimates that seven sites composed this community. Most of the structures, 111 rooms and 11 of the 12 kivas, are located at either Square Tower House or Little Long House (Site 5MV647). Rohn estimates the population of Square Tower House at 75–100 (1977: 278) and the entire community at about 120–150 (1977: 285).

The vegetation includes mainly pinyon-juniper woodland and shrubs.

### History of investigation

Square Tower House was one of the first cliff dwellings discovered by Richard Wetherill and Charlie Mason during their search for stray cattle in December, 1888 (Roberts 1993; Smith 2002).

The site was described in some detail by Gustaf Nordenskiöld in *The Cliff Dwellers of Mesa Verde* as a result of his work in 1891 in the area of today's Mesa Verde National Park; however, he didn't excavate or draw a plan of this site. The site was excavated in 1919 by Jesse W. Fewkes (Fewkes 1920; Rohn 1977: 80), although there is no official publication or plan of the site from these excavations. According to Munson (2008), an unpublished report, *Antiquities of the Mesa Verde National Park: Square Tower House and Fire Temple* (Unpublished manuscript on file at the National Anthropological

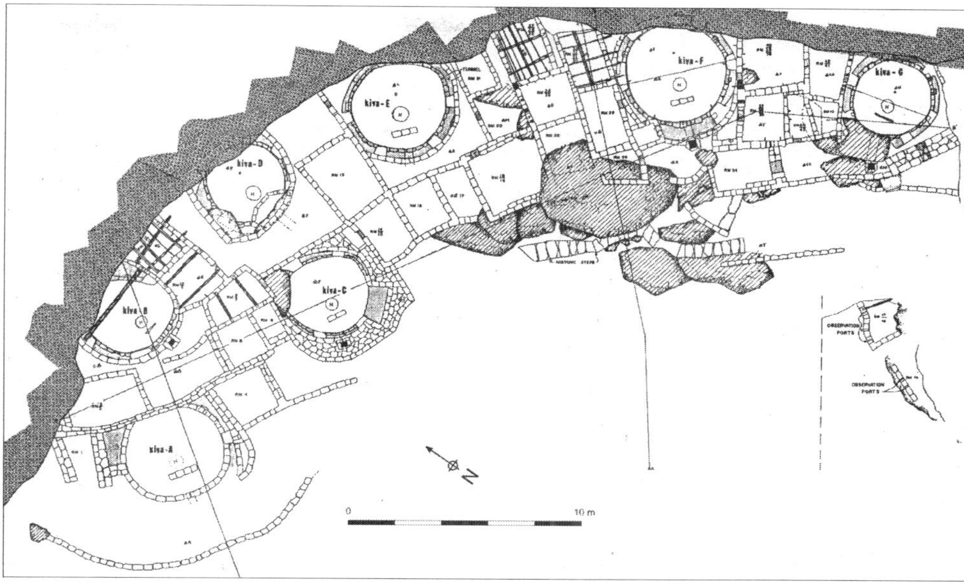


Fig. 9. Plan of the Site 5MV650, Square Tower House (Mesa Verde National Park modified by A. Danecki)

Archives), was written by Fewkes and was probably submitted in 1922. However, this report is difficult to access.

Between 1910 and the 1930s a trail to the site and other facilities were established to make the site more accessible to tourists. Stabilization work was also conducted (Torres-Reyes 1970). Today the site is usually closed to tourists; however, it can be easily seen from an overlook on the mesa top.

In 2006 or 2007, a large boulder or rock detached from the alcove face and fell in the western part of Square Tower House, damaging Room 1 and a two-story structure (rooms 2 and 3), as well as Kiva A. The Mesa Verde National Park Preservation Crew is currently working to stabilize the damaged structures (http://archive.cyark.org/mesa-verde-info#info).

In recent years electronic scanning and documentation of the architecture of Square Tower House has been undertaken by CyArk, a non-profit organization that "collects, archives and provides open access to data created by laser scanning, digital modeling, and other state-of-the-art technologies" (http://archive.cyark.org). The site was documented and digitalized by CyArk; most work was done in the vicinity of the square tower (rooms 30–33).

## History of the occupation of the site

The architectural style, pottery types, and tree-ring dates indicate that the village dates from the late Pueblo III period (Database-LTRR 2007; Rohn 1977: 245, 285). The earliest tree-ring dates are from the twelfth century A.D., primarily from the 1180s and 1190s, and the early part of the thirteenth century (A.D. 1203–1213). However, most of the construction and the heaviest occupation of the village apparently occurred in the thirteenth century A.D. Several samples dated to the A.D. 1220s, 1240, 1260s (Database-LTRR 2007; Rohn 1977: 245), some late dates (A.D. 1279–1281) are from Kiva G and the square tower. The latest tree-ring dates from Square Tower House are from rooms 1 and 3/2 (A.D. 1269) and from Room 5 (A.D. 1270).

## Description of the site

### *Site layout*

The site consists of about 70–80 rooms and at least seven kivas[8] (Lipe 2002: Table 10.2; Rohn 1977: 80). The dominant structure in the alcove is the four-story square tower for which the site was named. This tower was probably the tallest structure in the park area (Wenger 1980: 46). In front of this structure are traces of the former presence of two other buildings: a three-story building attached to the square tower and a two-story building in front of the three-story building. The roofs of these structures formed a series of terraced rooftops or stairsteps that began with the two-story building at the front of the village and ended at the uppermost rooftop of the four-story building. Today only this tallest one attached to the cliff face remains; the two shorter ones have since collapsed (Rohn and Ferguson 2006: 112). These buildings probably contained at least some domestic rooms.

In Fewkes' plan from a 1922 unpublished manuscript (Munson 2008), Kiva E – one of the kivas near the cliff edge at the outer part of the site – is shaped like a capital D (D-shaped); however, it is difficult to evaluate the unusual shape of this structure without further studies of Fewkes' report and architectural analysis.

Nordenskiöld mentioned intact kiva and room roofs (Nordenskiöld 1990 [1893]: 56–57; Rohn 1977). However, many roofs were on the verge of collapse (Nordenskiöld 1990 [1893]: 57). Today two kivas, B and F, have partly intact roofs; this preservation facilitated the reconstruction of kiva roofs at other sites such as Spruce Tree House (Rohn and Ferguson 2006: 112). Nordenskiöld also claimed that the masonry at the site was of good quality and precisely constructed (Nordenskiöld 1990 [1893]: 56).

### *Access to the site*

The site was one of the most difficult to access in what is now Mesa Verde National Park. There are two main routes or trails to Square Tower House from the mesa top, on which there were farming areas, above the ruin (Rohn and Ferguson 2006: 112–113). One route led from the southeastern part of the village along the base of the cliff and from there proceeded to the top of mesa. Part of this trail consisted of hand-and-toe holds. The second route connected Square Tower House with Little Long House, which was northwest of Square Tower House; these two settlements were probably inhabited at the same time (Rohn 1977). Now these trails are at least partly covered by piñon-juniper woodland.

[8] The numbering and names of the particular rooms in Square Tower House are derived from Munson 2008 and the CyArk website (http://archive.cyark.org).

Some aforementioned structures located above and to the right of the main area of Square Tower House are very difficult to access. The difficult access of Square Tower House, along with the attractiveness of the site, led to a decision in the 1910s and 1920s to construct trails and a balustrade with ladders conveniently set to aid those who wished to visit the ruins (Torres-Reyes 1970). However, today the site is off limits to tourists.

Nordenskiöld and other early researchers also described rooms located at the steepest part of the cliff face, above and to the right of the site; access to these structures was possible only by climbing or by using a very tall ladder (Fewkes 1920; Nordenskiöld 1990 [1893]: 58; Rohn and Ferguson 2006: 113). Jesse W. Fewkes called this the "crow's nest."

### *Availability of water*

The main water source for Square Tower House was a strong spring issuing from the steep canyon wall just below the village. Close to another site, Little Long House, there was also a "seep augmented by two reservoirs–one natural and one artificial" (Rohn 1977: 285) which probably consisted of a dam built by Puebloans on the bedrock above the sites and a natural spring in the draw near Little Long House (Rohn and Ferguson 2006: 112–113). These two sources might have provided water for the entire cluster of sites in the Square Tower House cluster (Rohn and Ferguson 2006: 112).

### *Evidence of defensive architecture*

It is difficult to describe elements such as walls, towers, or other structures from only fragmentary citations of unpublished reports. However, with this scanty information, Nordenskiöld's short descriptions from his work at Mesa Verde, and the author's personal observation of the site, it can be stated that Square Tower House resembled other cliff dwellings in the Mesa Verde National Park described in this chapter.

Some evidence of retaining walls is visible on the alcove floor at the edge of the cliff and walls enclosed particular complexes of buildings within the village that were not necessary for preventing sliding of sediment such as a wall that defined or enclosed the central part of the pueblo where Kiva C is located. On the Fewkes map a wall is identified as a retaining wall (Munson 2008). However, if this wall was built on large rocks and boulders as shown on the map, it probably was not intended to prevent erosion and should be called an enclosing or protecting wall, because it was at the front of the village. This issue, however, needs further study.

The square tower is a four-story structure (rooms 30–33, according to http://archive.cyark.org). The tower is 8 m (26 ft.) tall, and it was probably the tallest structure in the park area (Wenger 1980: 46). This structure was part of a complex of tall, multistory structures (see above). Other multistory buildings were constructed in front of the tower and probably on both sides as well, but they have since collapsed, and only the lower parts of them remain.

The westernmost structures in the cliff dwelling, rooms 2 and 3, were near the western entrance to the village and were at least two stories tall. Also in the western part of the site there is a complex of buildings with tall south walls, no doorways at the ground level, and at least one small rectangular opening that could be a window or loophole.

Kiva E is in the central part of the site and is enclosed by rooms 15–21 and the alcove wall at the back. There is evidence of a tunnel leading from this kiva into Room 21 (http://archive.cyark.org).

## Conclusions

Square Tower House is a mid-sized cliff dwelling in the Mesa Verde National Park. Signs of habitation of the alcove by ancient Pueblo people date from different times; however, the heaviest occupation occurred during the thirteenth century A.D. (Database-LTRR 2007; Rohn 1977), before the final abandonment of the village and the depopulation of the Mesa Verde area near the end of the thirteenth century A.D. The latest tree-ring dates from Square Tower House are from rooms 1 and 3/2 (A.D. 1269) and from Room 5 (A.D. 1270).

In the thirteenth century about 80 structures were built in this alcove. This settlement and smaller sites in the vicinity of Square Tower House are inferred by many archaeologists to have formed a cluster of related sites or a community. About 70–100 people are thought to have inhabited Square Tower House in the thirteenth century, and about 120–150 people formed the entire community (Rohn 1977: 278, 285). The number of structures within the community totals about 111 rooms and 12 kivas, and the largest settlements were Square Tower House and Little Long House (Site 5MV647).

Square Tower House was one of the cliff dwellings with the most difficult access in Mesa Verde National Park until the twentieth century when trails were built for tourists and for archaeologists working at the site, and even today the site is not the easiest to access. The location of the site in a cliff alcove on a steep talus slope, its difficult access, and particular features of the architecture at the site, have led many to theorize that the location was chosen at least in part for defensive purposes and for the protection of the residents. The first researchers at the site, such as Nordenskiöld (1990 [1893]: 58), assumed a defensive purpose for the village, and this remains one of the modern theories for the reason that the village was so located and built in such a manner.

This community of settlements had access to at least three springs as well as a dam built by Puebloans, which suggests that water was available within a short distance for the inhabitants of this community. The tallest structure in the village was the square tower for which the site was named; this four-story building (rooms 30–33) rises 8 m (26 ft.) above the floor of the alcove. The impression of its height may be augmented by the elevated position of its lowermost story on a boulder. This is also the tallest surviving structure in the park area.

Some structures in the settlement were two or three stories tall, the southern or outer walls of structures in the westernmost part of the pueblo lacked doorways and other openings on the ground level, and small rectangular openings (loopholes?) were noted in second-story walls. It is possible that some walls, such as the retaining walls, also served to define or enclose particular units within the settlement, including the wall built in the southern part of Kiva C in the central part of the village. Some walls visible in old photographs of the site and shown on Fewkes' map (Munson 2008), in the southern (outer) part of the pueblo, could have been built for protection, although this theory should be confirmed with additional study. At least one tunnel was built in the village, and it connected Kiva E and Room 21 (http://archive.cyark.org). This kiva is in the central part of the cliff dwelling, at the back of the alcove, and it is surrounded by the relatively tall walls of rooms 15–21.

## V.1.2. Mesa Verde Proper (Mesa Verde National Park): Wetherill Mesa

### V.1.2.a. Site 5MV1200 (Long House)

#### Location

Site type: cliff dwelling. This is the second largest cliff dwelling in Mesa Verde National Park (Fig. 10). Long House is on the west side of Wetherill Mesa in Long House Draw, a tributary of Rock Canyon. This part of Wetherill Mesa lies in the western portion of the Mesa Verde National Park.

The site was built in a shallow alcove, about 33 m (100 ft.) below the rimrock, approximately 165 m (500 ft.) above the bottom of Long House Draw. The elevation of the

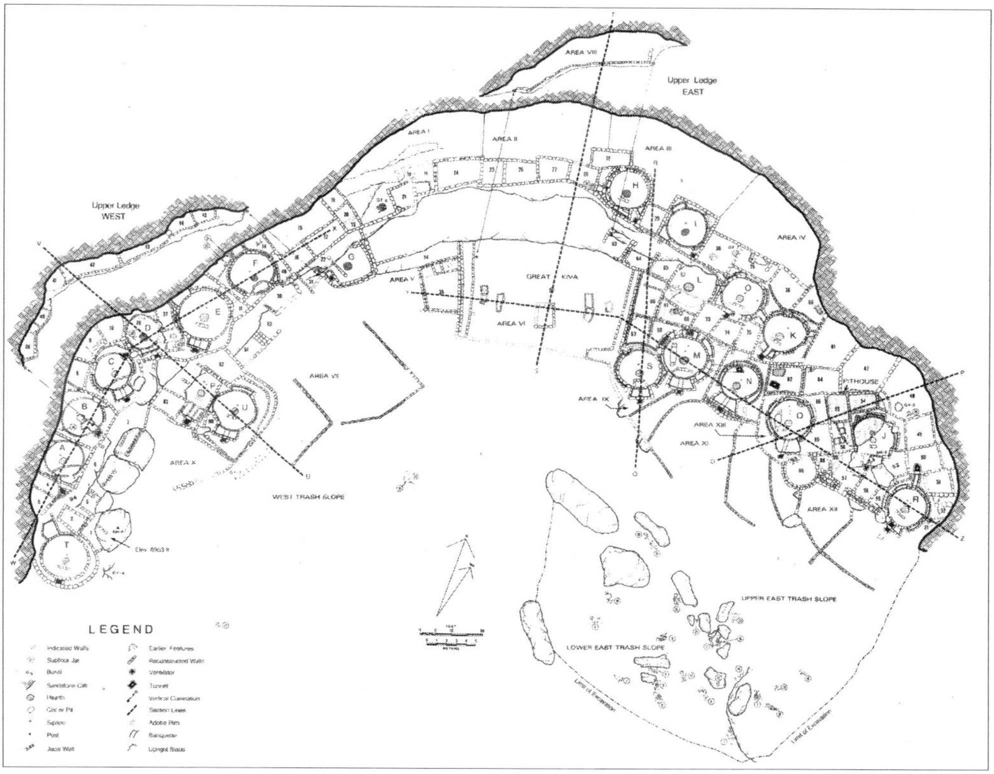


Fig. 10. Plan of the Site 5MV1200, Long House (after Cattanach 1980: Fig. 9 modified by the author)

site is approximately 2128 m, or 6983 ft. (Cattanach 1980: 1–2, 4). Most of the structures in the cliff dwelling face nearly due south, although some in the western part of the site face southeast.

Other sites in the vicinity of Long House also date from this period, and most are in rock shelters or alcoves (Cattanach 1980: 1, 3–4). This cluster of settlements, like others in Mesa Verde National Park, probably created a community of contemporaneous sites.

The vegetation near the alcove includes mainly dense pinyon-juniper forest as well as shrubs such as mutton grass and large sagebrush. Plants such as willow and reed were probably more abundant in this area in the past they are than today (Cattanach 1980: 1).

## History of investigation

Long House was discovered during the winter of 1889–1890 by Wetherill family members and Charlie Mason; inscriptions on the wall of the alcove also confirm exploration of the site by the Wetherills in 1891 (Cattanach 1980: 5; Smith 2002; Torres-Reyes 1970). In 1891 the site was partly excavated and described by Gustaf Nordenskiöld with the help of the Wetherills (Smith 2002; Torres-Reyes 1970). Nordenskiöld named the site "No. 15" and spent one month excavating there. He also prepared the initial map of the site (Nordenskiöld 1990 [1893]: III).

There are signs of late nineteenth and early twentieth century unofficial excavations and exploration of the site, although there are probably no written descriptions of these activities (Cattanach 1980: 6). Long House, like many other sites in the area, was subjected to pothunting. In the early 1920s, new trails were constructed to various sites, including one trail to Long House; at least once, in 1970, the trails to Long House were rebuilt (Torres-Reyes 1970).

The site was professionally excavated during the Wetherill Mesa Project from 1958 to 1962, and those excavations were directed by George S. Cattanach, Jr. A detailed map of the site was also prepared during this project, and necessary stabilization was conducted as well (Cattanach 1980).

## History of the occupation of the site

The earliest known Puebloan component was tree-ring dated to the Basketmaker III period. In A.D. 648 or later, a pithouse and some associated structures were built (Street 2001a, vol. 1: 74). Evidence of Pueblo I, Pueblo II, and possibly early Pueblo III (A.D. 750–1100/1150) occupations of the alcove are also present; however, the alcove was not occupied continuously (Cattanach 1980: 1, 4, 9). Recent dendrochronological studies such as that by Street (2001a, vol. 1: 196–198) suggest that the earlier component was probably more robust than was assumed previously.

But it is beyond question that the most intense occupation of the alcove and the one most visible in archaeological data and in the tree-ring record is the Pueblo III occupation, which dates from A.D. 1200 to 1280 (Cattanach 1980; Street 2001a, 2001b). A lack of tree-ring dates between A.D. 1206 and 1245 may indicate, as Street suggests (2001a, vol. 1: 198) partial abandonment of the settlement. From A.D. 1246 to 1248 construction resumed. Construction and remodeling intensified between A.D. 1260 and the 1270s (Street 2001a, vol. 1: 199). According to Street's dendrochronological study of Long

House (2001a, vol. 1: 198–199), most of the settlement burned and was destroyed in A.D. 1261 or a little later, including kivas M and O, which contained some "disaggregated individuals interred under burnt collapsed kiva roofing." Tree-ring dates indicate that after A.D. 1260/1261, destroyed parts of the village were rebuilt (Street 2001a, vol. 1: 199). The latest date for the village comes from a beam cut in the winter of A.D. 1279 (Street 2001a, vol. 1: 201).

## Description of the site

### *Site layout*

Approximately, 150 rooms and 21 kivas are contained in this alcove, as well as a large plaza in the central part of the cliff dwelling, and other spaces such as work areas (Cattanach 1980: 1, 9). Many of the structures built within the alcove conform to the natural topography and also to the structures that had been built there previously. Some parts of the alcove floor are fairly level, although in many places the floor slopes downward toward the front edge of the alcove (Cattanach 1980: 9).

Most of the structures are under the roof of the alcove, but the western and eastern ends of the site are somewhat exposed to the elements and not protected by the cliff overhang. Kiva U and associated structures are outside the alcove at the edge of the talus slope. Most midden areas are on the talus slope below the site. Numerous burials were noted within the eastern midden during archaeological excavations; others were found in rooms and kivas (Cattanach 1980: 11, 141–149).

Some structures are located on two upper ledges within the alcove (Cattanach 1980: 10–11, Fig. 1; Nordenskiöld 1990 [1893]: 27–28). On the ledge in the western part of the pueblo (West Ledge Ruin) are seven rooms built off of one long wall that parallels the rim of the ledge. A wall with loopholes extends across the entire front of the eastern ledge (East Ledge Ruin) but it is difficult to estimate the total number of structures on this ledge (Cattanach 1980: 136–138). The eastern ledge is ca. 17.5 m (53 ft.) above the plaza surface. Few structures were built on the upper level of the middle of the alcove probably at least partly because of numerous seeps that were enhanced by the inhabitants and because of poor lighting (Cattanach 1980: 74). The structures in the western part of the pueblo have a higher kiva-to-room ratio than the eastern part, but perhaps not all of these structures were in use at the same time (Cattanach 1980).

### *Access to the site*

The village could be accessed from both western and eastern ends of the alcove, and the inhabitants probably used trails from the mesa top down the cliff face. Portions of these trails are formed of hand-and-toe holds or steps carved into the rock, and other portions are on the gradual talus slope (Cattanach 1980: 6; Nordenskiöld 1990 [1893]: 24). Although Nordenskiöld states that there were more difficult parts of the trail that led to the western part of the village, which might have been the main trail to the alcove, he also claims that in general the descent from the mesa top was not very difficult. Some areas within the village, such as the ledges, were difficult to access especially the eastern ledge (Cattanach 1980: 6). Modern trails to the site, specially designed for tourists, were built in the early 1920s and were later rebuilt at least once, in 1970 (Torres-Reyes 1970). The main modern trail accesses the southwestern end of the site.

### *Availability of water*

The inhabitants of Long House enhanced the natural seeps at the back of the alcove modifying them to hold more water. They pecked and hollowed small holes and pits for catching the water that percolated through the porous stone. Although these seeps were a good source of water, they were probably not sufficient for all of the inhabitants year-round (Cattanach 1980: 1–2, 74; Nordenskiöld 1990 [1893]). Residents could have also obtained water at springs in Rock Canyon below the cliff dwelling. Today the nearest spring outside the alcove is located a few kilometers down the canyon, but it is not possible to state with certainty the conditions in the thirteenth century A.D. The clearing of trees and shrubs on the mesa top above the alcove would have allowed a greater quantity of water to percolate both through the sandstone to the back of the alcove and to the springs in the canyon.

### *Evidence of defensive architecture*

Many defensive structures, including towers, a "curtain wall," balconies, and loopholes were built during building intensification period during the latter portion of village occupation, from A.D. 1260/61 to 1279 (Street 2001a, vol. 1: 199). Street (2001a, vol. 1: 200) also suggests that a dual division of the settlement occurred about A.D. 1270–1277, although this theory requires additional study.

Numerous walls in Long House are called retaining walls. It is difficult to determine, however, if these structures served only to prevent sediment from sliding down the slope and to help stabilize buildings, or whether some might have been built to mark the boundaries of household units or serve a defensive function. Most of these walls were probably not tall; however, it is difficult to estimate the original height of many of the walls because of poor preservation. Some household units or complexes are defined by this type of wall, such as the wall west and southwest of Kiva Q (Cattanach 1980: 105) or the thick wall south of Kiva N (Cattanach 1980: 96–98). A wall that reached nearly to the roof of the alcove was noted by Nordenskiöld (1990 [1893]: 26) in front of Kiva I (Kiva 32 on Nordenskiöld's map).

Kiva U, on the talus slope immediately below the main level of Long House, was enclosed and supported by three massive walls that were probably built as retaining walls to prevent the structure from sliding downslope (Cattanach 1980: 124).

East Ledge Ruin is situated approximately 17.5 m above the plaza surface and could only be accessed by ladders that probably rested on the roof of Room 64 or perhaps on the walls of Kiva I (Cattanach 1980: 138). One wall extends nearly the entire length of the rim of this ledge. Few traces of structures can be observed behind this wall. The wall is 1.1–1.2 m (3.4–3.6 ft.) tall, 50 ft. long east-west, and 3.5 ft. long north-south, after it turns at the eastern end of the ledge. Twenty-one loopholes, at various elevations, were constructed in this wall; most are rectangular or square (Cattanach 1980: 136–139; Nordenskiöld 1990 [1893]: 28). They are roughly 10–15 cm x 10–15 cm (ca. 0.3–0.5 ft. x 0.3–0.5 ft.). Although they are angled in various directions, all command a view of some strategic location, including entrances into the alcove, the slope and canyon below the alcove, several nearby sites, and the mesa top.

Loopholes are also present in the West Ledge Ruin where seven rooms were identified (rooms 39–45). These rooms are separated into two units because of a break in the ledge. One unit consists of two rooms and the other of five rooms. The access to the ledge was by means of a ladder, and the most convenient place to rest the ladder was on the roof of Kiva C. The wall of West Ledge Ruin continues nearly the entire length of the ledge, although there are some breaks in the wall, and in most areas the wall reaches the roof of the alcove (Cattanach 1980: 15, 32–37). The loopholes were placed relatively low in the wall, approximately 0.3–0.8 m (1–2.5 ft.) above the ledge, and most view south and east across the site to the western and easternmost ends of the site.

There are at least two structures in Long House called "tower." One is Room 4, at the westernmost end of the site, at the back of the alcove (Cattanach 1980: 17–21, Fig. 1). This structure was built on a flat bedrock platform, is four stories tall, and the roof of the alcove forms the roof of the uppermost room. The tower is better preserved than other structures at the site. Entrance to this structure was probably through a roof hatchway, the doorways in the first and second stories, or through the adjacent Room 3 (Cattanach 1980: 17–20). The tower shares its southern wall with Room 3, which was probably connected with Kiva T (Cattanach 1980: 17, 123). Nordenskiöld pointed out that as many as three rooms formed this tower, consisting of rooms 3–5 (Nordenskiöld 1990 [1893]: 24–25). Room 60, the "circular tower," is in the eastern part of Long House (Cattanach 1980: 40–41) and was built on a large boulder. Its original height is difficult to estimate because this structure is poorly preserved.

Some structures, such as two kivas or a kiva and a room, were connected by an underground tunnel: tunnels link Kiva R and Room 50; probably Kiva T and Room 3; Kiva N, Kiva M, and Room 87; and Kiva Q and Room 93. Kivas R and T are the first structures encountered by anyone entering the site from the east or west, respectively. The presence of these tunnels might indicate their use as "emergency exits" to more secure rooms during an attack on the village (Cattanach 1980: 17).

Kiva T and Room 3 are at the western end of the site. Room 3 is behind Kiva T at the back of the alcove, and some evidence indicates that these two structures are linked by a tunnel (Cattanach 1980: 17, 123). Kiva R is at the eastern end of the site and is connected by a tunnel to Room 50 at the back of the alcove (Cattanach 1980: 17, 116–119, 121–123). The dimensions of the tunnel between Kiva R and Room 50 are ca. 2.1 m (7 ft.) long, 0.40–0.60 m (1.1–1.9 ft.) wide, and a maximum of about 1 m (3 ft.) tall. The walls of this tunnel are masonry and its floor it is bedrock leveled with sediment.

Tunnels connect Kiva N to both Kiva M to the west, the largest kiva on the site, and to Room 87 to the east (Cattanach 1980: 93–94, 96–98). The tunnel connecting the two kivas is 3.3 m (10 ft.) long, and the opening of the tunnel in Kiva N was sealed. The opening in Kiva M might also have been sealed, but poor preservation precludes definitive assessment. The width of this tunnel is ca. 0.45–0.65 m (1.5–2 ft.) and its height is approximately 0.70–0.90 m (2.2–2.7 ft.) (Cattanach 1980: 94). The passageway connecting Kiva N and Room 87 is 1.8 m (5.5 ft.) long. This tunnel or passageway was probably built during remodeling of the room, and a second story, and perhaps a third story, was added to increase the height of the structure (Cattanach 1980: 96–98).

Kiva Q is connected by tunnel with a small structure, Room 93, and indirectly with Room 60, the circular tower. Room 93 was probably constructed to provide access between this kiva and the tower; the tower could not be directly accessed by tunnel because it is located on a large boulder (Cattanach 1980: 104–109). A tunnel may link Kiva K and Room 81 as well as kivas O and K, although the existence of this latter link is not strongly supported by archaeological data (Cattanach 1980: 86–87, 101, 415).

## Conclusions

Long House, located on the west side of Wetherill Mesa, was the second largest cliff dwelling in what is now Mesa Verde National Park. Although there is evidence of heavy use of the alcove beginning in the Basketmaker III period, about the middle of the A.D. 600s, and again from the Pueblo I through the early Pueblo III period, occupation intensified in the thirteenth century A.D. (Cattanach 1980; Street 2001a, 2001b). The available tree-ring dates indicate two periods of increased building activity during the thirteenth century A.D. – one in the late 1240s and another that lasted from the early 1260s through the late 1270s – and the latest tree-ring date is A.D. 1279 (Street 2001a, vol. 1: 199).

Like other Pueblos of this time period in this area, the village was constructed in a cliff alcove. Access to the settlement from the mesa top led to the western and southern ends of the pueblo, and parts of these routes were formed by hand-and-toe holds. Small sites, mainly in difficult-to-access alcoves, are also considered to have been within the Long House community (Cattanach 1980: 1, 3–4).

Some buildings and architectural features within Long House might have been designed and used for defense and protection of the inhabitants. Many of these structures, including towers (such as rooms 4 and 60, at the western and eastern ends of the pueblo, respectively), walls in front of particular household units, balconies, and loopholes, were at least partly constructed during a building intensification period and the last stage of occupation of the village, from A.D. 1260/1261 to 1279 (Street 2001a, vol. 1: 199). Tunnels connect some kivas to other kivas, and some tunnels connect kivas to rooms. Both towers were probably connected to nearby kivas through intermediary rooms. There are also other tunnels within the site (Cattanach 1980: 415). Loopholes in walls on upper ledges in the alcove probably served defensive purposes, especially considering that the these openings were angled toward strategic locations: downslope below the alcove, the canyon itself, the mesa top, other sites near Long House, and locations within the pueblo such as the entrances (Cattanach 1980).

The lack of doorways in many ground-level rooms, in the upper level of Long House for example, was pointed out by Nordenskiöld as possible evidence that the inhabitants of the pueblo were afraid, or at least thought about the possibility, of hostile attacks (Nordenskiöld 1990 [1893]: 26). Nordenskiöld noted that a lot of human bones were "strewn in numbers" in different parts of the pueblo. It is possible that these remains were disturbed by early pothunters, but Nordenskiöld stated that it looked as though the inhabitants of the pueblo were defeated by enemies and the scattered remains were evidence of the attack. Though it is difficult today to determine for certain, Nordenskiöld's inference is worth considering nonetheless, because he was one of the first Euro-Americans to see the site after its discovery. Nordenskiöld's theory may be supported by new studies by Street (2001a, 2201b). If Street's interpretation (Street 2001a, vol. 1: 198–199) of the tree-ring dates is correct, then it may be concluded that most of the village was probably destroyed and some structures burned (with disarticulated human remains in at least two kivas) between A.D. 1260 and 1261. After that, it seems that the pueblo was rebuilt and some new architectural features were added, including towers, balconies, loopholes, and walls that could have defined some household units or larger parts of the settlement.

## V.1.2.b. Site 5MV1229 (Mug House)

### Location

Site type: cliff dwelling. The site (Fig. 11) is located in a shallow alcove on the western side of the Wetherill Mesa overlooking Rock Canyon; the site is situated on the east side of the canyon. The alcove is approximately 200 m (640 ft.) above the bottom of Rock Canyon (Fiero 2002; Rohn 1971). The talus slope below the site is steep and formed of rock fragments and boulders.

The alcove measures approximately 60–67 m (ca. 200 ft.) long and 12–13 m (ca. 40 ft.) deep. The mesa top is ca. 27 m (90 ft.) above the floor of the alcove, and the cliff face above the alcove roof is nearly vertical. The elevation of the site is 2195 m (7200 ft.) above sea level. The site faces mostly west, although some parts of the site face southwest, especially the northern part of the site.

Some smaller sites in the vicinity of Mug House are in locations very difficult to access (Nordenskiöld 1990 [1893]: 36). Rohn (1965: 68; 1971: 31) proposed that three or

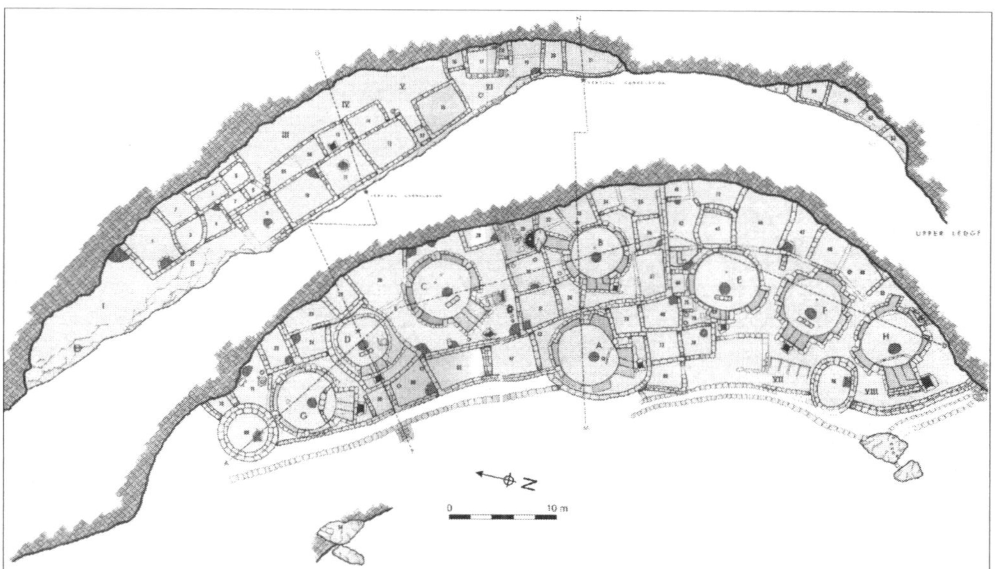


Fig. 11. Plan of the Site 5MV1229, Mug House (after Rohn 1971: 28–29, modified by A. Danecki)

four small alcove sites north of Mug House, such as Site 5MV1227 and Site 5MV1228 (Adobe Cave), should be considered part of the Mug House community, as should Mug House Reservoir (Site 5MV1586), which is ca. 180 m (600 ft.) south of Mug House. A large area of the mesa top was probably used by the residents of Mug House for crop fields (Rohn 1965: 68).

The vegetation in and around the site includes mainly pinyon-juniper woodland and some shrubs such as mountain-mahogany, bitterbrush, fendlerbush, and serviceberry (Rohn 1971: 5).

## History of investigation

This site, like many others in the present Mesa Verde National Park, was discovered by Wetherills and Charlie Mason, probably in the winter of 1889/1890. Also, the first collection of artifacts and possible non-professional excavations at the site were conducted by the Wetherill brothers. The name of the site originated from numerous vessels and three or more mugs tied together that were found at the ruin by the Wetherills (Nordenskiöld 1990 [1893]: 35; Rohn 1971: 1).

The first excavations at Mug House were conducted by Nordenskiöld in 1891. He excavated little of the site, described it only briefly, and did not prepare a map (Nordenskiöld 1990 [1893]: 35–36). He also described the condition of Mug House; rocks that had fallen from the roof of the alcove buried most of the site.

In 1928, Jesse Nusbaum, then superintendent of Mesa Verde National Park, conducted short-term excavations of some sites including Mug House, although no details of this work are available (Smith 2002). In 1934 or 1935, J.A. Lancaster directed a stabilization project at this site (Rohn 1971: 6; Torres-Reyes 1970). Mug House was also surveyed by the Gila Pueblo Survey. Beginning in the early 1930s tree-ring samples were collected from the site on several occasions (Dean 2001: 4).

Extensive excavations and stabilization were conducted at Mug House in 1960–1961 as part of a larger Wetherill Mesa Archeological Project; the entire project lasted from 1959 to 1972. Photographing and mapping of the site preceded excavations. This project also included fieldwork at a nearby reservoir, the Mug House reservoir (Site 5MV1228), and at other sites near Mug House. A report was published on these excavations (Rohn 1971).

Rohn (1971: 6) suggests that, in the early days of exploration in the Park area, there were additional undocumented, non-professional excavations and pothunting at Mug House just as in other sites in Mesa Verde, contributing to the site's destruction (Torres-Reyes 1970). Recently, Mug House and other sites in Mesa Verde National Park were included in a plaster preservation research program that was supported by The Getty Grant Program (http://www.nps.gov/meve/historyculture/partnerships.htm) and conducted by the National Park Service and the Architectural Conservation Laboratory and Research Center (ACL) of the University of Pennsylvania.

## History of the occupation of the site

The chronology of the site encompasses a long span of time, from the eighth to the thirteenth century A.D., although this span probably includes several discrete occupations rather than one continuous occupation (Rohn 1971; Street 2001a). This chronology was derived primarily from architectural style, pottery types, and dendrochronology. The earliest tree-ring dates are from the A.D. 700s; these samples were probably beams salvaged from earlier structures or were procured as deadfall, because the building where they were collected actually dates from about the middle of the thirteenth century A.D. (Rohn 1971).

Several tree-ring dates from the eleventh century A.D. indicate that the alcove was occupied sometime during that century. Probably about the middle of the eleventh century A.D. at least one small house unit and a kiva were constructed in the alcove; this residential component was similar to others located on mesa tops at that time (Rohn 1971: 19). Street (2001a, vol. 1: 74) even suggests that the eleventh century A.D. component of Mug House is a bit overlooked compared to the thirteenth century A.D. phase of the occupation, a situation that is, in his opinion, similar to that of Long House.

However, it is clear that most of the human activity and construction occurred in the thirteenth century A.D. with the earliest tree-ring date from that century being A.D. 1204, and subsequent dates cluster from the A.D. 1220s and 1230s to the 1270s (Rohn 1971; Dean 2001: 6). The latest date for the site is probable A.D. 1276 (or A.D. 1277), and is associated with the rebuilding or repair of Room 9 on the upper ledge (Dean 2001: 11; Rohn 1971).

During the first half of the thirteenth century A.D. there was a relatively low level of building activity; construction increased significantly and peaked between A.D. 1250 and 1276; most of the construction of Mug House occurred between A.D. 1250 and 1266 (Dean 2001: 6). The final buildings to be constructed were generally at the back of the shelter, at its mouth and ends, and probably on the upper ledge. Kiva E and some buildings adjacent to it, at the southern part of the village and midway between the rear of the alcove and its front edge, were probably the last structures built, as indicated by tree-ring dates; that part of the site is on the southern side of the dual division proposed by Rohn (Dean 2001: 11; Rohn 1971: 31, 39–40, and see below). The description of the site presented below refers only to the thirteenth century A.D. occupation of Mug House.

## Description of the site

### *Site layout*

According to Rohn (1971: 43), at least 94 structures were built within the alcove, and among them were at least eight kivas and two or three towers. Structures were built on two main levels. Most structures appear to rest on the lower or ground level of the shelter. Many buildings were more than one story tall, and some were probably as tall as three stories. The upper ledge or level in the northern part of the site houses many rooms and rises approximately 4.5–5.0 m (ca. 15 ft.) above the lower floor of the alcove (Fiero 2002; Rohn 1971). Four rooms, probably used for storage, were built on a smaller ledge in the southern part of the alcove (Fiero 2002).

Rohn suggested that some groups or clusters of buildings (suites) that might represent household living quarters had their own courtyards, while others shared a courtyard with other households or units (Rohn 1965: 65–68; 1971: 31). Rohn also observed evidence of a "dual division" running east-west that divided the village into two parts. This division is reflected in differential construction of kivas in these two parts and also in the location and construction of rooms in the central part of the site – rooms 35, 36, and 37 (Rohn 1971: 28–29, 40). The division is also apparent in the access between the two areas: it appears that the only route between the two sections was around the west side of Room 80 along the outermost terrace at the edge of the village (Rohn 1971: 31, 39–40). In consequence, the northern part was somewhat isolated from the southern one. The southern part was smaller and tree-ring dates suggest that many of the buildings there were built during the final stage of occupation of the settlement; however, the unequal number of samples from different parts of the site might be leading to an erroneous conclusion (Dean 2001, Rohn 1971).

The village midden was below the alcove on the steep talus slope; during archaeological excavations many burials were recorded there.

### *Access to the site*

The Mug House alcove was relatively difficult to access. Two main routes led from the top of the mesa to the village and probably other routes led down the canyon. One route accessed the village from south, and the other approached the alcove from the north. Smaller sites and a water basin are situated along these routes (Rohn 1971: 4, 86). The southern route consists partly of hand-and-toe holds cut into a sandstone boulder.

The northern and southern upper ledges of Mug House could have been reached by ladders that rested on the roofs of buildings or on the floor of the alcove. Evidence of at least one ladder location was observable – ladder grooves were noted between Rooms 12 and 15 (Rohn 1971: 62).

As mentioned above, communication between the northern and southern parts of the village was not easy because of the probable division of the settlement and the tall room walls along the division line. During at least one phase of village occupation in the thirteenth century A.D., it is likely that only one route allowed access between the two parts of the settlement (Rohn 1965: 66; 1971: 31, 39–40). The access route in the western part of the pueblo was near the edge of the alcove, which restricted connections between the two parts and probably caused difficulty in communication and that was compounded by particular difficulties in communication between different room suites or households, as suggested by Rohn (1965: 66).

### *Availability of water*

No water source such as a seep spring existed in the alcove itself (Nordenskiöld 1990 [1893]; Rohn 1971). Nordenskiöld (1990 [1893]: 22–23) claimed that, during his excavations in Mug House, he brought water from a distance of one kilometer. However, the residents of Mug House had constructed a rectangular masonry reservoir (Site 5MV1586) as well as other water-control devices near Mug House (Rohn 1971; Wright 2006).

The reservoir, located below and approximately 200 m (ca. 640 ft.) south of the alcove, probably utilized a natural depression that was augmented by enclosing the depression with a stone wall. The reservoir measures 7 m long, by 3 m width by 1 m deep (Fiero 2002; Rohn 1971). Most of the water that collected in the reservoir originated from a basin on the mesa top above where ancient Puebloans probably collected runoff. To control erosion on the mesa top near this basin and to avoid silting, they built four check-dams. The water from the mesa-top basin could have flowed down to the rectangular reservoir through two channels notched into the bedrock canyon rim that merged near the cliff face so that the water could fall directly into the reservoir (Hanel 2007; Wright et al. 2008). Rohn (1971: 65) estimated that the reservoir could hold 23,000–27,000 liters of water.

This water-control system might have been built between 1200 and 1240 A.D. (Wright et al. 2008). During his research on this reservoir, Kenneth Wright from Wright Paleohydrological Institute conducted an experiment that consisted of an attempt to flow water from the mesa top through the channel near the cliff face and then down the cliff into the rectangular reservoir (Hanel 2007). The results demonstrated that this was an effective method of filling the reservoir especially after rainfall. Wright and his team concluded, on the basis of the annual precipitation on the Mesa Verde escarpment and dendrochronological records, that their "hydrologic analyses of average annual rainfall runoff showed that: 27 times, on average, there would be 200 gallons of water flowing to the cliff-side notch; seven times, there would be 500 gallons; four times, there would be 900 gallons; and twice, there would be a yield of 1,200 gallons" (Wright et al. 2008).

Wright claims that this water-management system, although quite simple, was very effective for the inhabitants of Mug House:

> the Ancestral Puebloans were good engineers and diligent at water harvesting. They practiced successful erosion control measures to protect their water supply cistern from excessive siltation. Their water supply system, while simple in design and construction, was effective in providing domestic water in an arid environment (Wright et al. 2008).

### *Evidence of defensive architecture*

The Mug House alcove contains evidence of several retaining walls built at different times during the thirteenth century A.D., although it is not clear whether they were designed for defense or to prevent erosion in the alcove. Rohn (1971: 64) suggests that they were used primarily to level the surface and to "prevent loose fill beneath the front rooms from bleeding slowly downslope." This might have been the main purpose of two long walls that were built during the final stage of village occupation in the western or outer part of the settlement near the edge of the alcove just above the steep talus slope. An even stronger argument could be made for walls built around kivas C and D, beneath rooms 60 and 66.

However, it is significant that the outermost room walls facing west across nearly the entire pueblo formed a line that could have impeded access to the interior of the village. The situation is the same for the northern and southern upper ledges. Also, most of the structures in the outer part of the pueblo near the edge of the alcove are rooms, whereas most of the kivas were constructed at the rear of the alcove or between the edge and back of the alcove.

A minimum of two masonry towers were built in Mug House; they are toward the front of the overhang at the extreme ends of the alcove at the village-access locations (Rohn 1971). Room 60 is a circular tower at the north end of the site, and Room 76, which is rather oval, is situated at the south end (Rohn 1971: 86). The northern tower is about 2.5 m (8.5 ft.) in diameter, and the southern tower measures 2.1 by 2.7 m (7 by 9 ft.). It is difficult to estimate the original height of these towers, because their walls are poorly preserved; however, there is evidence that the northern tower was at least two stories tall (Rohn 1971: 86).

Both towers have double-coursed masonry walls ca. 40–60 cm (1.3–1.9 ft.) thick. The structures are near the village-access points and are situated such that a maximum of only 80–90 cm (ca. 3 ft.) of space lies between each of the towers and the outer retaining wall and the steep slope below (Rohn 1971: 86). The doorways of the towers faced the interior of the village; the doorway of the northern tower opens onto the roof of Kiva G. The southern tower is included in the line of the inner retaining/protecting wall. The northern tower is at the northern end of the site where the inner retaining wall ends.

According to archaeologists working at Mug House, only three loopholes have been preserved (Rohn 1971: 54), but an unknown number of additional loopholes could have been present in masonry that has collapsed. There are no openings such as loopholes in the walls of the two extant towers; however, these structures, especially the southern one, are preserved to a relatively low height (Rohn 1971: 86).

Although no balconies have survived at Mug House, several were probably present originally. For example, the second- and third-story rooms in structures 36/2, 37/2, 22/2, 24/2, 69, 30/2, and 74/2 would have been much more easily accessible if balconies had existed there (Rohn 1971: 57). Probable ladder grooves are visible at the edge of the sandstone ledge between rooms 12 and 15 and also above Room 29, which would have provided access to the upper ledges in the alcove (Rohn 1971: 62). Ladders also permitted access to the upper portions of particular buildings and could be easily pulled up for security. About 15 wooden "hand loops" had been set into the exterior walls of rooms 10, 11, 12, and 15. Rohn (1971: 62–63) suggests that these features were designed to help residents enter the upper ledge, although this required traversing a narrow passage ca. 30 cm (1 ft.) wide that might have been quite hazardous. Other hand loops at the site (Rohn 1971: 56–57) were set into walls in rooms 33 and 45/2.

## Conclusions

This alcove was inhabited during different time periods beginning in the A.D. 700s, although the most intense occupation and the construction of the reservoir below the alcove occurred in the thirteenth century A.D.; the final abandonment of the village may have occurred in the early A.D. 1280s (Dean 2001; Rohn 1971). Data gathered during excavations associated with the Wetherill Mesa Archaeological Project suggest that not all of the structures in Mug House were occupied at the same time in the thirteenth century A.D. However, it is probable that a fairly large population resided in this village until the final years of occupation (Rohn 1971). Many tools and utensils were left on the floors of the buildings, probably because the inhabitants could not take these belongings, or perhaps the residents planned to return (Rohn 1971).

Archaeological data from the Wetherill Mesa project reveal no evidence of violence that might have stimulated abandonment of the village. However, the location of the settlement in an alcove that was difficult to access, the types of architecture, and the layout of the village reflects a concern for defense and protection by Puebloans living there in the thirteenth century A.D. Some structures were located on difficult-to-access ledges in the northern and southern parts of the alcove. The two extant towers in Mug House were ideally situated for defense at the northern and southern ends of the alcove at the only reasonable entry points (Rohn 1971: 86). And although Rohn suggests that the towers served ritual or ceremonial functions, these structures might have been built for protection (especially because of their location in strategic places close to entry points to the pueblo); however, it is possible that ceremonial use of some structures was associated with defense, such as at Balcony House.

Many researchers interpret the walls in the outer part of the pueblo as retaining walls that prevented slippage and erosion of the sediment, but some inner walls also might have been built to enclose or stabilize the areas behind them. I would also postulate a defensive function for these walls. The long south wall, as the outermost wall, could have served to level the floor of the alcove and minimize sediment loss, or even to prevent people from falling down the talus slope. The inner walls on both the lower and upper levels might also have served defensive functions, as suggested by the layout of the rooms in one row facing the outer or western part of the pueblo.

## V.1.3. McElmo-Monument

### V.1.3.a. Site 5MT5006 (Yucca House)

#### Location

Site type: Village built on flat/open area around the spring. The site (Fig. 12) is located at the transition between the bottom of Montezuma Valley and the slopes of Ute Mountain; to the east is Mesa Verde proper, and to the north is McElmo Creek (Glowacki 2001: 2, 4). The elevation of the site ranges between 1760 and 1804 m (5775–5920 ft.). The eastern part of the site, Lower House, is situated at a lower elevation than the western part, which is the West Complex that includes Upper House.

There are several sites in the vicinity of Yucca House that may be considered as part of Yucca House community. This includes, for example, Ismay, Watson and Grinnell sites (Luebben 1982, 1983; Luebben and Nickens 1982).

The vegetation on and near the site includes sagebrush, four-winged saltbush, cacti such as claret cup cactus, and grasses. Because two springs are present on the site, many plants grow there; however, no yucca grows on the site today.

#### History of investigation

William Henry Jackson wrote the first description of the site, and a detailed map was prepared by William Henry Holmes during the Hayden Survey in 1874 and 1878 (Glowacki 2001: 6–7; http://www.nps.gov/yuho). Holmes named the site "Aztec Springs," because at the time the populace believed that ruins in the Southwest such as Yucca House might have been built by ancient Aztecs from Mexico. In 1919, a description and a map of the site were published by Jesse W. Fewkes in *Prehistoric Villages, Castles and Towers of Southwestern Colorado* as a result of his study of the site in 1918 (http://www.nps.gov/yuho). The site became Yucca House National Monument in 1919,

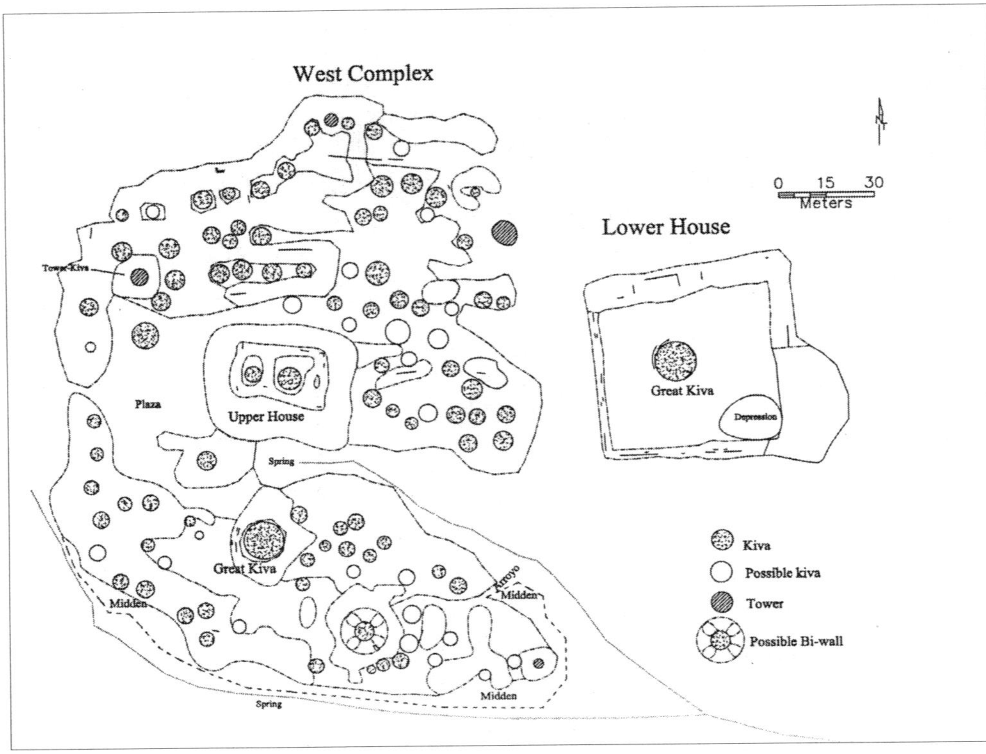


Fig. 12. Plan of the Site 5MT5006, Yucca House (after Glowacki 2001: 3, Fig. 2 modified by A. Danecki)

but at that time the monument did not encompass the entire site, only 9.6 acres. Most of the land for the monument was deeded by landowner Henry Van Kleeck. In 1990, Hallie Ismay, who owned the land surrounding the site, donated 24.27 acres of the site to the park (http://www.nps.gov/yuho).

In 1953, archaeologist Philip Van Cleave submitted charcoal samples from Yucca House and other sites in Mesa Verde National Park to the Laboratory of Tree-Ring Research in Tucson for dating (Glowacki 2001: 9). In the 1950s, unofficial excavations were conducted in the southern part of the Upper House, and Van Cleave probably visited the site during this time (Glowacki 2001: 41). In 1964, the northwest corner of Lower House was exposed and stabilized by a crew supervised by Al Lancaster. In the same year the West Complex was tested archaeologically by a team supervised by Al Schroeder (Glowacki 2001: 9–13).

In 2000, Donna Glowacki supervised the Yucca House Mapping Project, a joint research effort by Mesa Verde National Park and the Crow Canyon Archaeological Center, Cortez, Colorado (Glowacki 2001). The site was surveyed and mapped, and two remote sensing techniques, electrical resistivity and magnetic field gradient surveys, were used in an attempt to detect subsurface features at the site. Plans for managing the site are partly described in the First Annual Centennial Strategy for Yucca House National Monument (Wiese 2007).

## History of the occupation of the site

The chronology of particular parts of the pueblo is problematic. However, a post-1250s occupation of the West Complex is suggested by the predominance of McElmo and Mesa Verde Black-on-White pottery sherds and a high percentage of bowl sherds spotting exterior designs. Architectural styles are characteristic of the same period, and tree-ring dates from the thirteenth century A.D. indicate that the settlement was inhabited during most of that century (Glowacki 2001: 38, 42), probably until the final depopulation of the region about A.D. 1270/1280s. As indicated by the architecture and the building materials used, Lower House and Upper House in the West Complex might have been the earliest structures built in the village (Glowacki 2001: 39, 41–44). Construction of Upper House might have begun during the Chaco heyday (A.D. 1050–1150), although tree-ring dates indicate that the latest building activity occurred in this structure during or after A.D. 1263 (Glowacki 2001: 38).

## Description of the site

### *Site layout*

The site is divided by archaeologists into two parts: West Complex and Lower House (Glowacki 2001: Fig. 9–11). West Complex is much larger than Lower House, which consists mostly of a large square plaza containing a Great Kiva that measures 12 m (39 ft.) in diameter. The plaza is enclosed by rubble that indicates the probable existence of rooms or other structures along at least its northern and northeastern sides. The interior dimensions of the plaza are 53 m (174 ft.) by 47 m (154 ft.) (Glowacki 2001: 20). The characteristics of the visible rubble suggest that the rooms could have been two stories tall. In the southeastern corner of the plaza is a depression that might have been a small reservoir. This plaza, enclosed by roomblocks and walls, is unusual in the central Mesa Verde region; the most similar constructions can be found in the Kayenta region of northern Arizona (Glowacki 2001: 44).

The West Complex is built around a spring whose drainage bisects the site. This complex contains approximately 450–600 rooms, about 104 kivas, an additional Great Kiva, at least two towers, one tower-kiva, a possible bi-wall structure, at least one plaza, and an architectural block called Upper House, which is a massive rectangular structure with two enclosed kivas. Upper House probably dominated the pueblo, for it was a minimum of two stories tall and was situated just north of the spring.

Surprisingly, test excavations in 1964 in the West Complex revealed that a portion of the Upper House, which dates from the Pueblo III period, was built of adobe bricks, which were rarely used for construction during that time (Glowacki 2001: 9–13, 41). The dominant building material was stone, including sandstone, Juana Lopez limestone, and diorite. Sandstone dominated in the construction of Lower House, the great kiva, and the enclosing walls (Glowacki 2001: 39).

### Access to the site

The present entrance is at the eastern edge of the site. Ancient entry locations into the pueblo are difficult to define without archaeological excavation; however, indications on the modern ground surface suggest that access to the village was restricted to a few openings. Most of the outer walls of roomblocks and segments of what were probably enclosing walls or walls in the West Complex might have formed a solid barrier against entry into the pueblo. One gap only is visible in the walls on the western side of the complex; this opening provided entry to the plaza west of Upper House.

### Availability of water

Yucca House boasts two springs, and the abundant moisture fosters the growth of vegetation on the site. One spring is in a large depression in the middle of the site that holds water even in the driest years (Glowacki 2001: 22). Water from this spring flows through the central portion of the site. The second spring flanks the southern edge of the site. The two drainages converge southeast of the site (Glowacki 2001: 5, Fig. 9). The depression in the southeastern corner of the plaza in Lower House might have been small reservoir built to hold groundwater (Glowacki 2001: 20). The presence of these water sources was probably one reason that Ancestral Puebloans chose this location for a village.

### Evidence of defensive architecture

The plaza in Lower House was enclosed by roomblocks on the northern and eastern sides and by an enclosing wall along the southern and western sides (Glowacki 2001: 20). The records of Lancaster and Schroeder during his stabilization of part of the site in 1964 suggest that the roomblock walls were massive (Glowacki 2001). The height of the enclosing-wall rubble is only about 0.22 m. An earthen mound may reflect the presence of a retaining or enclosing wall at the southeastern edge of the plaza (Glowacki 2001: 20, 40).

In the West Complex, enclosing walls may be present both north and south of the spring. Evidence of a massive enclosing or retaining wall is visible in the northern part of this complex (Glowacki 2001: 22). The exact extent and scale of such constructions are difficult to determine on the basis of survey maps, further study is therefore needed. In some areas of the West Complex, sections of free-standing walls connect one building to the next, forming massive, continuous barriers.

A minimum of three circular towers were constructed in this village. One is in the extreme southeastern corner of the site, between the two springs, and another is in the extreme northern part of the site. The third tower, called a tower-kiva on a map created in 2000 (Glowacki 2001), is in the northwestern part of the site, and is about 4.5 m (15 ft.) in diameter. Additional towers may be present at the site; not all of the remaining circular structures are known to be kivas (Glowacki 2001: 22).

Evidence of several tunnels connecting kivas to rooms and towers has been documented at the Ismay and Watson sites (Luebben 1982), which might have been part of a Yucca House community. At the nearby Grinnell Site, the disarticulated and fragmented remains of at least seven people were discovered in one of the kivas (Luebben 1983; Luebben and Nickens 1982).

### Conclusions

Yucca House was one of the largest villages in the central Mesa Verde region in the thirteenth century A.D., although part of the settlement might have been constructed as early as the twelfth century A.D. (Glowacki 2001). The presence of multiple springs and a high water table probably were important reasons to construct a pueblo there. It is worth mentioning that Yucca House is located near "the southern edge of the central Mesa Verde region, at the gateway of a primary conduit – Montezuma Valley – into the heart of the Mesa Verde region" (Glowacki 2001: 41). That location was probably very important for the inhabitants of the village and might have determined its function.

Portions, if not most, of the settlement had massive, continuous outer walls formed by enclosing or retaining structures and by the exterior walls of particular roomblocks (Glowacki 2001: 22). This configuration is clearly visible in the West Complex both north and south of the drainage that bisects the site and might have served defensive purposes.

The locations of at least three towers at the southeastern, northern, and northwestern edges of the site suggest that these buildings were used for lookout or defense. The tower called a tower-kiva is in the northwestern part of the West Complex. Part of the pueblo might have been burned; many building stones in the southern part of the West Complex are fire-reddened and blackened (Glowacki 2001: 41).

## V.1.3.b. Site 5MT765 (Sand Canyon Pueblo)

### Location

Site type: canyon-rim settlement. Sand Canyon Pueblo (Figs 13, 14) is situated at the head of a small tributary canyon that drains southward into upper Sand Canyon. The site is approximately 19 km (12 mi) west-northwest of the town of Cortez, Colorado. The total area of the site is approximately 2.2 ha (5.4 acres). The elevation of the site is 2073 m (6800 ft.). Most of the structures in the site face south (Kuckelman et al. 2002: 389; CCAC 2004).

Southwest of Sand Canyon Pueblo is Site 5MT10246 (Lester's Site). This nearby site was probably part of Sand Canyon Pueblo. An isolated kiva, Kiva 1601, is approximately 38 m north of the site (CCAC 2004). Sites 5MT16844 and 5MT16845 are southeast of the pueblo; the latter site contains a reservoir. Sand Canyon Pueblo was probably the center of a larger community of settlements clustered near the upper part of Sand Canyon and in nearby smaller canyons, spurs of Sand Canyon. Some of these small habitations were in open areas, and others were in cliff alcoves.

The vegetation on and near the site includes mainly pinyon-juniper woodland, sagebrush, and a variety of shrubs. The site is today covered primarily by pinyon-juniper woodland.

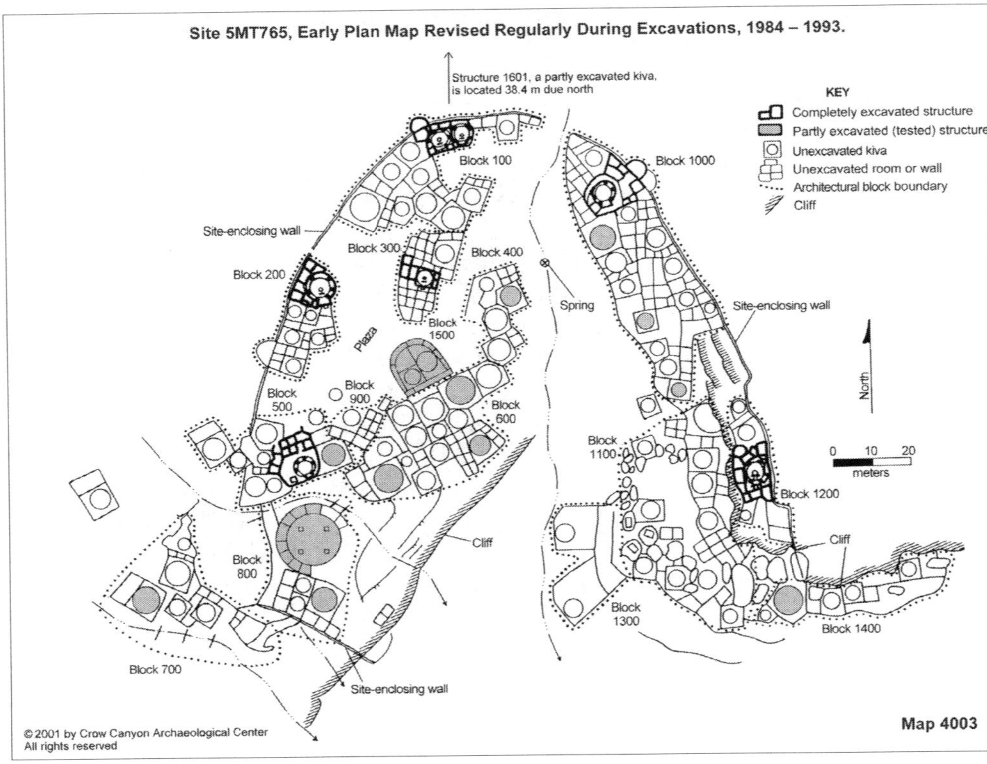


Fig. 13. Plan of the Site 5MT765, Sand Canyon Pueblo. Courtesy of Crow Canyon Archaeological Center

## History of investigation

The first published description of Sand Canyon Pueblo was prepared in the early twentieth century and was published by T. Mitchell Prudden (1903). The site was later visited and described by Jesse W. Fewkes who named the site Johnson Ruin after a homesteader who lived nearby (Fewkes 1919: 18). Beginning in 1967 the site was surveyed several times, and stabilization of the site took place in 1975 and 1978 (Crow Canyon Archaeological Center 2004; Lipe and Kuckelman 2007). In 1983, a new map of the site, a research plan, and a proposal for a multiphase program of testing, excavation, and survey at Sand Canyon Pueblo and in the surrounding area was prepared. In 1985, with the aid of aerial photographs, a contour map of the site was prepared (Bradley 1992: 80).

Excavation was conducted at the site by CCAC from 1984 through 1989 and from 1991 through 1993 (Bradley 1992; Lipe and Kuckelman 2007; Ortman and Bradley 2002: 42–43) as a part of the Sand Canyon Archaeological Project. About five percent of the site was excavated during the project. The first six seasons of fieldwork focused on rooms and kivas, as well as on public architecture such as the great kiva and the D-shaped building, or Block 1500 (Bradley 1992; Kuckelman, ed. by 2007). From 1991 through 1993 the project focused more intensively on public architecture (Lipe and Kuckelman 2007).

## History of the occupation of the site

The chronology of this village was determined from pottery types, architectural analysis, and on tree-ring dates from samples collected during the excavations conducted by Crow Canyon Archaeological Center in 1980s and 1990s (e.g., Lipe, ed. by 1992; Kuckelman, ed. by 2007). Tree-ring cutting dates for Sand Canyon Pueblo indicate construction between the late 1240s or early 1250s A.D. and the late 1270s or 1280 A.D., which was probably the span of occupation of the settlement (Kuckelman et al. 2007; Ortman and Bradley 2002: Table 3.2; CCAC 2004).

Probably the first structures built in the village were two circular towers, towers 212 and 1203, the D-shaped building, a village-enclosing wall, and Great Kiva 800 (Bradley 1996: 245; Kuckelman et al. 2007). The two towers were probably built before the buildings adjacent to them. The village-enclosing wall was built in at least two construction episodes, and it is probable that, late in the occupation of the village, the dimensions of the gateways in the wall were reduced, and towers were built against the exterior face of the wall.

The latest tree-ring date from Sand Canyon Pueblo is A.D. 1277vv, a non-cutting date (Kuckelman et al. 2007) from a sample collected at the northeast edge of Block 700. It is probable that the village was depopulated soon after this date. Kuckelman (2008: 117) suggests that one-fourth to three-fourths of the population of the pueblo migrated before the final depopulation of the village.

## Description of the site

### *Site layout*

Sand Canyon Pueblo is situated on and around the head of a tributary of Sand Canyon and around a spring; the canyon in which the spring is located bisects the site. The site comprises at least 420 rooms, 90 to 100 kivas, and 14 towers, as well as public architecture such as a great kiva, an enclosed plaza, and a D-shaped bi-wall structure (Bradley 1993; Kuckelman, ed. by 2007; Ortman and Bradley 2002). Structures are located on the canyon rim, below the rim, on the talus slope, and on boulders. The site is enclosed on the north, west, southwest, and east by a masonry wall.

The division of the village, by the canyon, into two sides has led some archaeologists to suggest that the site was intentionally built in that manner and the division was an integral part of the layout of the settlement (Kuckelman, ed. by 2007).

The example of public architecture in Sand Canyon, great kiva (Great Kiva 800), was probably one of the earliest structures built in the village and contained architectural features not found in residential kivas in the area, such as a low masonry bench, floor-based masonry pillars, and a large masonry-lined floor vault. The great kiva at Sand Canyon Pueblo was probably not roofed (Kuckelman et al. 2007).

Another type of public architecture at this site is the D-shaped structure, Block 1500, a bi-wall construction made up of multiple, contiguous arc-shaped surface rooms forming a capital "D" and two kivas within this "D" (Ortman and Bradley 2002: 55–62). This block was centrally located within the village and was not far west of the spring. The block rose at least 3.5–4.0 m in height and was probably at least two stories tall

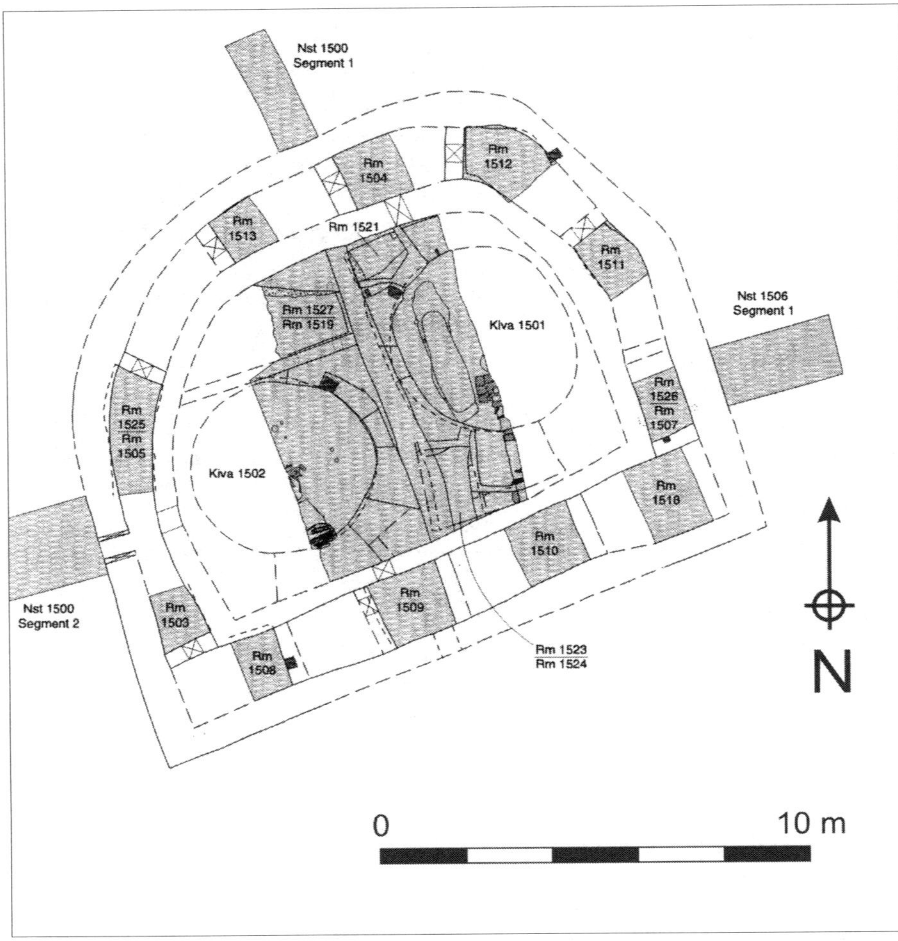


Fig. 14. Block 1500 in Sand Canyon Pueblo, D-shaped structure similar to Structure 700 at Goodman Point Pueblo (after Ortman and Bradley 2002: 56 modified by A. Danecki)

(Kuckelman et al. 2007). The architecture of this structure and the artifacts found there during excavations suggest that this building served a special function, perhaps also ceremonial (Bradley 1996: 246).

## *Access to the site*

Access to the village was, at least to some extent, protected from the north, east, and west by the village-enclosing wall. Although it is difficult to estimate the exact number of gates or doorways in the wall, several lines of evidence suggest that these were few in number (Kuckelman et al. 2007). One such opening, in the western part of the wall, is Feature 1 in Nonstructure 201. As concluded after the excavations, "the gap was reduced substantially by the addition of masonry to both sides of the opening, after 40 cm of sediment had been deposited naturally at its base. It is also likely that the width of a large gap that might have originally been present in the wall in the vicinity of the main drainage was reduced significantly midway through the occupation of the village" (Kuckelman et al. 2007). Tower 212, situated near this gap or gateway, might have served to protect this possible entrance.

### *Availability of water*

The unnamed spring in the center of the pueblo was probably a permanent water source for the inhabitants of the pueblo and was presumably the main source of domestic water for the villagers (Kuckelman et al. 2007). It is probable that other seep springs were also present in the vicinity of Sand Canyon Pueblo. A gap in the north section of the village-enclosing wall today is likely to have also been present during the occupation of the village, and it was probably designed to accommodate the flow of water down the drainage (Kuckelman et al. 2007). If there was no gap in this portion of the wall, runoff moving down the drainage would have accumulated behind the wall, forming a reservoir.

A dam and reservoir were constructed at Site 5MT16845, just southeast of Sand Canyon Pueblo.

### *Evidence of defensive architecture*

The village was enclosed on the north, east, west, and southwest by a massive, arc-shaped masonry wall. The presence of this wall, which defined nearly the entire boundary of the pueblo, along with the limited number of entryways in the wall, suggests that the wall could have served as protection against intruders (Kenzle 1993, 1997; Kuckelman et al. 2007). The enclosing wall defined the boundary of the settlement, and only a few structures were built outside the wall. The wall also enclosed the spring near the center of the village. The exposed height of particular sections of the wall, as recorded during excavations, ranged from 0.9 m to 2.4 m and the recorded width from 0.50 to 0.75 m (Kuckelman et al. 2007).

Many buildings were built against the inside face of the enclosing wall; however, only a few structures – D-shaped towers – were abutted to the outside face. Most sections of this wall were built with larger and more-irregular stones than those used in other walls in the pueblo, which may indicate that sections of the enclosing wall were constructed very quickly or "at least without formalized style" (Bradley 1992: 95, 97; Kuckelman et al. 2007). One labor estimate indicates that the wall might have been built by about 30 people during a period of two months (Bradley 1992: 93–96).

Although the entire village-enclosing wall was probably not built in one episode, data suggest that the wall was built in large sections (Bradley 1992: 95; Kuckelman et al. 2007). Some part of the wall might have been added, or the wall was partly remodeled, late in the occupation of the village; for example, the section of "site-enclosing wall in the eastern half of Block 100 appears to have been added in a separate construction event, possibly about A.D. 1271, and might have been designed to further restrict access by outsiders down the drainage to the spring" (Kuckelman et al. 2007).

At least 14 towers were constructed in different areas of Sand Canyon Pueblo. Some, such as Tower 212 (later remodeled into a kiva) and Tower 1203, were circular in plan; others, such as towers 101 and 1019/1008, were D-shaped and abutted the outside face of the village-enclosing wall in the northern part of the pueblo (Kuckelman et al. 2007; CCAC 2004). Access to at least some towers was restricted and controlled by the inhabitants of the pueblo. The ground-level story of two excavated towers could have been entered only from inside the village through an opening in the village-enclosing wall. There was a possibility of entry into the upper levels of the towers such as in Tower 1019/1008 (Kuckelman et al. 2007).

Because of the poor preservation of the enclosing wall and the limited nature of the excavations, it is difficult to determine the number of loopholes that might have once been present. However, three loopholes were recorded during excavations (Kuckelman et al. 2007). They are clustered in the section of village-enclosing wall in Block 1000 and were constructed when the enclosing wall was built. They are oriented at different angles and their main purpose was probably "to enable someone from inside the site-enclosing wall to view slightly different areas of the landscape outside the wall before the tower (Tower 1019/1008) was built" (Kuckelman et al. 2007). Later, the tower was built and the probable function of the loopholes in providing views of surrounding landscape was probably transferred to the tower, from which the view of the landscape might have been much improved.

## Conclusions

Sand Canyon Pueblo was one of the largest villages (community centers) in the central Mesa Verde region during the thirteenth century A.D., and it was probably a regional, political, religious, and economic center for a community of smaller habitations in the Upper Sand Canyon area; however, most of the population of this community probably lived in Sand Canyon Pueblo itself (Bradley 1992: 97; Ortman and Bradley 2002). The pueblo was inhabited by about 400 to 600 people.

The general plan of the site resembles the letter "D," and the presence of a D-shaped structure within the site that is similar to those at other sites in the Mesa Verde area has led some archaeologists to compare it with other sites in the region. Sand Canyon Pueblo was divided by the canyon that contained the community spring. The majority of the structures east of the drainage are standard or domestic rooms and kivas, and most of the public architecture, including the D-shaped structure, the great kiva, and the plaza, are located west of the drainage (Bradley 1992: 96–97; 1996: 245). This layout has led some archaeologists to conclude that the arrangement of structures in the village was preplanned and organized (e.g., Ortman and Bradley 2002) to include areas for domestic, ritual, and community activities as indicated by the layout of the village-enclosing wall and its spatial relation to cliffs and ledges as well as to the layout of particular roomblocks and public architecture.

As inferred on the basis of dendrochronology, the village was founded in the late A.D. 1240s or the early 1250s, and the latest tree-ring date from the site is a noncutting date of A.D. 1277 (Kuckelman, ed. by 2007; Ortman and Bradley 2002). The latest tree-ring dates correspond well with late tree-ring dates from other sites in the central Mesa Verde region. Sand Canyon Pueblo was depopulated in at least two stages; one-fourth to three-fourths of the inhabitants of the pueblo probably migrated sometime before the final depopulation of the settlement (Kuckelman 2008: 117). If occupation of the pueblo ended as the result of an enemy attack (Kuckelman, ed. by 2007), the reduced population of the settlement might have seriously hampered the defense of the village.

That the residents were concerned about danger is evidenced by the location of the pueblo on the canyon rim, the incorporation of the spring into the central part of the village, and the presence of a massive wall that encompassed most of the settlement (Bradley 1992: 95; Kenzle 1993, 1997). The need for defense may be also seen in the presence of circular and D-shaped towers. Some are outside the village-enclosing wall and are abutted to it. These towers might have been built for defense or at least to provide a good view of the surrounding areas, and some were built such that, on the ground level, they could be entered only from inside the enclosing wall. Loopholes were constructed in the village-enclosing wall as well (Kenzle 1993).

The remains of nine individuals were found in Blocks 100, 800, and 1000 during the Sand Canyon Archaeological Project excavations, and the archaeological context indicates that these individuals died as a result of violence that probably occurred during one event at the end of the occupation of the village (Bradley 1992: 84; Kuckelman 2010; Kuckelman et al. 2002: 492). A similar attack ended the occupation of Castle Rock Pueblo, a contemporaneous community center approximately 7.4 km southwest of Sand Canyon Pueblo (e.g., Kuckelman et al. 2002).

## V.1.3.c. Site 5MT604 (Goodman Point Pueblo)

### Location

Site type: canyon-rim settlement. Goodman Point Pueblo (Fig. 15) is situated approximately 16 km (10 mi) west-northwest of Cortez, Montezuma County, southwestern Colorado (Connolly 1992; Kuckelman et al. 2004). The elevation of the site is 1920 m (ca. 6300 ft.) above sea level.

Goodman Point Pueblo is within the Goodman Point Ruins Group Unit, a 58-hectare (142 acres) area that is part of the legally protected Hovenweep National Monument. This monument is a complex of ancient Pueblo sites situated on the Colorado-Utah border. A total of 39 additional ancestral Pueblo sites – including an isolated great kiva (Harlan Great Kiva) located 500 m west-southwest of Goodman Point Pueblo – and two historic sites were also recorded within the 58-hectare Goodman Point Unit (Kuckelman et al. 2004; Coffey 2009; Coffey and Kuckelman 2006). The ancient sites include small farmsteads and vestiges of ancient roads and farmlands, and it is possible that "Goodman Point Pueblo served as the center of what was perhaps the most populous community in the Mesa Verde region between A.D. 1260 and 1275" (Kuckelman et al. 2009).

A few historic sites, mostly small refuse deposits and two-track roads from early Euro-American settlers in the nineteenth and twentieth centuries, are also within the Unit (Connolly 1992).

The major flora typical of the area includes juniper, pinyon (with edible nuts), sagebrush, and rabbitbrush; this vegetation grows on the slopes within the canyon as well as on the canyon rim and the rolling uplands away from the rim.

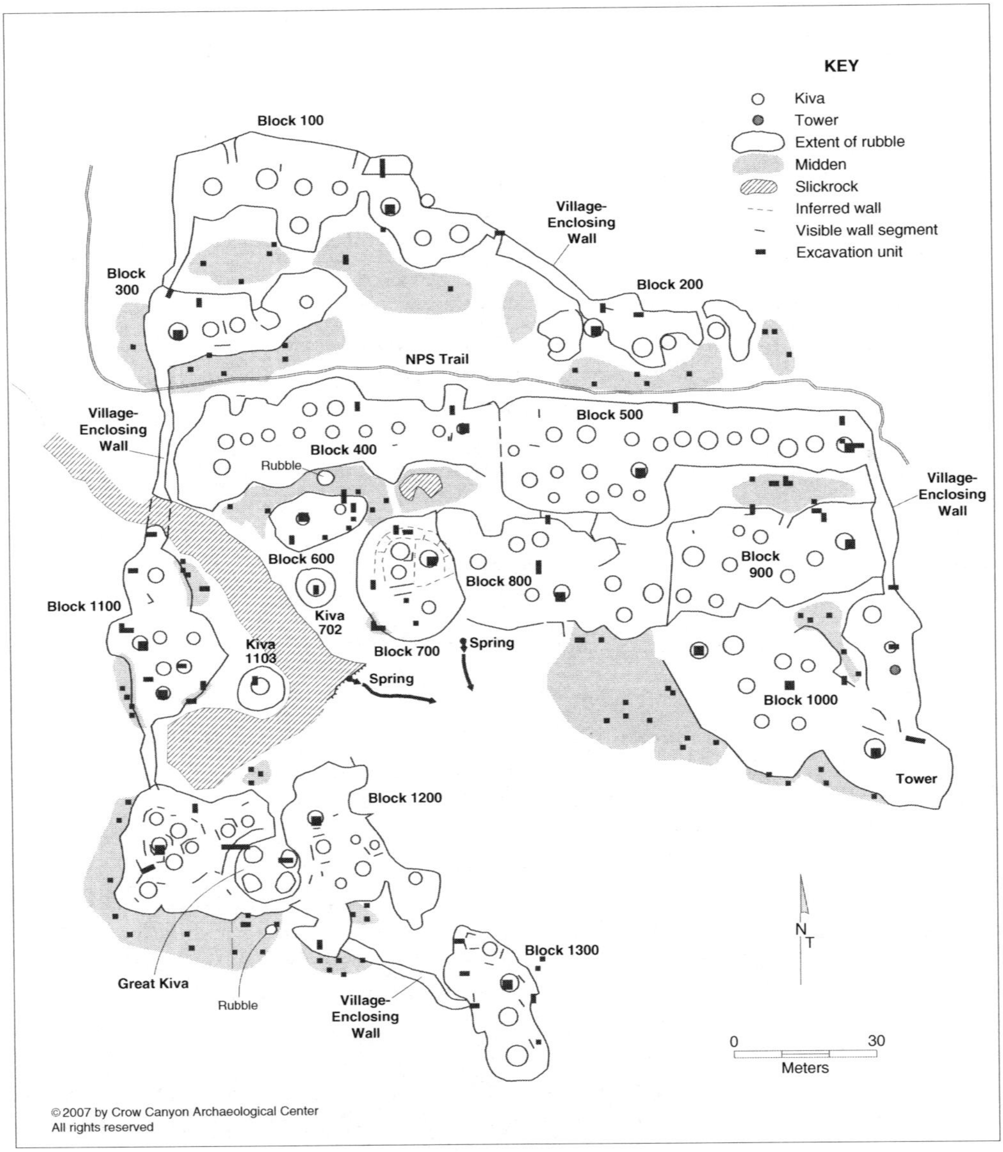


Fig. 15. Plan of the Site 5MT604 (Goodman Point Pueblo). Courtesy of Crow Canyon Archaeological Center

## History of investigation

Goodman Point Pueblo, the largest site in the Goodman Point Unit of Hovenweep National Monument, has been protected by the federal government since 1889 and thus at present is one of the best preserved sites in the region (Connolly 1992; Kuckelman et al. 2004; Varien 2006). The site was added to the National Register of Historic Places as a historic dwelling featuring residential buildings as well as public architecture such as a great kiva, several plazas, and a D-shaped building that was at least three stories tall and was the tallest structure in the village (Kuckelman and Coffey 2007). The name of the Unit and the site was derived from Henry Goodman, a foreman of the Lacy-Coleman Cattle Company, who brought many thousands of head of cattle through the Goodman Point area in the 1870s, but who never lived in the area himself. T. Mitchell Prudden (1903) and Jesse W. Fewkes (1919: 17–18) provide early descriptions of the site, and Fewkes observed that the site was divided by the canyon-head drainage into northern and southern parts. In the 1930s Charles Lindbergh took aerial photographs of Goodman Point Pueblo and other areas of the Mesa Verde region (Kuckelman et al. 2004).

Before the Crow Canyon Archaeological Center (CCAC), Cortez, Colorado, began its work in the Goodman Point Unit, research in the Unit had been limited to control and management of the land by the federal government and to surveys and surface collections by Pinkley in 1951, McLellan and Hallisey in 1967, and by an unknown researcher in 1969 (Kuckelman et al. 2004). In 1986, archaeologists from CCAC surveyed the sites in the Unit and mapped Goodman Point Pueblo as part of the Sand Canyon Project, a large research project within the locality. In 2003, archaeologists with CCAC and the Southeast Utah Group of the National Park Service (SEUG-NPS) conducted a more-detailed survey of the cultural resources in the Unit. The information from this survey was used to design six years of excavation research on 16 sites within the Unit.

In 2005, archaeologists from CCAC began a six-year research project called *The Goodman Point Archaeological Project: Community Center and Cultural Landscape Study* (Coffey and Kuckelman 2006; Kuckelman and Coffey 2007; Palonka and Kuckelman 2008). The excavation of sites in the Goodman Point Unit is designed to reveal the history of settlements of the Pueblo Indians in the Goodman Point community. Four years of the project (2005–2008) focused on investigating Goodman Point Pueblo. The latter three years (2008–2010) are devoted to the examination of other ancient remains in the Unit – 15 smaller habitations and the remains of such features as ancient roads, trails, and farming fields that were detected during surveys and in aerial photographs. The Goodman Point Unit is managed today by the Southeast Utah Group of the National Park Service (SEUG-NPS).

## History of the occupation of the site

The landscape within the Goodman Point Unit was very sparsely inhabited by Ancestral Pueblo Indians as early as the Basketmaker III period (A.D. 500–750) as indicated by the pottery types and architectural styles observed during survey (Coffey 2009; Kuckelman et at. 2004; Kuckelman et al. 2009). Population density increased during the Pueblo II period (A.D. 900–1150), and the peak density was during the Pueblo III period (A.D. 1150–1300) (Kuckelman et al. 2004; Kuckelman et al. 2009).

On the basis of the research conducted thus far, it seems that Goodman Point Pueblo was constructed and occupied during the late Pueblo III period. There were 427 tree-ring samples collected in the site during three seasons of excavations (2005–2007). Tree-ring dates from the site confirm the dating established roughly on the basis of pottery and architecture and suggest that the village was founded about A.D. 1260, grew very rapidly during the 1260s, and was probably vacated, when the Mesa Verde region was depopulated about A.D. 1280 (Kuckelman et al. 2009; Personal communication with Kristin A. Kuckelman 2008).

Some of the midden deposits from the northernmost part of the site tested thus far were very shallow and contained sparse quantities of artifacts, such as those in Blocks 100, 200, and 300 which formed the north and northeast boundaries of the village. This suggests relatively briefer occupation of those roomblocks and supports an inference that the village could have been founded at the canyon rim (where the accumulation of refuse is relatively larger) and expanded northward through time (Kuckelman et al. 2009; Palonka and Kuckelman 2008: 143). The architectural blocks along the canyon rim were probably occupied for the longest period of time

## Description of the site and analysis of the architecture

### *Site layout*

Goodman Point Pueblo contains 13 architectural blocks; each block comprises a cluster of adjacent dwelling and storage structures (rooms and kivas), associated middens (refuse areas), and outdoor use areas (Kuckelman et al. 2009; Palonka and Kuckelman 2008, 2009). Surveys and archaeological excavations at Goodman Point Pueblo have revealed several types of public architecture: a great kiva, several plazas, a D-shaped building (bi-wall structure) in 700 Block that was probably three stories tall, and bi-wall structures in blocks 600 and 1100 (Kuckelman et al. 2009).

Blocks 100, 200, and 300 are located in the northern part of Goodman Point Pueblo, and Block 100 is the northernmost of the three. Sections of village-enclosing wall link these blocks with each other and with Block 400 to the south. The central portion of the village was formed by blocks 400, 500, 600, 700, and 800. These blocks are east of a very shallow drainage that bisected the village. The eastern part of Block 500 and blocks 900 and 1000 formed the eastern edge of the village, and Block 1000 was the southernmost block in the pueblo. These blocks were almost certainly, like blocks 100, 200, and 300, used for residential purposes. Block 1100 formed part of the western edge of the pueblo and is situated between two shallow drainages that crossed the western part of the village and that converge just above Juarez Spring. This block is unusual in that its long axis runs north-south instead of the typical east-west orientation. Blocks 1200 and 1300 as well as great kiva are located in extreme southeast and southern parts of the site.

The site wraps around the head of a small tributary canyon on the west rim of Goodman Canyon. Juarez Spring issues from the canyon head at the center of the site. The larger portion of the site is on the north rim of the canyon; however, a few architectural blocks (blocks 1200 and 1300) and a great kiva are located on the south rim. Archaeological surveys and excavations documented several types of public architecture at Goodman Point Pueblo: a great kiva, multiple plazas, and a D-shaped bi-wall building in Block 700 that was originally at least three stories tall (Kuckelman et al. 2009; Palonka and Kuckelman 2008, 2009).

### Access to the site

Most of the village was enclosed by a masonry wall; the number and locations of gates or entryways is difficult to determine. The most likely locations of entryways or breaks in the village-enclosing wall are along the north, northeast, and the west edge of the pueblo.

### Availability of water

Juarez Spring issued from the west-central portion of the settlement into the canyon that divided the pueblo into two parts and was probably the primary source of potable water for the residents of this village. A reservoir might have been built in the vicinity of the settlement. Other seep springs probably existed nearby.

### Evidence of defensive architecture

The data at hand indicate that the village was enclosed by discrete sections of one-story tall stone wall that linked the ends of successive roomblocks. The section of enclosing wall that links blocks 100 and 300 was observed to abut the northwest corner of Block 300; it is, therefore, reasonable to infer that roomblocks were built first and sections of enclosing wall were then constructed as needed to bound extramural spaces within the village. However, the eastern village-enclosing wall was built first, then structures were abutted to the inside face of this wall (Coffey and Kuckelman 2006).

Excavations exposing sections of the village-enclosing wall in blocks 300, 500, 900, and 1000 indicate that this wall was a minimum of one story tall and was 50 to 60 cm thick. Many of the stones visible in both faces of the wall were shaped; however, in general, these stones were not as finely shaped and dressed as the stones used to construct rooms and kivas. Refuse – including ash and charred maize kernels – was found just inside the village-enclosing wall in Block 900, but no refuse was found just outside this same section of wall.

One cluster of adjoining structures was built outside the village-enclosing wall east of Block 1000, and this is the only architecture located outside the village boundary as delineated by this wall. On the basis of excavations, it appears that the most prominent structure in the cluster was a tower, which was built on a boulder or sandstone ledge, and that a minimum of one room and a kiva are also present in this cluster. The use of this cluster of structures, and the reason for its unusual location, has not been discovered.

Two free-standing buildings (702 and 1103) originally thought to be towers were revealed through test excavations to be kivas within above-ground masonry structures. Most structures that were still called towers after fieldwork was completed at this site are rectangular multistory rooms, such as rooms 105 and 308, within roomblocks.

## Conclusions

Goodman Point Pueblo was one of the largest thirteenth century A.D. Puebloan settlements in the Mesa Verde region (Varien 1999; Varien et al. 2000). Numerous smaller settlements in the vicinity of Goodman Point Pueblo indicate the spatial extent of the

Goodman Point community during the time before Goodman Point Pueblo was constructed.

Detailed mapping of the site has located 114 kivas (most were residential), several hundred rooms used for working and storage, and several structures that appear to have been used for special purposes. The quantity of kivas suggests that approximately 550 to 800 people inhabited the village during the height of occupation. The majority of the buildings were built on bedrock. Numerous structures in the village were two stories tall, and several were three stories, as evidenced by the extant height of the walls and the estimated original height as calculated from the volume of rubble associated with these buildings.

Several types of data, including tree-ring dates, the prevalence of Mesa Verde Black-on-white pottery, and McElmo-style architectural characteristics, indicate that this was a late Pueblo III village that was founded about A.D. 1260 and grew rapidly during the 1260s; occupation of this settlement probably ended when the Mesa Verde region was entirely depopulated about A.D. 1280/1290 (Palonka and Kuckelman 2008). It is likely that the portion of the village along the canyon rim was built first, and then the settlement quickly expanded northward.

Goodman Point Pueblo was largely enclosed by a stone wall. In the eastern part of the village, this wall was built before the adjacent roomblocks. In other areas of the village, the blocks were built first, and sections of village-enclosing wall were abutted to these blocks. Only one group of structures was built outside this wall-a cluster including a tower, kiva, and associated rooms east of Block 1000. There is evidence of at least one tower, in the southeastern part of the site; two isolated structures that flanked the spring were probably kivas instead of towers, as revealed by excavations conducted in 2005 and 2006.

## V.1.3.d. Site 5MT5 (Yellow Jacket Pueblo)

### Location

Site type: canyon-rim settlement. The site (Fig. 16) sits at is at the confluence of two canyons that become Yellow Jacket Canyon, on the canyon rim, on the talus slopes below the rim, and on the upland promontory north of the canyon rim at the confluence of two drainages. The elevation of the upper part of the site is approximately 2072 m.

The vegetation in the vicinity of the site includes primarily sagebrush, pinyon, juniper, and smaller plants such as willow, oak, and various shrubs that grow berries (Lange et al. 1986: 18).

### History of investigation

The site was mentioned by early explorers in the second half of the nineteenth century A.D., and it was visited and described by the Macomb Expedition in 1859, the Hayden Survey in 1874, and T. Mitchell Prudden, Jesse W. Fewkes, and Alfred V. Kidder in the early twentieth century (www.crowcanyon.org).

The first excavations at the site were conducted in the great tower complex (also called Square Mug House) in 1931 as a field school associated with the museum of

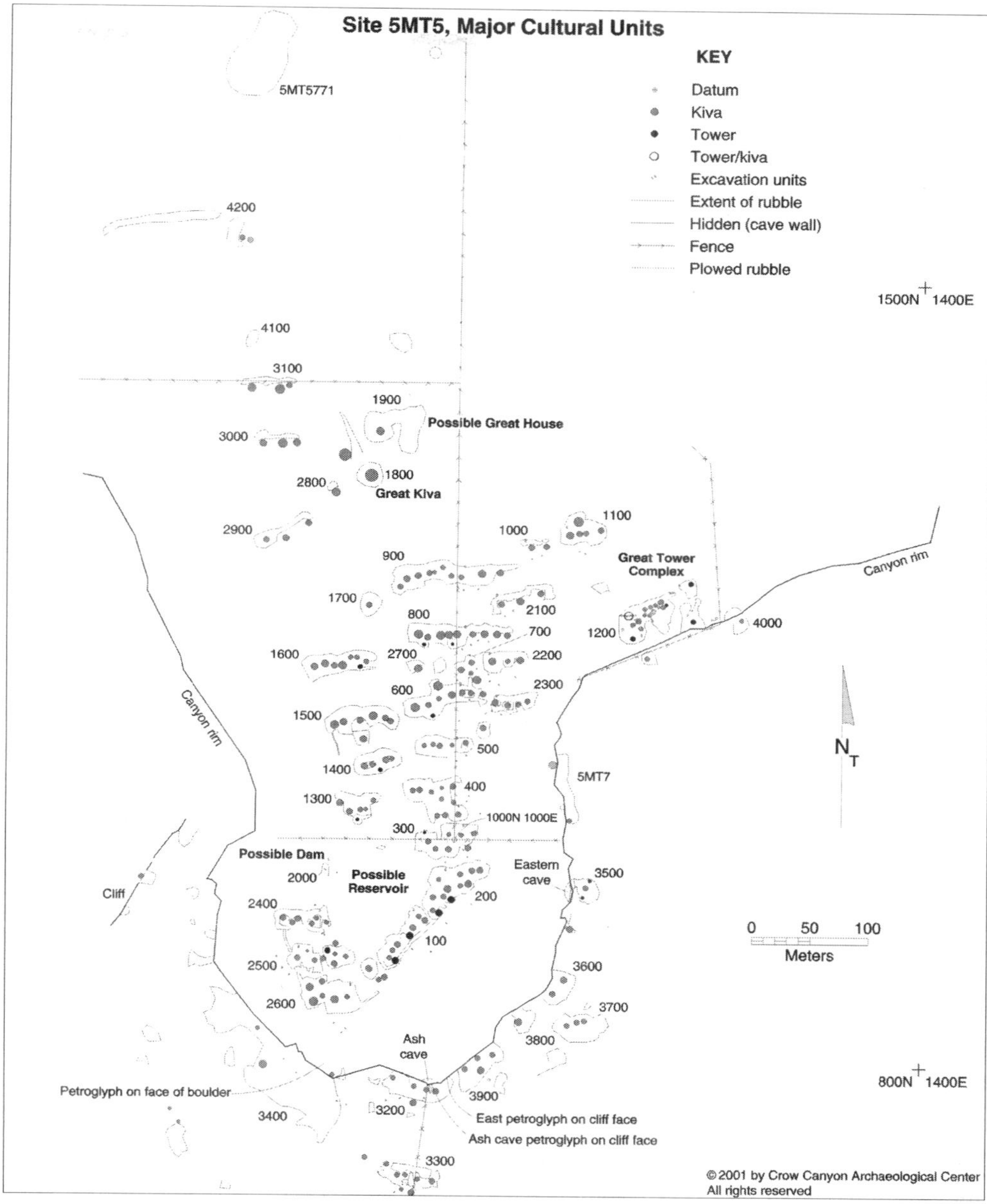


Fig. 16. Plan of the Site 5MT5 (Yellow Jacket Pueblo) with major cultural units. Courtesy of Crow Canyon Archaeological Center

Western State College in Gunnison, Colorado (Kuckelman, ed. by 2003). During the first half of the twentieth century nonprofessional excavations at the site that destroyed many burials (Kristin A. Kuckelman, personal communication).

Archaeological fieldwork was also conducted at small sites in the vicinity of Yellow Jacket Pueblo, such as sites 5MT1, 5MT2, and 5MT3, over the course of many years

(1954–1991) under the supervision of Joe Ben Wheat of the University of Colorado Museum (Kuckelman, ed. by 2003; Lange et al. 1986: 20–28; Mobley-Tanaka 1997: 1–3). In 1981, the main portion of Yellow Jacket Pueblo was mapped by Arthur H. Rohn (www.crowcanyon.org). Research on possible archaeoastronomical alignments at Yellow Jacket Pueblo and between this site and smaller sites within the Yellow Jacket community was conducted by J.M. Malville (1991).

Between April 1995 and October 1997, excavations were conducted at Yellow Jacket Pueblo by the Crow Canyon Archaeological Center, Cortez, Colorado, under the direction of Kristin A. Kuckelman. The great tower complex was partly re-excavated. Approximately two-thirds of the site has been owned and managed by The Archaeological Conservancy since 1983, and the remainder of the site is owned by several private landowners. Crow Canyon's excavations were limited primarily to the area owned by The Archaeological Conservancy and to one parcel of land on the southwest talus slope then owned jointly by Joe Tipton and Jack Hawkins. The total area of the site tested by Crow Canyon's excavations is 167 $m^2$, which is 0.04 percent of the total site area of 100 acres (Kuckelman, ed. by 2003; Lange et al. 1986: 14).

## History of the occupation of the site

The site was inhabited by Ancestral Pueblo people from at least the late Pueblo II period through the Pueblo III period (approximately A.D. 1060 to 1280) until Puebloan occupation of the region ended near the end of the thirteenth century A.D. (Kuckelman and Ortman 2003). However, building activity increased about A.D. 1180 and the population of the village peaked during the thirteenth century A.D. (Kuckelman and Ortman 2003, Varien and Ortman 2005). Most of the structures within the settlement were in use at least until A.D. 1260 and probably later.

The chronology of the site was determined primarily from pottery types and architectural styles, because only a few tree-ring dates are available for the site. The few samples available dated from the tenth and the twelfth centuries and from the mid-thirteenth century A.D. (Kuckelman and Ortman 2003; Database – LTRR 2007). The earliest dates are probably from reused beams, because the pottery and architecture associated with these dates indicate that the structures were built later than the tenth century A.D. The latest date, A.D. 1254, dates construction of the great tower complex (Kuckelman and Ortman 2003).

Although a few sherds from the Basketmaker III and Pueblo I periods were found during Crow Canyon's excavations, these were too sparse to indicate habitation during those periods (Kuckelman and Ortman 2003: par. 20). It is probable that at least part of the settlement was abandoned between A.D. 1140 and 1180 (Kuckelman and Ortman 2003) when a drought struck the Mesa Verde region (Lipe and Varien 1999b: 299). However it is also possible that the village was inhabited continuously for several generations as is indicated by some recent studies (Varien and Ortman 2005: 146–148).

## Description of the site

### *Site layout*

During the more than two hundred years of occupation, the distribution and number of structures, including residential, ceremonial, and public architecture, changed at Yellow Jacket Pueblo. During the late Pueblo III period, in the thirteenth century A.D., there were probably more buildings and a larger population than ever before in this village (www.crowcanyon.org). The settlement contained at least 42 roomblocks (most are oriented east-west), 195 kivas, many midden areas, one great kiva, 18 towers, one bi-wall tower kiva, five dams, and one large reservoir. Probably not all structures were in use at the same time. The public architecture in this settlement included towers, plazas, a bi-wall structure, a great kiva (Architectural Block 1800), and probably a Chacoan great house (Architectural Block 1900). Most of the structures are located on the rim of Yellow Jacket canyon, but many are situated on the talus slope below the rim. Evidence of at least two ancient roads that originate near the Chacoan great house was detected with the assistance of aerial photographs and topographic maps (Kuckelman 2003).

In the thirteenth century A.D., the village consisted of a series of discrete architectural blocks. Each block was composed of rooms, kivas, courtyards, and one or more middens; some blocks also contained towers, extramural walls, or other features. Architectural Block 1200 (the great tower complex) was one of the largest and probably most important blocks located near one of the village seep springs. Four or five towers were incorporated into this block, including a two-story tower that was probably one of the tallest structures in the village. At least three open spaces in different areas of the village might have served as plazas for gatherings or other public activities (Kuckelman 2003).

The ratio of rooms to kivas at Yellow Jacket Pueblo probably changed through time, but it seems to have been lower than in other settlemtents in the Mesa Verde region (Kuckelman 2003; Lange et al. 1986). The architectural block at Yellow Jacket with the highest ratio was probably the Chacoan great house (Architectural Block 1900) that in all likelihood was built sometime between A.D. 1075 and 1135 (Kuckelman 2003)

Two large rectangular slabs or monoliths, one of which is still standing, have been associated with astronomical observations by some researchers (Malville 2006). Three rock art images, or petroglyphs, of anthropomorphic stick figures have been documented on the cliff face and boulders along the canyon rim. Several small habitation sites near Yellow Jacket Pueblo are inferred to have been part of a Yellow Jacket community in which Yellow Jacket Pueblo was the community center (Kuckelman, ed. by 2003; Mobley-Tanaka 1997: 3–4).

### *Access to the site*

The settlement might have been entered from the north, northwest, or northeast across the uplands; the pueblo was protected to the west, east, and south by the cliff face and talus slopes.

### *Availability of water*

Two dependable springs are present in the eastern part of the site; one is in the eastern part of the great tower complex, and one is in the bottom of Yellow Jacket Canyon. The canyon spring was also used during historic times near the end of the nineteenth and in the early twentieth centuries by American travelers and settlers, who described it as a very good source of water. A third spring was present in Tatum Draw along the west edge of Yellow Jacket Pueblo (www.crowcanyon.org). Shallow drainages also bisect the site; one bisects the great tower complex, where four masonry dams were constructed across a drainage. The lower three of these dams would also have served to slow the flow of water from the spring surrounded by this complex (www.crowcanyon.org). A large depression in the southern portion of Yellow Jacket Pueblo might have served as a reservoir. An earth-and-rubble dam was documented at the western edge of this depression.

### *Evidence of defensive architecture*

This village does not appear to have been surrounded by an enclosing wall. However, sections of extramural walls did enclose the space between particular roomblocks (Kuckelman 2003). In the southern part of the settlement a wall connected some blocks (Lipe and Varien 1999b: 321, Fig. 9–9). In addition, the outer walls of some roomblocks were probably effective barriers against easy access into the building.

A minimum of 19 circular towers were constructed in 11 different architectural blocks within the village. Of these, 18 average 4.1 m in diameter and range in diameter from about 2.5 to 6.0 m. The only tower tested archaeologically is the one larger tower in Block 1200, or the great tower complex (Kuckelman 2003). Probably only two towers, this large one in Block 1200 and another in Block 2500, were at least two stories tall, and the others were probably single story.

Towers were located in a variety of contexts within the village. One tower was probably attached to the north wall of Block 300, and one was incorporated into a roomblock in Block 2500. A tower was situated at each of the four corners of Architectural Block 1200, or the great tower complex, and another is adjacent to the spring (Kuckelman 2003).

Excavations by the University of Colorado at Site 5MT3, one of the small sites located across Tatum Draw southwest of Yellow Jacket Pueblo and considered part of the Yellow Jacket community, revealed numerous subterranean tunnels that connected kivas with rooms; a kiva in House I that was probably one of the final kivas used in the settlement was connected by tunnels to both a surface room and a subterranean room (Lange et al. 1986: 36). Most of the towers at Yellow Jacket Pueblo are near enough to kivas to have permitted such underground connections, although the existence of such features has not been not confirmed archaeologically (Kuckelman 2003).

## Conclusions

Yellow Jacket Pueblo was inhabited beginning at least by the mid-A.D. 1000s and continued through the late thirteenth century A.D., when the Mesa Verde was depopulated by the Ancestral Pueblo people. This village was thus occupied for more than 200 years.

The peak of building activity as well as the maximum population occurred probably by A.D. 1225, when 850–1350 people might have been living in the village. The early timing of this population peak shows that Yellow Jacket Pueblo was perhaps the first large community center to form in the central Mesa Verde region during the late Pueblo III period (Kuckelman, ed. by 2003). During the thirteenth century A.D., this was probably the largest village in the central Mesa Verde region and its large size might have been its primary defensive attribute. The existence of multiple dependable water sources within the settlement and nearby is probably the primary reason for the location and success of this pueblo.

In some architectural blocks, such as Block 1200 (the great tower complex), a combination of tall structure walls that were connected to extramural walls and some associated towers, might have been enough of an obstacle against easy entry into a complex of buildings such as this. The great tower complex, constructed during the second half of the thirteenth century A.D. and included a bi-wall structure and numerous rooms, kivas, and towers, was one of the final blocks built in the village. This block enclosed a spring that was the most important or one of the most important water sources for the residents of this settlement. Five of the 18 or 19 towers in the village were located in this architectural block in key defensive positions for the block and the spring enclosed therein (Kuckelman, ed. by 2003).

## V.1.3.e. Site 5MT11842 (Woods Canyon Pueblo)

### Location

Site type: canyon-rim settlement. The site (Figs 17, 18) is located on the rim of Woods Canyon and also on the steep talus slope and canyon bottom below the rim. Woods Canyon is a tributary of Yellow Jacket Canyon. "North boundary is immediately north of the canyon rim; east boundary is a maximum of 50 m west of a side drainage; west boundary is up to 50 m east of another side drainage; south boundary is in canyon bottom, approximately 25 m north of the main drainage of the canyon" (www.crowcanyon.org). The site is approximately 5 km (3 mi) southwest of the present-day town of Yellow Jacket, Montezuma County, Colorado. The elevation of the site is 1974 m (6400 ft.). The talus slope where part of the site is situated faces south.

The vegetation on the site includes primarily pinyon, juniper, cliffrose, mountain mahogany, broadleaf yucca, prickly pear, big sagebrush, rabbitbrush, snakeweed, cheatgrass and other grasses, as well as willows and sedges that grow in the bottom of the canyon (Lipe 1995b: 1).

### History of investigation

The first published description of the site comes from *Prehistoric Villages, Castles and Towers of Southwestern Colorado,* a publication by Jesse W. Fewkes (1919: 32), who also published a map of the site (Lipe 1995b: 7). In 1993, the site was mapped and surveyed by the Crow Canyon Archaeological Center, Cortez, Colorado, under the direction

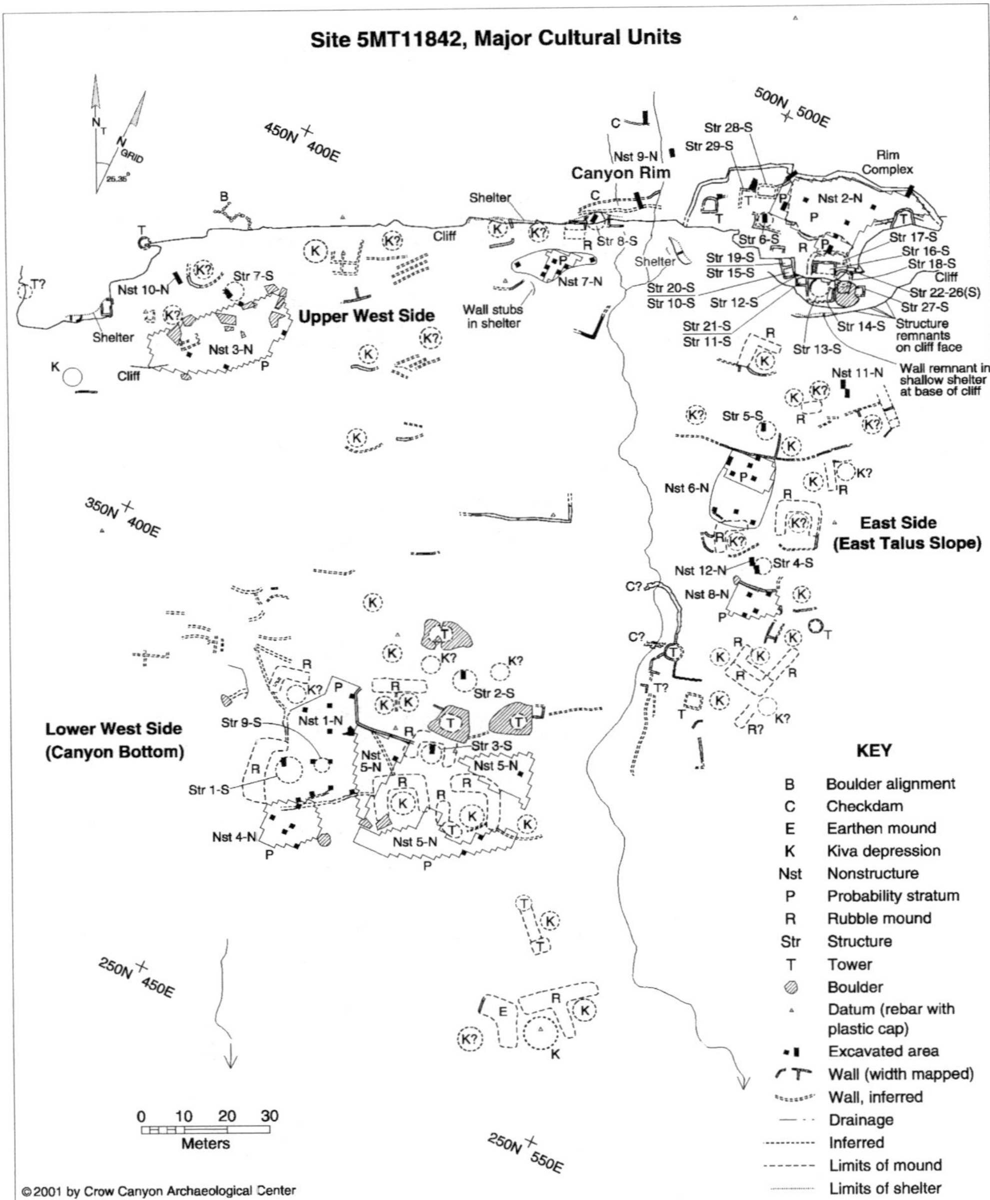


Fig. 17. Plan of the Site 5MT11842 (Woods Canyon Pueblo). Courtesy of Crow Canyon Archaeological Center

of William D. Lipe. From 1994 to 1996 Crow Canyon conducted test excavations at the site under the supervision of Richard Wilshusen, Mark Varien, and Melissa Churchill (www.crowcanyon.org). Aerial photographs of the site were taken during the Montezuma County Regional Survey and Preservation Program (Lipe 1995b: 8). Between 1997 and

1998 a crew from Crow Canyon conducted additional documentation of the architecture, and roofing beams were cored (www.crowcanyon.org). A Master's thesis was prepared on Woods Canyon Pueblo in the context of other settlements in the Mesa Verde region (Kelley 1996).

## History of the occupation of the site

Pottery types and architectural styles at the site are characteristic of the Pueblo III period. Several tree-ring dates suggest that the village was constructed between A.D. 1225 and 1280 (Lipe 1995b: 2; Kelley 1996: 82–104). However, an earlier component dates from about A.D. 1140/1150 to A.D. 1225 (Churchill and Ortman 2002). Between A.D. 1140 and 1225 the settlement was centered in the canyon bottom, whereas in the period 1225–1280 building construction proceeded up the talus slope, and the "canyon bottom fell into disuse a few decades before the end of the occupation of the site" (Churchill and Ortman 2002). Building activity probably reached the canyon rim by the mid-A.D. 1200s.

Some tree-ring dates are in the A.D. 1260s, and the two latest dates are A.D. 1274, which indicates that at least part of the settlement was still inhabited around this date or even later (Lipe 1995b: 2; Database – LTRR 2007). Many of the dated tree-ring samples came from structures located on the canyon rim (Kelley 1996: 83), and numerous structures in this complex were built during the final stage of the occupation of the village (Churchill and Ortman 2002). The pottery assemblage from the site also indicates that the settlement was occupied primarily between A.D. 1225/1230 and the 1280s (Kelley 1996: 84–104).

## Description of the site

### *Site layout*

The site, classified as a canyon-oriented village (Kelley 1996; Lipe 1995b: 1), is located on the north rim of Woods Canyon, and was built around a spring whose drainage bisects the site north-south. Woods Canyon Pueblo occupies several topographic locations (Lipe 1995b: 2–6; Kelly 1996: 23–81; Churchill 2002; www.crowcanyon.org): part of the site, the Rim Complex or Unit, according to Lipe, is on the canyon rim and was enclosed by a stone wall; part of the site is on the talus slope below the canyon rim; a portion is at the base of the cliff; and the remainder is in the canyon bottom. Most structures are visible on the ground surface, although many of those on the talus slope are difficult to identify (Lipe 1995b: 5).

Woods Canyon Pueblo contains an estimated 120 to 220 rooms, 28 to 50 kivas, and 14 to 16 towers. Public architecture is also present, such as a D-shaped building and a plaza in the Rim Complex and other possible plazas in the canyon bottom. Evidence of terraces and retaining walls, possibly for agriculture and erosion control, is visible on the talus slope, and traces of several enclosing walls have also been noted (Lipe 1995b: 1; www.crowcanyon.org). Some buildings were multi-story, including structures at the base of the cliff.

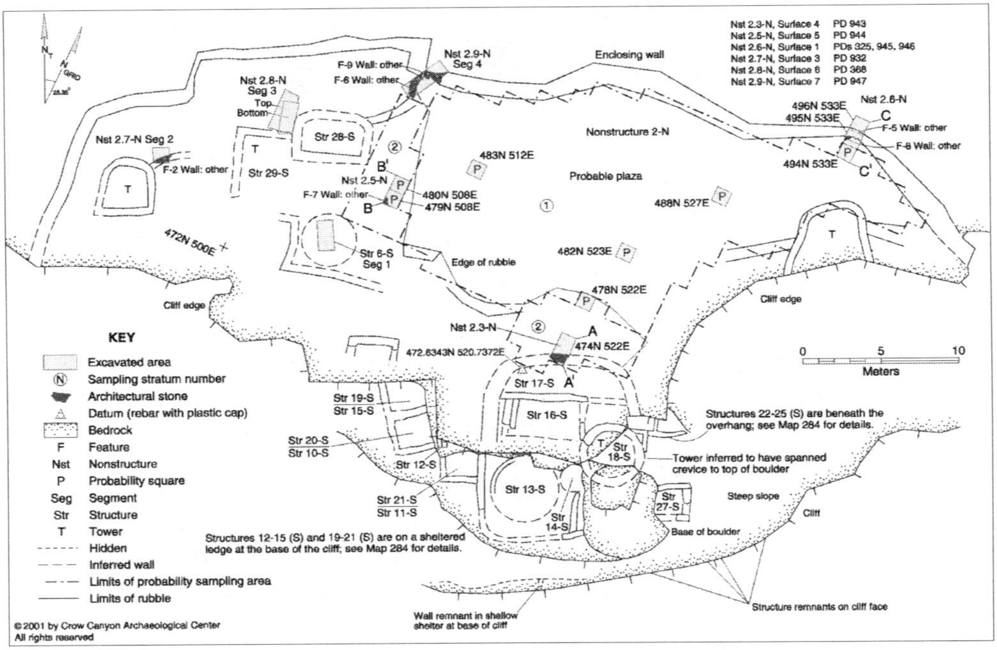


Fig. 18. Rim Complex in Woods Canyon Pueblo. Courtesy of Crow Canyon Archaeological Center

## *Access to the site*

Access to the village, or at least to the Rim Complex, was protected by a wall that entirely enclosed this complex (Churchill, ed. by 2002, Lipe 1995b: Fig. 4). This wall might have been as much as 1.5 m tall (Churchill, ed. by 2002). Access to the portion of the pueblo in the bottom of Woods Canyon was through the bottom of the canyon itself.

## *Availability of water*

The stream in the canyon bottom was probably present during occupation of the pueblo, and might have provided a permanent water source for the inhabitants in the thirteenth century A.D. (www.crowcanyon.org). This stream was fed by several springs. Intermittent water sources include the spring whose drainage bisects the site; this drainage extends from the mesa top to the canyon bottom. Other springs were in proximity to the pueblo, including a large spring east of the site. Several checkdams were built near the springs within the pueblo (www.crowcanyon.org).

A reservoir (Site 5MT12086) created by an earthen and masonry dam was built approximately 750 m northeast of Woods Canyon Pueblo (Wilshusen et al. 1997: 667–675). Although the reservoir was constructed between A.D. 1125 and 1175, it might have also been used by Pueblo people during the A.D. 1200s (www.crowcanyon.org).

### *Evidence of defensive architecture*

The Rim Complex, which includes structures on the canyon rim and directly below the rim, was enclosed to the north, east, and west by a stone wall. The wall enclosed all parts of the village on the canyon rim, and it ended at the cliff face. This wall was made of large, tabular or blocky pieces of unshaped sandstone (Churchill, ed. by 2002). The present height of the wall is 0.84 m, but on the basis of associated rubble, Churchill (ed. by 2002) estimated that the wall had been at least 1.5 m tall originally. Three towers were constructed at the northern edge of this complex. An additional tower is located on the canyon rim at the southeastern edge of the complex. Several other buildings, a D-shaped structure, and a possible plaza north of the D-shaped building, are also included in the Rim Complex (Lipe 1995b: 3–4, Fig. 4). Tree-ring dates and other evidence indicate that the structures within this complex were built during the last phase of the occupation of the pueblo (Churchill, ed. by 2002).

Walls on the talus slope might have been used to construct agricultural terraces or as retaining walls to prevent erosion (Churchill, ed. by 2002; Kelley 1996; Lipe 1995b). Some sections of walls might have connected particular structures or roomblocks (Kelley 1996: Figs 3.3 and 3.4). Some towers were constructed in the bottom of the canyon, primarily on large boulders; others were built on the canyon rim west of the Rim Complex, and near the base of the east talus slope (Churchill, ed. by 2002; www.crowcanyon.org). The towers in the canyon bottom might have been the last structures built there or, if they were contemporaneous with other buildings in this area of the settlement, they would have been built between the late A.D. 1100s and the early 1200s (Churchill, ed. by 2002).

## Conclusions

Woods Canyon Pueblo, a community center in the central Mesa Verde region during the thirteenth century A.D., is an example of a village constructed on both the canyon rim and the talus slope. The unit pueblos at Woods Canyon Pueblo are scattered rather than being clustered into architectural blocks such as those at Sand Canyon Pueblo (Churchill, ed. by 2002). The Rim Complex might have been built slightly later than the buildings on the upper west side and east talus slope, and construction in this area apparently continued into the late A.D. 1270s. Construction of the Rim Complex was probably the last major building effort at the pueblo (Churchill, ed. by 2002)

The largest concentration of human remains on the site was found on the floor of a kiva, Structure 5–S. The data suggest that these individuals died over a short span of time and were buried in one place. Cynthia S. Bradley (2002) suggests that these individuals might have died as a result of disease or epidemic rather than violence, because there is no evidence of violence on the bones.

Archaeobotanical data (Rainey and Jezik 2002) indicate that the Rim Complex might have been used differently from the rest of the village. For example, food might have been rarely prepared in this part of the settlement, although a relatively greater variety of woods were used for fuel here (Rainey and Jezik 2002). I suggest that the Rim Complex was used for public activities, including the serving of food that was prepared outside the complex. If fire or smoke was used to communicate with other sites, this complex, with its tall structures (four towers and the D-shaped building) positioned on a canyon rim, would also have been a good place for activities such as this.

## V.1.3.f. Site 5MT1000 (Seven Towers Pueblo)[9]

### Location

Site type: canyon-rim settlement. The site (Fig. 19) sits on a canyon rim that forms a low cliff in some parts of the site and on the talus slope below the rim. Part of the rim is collapsed. The site is at the head of a small unnamed tributary of Negro Canyon.

Site dimensions are approximately 210 x 195 m, an area of 29 766 m² (7.36 acres). The site is defined as extending approximately 25 m beyond the architectural features located on the canyon rim and includes an artifact scatter. The elevation of the site is 1871 m (6140 ft.). The canyon where the site is located faces south-southwest.

The vegetation on and around the site includes pinyon and juniper trees, sagebrush, four-wing saltbush, bitterbrush, tamarisk, cheatgrass, snakeweed, and rabbitbrush.

### History of investigation

The site was surveyed in 1967 by Paul Folse, Mesa Verde Research Center, University of Colorado, and also by the Bureau of Land Management during the Mockingbird Mesa Class III Survey of 1981–1984. In 1994 William D. Lipe re-surveyed the site, and Lipe and Scott Ortman conducted yet another survey. Rocky Mountain Aerial Survey of Englewood, Colorado, photographed the site. Compared to other sites in the region, the site is well preserved, partly because it has suffered only minor damage from looting. However, erosion, probably caused partly by livestock, has taken a toll; the site is also threatened by wind-and-water erosion, especially the part of the site on the talus slope.

### History of the occupation of the site

Pottery types and architectural style indicate that this settlement was constructed and occupied during the Pueblo III period, and probably most intensively occupied in the late Pueblo III period, between A.D. 1240 and 1280. Most of the masonry is classic Pueblo III McElmo style, and the pottery is dominated by Mesa Verde Black-on-White, although McElmo Black-on-White is also present. The site was probably inhabited until the Mesa Verde area was depopulated near the end of the thirteenth century A.D.

### Description of the site

#### *Site layout*

Part of the site is situated on the canyon rim, but the largest portion is on the steep talus slope just below and south of the rim. Boulders are present on the slope within the site boundary. The site is also divided by multiple drainages; the main drainage bisects the

[9] Data for the site are from Lipe 1995c (*National Register of Historic Places Registration Form – Seven Towers Pueblo*).

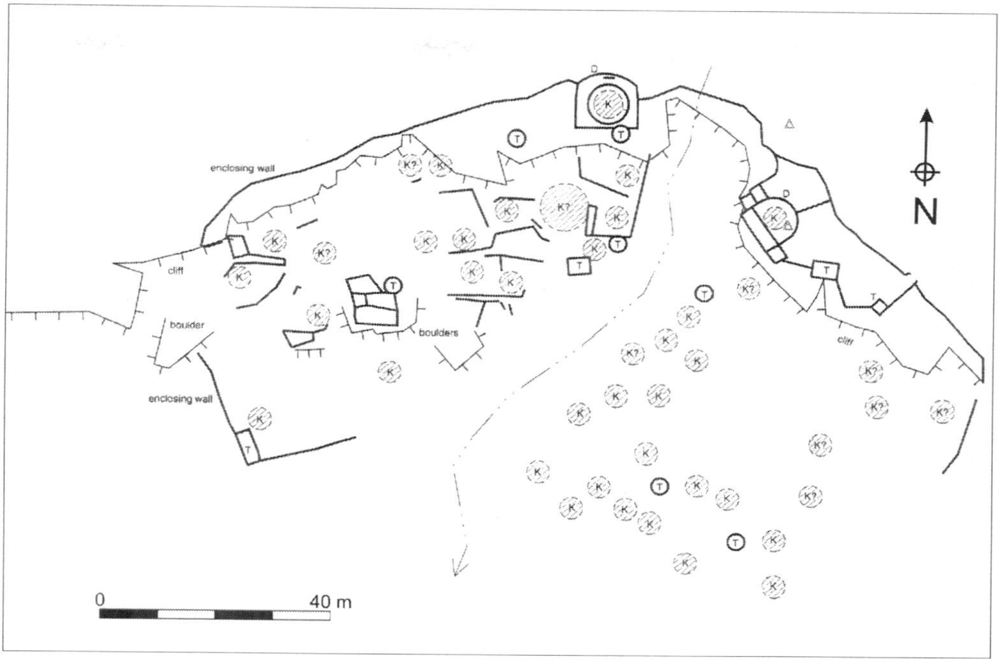


Fig. 19. Plan of the Site 5MT1000, Seven Towers Pueblo (after Lipe 1995b: Figure 3 modified by A. Danecki)

site into similar parts, although the ruins in the western part of the site are more visible on the modern ground than those in the eastern part.

The site contains the remains of 128–210 rooms, an estimated 42 kivas, one probable great kiva, and 11 towers, which is four towers more than is indicated by the name of the site if, of course, all 11 of these structures were actually towers. Two large D-shaped buildings that were probably two stories tall sit on the canyon rim on either side of the drainage that divided the settlement. Each of these structures is formed by an exterior row of rooms surrounding a kiva. The midden in the eastern part of the site looks more extensive than that in the western part.

### *Access to the site*

The village could be reached from the top of Mockingbird Mesa, but there is an enclosing wall that separates the northern part of the site on the canyon rim from the rest of the mesa top. The other main access is from the south and involves hiking from the bottom of Negro Canyon or other access points.

### *Availability of water*

The site is situated at the head of a small tributary of Negro Canyon. The site is bisected by drainages, and the central drainage contains a seep. The abundance of vegetation just below the canyon rim in this central drainage may indicate that ground water is near the surface (Lipe 1995b). It is probable that a seep spring was present during occupation of the settlement. The nearest permanent water source, a spring, is in Negro Canyon, 3 km (1000 ft.) southwest of this site. Water-control features such as terraces or checkdams might be associated with this site, but this has not been verified.

### *Evidence of defensive architecture*

The village might have contained as many as 11 towers; four are located on the canyon rim, the others are on the talus slope, mostly on large boulders. These towers are similar to those found in Hovenweep National Monument on the Utah-Colorado border. Remains of an enclosing wall are visible on the canyon rim and talus slope. Without further research it cannot be determined if the part of the settlement located on the talus slope was entirely, or only partly, enclosed by the wall; also it is not clear whether the wall on the canyon rim was connected to the wall on the talus slope. The enclosing wall on the rim trends east-west and is parallel to the rim and cliff face. Archaeological investigations thus far suggest that the wall was not tall. Multiple kivas were outside the enclosing wall.

### Conclusions

The site is situated on the canyon rim and talus slope, although the main part of the village was located below the rim. Seven Towers Pueblo is a large site with public architecture such as D-shaped buildings, a plaza, and a great kiva, as well as other distinctive structures like towers and enclosing walls. This was among the larger villages on Mockingbird Mesa and reached its peak population during the late Pueblo III period.

Some structures, such as towers, enclosing walls, and perhaps the D-shaped structures, might have functioned as defensive structures, ceremonial buildings, or both. The location of D-shaped structures on both sides of the drainage is similar to the location of similar structures at Sand Canyon and Goodman Point pueblos. D-shaped structures, as well as other structures mentioned above, could have been used for a variety of purposes. Similar to many other community centers constructed in the Mesa Verde area during the thirteenth century A.D., this site reflects the aggregation of population and the choice of a canyon rim for settlement. The position of the site, surrounding a spring, may indicate that this location was chosen for the availability of water as well as for its defensible landscape.

## V.1.3.g. Site 5MT338 (Cannonball Ruin)

### Location

Site type: canyon-rim settlement. The site (Fig. 20) is situated on the canyon rim and talus slope below the rim at the head of Cannonball Canyon in the central portion of Cannonball Mesa. Cannonball Canyon is a tributary of Yellow Jacket Creek. The site sits at an elevation of approximately 1634 m (5360 ft.). Parts of the talus slope where some structures are located face south and southwest.

The vegetation in the canyon includes mainly, willow, squawbush, and rabbitbrush. On the mesa top, the vegetation includes shrubs such as big sage, four-wing saltbush,

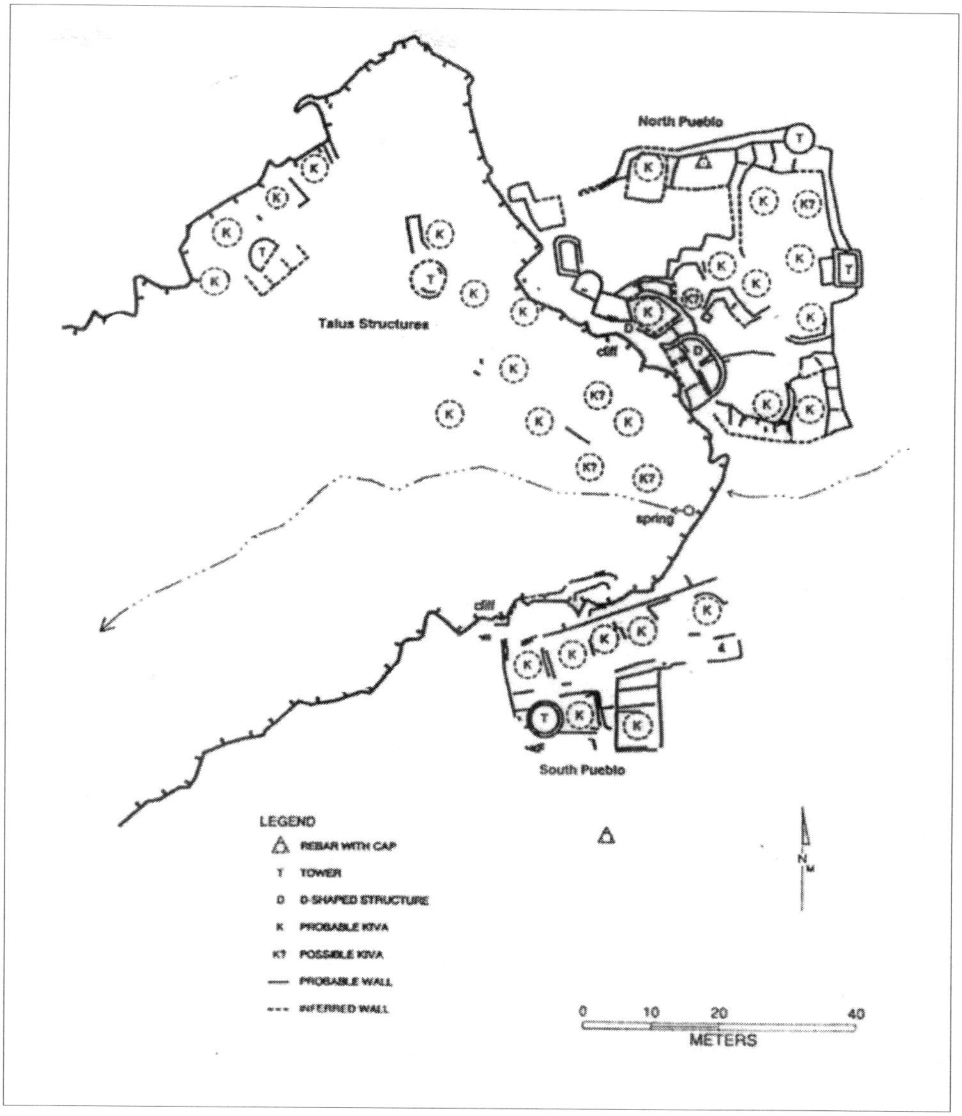


Fig. 20. Plan of the Site 5MT338, Cannonball Ruin (after Lipe 1996: Fig. 2 modified by A. Danecki)

shadscale, blackbrush, rabbitbrush, and bursage, as well as sparse grasses, and some pinyon and juniper (Lipe 1996: 3–4).

## History of investigation

The first records and descriptions of the site come from a survey directed by Edgar Hewett but conducted in the field by Sylvanus G. Morley, Alfred V. Kidder, and John G.

Fletcher in 1907 (Lipe 1996; Morley 1917). In 1908, the southern part of the site, called the South Pueblo, was excavated by Morley. The report of these excavations was published in *American Anthropologist* in the fall of 1908 (Morley 1908). Morley also prepared a map of the part of the pueblo he excavated. Collections from these excavations are curated at the Colorado Historical Society and the University of Colorado Museum (Lipe 1996: 6).

The site was surveyed in 1966 and 1978 by crews from the University of Colorado, who also prepared new map of the site. In 1977, a crew stabilized and "reset" the doorway of Tower A. In 1994 and 1995 the site was re-surveyed, prepared for aerial photography, and was mapped, first by a crew under the direction of William D. Lipe, and later by a crew from the Crow Canyon Archaeological Center under the direction of William D. Lipe and Scott Ortman. As part of this last research, aerial photography was conducted by Rocky Mountain Aerial Surveys of Englewood, Colorado, and more detailed map of the site was prepared by Neal Morris (Lipe 1996: 6).

During the survey of sites analyzed for the dissertation, the author visited the site with an archaeologist from the Crow Canyon Archaeological Center, Kristin A. Kuckelman, in April 2009; two fresh looters' pits were noted (and reported to the Bureau of Land Management) in one of the D-shaped structures on the canyon rim in the north-central part of the site. Evidence of vandalism and looting was also noted in recent decades (Lipe 1996: 5), and a comparison of the photographs taken during Morley's excavations in 1908 with the current condition of the architecture reveals that the site has suffered a substantial amount of destruction during the past 100 years. For example, in the historic photographs Tower A is much taller and more complete (Morley 1908: Pl. XXXVI, XXXVIII).

## History of the occupation of the site

The site dates from the Pueblo III period (A.D. 1150–1300). Although no tree-ring samples have been collected from the site most of the building activity and the heaviest site occupation, appears to have occurred during the late Pueblo III period, probably between A.D. 1240 and 1280 (Lipe 1996: 4, 12; Morley 1908). This dating is indicated by the presence of classic, late Pueblo III Mesa Verde architectural style and a pottery assemblage dominated by Mesa Verde Black-on-white sherds.

## Description of the site

### *Site layout*

Most of the structures sit on the canyon rim at the head of Cannonball Canyon, but some structures are on the talus slope below the rim. Two free-standing structures, or towers, are situated on boulders that rest on the talus slopes within the canyon. At least 110–130 rooms, 32 kivas, and six structures called towers are within the site boundaries (Lipe 1996: 2). Three D-shaped structures, probable public architecture, have also been identified; two such structures are large and adjoined to each other and are in the north-central part of the site on the canyon rim. (Lipe 1996: 2, Figs 1–3). Most of the portion of the village that was on the canyon rim was enclosed by a wall.

Cannonball Ruin is bisected by a drainage, and some asymmetry is visible in terms of the types and arrangement of architecture present on either side of this drainage. The site was divided by archaeologists into sections on the basis of the location of particular structures. Structures in the southernmost section on the canyon rim and talus slope are called South Pueblo, and the structures directly at the head of the canyon are called North Pueblo (Lipe 1996). North Pueblo is larger than South Pueblo and includes more structures that could have been public architecture, such as D-shaped structures, towers, and a possible plaza (Lipe 1996: 3).

### *Access to the site*

Access to this settlement was possible from the north, east, and south across the top of the mesa, and from the west up Cannonball Canyon. Access from the west must have followed steep canyon slopes. The areas of the village on the canyon rim were mostly or entirely enclosed by a wall built on a relatively flat area of the mesa top. It is difficult to estimate the number of gates or openings through this enclosing wall. However, during his excavations in 1908, Morley noted no doorways in the exterior room walls of South Pueblo, nor were there any doorways in first story rooms that faced the mesa top; all doorways faced the canyon (Morley 1908: 598).

### *Availability of water*

A plentiful spring is present in the low alcove or shelter below the site at the head of the canyon near the center of the site. Shallow depressions in the floor of the shelter are continuously filled with water. There is also a pool in the canyon just below the shelter. According to Kristin A. Kuckelman (personal communication, 2009), even in the driest summers, water drips from the roof of the alcove and the supply of water is plentiful. East of the site Morley noted a reservoir and several "irrigating ditches" (Morley 1908: 598), and possible evidence of a dam and other water control features were recorded during more recent surveys of the site (Lipe 1996: 3).

### *Evidence of defensive architecture*

Data indicate that a wall enclosed all structures built in the North Pueblo. This wall probably continued to the canyon rim (Lipe 1996: 2). No evidence of a similar wall has been detected around the South Pueblo, although it is probable that the outer walls of particular structures in this section were joined together and created a continuous exterior masonry wall (Lipe 1996: 2; Morley 1908).

Still standing in the South Pueblo is a wall that was built on the talus slope (possibly part of Room 30) facing the canyon and the northern part of the pueblo. The North Pueblo contains evidence of massive retaining walls that formed terraces where many structures were built (Lipe 1996: 3).

At least six structures at Cannonball Ruin might be called towers. Two were built on large boulders or detached portions of the canyon rim, and the remainder are situated on or near the canyon rim. At least three towers are circular in plan. One sits on a large boulder on the talus slope below the rim of the canyon. Two towers are located at the extreme outer corners of roomblocks, were joined to other structures, and were incorporated into village-enclosing walls. One of these two towers is at the northeastern corner of the site, and the other, Tower A, is situated at the southwestern corner of the site (Lipe 1996: Figs 2–4). Tower A, whose walls even in 1908 stood 3 m tall, probably dominated the other the structures in the South Pueblo (Morley 1908: 599). The tower doorway faced southeastward and opened into Room 1. Morley proposed, on the basis of wall abutments, that Tower A was the oldest structure in the southern part of the site (Morley 1908: 601). A different structure, in the southeastern part of the South Pueblo and indicated by one visible wall, stood about 4.5 m tall in 1908 (Morley 1908: 599). The tower in the eastern part of the North Pueblo is rectangular. The tower in the northern part of the pueblo on the talus slope has a D-shaped plan.

Several loopholes were noted by the author during a survey in 2009. One loophole viewing east was noted in the eastern wall of the rectangular tower in the eastern part of the North Pueblo, and another was visible in the tower perched on a large boulder below the canyon rim in the northern part of the pueblo. The two possible loopholes in extant walls of the tower on the boulder face different directions-one affords a view of the canyon bottom, and the other is oriented toward the alcove containing the spring. The loopholes in the eastern rectangular tower provide views at different angles toward the east and southeast. Through these loopholes, one has a very good view of the surrounding mesa top and, during ancient times, probably of farm fields and water control features. Larger openings in the northern wall of the South Pueblo along the canyon rim might have been loopholes or windows (Morley 1908: Pl. XXXVIa).

Three D-shaped structures, in addition to the D-shaped tower, are located in the North Pueblo on the canyon rim. Two are conjoined and are larger than the third structure, which is just northwest of the conjoined structures. The largest of these D-shaped buildings was a minimum of two stories tall (Lipe 1996: 3). It seems reasonable to assume that the conjoined D-shaped structures were the largest buildings in the village.

## Conclusions

Cannonball Ruin was medium-sized village in the central Mesa Verde region during the thirteenth century A.D. The site is situated on and below the canyon rim at the head of Cannonball Canyon and is bisected by a drainage. The site was partly excavated in 1908 by Morley (1908), and later research involved surveys only (e.g., Lipe 1996).

That defense was a concern of the inhabitants of Cannonball is indicated by the location of the settlement on a canyon rim around a canyon head, the presence of strong spring within the village, the construction of architectural features such as towers with loopholes that were located on the canyon rim, on boulders, and on the talus slope below the canyon rim, and the presence of an enclosing wall around at least the North Pueblo (Lipe 1996: 4, 8; Morley 1908: 597–598). These towers resemble those at several sites within Hovenweep National Monument, near Cannonball Ruin, along what is now the Utah-Colorado border (Lipe 1996: 2). Three towers are at the extreme ends of the pueblo and were incorporated into the outer walls of the village, and provided good eye communication with nearby areas. If the towers constructed on boulders and on the talus slope were defensive, they must have been designed for protection against attackers coming up the canyon bottom. Besides the structures mentioned above that might have afforded protection in case of attack, it is possible that the large, conjoined D-shaped structures in the North Pueblo were among the tallest buildings in the village and that they functioned as defensive structures in time of danger.

## V.1.3.h. Sites M-1, M-2, M-3 (Moon House)

### Location

Site type: cliff dwelling. This complex (Figs 21–22) of three sites is located in separate sandstone alcoves or shelters overlooking McLoyd's Canyon. The canyon is on the east side of Cedar Mesa, an upland area in San Juan County, southeastern Utah (Bedell 2000: 28). The elevation of Cedar Mesa is approximately 2000 m (6500 ft.), but ranges from 1700 m (5300–5600 ft.) to ca. 2120 m, or 6950 ft. (Bedell 2000: 29; Bloomer 1989: 26; Matson et al. 1988: 247); the level of precipitation and the agricultural potential vary with elevation. All three sites face south, although the aspect of Site M-3 is south and southeast.

The vegetation on and near the site includes mostly pinyon-juniper woodland and sagebrush, but also mountain mahogany, Gambel's oak, variety of cacti, yucca, sparse willow, and cottonwood in the canyon bottoms.

### History of investigation

Cedar Mesa was initially explored in the 1890s by Wetherill family members (Bedell 2000: 33), and more-professional work was conducted in the twentieth century. The first official descriptions of sites M-1 and M-2 were recorded in 1964. In 1974 Moon House was surveyed and mapped as part of the Cedar Mesa Project of the Museum of Northern Arizona, which was supervised by R.G. Matson, who was from the University of British Columbia and by William D. Lipe (Bedell 2000: 33–41; Bloomer 1989: 34–35; Matson et al. 1988: 245–246). The Cedar Mesa Project lasted from 1972 to 1975. During this survey, artifacts and tree-ring samples were collected; many well-preserved roofing beams and jacal walls were encountered. McLoyd's Canyon and Grand Gulch were included in the survey because of the relatively well-preserved architecture in those canyons (Bedell 2000: 38).

In 1986, William W. Bloomer re-surveyed Moon House and produced descriptions, notes, and photographs of the architecture (Bloomer 1989: 21–22, 36–37). In that same year, archaeological reconnaissance was conducted at several sites in McLoyd's Canyon, including Moon House (Bloomer 1989: 37–48).

### History of the occupation of the site

Although some tree-ring samples predate A.D. 1200, most date between A.D. 1220 and the late 1260s (Bloomer 1989: 58). The central portion of the Moon House (Site M-1) appears to have been occupied the latest; several habitation and storage rooms were constructed in A.D. 1264, 1265, and 1267. The two other areas of Moon House were contemporaneous with the central area (Bloomer 1989: 2). At least 32 rooms in the Moon

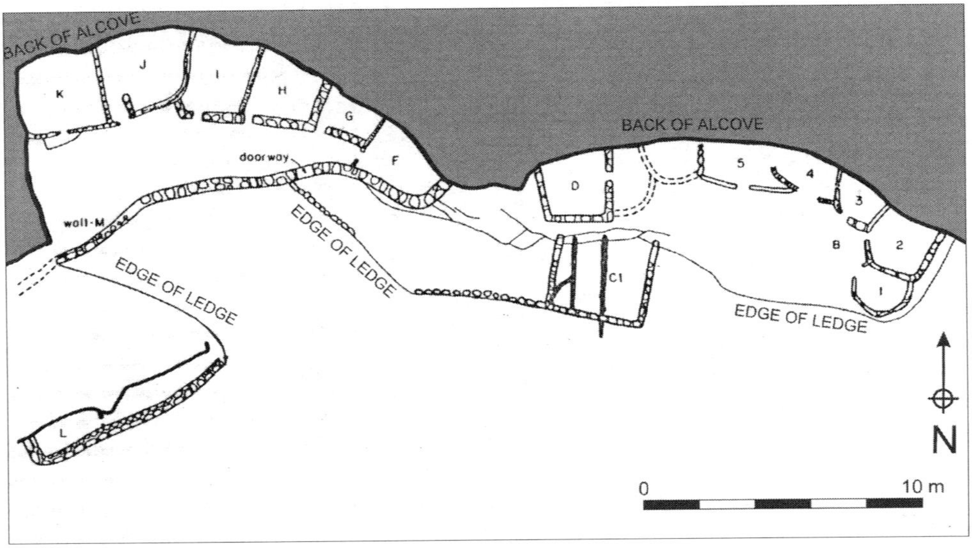


Fig. 21. Plan of the Site M-1 at Moon House complex (after Ahlstrom 1985: Fig. 49 modified by A. Danecki)

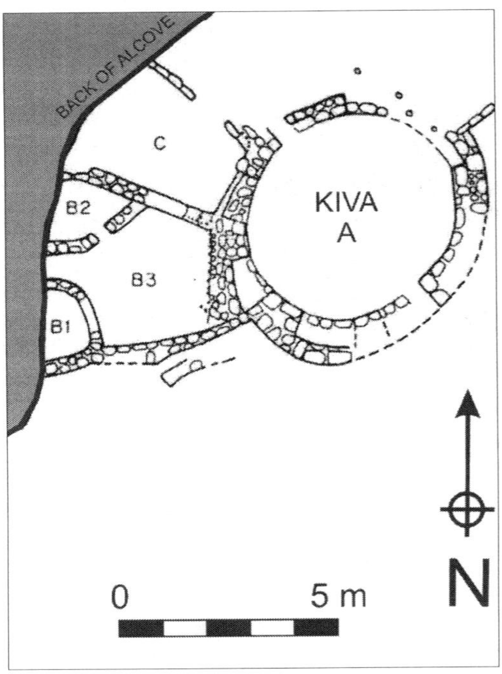


Fig. 22. Plan of the Site M-3 at Moon House complex (after Ahlstrom 1985: Fig. 50 modified by A. Danecki)

House complex were still in use in the late A.D. 1260s, during what was probably the terminal phase of occupation of the complex (Bloomer 1989: 65). The latest date for Moon House is A.D. 1268 (Bloomer 1989: 58).

The timing of building activity at Moon House corresponds with increasing construction in other canyon sites at Cedar Mesa in the mid- A.D. 1200s (Bedell 2000: 44). Moon House and most of the other settlements in southeastern Utah were probably abandoned during the A.D. 1260s, which was about 10–20 years earlier than those in southwestern Colorado (Lipe 1995a; Varien et al. 1996: 103).

## Description of the site

### *Site layout*

Moon House comprises three shelters or alcoves within a 0.5 km strip in McLoyd's Canyon. Site M-1 (42-SA-5005) contains many residential rooms and was probably the main habitation area for the complex. Site M-3 is west of Site M-1 and houses a kiva with associated rooms. Approximately 200 m east of Site M-1 is Site M-2 (42-SA-5004), which contains several rooms that could have been used for storage (Bloomer 1989: 1–2). In the late phase of occupation, the function of some rooms might have changed from residential to storage (Bloomer 1989: 67).

Both jacal and two or three types of masonry construction were used to build the structures at Moon House (Bloomer 1989: 1, 49–53); construction techniques also reflect the chronology of the site.

### *Access to the site*

All three alcoves of Moon House are situated high in the north cliff face of the canyon; access to the site is restricted, by the vertical cliff face, to specified routes that involve trekking and climbing (Bloomer 1989: 29). These alcoves are approximately 100–120 m (400 ft.) above the canyon bottom.

The interior of Site M-1 can be accessed through only one entryway in an outer wall extending along the front edge of the alcove. Communication between alcoves M-1 and M-2 was possible by means of a ledge between these two sites (Bloomer 1989: Fig. 4).

### *Availability of water*

Springs are present just below the complex and nearby in McLoyd's Canyon, and also in small tributaries to McLoyd's Canyon (Bloomer 1989: 28, Fig. 5).

### *Evidence of defensive architecture*

A wall that might have protected access to the settlement extends nearly the entire length of the alcove where Site M-1 is located. Loopholes are present in Moon House as well as in some other sites in McLoyd's Canyon, such as Site SA-1369, and might have served defensive purposes (Bloomer 1989: 47–48). Some loopholes in the outer wall of M-1 are trained on the main route to the village (http://www.cs.uwaterloo.ca/~shallit/moonhouse.html).

### Conclusions

Moon House was one of the largest cliff dwellings in the thirteenth century A.D. in what is today southeastern Utah, and it is possible that it was the latest of the large villages in McLoyd's Canyon in the late thirteenth century (Bloomer 1989: 22). Early in the occupation of this complex, all three sites were residential; later, their functions differed (Bloomer 1989: iv, 2, 67). The high ratio of storage rooms to living rooms (5:1) indicates that Moon House might have been an important place to store food for a population larger than that inhabiting these alcoves (Bloomer 1989: iv). William D. Lipe suggested that the site might have been used seasonally as a center for the storage and distribution of food for a larger community (Bloomer 1989: 22).

The location of Moon House, the difficult access, and the defensive features incorporated into especially the late constructions in the complex, all suggest a great concern for the protection and defense of the inhabitants. The layout of the complex, including habitation, ritual, and storage buildings located in three separate alcoves, is similar to nearby clusters of sites in McLoyd's Canyon (Bloomer 1989: 47) such as complex SA-5009, and M-21 and M-22.

# V.2. ANALYSIS OF SITES IN LOWER SAND CANYON LOCALITY (CASTLE ROCK COMMUNITY)

## V.2.1. Site 5MT1825 (Castle Rock Pueblo)

### Location

Site type: village situated on the top, and around the base, of a butte. Castle Rock Pueblo (Fig. 23) is in Montezuma County in the southwestern part of Colorado. The site lies about 7.5 km (4.5 mi) southwest of Sand Canyon Pueblo, one of the largest settlements in the area during the occupation of Castle Rock Pueblo in the thirteenth century A.D. (Kuckelman, ed. by 2000).

The site is near the floodplain of McElmo Creek. The terrain south of the site slopes downward about 5 to 10 degrees toward McElmo Creek, which is 0.5–0.6 km (ca. 2000 ft.) south of the site. The elevation of Castle Rock Pueblo is 1682 m (5520 ft.), and the site is one of the highest points in the immediate area (Kuckelman, ed. by 2000; Kuckelman et al. 2002: 488).

Castle Rock Pueblo might have been the center of larger community of around 30–40 sites located in lower part of Sand Canyon and Rock Creek Canyon (Ortman 2008; Palonka 2009, 2010).

The natural vegetation on and near site includes pinyon and juniper woodland as well as sagebrush, grasses, winterfat, prickly pear cactus, and four-wing saltbush.

### History of investigation

Information about Castle Rock Pueblo was first published in the reports of the Hayden Survey expeditions to Colorado, supervised by William H. Jackson and William H.

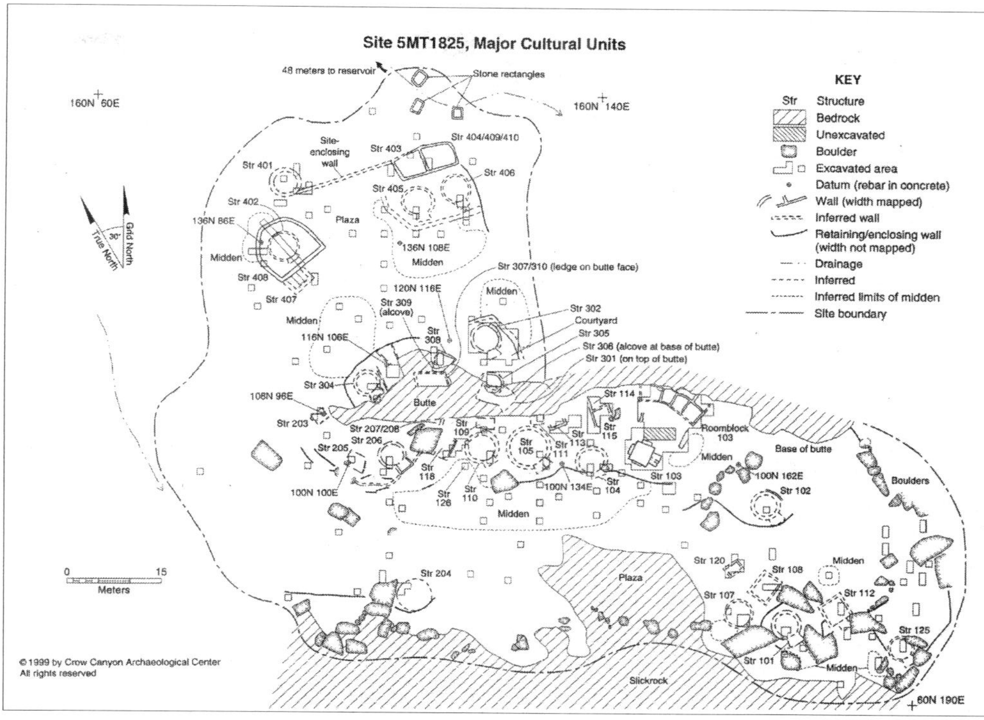


Fig. 23. Plan of the Site 5MT1825 (Castle Rock Pueblo). Courtesy of Crow Canyon Archaeological Center

Holmes in 1874 and 1875. The expedition to southwestern Colorado was part of a larger survey organized by Ferdinand V. Hayden to explore areas of the North American West and included mapping, painting, and photographing visited sites, as well as gathering a wealth of knowledge about the region's natural history.

During this expedition, Castle Rock Pueblo was visited and described by the survey party. W.H. Jackson photographed the site (Holmes 1876, 1878; Jackson 1876a, 1876b; Jackson and Holmes 1981); these images provide invaluable information about walls and structures that no longer exist as a result of vandalism and erosion. During this survey the site was named Battle Rock. Battle Rock is a long, narrow butte and the site itself is often called Battle Rock by local residents; however, there are two buttes called Battle Rock that are very near each other.

In 1874, the journalist Ernest Ingersoll, who accompanied the Hayden Expedition, published several articles in newspapers on the East Coast. One of the most important of his articles concerning Castle Rock Pueblo is one published in the *New York Tribune* on November 3, 1874 (Kuckelman, ed. by 2000). This article contained a legend told to the Hayden expedition by John Moss, the first Indian agent for the Hopi people from 1864 to 1868, about an ancient battle that took place at Battle Rock between the ancestors of Hopi (Moqui) inhabitants of the village and the ancestors of probably the Ute Indians (for the story, see Chapter IV.3). In 1891, the site was photographed by the H. Jay Smith exploring party and photographed again in 1906 by T. Mitchell Prudden (www.crowcanyon.org).

Archaeological surveys of Castle Rock Pueblo were conducted in 1965, 1975, and 1988. The 1965 survey was conducted by the Mesa Verde Archaeological Research Center, Department of Anthropology, University of Colorado. The site was assigned a number, 5MT1825, and in 1968, a survey form was completed (www.crowcanyon.org).

In 1975, a survey and a Ruins-stabilization Inventory Form was completed for the Lower Sand Canyon area by the Mesa Verde Research Center. Castle Rock Pueblo was then recommended for stabilization (Martin 1976; Varien, ed. by 1999, www.crowcanyon.org). In 1988, a survey was conducted by Native Cultural Services as part of the Sand Canyon Inventory project (Gleichman and Gleichman 1989). An additional survey of the Lower Sand Canyon area, including Castle Rock Pueblo, was conducted by the Crow Canyon Archaeological Center (CCAC), Cortez, Colorado in 1990 as part of the Sand Canyon Archaeological Project Site Testing Program (Adler and Metcalf 1992; Varien, ed. by 1999).

From 1990 to 1994, CCAC conducted excavations at the site. The first phase of that work was conducted in 1990 and 1991, and included mapping the site and initial test excavations. The second phase, between 1992 and 1994, included more intensive excavations to more thoroughly investigate, among other things, several structures discovered during the testing phase. About five percent of the site was tested archaeologically (Varien, ed. by 1999). The results of these excavations are accessible through the CCAC web site at www.crowcanyon.org (Kuckelman, ed. by 2000; Varien 1999). There are also more recently published articles that consider Castle Rock Pueblo in a broader context and tell of evidence of warfare at this site.

Like many other sites in the Mesa Verde region, the site has suffered from vandalism and looting. Effects of these activities are especially noticeable if we compare the photographs taken by W.H. Jackson in the 1870s with the present condition of the site. Specific walls and structures, including possible towers, that were recorded and photographed by Jackson now no longer exist or are much reduced in height. Some of this damage occurred in the past few decades. Local residents remember surface collecting and excavating burials 20 to 30 years ago at the site.

However, most subsurface deposits are intact despite vandalism, looting, and intensive surface collection at the site. Today the site is within a large area used for recreation and, as a result, artifacts are still being picked up from the modern ground surface. The site is within the Canyons of the Ancients National Monument which is managed by Bureau of Land Management.

## History of the occupation of the site

The chronology of the site was established on the basis of tree-ring dates, pottery types, and architectural styles. Tree-ring samples were collected during archaeological excavations conducted in the 1990s. Tree-ring dates indicate that Castle Rock Pueblo was inhabited during the second half of the thirteenth century A.D. (Kuckelman, ed. by 2000). The village was probably founded in A.D. 1256, or a little later, and was occupied until sometime after A.D. 1274, which is the latest date for the site. However, the village might have been occupied until the mid-1280s (www.crowcanyon.org). The latest date for the site corresponds with the latest dates from sites in Mesa Verde National Park, although the latest date for the entire region is 1280.

The earliest tree-ring date for Castle Rock Pueblo is for Structure 204, a partly underground kiva that was at the southwestern edge of the settlement. In A.D. 1260/1261 Structure 206 and nearby structures were built in the south-central part of the site south of the butte. Structures north of the butte such as structures 302, 306, possibly Structure 305 (a tower) and another tower were built about A.D. 1264 (Kuckelman, ed. by 2000).

The available tree-ring dates suggest that the settlement was not built quickly, or entirely in the first stage of occupation in late A.D. 1950s and early 1260s. In the 1260s, building activity increased and probably continued until the village was depopulated. Kuckelman (ed. by 2000) suggests also that "all structures in the village except Structures 108, 126, 304, and 308 were still in use until the occupation ended."

The latest tree-ring date, A.D. 1274vv, comes from Structure 304, a kiva north of the butte in the north-central part of the site. This date indicates that this kiva was either built or repaired after A.D. 1274. It is probable that other structures near this kiva were also still in use during this time, along with Structure 307/310, a tower (Kuckelman, ed. by 2000).

## Description of the site

### *Site layout*

Castle Rock Pueblo is situated on and around the base of a 20 m (65 ft.) tall butte, the lower section of which is Entrada Formation; the sandstone slickrock below the talus slope Navajo Formation (Varien, ed. by 1999). Most structures were built on the talus slope north and south of the butte and some are abutted to the butte face. Some buildings were also constructed on the butte itself and on a large boulder south of the butte.

The site consists of more than 60 structures, including a minimum of 40 rooms, 16 kivas, nine towers, a D-shaped building, several sections of enclosing or retaining walls, at least two plazas, and several midden areas (Kuckelman, ed. by 2000; www.crowcanyon.org). However, because a great deal of the rubble was removed from the site in historic times, it is difficult to estimate the exact number of structures that might have been present during the occupation of the village.

One possible plaza is near the north edge of the site; the other possible plaza is south of the butte, and the southern edge of this plaza is defined partly by "an intentionally placed row of boulders" (Kuckelman, ed. by 2000). At least two dams and associated reservoirs are located in an arroyo that runs along the north edge of the site. This village was probably the center of a larger community of settlements in the Sand Canyon locality, which includes Sand Canyon itself, East Rock Canyon, other smaller canyons, and other areas. There were probably about 40 small habitations in the vicinity of Castle Rock Pueblo.

### *Access to the site*

The access to particular parts of the village differed, because some structures were at the base of the butte and some were on top. The structures most difficult to access were atop the butte, on a ledge midway up the north face of the butte, and on a boulder south of the butte. Structures on top of the butte could have been accessed from the northern face of the via ladders on the roofs of two towers: Structure 305 and Structure 307/310

(Kuckelman, ed. by 2000). At the base of the north face of the butte, a cluster of structures had been built as additional protection along the access route to the top of the butte. These buildings were abutted to the north face of the butte and thus faced north, which was not typical of construction during the Pueblo III period. Access to the top of the butte was not possible from the south.

### *Availability of water*

The primary water source was McElmo Creek, approximately 600 m (2000 ft.) south of the site. This creek might have served as a permanent or at least a seasonal water source during the occupation of the village in the thirteenth century A.D. (Kuckelman, ed. by 2000; Varien, ed. by 1999). The floodplain of McElmo Creek could have served as a good farming area during the Puebloan occupation of the area.

The remains of two stone-and-earth dams are approximately 40 m (131 ft.) north of the site in an unnamed intermittent drainage. They were probably built by the inhabitants of Castle Rock Pueblo to impound runoff relatively near the village (Kuckelman, ed. by 2000; Kuckelman et al. 2002). The dams were constructed in a natural bedrock drainage from which runoff drained southward, along the north edge of Castle Rock Pueblo.

### *Evidence of defensive architecture*

Some areas of the settlement were enclosed or bound by stone walls. The wall was probably not tall, although it is difficult to estimate the original height. Segments of this wall were documented along the north and south edges of the site (Kuckelman, ed. by 2000; www.crowcanyon.org).

An estimated nine towers were constructed at Castle Rock Pueblo; this estimate resulted from excavations conducted at the site from 1990 to 1994 by the Crow Canyon Archaeological Center (Kuckelman, ed. by 2000; Kuckelman et al. 2002: 488). Six of these (structures 207/208, 301, 305, 307/310, 401, and 404/409/410) were tested during excavations, and three additional structures are known only from nineteenth-century photographs taken by W.H. Jackson (Kuckelman, ed. by 2000). Structure 207/208 is between the southwestern face of the butte and a boulder, and it is protected by these natural barriers. Structure 307/310 was situated on a ledge midway up the north face of the butte. Structure 305 abuts the north face of the butte. Structure 401 is positioned at the northwest edge of the site, whereas Structure 404/409/410 is in the northern part of the site and is attached to a section of village-enclosing wall. All of these structures might have been two stories tall; however, this is difficult to prove given the current state of preservation. An exception is Structure 305, for which there is evidence of a second story, and the 3.5-m-tall Structure 404/409/410 which shows evidence of a second or even third story in historic photographs (Kuckelman, ed. by 2000; www.crowcanyon.org).

Towers were constructed in different areas of the settlement. At least three were built on the top of the butte-Structure 301 plus two structures known only from historic photographs. The others were built on the northern and western sides of the village. Structure 301 might have protected the northern approach to the butte (Kuckelman, ed. by 2000). Structures 305 and 307/310, along with Structure 301, might have also protected access to the butte from the north. Kuckelman (ed. by 2000) concluded that the structures considered to be towers at Castle Rock Pueblo were built to increase the defensibility of the village; at least three were situated on the butte top in difficult-to-access locations. Structure 408 might have been a tower, but even though it was circular, it was not very tall (Kuckelman, ed. by 2000). Its location is indicative of defense.

The number and locations of loopholes originally present in the village is difficult to estimate because of the poor preservation of much of the architecture and of the limited exposure of walls during testing by Crow Canyon. Two loopholes were documented in Structure 404, a tower, and they were angled north and east or southeast across the drainage that delineates the northern boundary of the settlement (www.crowcanyon.org).

## Conclusions

Castle Rock Pueblo located in Lower Sand Canyon area north of McElmo Creek in the Mesa Verde region was the large village (community center) in the thirteenth century A.D. The village was probably founded in the A.D. 1250s, as indicated by tree-ring dates. The latest tree-ring date is A.D. 1274vv. The total number of residents has been estimated at about 75–150 (Kuckelman, ed. by 2000). Excavations conducted in the 1990s revealed that the settlement was attacked as indicated by human remains representing at least 41 unburied individuals, some showing signs of violent death, as well as burned structures. These data correspond with the oral tradition of Hopi people that was recorded in the 1870s about an ancient battle that could have taken place at Castle Rock (Kuckelman, ed. by 2000; Kuckelman et al. 2002). This attack probably ended the occupation of Castle Rock Pueblo, similarly like a contemporaneous community center (Sand Canyon Pueblo) located northwest of Castle Rock Pueblo (e.g., Kuckelman et al. 2002).

A rock art panel on the north face of the butte depicts three people fighting (Figs 50, 51). "The three figures have rectangular or globular bodies that may represent warriors' shields. The figure in the center and the figure on the right hold bows and arrows, stand back-to-back, and appear to be defending each other. The figure in the center seems to be shooting an arrow toward the figure on the left The figure on the left, with his legs in front of him, appears to be falling away from the central figure and holding up a shield in defense against the arrow" (Kuckelman, ed. by 2000).

Kuckelman infers that this panel was created during the occupation of the settlement, or it was made by the survivors or attackers after the battle at Castle Rock Pueblo that forced the surviving residents to migrate.

Although the location of Castle Rock varies in some respects from other large sites in the region, the site shares some traits such as the presence of public architecture (for example, a D-shaped structure and plazas) and evidence of a concern for the protection of the inhabitants of the pueblo. A concern for defense can be seen in the location of the settlement on and around a 20-m-tall butte as well as in the presence of loopholes, several sections of village-enclosing walls, and nine towers, at least three of which are located on the butte top. Access to the village was protected from the south and north by particular structures, and access to the top of the butte was restricted by the presence of structures at the base of the butte, and the necessity of using ladders on rooftops.

Table 1. Location, elevation, and aspect of the large sites analyzed in the book

| No. | Site name | Site type/location | Elevation above sea level | Aspect of the site |
|---|---|---|---|---|
| 1 | 5MT5 (Yellow Jacket Pueblo) | Mesa top and canyon-rim | 2072 m (6800 ft.) | South |
| 2 | 5MT338 (Cannonball Ruins) | Canyon-rim settlement | 1634 m (5360 ft.) | South and southwest |
| 3 | 5MT604 (Goodman Point Pueblo) | Canyon-rim settlement | 1920 m (ca. 6300 ft.) | Different (mostly south?) |
| 4 | 5MT765 (Sand Canyon Pueblo) | Canyon-rim settlement | 2073 m (6800 ft.) | Mostly south |
| 5 | 5MT1000 (Seven Towers Pueblo) | Canyon-rim settlement | 1871 m (6140 ft.) | South and southwest |
| 6 | 5MT1825 (Castle Rock Pueblo) | Site on top and around a butte | 1682 m (5520 ft.) | Different (mostly south) |
| 7 | 5MT5006 (Yucca House) | Canyon-rim settlement | 1760–1804 m (5775–5920 ft.) | Different |
| 8 | 5MT11842 (Woods Canyon Pueblo) | Canyon-rim settlement | 1682 m (5520 ft.) | Mostly south |
| 9 | 5MV615 (Balcony House) | Cliff dwelling | 2085m (6840 ft.) | East and northeast |
| 10 | 5MV625 (Cliff Palace) | Cliff dwelling | 2070 m (6790 ft.) | West, southwest, and partly south |
| 11 | 5MV640 (Spruce Tree House) | Cliff dwelling | 2097 m (6880 ft.) | West and southwest |
| 12 | 5MV650 (Square Tower House) | Cliff dwelling | 2073 m (6800 ft.) | South and southwest |
| 13 | 5MV 1200 (Long House) | Cliff dwelling | 2128 m (6983 ft.) | South and partly southeast |
| 14 | 5MV1229 (Mug House) | Cliff dwelling | 2195 m (7200 ft.) | West and partly southwest |
| 15 | M-1, M-2, M-3 (Moon House Complex) | Cliff dwelling | 1707 m (5600 ft.) | South and southeast |

## V.2.2. Small sites in Lower Sand Canyon locality

During the thirteenth century A.D., the largest settlement or community center in the Lower Sand Canyon (Castle Rock Community) locality was Castle Rock Pueblo (Site

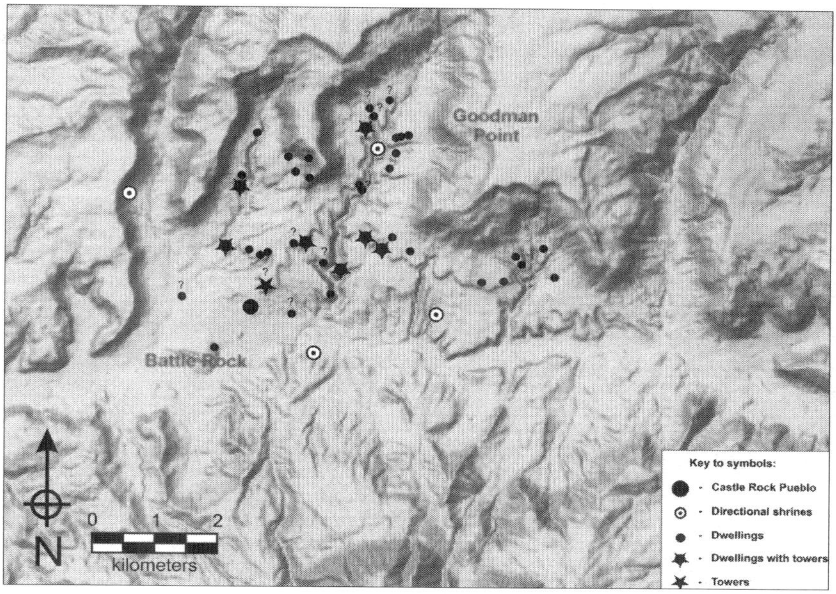


Fig. 24. Location of sites in the Lower Sand Canyon area dating between A.D. 1225 and 1290 analyzed in this book (sites with question mark are with not certain chronology) (drawing by M. and M. Przybyła)

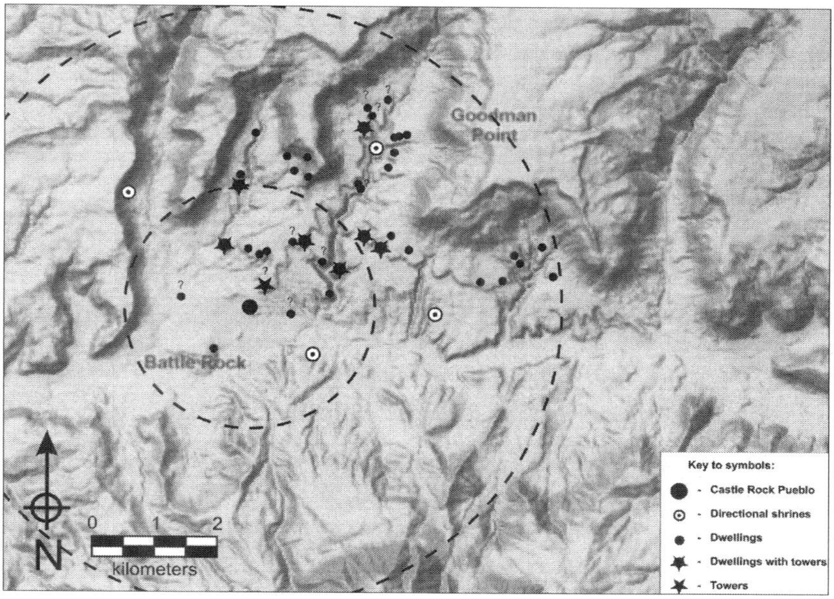


Fig. 25. Map showing 1-, 2-, and 4-kilometer radii centered on Castle Rock Pueblo, showing the distances between the community center and the small sites in the community (drawing by M. and M. Przybyła)

5MT1825). In the vicinity of Castle Rock Pueblo, there were several dozen smaller sites, including habitations as well as limited activity sites (Adler and Metcalf 1992; Gleichman and Gleichman 1989; Lipe and Varien 2003). I use the term "Castle Rock Community" to refer to Castle Rock Pueblo and numerous small sites in the same vicinity in the Lower Sand Canyon area (Figs 24, 25) (Ortman 2008: 129; Palonka 2010; also personal communication: William D. Lipe, Mark D. Varien, and Scott G. Ortman).

## Location of sites in Lower Sand Canyon locality

The precise boundary of the community is difficult to establish. In my analysis of sites from the Lower Sand Canyon area, I estimate the approximate area of the Castle Rock community on the basis of Varien's estimates of the size of community catchments in the Mesa Verde region (Varien 1999; Varien and Potter 2008) and the boundary of the Castle Rock community follows Ortman's (2008) proposal of the boundary as marked by four shrines. The shrines are located to the north, west, east, and south of Castle Rock Pueblo. The shrines that Ortman considers community boundary makers are stone circles approximately 5 m in diameter, each is situated "in a significant location, one that relates Castle Rock to the cardinal directions, the surrounding landscape, and prominent topographic features on the horizon" (Ortman 2008: 134). The topographic features mentioned by Ortman may be, for example, mountains such as Sleeping Ute Mountain. Three of these shrines or stone circles open toward Castle Rock Pueblo and one opens toward Sleeping Ute Mountain. The shrines considered community boundary markers had ritual and spiritual functions and are also known from the ethnographic literature of different Pueblo societies such as the Hopi, Zuni, Keres, and Tewa (Ortiz 1969; Ortman 2008: 138–146). These shrines probably functioned as well in the period before contact with Europeans (Ortman 2008).

The western shrine (Site 5MT15184) is at the eastern edge of a mesa above Rock Canyon and Rock Creek approximately 4 km northwest of Castle Rock Pueblo. The eastern shrine is situated on top of a low hill above McElmo Creek 4 km east of the pueblo. The northern shrine (Site 5MT2796) is about 4 km north of the pueblo "on a knoll above the inner gorge of Sand Canyon." The southern shrine is "on top of a ridge where the northern slopes of Ute Mountain meet McElmo Creek" about 2 km southeast of Castle Rock Pueblo (Ortman 2008: 134–138).

The Lower Sand Canyon area is in Montezuma County, in the southwestern part of Colorado, and encompasses the central and southern part of Sand Canyon and smaller canyons, especially East Rock Canyon (East Fork Canyon) that drains southward toward McElmo Creek, the seasonal stream and small canyon between Sand Canyon and Goodman Canyon. McElmo Creek is in the southern part of Lower Sand Canyon, flows westward from the Montezuma Valley, and empties into the San Juan River in southeastern Utah.

The Lower Sand Canyon area is part of a larger area within the central Mesa Verde Region called the Sand Canyon locality (Gleichman and Gleichman 1992; Lipe 1992; Ortman 2008). North of the Lower Sand Canyon locality is the McElmo Dome and to the south is Sleeping Ute Mountain. Ortman (2008: 127–128) also describes Lower Sand Canyon as "neatly defined as a low-lying area of red-rock canyons, with the slopes of Sleeping Ute Mountain rising to more than 2,800 m (10,000 ft.) on the southern horizon." The elevation of the area ranges between about 1700–1800 m (5600–5800 ft.) near the McElmo Creek floodplain and about 1650 m (5400 ft.) in East Rock (East Fork) Canyon to about 1850 m (about 6100 ft.) and about 2100 m (7000 ft.) in the northern part of the area (Adler and Metcalf 1992: 52–53; Gleichman and Gleichman 1992: 58–62, Fig. 3.1; Ortman 2008: 127).

During the Puebloan occupation of the Lower Sand Canyon area the McElmo floodplain was probably a good place to farm (Lipe and Varien 2003: 1–2). Other areas near particular sites also had good farming potential, especially those on uplands or other areas of adequate rainfall in the higher part of the Lower Sand Canyon area. The requirements for successful farming in the area are primarily a minimum of 120 frost-free days and about 14 inches of precipitation per year. This amount of rain falls at elevations above 1800 m, or 6000 ft. (Adams and Petersen 1999; Lipe and Varien 2003), and farmlands at lower elevations probably relied on a high water table or on runoff from slopes or stream courses (Lipe and Varien 2003).

Below is a short analysis of 42 small sites based on detailed analysis presented in the doctoral dissertation (Palonka 2009) within the Castle Rock community of the Lower Sand Canyon locality that date from the thirteenth century A.D. as indicated by pottery types, architectural styles, and tree-ring dates, although tree-ring dates are available for few sites from this area. The data were obtained primarily from an electronic database prepared by Scott G. Ortman, Crow Canyon Archaeological Center, Cortez, Colorado, and from an analysis of survey site files obtained courtesy of the Anasazi Heritage Center, Dolores, Colorado, and the Crow Canyon Archaeological Center, Cortez, Colorado, as well as on survey reports (Adler and Metcalf 1992; Gleichman and Gleichman 1989), and my personal observations in May 2009 (e.g., Palonka 2010).

The data for each site described below derive mostly from survey site files (Archaeological Component Form, Inventory Record of Site, Stabilization Inventory Form, Cultural Resource Reevaluation Form, Management Data Form, Prehistoric Archaeological Component Form) and Final Nomination Form or National Register Files obtained courtesy of the Bureau of Land Management, Anasazi Heritage Center, and through the invaluable help of William D. Lipe (Department of Anthropology, Washington State University, Pullman), Mark D. Varien, Scott G. Ortman (Crow Canyon Archaeological Center), and Linda Farnsworth (Anasazi Heritage Center, Bureau of Land Management).

The data in the above-mentioned site files derive from surveys undertaken in the area since 1965 (see below) and were prepared by a variety of individuals who will not be cited in the text. Data from other sources and publications are cited in the text. These additional data come from unpublished survey reports (Adler and Metcalf 1992; Gleichman and Gleichman 1989), National Register of Historic Places Registration Form for Sand Canyon Archaeological District (Lipe and Varien 2003) and the Sand Canyon Archaeological Project Site Testing Program (Varien, ed. by 1999). Also, the history of archaeological investigations conducted at these sites is similar, and to avoid repetition will be presented only once.

The small sites in Lower Sand Canyon locality may be divided geographically on several groups located in canyons and areas between canyons (Palonka 2010):

1) Lower part of Sand Canyon that includes sites: 5MT125, 5MT126, 5MT127 (Vision House), 5MT129, 5MT135 (Sunny Alcove), 5MT181 (Mad Dog Tower),

5MT182, 5MT185, 5MT186 (Corncob Pueblo), 5MT257, 5MT261, 5MT262 (Saddlehorn Hamlet), 5MT1804, 5MT2796, 5MT2797, 5MT2801, with additional at least six sites with uncertain chronology (PII or PIII period): 5MT132, 5MT133, 5MT134, 5MT263, 5MT10992, 5MT10366;

2) East Fork of Rock Creek Canyon that includes sites 5MT264 (The Gallery, Serpent Quarters) with sites: 5MT1842 and 5MT1843, 5MT265, 5MT1826, 5MT1827, 5MT1828, 5MT1829, 5MT1831, Sites 5MT2799 and 5MT2800, 5MT2636, 5MT13251, 5MT14659, and site with uncertain chronology 5MT11023;

3) An unnamed canyon between Sand Canyon and Goodman Canyon that includes sites: 5MT1805 (Two Story House), 5MT1806 (Kiva in the Sky), 5MT1807 (Crescent House), 5MT1808 (Two Room House), 5MT1824, 5MT2644;

4) Sites located south of Castle Rock Pueblo on Battle Rock: 5MT1999, 5MT2000, 5MT2001, and 5MT2002.

Table 2. Location, site type, elevation, aspect of site, and distance to the nearest water source and possible function of the thirteenth century A.D. (Late Pueblo III) sites in Castle Rock Community. Distance to water sources is estimated on the basis of survey data

| No. | Site name | Elevation (above sea level) | Site type/Possible function | Aspect of the site | Distance to the nearest water source |
|---|---|---|---|---|---|
| 1 | 5MT125 | 1792 m (5880 ft.) | Cliff dwelling with isolated tower/ Habitation-lookout | South and south-east | 25 m (24 m below the site) |
| 2 | 5MT126 | 1792 m (5880 ft.) | Cliff dwelling/ Habitation single | South and south-west | 25 m (18 m below the site) |
| 3 | 5MT127 (Vision House) | 1798 m (5900 ft.) | Cliff dwelling/ Habitation multiple | South and south-east | In the site |
| 4 | 5MT129 | 1795 m (5890 ft.) | Cliff dwelling/ Habitation single | South | 275 m (64 m below the site) |
| 5 | 5MT135 (Sunny Alcove) | 1792 m (5880 ft.) | Cliff dwelling/ Habitation single | South and south-west | 20–40 m |
| 6 | 5MT181 (Mad Dog Tower) | 1789 m (8870 ft.) | Tower with associ-ated structures/ Habitation-lookout | Southeast | 425 m (55 m below the site) |
| 7 | 5MT182 | 1795 m (5890 ft.) | Cliff dwelling/ Habitation single | South | In the site and 45 m from the site |
| 8 | 5MT186 (Corncob Pueblo) | 1762 m (5781 ft.) | Cliff dwelling/ Habitation multiple | South | In the site and very close to it |
| 9 | 5MT257 | 1713 m (5620 ft.) | Dwelling on a bench against the cliff/ Habitation multiple | South | 75 m (probable also closer) |

| | | | | | |
|---|---|---|---|---|---|
| 10 | 5MT261 | 1707 m (5600 ft.) | Cliff dwelling with isolated tower/ Habitation-lookout multiple | South | 122 m (30 m below the site) |
| 11 | 5MT262 (Saddlehorn Hamlet) | 1769 m (5800 ft.) | Cliff dwelling with isolated tower/ Habitation-lookout | South and south-west | 475 m (77 m below the site) |
| 12 | 5MT264 (The Gallery, Serpent Quarters) (included Site 5MT1842 and 5MT1843) | 1707 m (5600 ft.) | Cliff dwelling with isolated tower (Site 5MT1842)/ Habitation-lookout multiple | South and south-east | 3 m |
| 13 | 5MT265 | 1768 m (5800 ft.) | Cliff dwelling/ Habitation multiple | East | A few meters east of the site |
| 14 | 5MT1804 | 1767 m (5797 ft.) | Cliff dwelling/ Habitation single | West and south | ? |
| 15 | 5MT1805 (Two Story House/Broken Beam Pueblo) | 1804 m (5915 ft.) | Cliff dwelling/ Habitation multiple | South | ? |
| 16 | 5MT1806 (Kiva in the Sky) | 1804 m (5915 ft.) | Cliff dwelling/ Habitation single | South | ? |
| 17 | 5MT1807 (Crescent House) | 1804 m (5915 ft.) | Cliff dwelling/ Habitation single | South and west | In the site |
| 18 | 5MT1808 (Two Room House) | 1804 m (5915 ft.) | Cliff dwelling/ Habitation single | South and south-east | In the site |
| 19 | 5MT1824 | 1800 m (5900 ft.) | Cliff dwelling/ Habitation indetermi-nate | Southwest | In the site |
| 20 | 5MT1825 (Castle Rock Pueblo) | 1682 m (5520 ft.) | Site on top and around a butte/ Habitation-community center | Different (mostly south) | 600 m south of the site |
| 21 | 5MT1826 | 1750–1770 m (ca. 5800 ft.) | Cliff dwelling/talus slope/Habitation single | South and south-east | Probably a few meters of the site |
| 22 | 5MT1827 | 1750–1770 m (ca. 5800 ft.) | Cliff dwelling/talus slope/Habitation single | South and south-west | Several hundred meters west of the site |
| 23 | 5MT1828 | 1750–1770 m (ca. 5800 ft.) | Cliff dwelling/talus slope/Habitation single | Southwest | Probably a few meters of the site |
| 24 | 5MT1829 | 1795 m (5892 ft.) | Cliff dwelling/ Habitation multiple | West | Several hundred meters west of the site |

| | | | | | |
|---|---|---|---|---|---|
| 25 | 5MT1831 | 1700 m (5600 ft.) | Cliff dwelling/ Habitation single | South | In the site |
| 26 | 5MT1999 | 1706 m (5600 ft.) | Cliff dwelling/ Habitation indetermi-nate | East and north-east | Near the site |
| 27 | 5MT2000 | 1706 m (5600 ft.) | Cliff dwelling/ Habitation single | East and north-east | Near the site |
| 28 | 5MT2001 | 1706 m (5600 ft.) | Cliff dwelling/ Habitation indetermi-nate | East and north-east | Near the site |
| 29 | 5MT2002 | 1706 m (5600 ft.) | Cliff dwelling/ Habitation multiple | East and north-east | Near the site |
| 30 | 5MT2636 | 1877 m (6160 ft.) | Cliff dwelling/ Habitation multiple | South | Probably a few meters of the site |
| 31 | 5MT2644 | 1774 m (5820 ft.) | Site on talus slope/ Habitation single | West | Probably a few meters of the site |
| 32 | 5MT 2796 | 1785 m (5855 ft.) | Site on a knoll/Shrine | Southeast | 300 m north of the site |
| 33 | 5MT2797 | ca. 1790 m (8870 ft.) | Tower with associ-ated structures/ Habitation-lookout multiple | Mostly south | Probably a few meters of the site |
| 34 | 5MT2799 and 5MT2800 | 1798 m (5900 ft.) | Tower with associ-ated structures/ Lookout | South and south-east | Below the site |
| 35 | 5MT2801 | 1676 m (5500 ft.) | Cliff dwelling/ Habitation single | South | 350 m south of the site |
| 36 | 5MT10992 | 1655 m (5430 ft.) | Site on talus slope/ Habitation single | West | 260 m from the site |
| 37 | 5MT11023 | 1780 m (5840 ft.) | Site on talus slope/ Habitation single | Southwest | 457 m from the site |
| 38 | 5MT13251 | 1843 m (6049 ft.) | Site on talus slope/ Habitation single | South and south-east | 442 m from the site |
| 39 | 5MT14659 | | Site on talus slope/ Habitation single | | ? |
| 40 | 5MT 15184 | | Edge of a mesa/ Shrine | | ? |
| 41 | Not known 5MT number | | Top of a low hill/ Shrine | | ? |
| 42 | Not known 5MT number | | Top of a ridge/Shrine | | ? |

# Chapter VI

# SUMMARY AND CONCLUSIONS

On the basis of the analytic data contained in Chapter V, as well as comparison with other areas and cultures presented elsewhere in this book, I conclude that in the thirteenth century A.D. in the central Mesa Verde region, population aggregation, specific architectural characteristics, and choice of site location were determined to a great extent by a need for defense and protection for both the residents of the area and their food supplies. Archaeological data – primarily excavation and survey reports and my own observations in the central Mesa Verde region, particularly in the lower portion of the Sand Canyon locality – are supported by other sources of information that include ethnographic and ethnohistoric records and Native American oral traditions. I also use ethnographic analogy with indigenous cultures in other parts of the Southwest and North America as well as other areas of the world, mostly prehistoric non-state societies in central-eastern and southern Europe.

My conclusions consist of several aspects of site configuration and architecture at large sites, mostly community centers, across the central Mesa Verde region as well as at small sites in the Castle Rock community. The associated data are presented in Chapter V and include site location, layout, access, availability of water, and presence of defensive structures and features such as towers, protecting walls, loopholes, and tunnels. In addition, I consider the possible identity of the attackers against whom the settlements in the central Mesa Verde region were protected and, through the manifestation of defensive architecture, I attempt to determine the scale of influence and impact of the conflict and violence on the depopulation of the Mesa Verde region near the end of the thirteenth century A.D.

## VI.1. LOCATION OF SITES AND THEIR ACCESSIBILITY

Many researchers have indicated that during the thirteenth century A.D. in the central Mesa Verde region settlement locations shifted from the mesa tops and uplands to canyon rims, cliff alcoves, and overhangs (e.g. Kuckelman 2002, 2006; Lipe and Varien 1999; Varien 1999; Varien et al. 1996). My analyses of large and small sites in the region focus on site location as one factor that may inform us about defensive actions and attempts by Ancestral Pueblo people to protect themselves. Site location is considered by archaeologists and anthropologists to be one of the most important and significant indications of attempts to defend and protect people and is often perceived in archaeological and anthropological theory as evidence of threat (Hard and Roney 2007; Jankuhn 2004; Keeley 1996; Keeley et al. 2007; Kurnatowska 2008; LeBlanc 1999; Otterbein 1970; Poleski 2008; Wilcox et al. 2001b). This phenomenon may be observed in many non-state and state societies cross-culturally (e.g., Ember and Ember 1992; Hard and Roney 2007; Otterbein 1970) as briefly discussed in Chapter III and which revealed an association between defensible site location and evidence of danger. Defense against a threat often involved relocating a settlement to a higher elevation or seeking protection in refuge settlements in times of danger.

This theory is supported by archaeological and ethnohistoric data for various Pueblo groups through time (e.g., Ahlstrom and Roberts 1995; Haas and Creamer 1993; LeBlanc 1999, 2001; McMahon 2000; Snead 2008; Wilcox 2005: 24–35; Wilcox et al. 2001a, 2001b) and for other native societies such as the Navajo, who constructed pueblitos, and the Apache, who built breastworks, in which defensible locations were used especially during times of danger (Adams et al. 2001; Towner 1999, 2004; Towner et al. 2001). Oral traditions of contemporary Native Americans also tell of moving to defensible locations during times of danger (Ferguson and Colwell-Chanthaphonh 2006: 116, 163; Haas and Creamer 1997: 253). As seen in archaeological and ethnographic data, some prehistoric and historic pueblos were relocated to previous locations, such as valley floors, after a threat such as the Pueblo Revolt of 1680 ended, but other settlements, such as those of the Hopi and Acoma, remained on their isolated and difficult-to-access mesa tops (Ferguson 2002: 36, 41; Haas and Creamer 1996: 206; Knaut 1997; Liebmann et al. 2005; Preucel 2002).

Also, data for many defensive sites of prehistoric and protohistoric non-state societies dating from the Neolithic, Bronze Age, Iron Age, and early Medieval Europe described in Chapter III demonstrate the widespread usage of strongholds and other types of defensive sites. Many of these sites were located in places difficult to access, such as hilltops or on islands in lakes, that were inhabited either permanently or only in times of danger. During the Bronze Age, Iron Age, and early Medieval times, the construction of defensive, fortified sites was somewhat dependant on the settlement stability, social change, and economic power necessary to build these fortifications (Buko 2005: 89; Dulinicz 2001:186–187; Kobyliński 1988: 206; Kurnatowska 2008: 313–315; Urbańczyk 2000). In many cases, the number of entry gates was limited, and for numerous sites, such as the Early Iron Age Biskupin stronghold in the Wielkopolska region of Poland, only one entry route existed (Kozłowski and Kaczanowski 1998: 181–182).

The large sites in the central Mesa Verde region examined in this book, most of which were community centers, follow the characteristic location pattern of sites constructed during the late Pueblo III period described briefly above and in more detail in Chapter V. Of the 15 sites examined, seven – sites 5MV615 (Balcony House), 5MV625 (Cliff Palace), 5MV640 (Spruce Tree House), 5MV650 (Square Tower House), 5MV1200 (Long House), 5MV1229 (Mug House), and M-1, M-2, M-3 (Moon House Complex) – are located in rather difficult-to-access cliff alcoves and overhangs. The Moon House Complex is on Cedar Mesa in southeastern Utah, and the other six are on Chapin and Wetherill mesas in Mesa Verde National Park in southwestern Colorado. The elevation of these cliff dwellings ranges between 1707 m (5600 ft.) and 2195 m (7200 ft.) while most of the sites are located on the elevation over the 2000 m and only one site (Moon House) is located on the elevation of 1707 m. They are oriented in a variety of directions: five sites face southwest, south, and west; Moon House faces south and southeast; and Balcony House faces east and northeast. The orientation of sites to the west-southwest was probably dictated by the need for maximum solar exposure during the winter and maximum shade during the summer (Morgan 1994: 139).

Access to these settlements was relatively difficult and only one or two main trails led to most of these alcoves. For many cliff dwellings, access routes allowed entry at both ends of the alcove. Only one route provided access to Balcony House and Site M-1 of the Moon House Complex. Access to Balcony House was further restricted in the final years of occupation when the construction of a massive masonry wall created a narrow tunnel entryway. Tree-ring dates indicate that this tunnel was probably built in the A.D. 1270s (Fiero 1998: 35; Parks and Dean 1998: 11–12). Access to nearly all of these sites included at least one route with places that could be traversed only with the aid of ladders or by means of hand-and-toe holds carved into the cliff face, or even ropes (Cattanach 1980; Ferguson 1996; Fewkes 1911: 14, 23; Fiero 1998: 35; Nordenskiöld 1990 [1893]; Rohn 1971; Rohn and Ferguson 2006).

Access was also restricted within some cliff dwellings. The upper ledges in Long House and the highest structures in Square Tower House are difficult to access even from within the alcove. Communication between different areas of some cliff dwellings was difficult, even where structures rested at the same level, such as in Balcony House (Fiero 1998: 33–34), Cliff Palace (Nordby 2001: 107; Roberts 1999), and Mug House (Rohn 1965: 66; 1971: 31, 39–40), where probably only one route allowed access between the northern and southern parts of the settlements. Some villages were additionally divided by walls that increased the difficulty of communication between room suites or households (these divisions did restrict access and movement, which may be significant for defense).

Six of the sites examined, sites 5MT5 (Yellow Jacket Pueblo), 5MT338 (Cannonball Ruin), 5MT604 (Goodman Point Pueblo), 5MT765 (Sand Canyon Pueblo), 5MT1000 (Seven Towers Pueblo), and 5MT11842 (Woods Canyon Pueblo), were constructed on canyon rims or canyon heads and enclosed springs, and most of these springs drained through the central part of the settlement. Site 5MT5006 (Yucca House) encloses two springs and was constructed partly on both sides and the rim of a very small canyon created by runoff from the springs. Site 5MT1825 (Castle Rock Pueblo) is located on the top and around the base of a 20-meter-tall butte that is the most prominent landform in the immediate area. The elevations of the large sites examined in this book range from about 1634 m (5360 ft.) to 2073 m (6800 ft.). The sites face various directions; however, most of the structures within these sites probably faced south.

It is difficult to determine the exact number of access routes to these villages; however, some evidence, such as the presence of enclosing walls and canyon-rim locations, suggests that few entryways existed for villages such as Sand Canyon and Goodman Point pueblos; entryway size was reduced late in the occupation of some villages (Kenzle 1993). Most of these habitations were constructed on canyon rims, but portions of the settlements were located on talus slopes below the rims, usually around the spring on both sides of the canyon.

Most of the small sites inferred to have been part of the Castle Rock Community in the lower part of Sand Canyon during the thirteenth century A.D. are located in three canyons: Sand and East Fork canyons, and a small canyon between Sand and Goodman canyons. Castle Rock Pueblo, the community center, is situated between East Fork and Sand canyons, and four other sites inferred to have been part of this community lie south of Castle Rock Pueblo on Battle Rock. One of four directional shrines is located in middle part of Sand Canyon and the other three lie outside Sand Canyon. Of the 42 sites examined (including shrines), 28 are located in difficult-to-access cliff alcoves and associated talus slopes, one (Castle Rock Pueblo) is situated on and around a butte 20 m tall, five lie on talus slopes, three sit atop a knoll, hill, or ridge, three that consist of towers and associated structures rest on relatively flat areas and gentle talus slopes, one site on the edge of the mesa, and one (Site 5MT257) is perched on a difficult-to-access bench against a cliff face. Most of these sites are difficult to access, although the sites with the most restricted access, and that require the use of a ladder several meters long to reach, are located in cliff alcoves. Site 5MT257, on a bench at the top of a steep talus slope, is also difficult to access. The elevations of the sites that formed the Castle Rock Community range from 1655 m (5430 ft.) to 1877 m (6160 ft.). Most face south, southeast, and southwest directions.

Most of the small sites examined in the lower portion of the Sand Canyon locality were accessible by one or two routes. The data suggest that the small sites in cliff alcoves were situated more defensively than the large cliff dwellings described above, in that the use of ladders was required to enter many of them. Hand-and-toe holds are associated with a few sites in the lower portion of the Sand Canyon locality and were found south of Site 5MT2799 (a tower), on the route to a tower at Site 5MT261, and at Site 5MT2801. Walls extend the entire length of the alcove and create only one entryway into sites 5MT256, 5MT1826, 5MT1831, and 5MT2801.

## VI.2. DEFENSIVE ARCHITECTURE AND SITE LAYOUT

Buildings and features that might have functioned as defensive structures in villages in the central Mesa Verde region during the thirteenth century A.D., as well as on other parts of the Colorado Plateau during various times, include mainly towers, protecting walls, village-enclosing walls, tunnels, loopholes, and presumably other constructions such as D-shaped buildings and other tall structures. These elements of the architecture of the Mesa Verde region are briefly characterized in Chapter III and are described for each of the analyzed sites in Chapter V. Although these architectural features might have been designed for uses other than defense, several lines of evidence suggest that a need for defense did stimulate their construction: an increasing number of these architectural features were built in the thirteenth century A.D. (Lipe and Varien 1999; Varien et al. 1996); the structures and features were built in defensible locations; the co-occurrence of nearly all of these features at most of the sites; the construction of these structures and features during a time of environmental perturbations; and the construction of these features during a time of increasing conflict and violence (e.g., LeBlanc 1999; Lekson 2002; Kuckelman 2002; Kuckelman et. al 2000, 2002) as indicated by skeletal evidence of lethal trauma and the destruction of some villages. These multiple lines of evidence lead to the conclusion that the primary function of most of these structures and features was the defense and protection of the inhabitants, the observation of areas outside the settlements, and communication between sites. Of course, these structures and features could have been used for other purposes as well.

It is worth noting that most structures were much taller originally and were taller even as late as the turn of the twentieth century than they are today (e.g., Cattanach 1980: 17, 40–41; Fewkes 1919; Morley 1908: 599). It is difficult to accurately infer the height and appearance of these buildings at the time the villages were inhabited and thus to evaluate their potential for defense; however, it is probable that entry, in the absence of a doorway in the first story, was rather difficult.

One of the main signs concerning possible defensive function of the site may be its size. In the thirteenth century A.D. in the Mesa Verde region many community centers (including most of the large sites analyzed in the book) were relatively large and inhabited by several hundreds of people (e.g., Lipe 2002; Wilshusen 2002). As the settlements became larger, aggregated, and more populated, at least some of them were well-planned in terms of layout and architecture (Lipe and Varien 1999b: 303; Varien et al. 1996: 100–101).

The process of the consolidation and aggregation of settlements is also characteristic trait of many non-state societies during times of danger and warfare, for example it is seen in the archaeological record in Early Medieval central Europe when it was connected with the beginning and the stage of development of stronghold construction (Buko 2005: 412).

## VI.2.1. Walls

Besides constructing sites in locations difficult to access, the construction of palisades, barricades, or stone walls was probably the most efficient and common method of defending villages. Some palisades or stone walls that were probably built for protection were constructed before the thirteenth century A.D. the central Mesa Verde region (Kenzle 1993, 1997; Lipe et al. 1999; Wilshusen 1999a: 180), and many others were built in various areas of the Southwest through time (e.g., Ahlstrom and Roberts 1995: 28–31; Farmer 1957; LeBlanc 1999; Lekson 2002; Schulman 1950; Wilcox 2005: 27–30).

During the Neolithic period in central-eastern and southern Europe numerous defensive settlements incorporated ditches and earthen or wooden enclosures, and they were built in locations that were easy to defend (Jankuhn 2004: 114–117; Keeley 2007: 84–85; Kozłowski, Kaczanowski 1998: 112–113; Kruk 2008). Archaeological and historic data indicate that similar defensive constructions were built later in European prehistory and in early historic times in which various types of fortifications utilizing earth, wood, or stone were the main feature for protecting settlements. Some of the spaces defined by fortifications were used as refuges only in time of attack.

Abundant data indicate that walls enclosed parts of villages or entire villages in the central Mesa Verde region in the thirteenth century A.D. The function, or functions, of these walls might be interpreted in several ways (Kenzle 1993, 1997) and probably varied from village to village. However, it is reasonable to infer that walls or sections of walls that enclosed entire canyon-rim settlements or parts of settlements were constructed to protect the residents or to restrict access into the pueblo (Kenzle 1993). Large canyon-rim sites examined in this book that were almost entirely enclosed by stone walls include Sand Canyon and Goodman Point pueblos, whereas villages partly enclosed by masonry walls include Cannonball Ruin and Yucca House, as well as Seven Towers, Woods Canyon, Castle Rock, and Yellow Jacket pueblos.

At many sites, stone walls linked the ends of successive roomblocks in such a way that roomblocks were incorporated into the line of the wall, and, in numerous cases, the presence of the wall defined nearly the entire boundary of the settlement. Data for some sites indicate that the enclosing walls were built before the adjacent roomblocks; such was the sequence of construction in the eastern part of Goodman Point Pueblo, although in other areas of this village, roomblocks were built first, and sections of village-enclosing wall were abutted to these blocks (Coffey and Kuckelman 2006). The village-enclosing wall around Sand Canyon Pueblo was constructed in large sections (Bradley 1992: 95; Kuckelman, ed. by 2007).

The height of village-enclosing walls, such as the one at Sand Canyon Pueblo, ranged from 0.5–0.6 m to about 2.4–2.5 m (Kuckelman, ed. by 2007). The sections of wall that enclosed Goodman Point Pueblo were at least one story tall (Kuckelman and Coffey 2007). However, the original height of these walls is difficult to determine, because the walls are poorly preserved. The widths of these walls also vary; some of the enclosing walls in the region were single-course dry-laid masonry, but many were probably wet-laid and were double-stone-with-core in cross section (Kenzle 1993). The exposed sections of village-enclosing wall at Sand Canyon Pueblo were 0.50 to 0.75 m wide (Kuckelman, ed. by 2007), and those at Goodman Point Pueblo were 0.50 to 0.60 m wide (Coffey and Kuckelman 2006). At Sand Canyon Pueblo, most exposed sections of wall were constructed of larger stones that were more irregular than those used in other walls exposed at the site, which may indicate that the sections of enclosing wall were built very quickly or "at least without formalized style" (Bradley 1992: 95, 97; Kuckelman, ed. by 2007). A similar situation might have occurred at other villages.

It is difficult to determine the exact number of openings constructed through these walls, although at Sand Canyon and Goodman Point pueblos the number appears to have been as few as possible (Kenzle 1993; Kuckelman, ed. by 2007). More problematic is interpreting protecting walls in cliff dwellings. Many alcoves contain "retaining" walls; however, the functions of these walls are not always easy to determine. Different explanations of the purposes of these structures include leveling the surface of the alcove, protecting the site from erosion and the washing of materials out of the alcove, preventing children from falling out of the shelter, helping to stabilize buildings, and defense. At some sites, such as Balcony House, Spruce Tree House, and Site M-1 in the Moon House Complex, the retaining wall extends the full length of the alcove. In some shelters the wall might have reached the ceiling of the alcove. This was the case at Balcony House (Fiero 1998: 26; Parks and Dean 1998: 11), in which a wall in North Plaza near rooms 4 and 5 extends from the floor to the roof of the alcove and might have been 6.7 m tall, an unusually tall feature in the cliff dwellings at Mesa Verde. In Long House a wall that nearly reached the roof of that alcove in front of Kiva 32 (Kiva I according to Cattanach 1980) was noted by Nordenskiöld (1990 [1893]). Walls were built along the entire length of upper ledges in some cliff dwellings including the upper ledge in Cliff Palace and two ledges in Long House; many of these walls contain loopholes.

In addition to retaining or protecting walls extending the entire length of an alcove in large cliff dwellings, smaller walls separated or protected access to particular buildings or complexes of buildings within villages. Also, walls enclosed particular complexes and roomblocks or were built at the front of particular household units. Such was the case in courtyard complexes J and M and the Speaker Chief's House in Cliff Palace (Nordby 2001), the walls in front of kivas Q and N in Long House (Cattanach 1980: 96–98, 105), and walls that enclosed particular complexes of buildings in Square Tower House (Munson 2008; Nordenskiöld 1990 [1893]). At some sites the use of such walls is associated with the physical division of the villages effected by walls, buildings, or open spaces, such as in Spruce Tree House, Cliff Palace, Mug House, Balcony House, and possibly Long House (Fewkes 1909; Fiero 1998; Nordby 2001; Nordenskiöld 1990 [1893]; Street 2001a). This physical barrier did not divide the village into halves, because in most cases one area contains more rooms and kivas than the other (Fiero 2002). This physical division of sites in the Mesa Verde region is manifested primarily in the architectural division of cliff dwellings, but is also present in canyon-rim settlements in the form of the settlement-bisecting drainage that contains the spring. This division is compared to the social duality present in modern Pueblos and represented by Winter People and Summer People (e.g., Ferguson 1996: 43–45; Nordby 2001; Rohn 1977). At Cliff Palace, Balcony House, and Long House, the creation of the physical dual division probably occurred near the end of the occupation of the village, during building episodes that occurred between A.D. 1278 and 1280 (Fiero 1998: App. C-1; Nordby 2001: 109; Street 2001a, vol. 1: 200).

A drainage bisected all canyon-rim villages was analyzed in this book. Some researchers infer that this was an intentional division of the pueblo by the inhabitants; however, it is difficult to determine if such a division was intentional, or if it was dictated by the need to surround the spring by constructing buildings on both sides of the canyon. The division of the village into two parts by the drainage that contained the spring bisecting Sand Canyon Pueblo has led some researchers to suggest that the settlement was intentionally built in that manner and that the division was an integral part of the site layout (Kuckelman, ed. by 2007).

At small sites in the lower portion of the Sand Canyon locality, in the proposed Castle Rock Community, evidence of retaining walls can be observed below some alcoves. Walls that were built along the entire length of the alcove are visible at sites such as 5MT256, 5MT1826, 5MT1831, and 5MT2801; the only entry into these alcoves is through these walls, and some of the walls reach nearly to the roof of the alcove. At two small cliff dwellings, sites 5MT1826 and 5MT1831, there is not much evidence of permanent habitation within the alcove, although there is evidence of structures below the shelters. These alcoves might have functioned as refuges for inhabitants living below the alcoves and also for people at other nearby small habitations. At other small sites in the area, such as Site 5MT135, room walls that were constructed parallel with the cliff face near the edge of the alcove might have protected the entrance.

## VI.2.2. Towers

Many towers were constructed in the central Mesa Verde region and in other regions of the Southwest, such as the Gallina region of New Mexico and Canyon de Chelly in Arizona, during particular time periods, and they were probably used for purposes such as ceremonies and for monitoring (Johnson 2003; Lipe and Ortman 2000: 110; Rohn 1977; Schulman 1950; Thompson 2004: 29). Some towers are inferred to have been used for defense or communication, or as lookout structures (Kenzle 1993; Lipe and Varien 1999; Thompson 2004; Thompson et al. 1997; Varien et al. 1996; Winter 1975, 1976, 1977). Many towers contained in the sites analyzed in Chapter V were more carefully constructed and incorporated stones that were more carefully pecked than did other buildings at these same sites; the careful construction probably resulted in the superior preservation of these buildings compared to other buildings at the sites. Towers at analyzed sites stood one or more stories tall, and in most towers, the lowermost story was one room. However, at sites 5MT264 and 5MT262, the ground story of the tower probably consisted of two rooms; this is an unusual construction design for this area, however.

Ethnohistoric accounts tell of the use of the tallest structures in the village for defense during attacks-in many settlements, towers were the tallest structures. D-shaped structures were also tall and might have been used defensively during attacks. Winship (1904: 241–242) mentions several sites and ruins no longer inhabited during the early Spanish expeditions that were built like a "fortress" with tall and finely constructed walls. He also quotes Spanish chronicles describing buildings in the Zuni village of Matsaki that were "higher than the others and set up above them like towers" with embrasures and loopholes for defending the roofs of different stories (Spielmann 1994: 51; Winship 1904: 45). During the late 1600s and early 1700s towers in Navajo pueblitos in the northwestern part of New Mexico were important for defense and communication (Bryan 2009; Towner 1999, 2004; Towner et al. 2001). Similarly, the primary functions of towers, usually the tallest structures in the settlements, constructed in Neolithic, Bronze Age, Iron Age, or Medieval defensive sites in Europe, were defense, observation of the surrounding areas, and/or communication with other settlements. Some towers were constructed near the gates of the villages (Kozłowski and Kaczanowski 1998: 181–182).

Nearly all of the 15 large sites analyzed in this book contained one or more structures that might be called towers. Towers were more numerous in canyon-rim settlements than in cliff dwellings possibly because of the greater space available for construction in canyon-rim settlements. There are 19 towers at Yellow Jacket Pueblo, 15 at Woods Canyon Pueblo, 14 at Sand Canyon Pueblo, 11 at Seven Towers Pueblo, nine at Castle Rock Pueblo, and a few towers in each of the other analyzed canyon-rim settlements. A relatively smaller number of towers, usually two to four, are found in large cliff dwellings.

At least some of the towers in large villages were probably used for defense, as indicated by their strategic positions at the extreme ends of alcoves at the only entryways into the cliff dwellings. Towers were constructed at the ends of Long House, Cliff Palace, and Spruce Tree House. Other towers were built along the outer portions of village-enclosing walls in canyon-rim settlements such as Sand Canyon Pueblo, Cannonball Ruin, and Woods Canyon Pueblo. Some towers were located higher than the other buildings in the pueblo; at Castle Rock Pueblo, towers were constructed on top of the butte and on a ledge midway up the north face of the butte. Towers marked the boundaries of particular complexes within canyon-rim villages such as Yellow Jacket Pueblo, where four or five towers were constructed at the corners of the great tower complex (Block 1200).

The function of some towers, such at those at Cannonball Ruin and Woods Canyon Pueblo, that are located in canyon bottoms or on large boulders below the canyon rim, is problematic; the use of these towers for defense is questionable, because the structures sit below the canyon rims and mesa tops. However, some canyon bottoms are more easily traversed than steep talus slopes or mesa tops. If attackers approached a canyon-head village by traveling up the canyon bottom, the location of the towers below the canyon rim and the fact that they face down the canyon would have made them useful as defensive structures. Such might have been the case at sites in Hovenweep National Monument and some canyon-rim sites analyzed in this book.

The presence of loopholes indicates that some of the towers at the analyzed sites, such as those on the east side of Cannonball Ruin, in the Rim Complex at Woods Canyon Pueblo, or on the butte at Castle Rock Pueblo, could have served as lookouts or for communication and signaling. The use of towers for communication is also proposed for the small sites in the Castle Rock community, because nearly all of these recorded towers were located either within or near sites that were intervisible with sites nearby. At least eight sites in the proposed Castle Rock community – 5MT125, 5MT181 (Mad Dog Tower), 5MT261, 5MT262 (Saddlehorn Hamlet), 5MT1831, 5MT2797, 5MT2799, Castle Rock Pueblo, and 5MT264 (The Gallery or Serpent Quarters) with Site 5MT1842 (tower) – contained towers, or towers were located in proximity to the sites.[10] I propose that the primary function of these towers was communication, because most are intervisible with nearby sites (see subchapter VII.4 for a more detailed description of this evidence), and that the secondary function was defense.

Some towers in the central Mesa Verde region not analyzed in this book, such as towers in Hovenweep National Monument, a free-standing tower on a large boulder or knoll in Navajo Canyon, and a three-story tower at Site 5MV1138 in Mesa Verde National Park, might have been used for communication or defense (LeBlanc 1999: 58–61), because their locations would have rendered them impractical for habitation. Intervisibility has been recorded for towers at Hovenweep National Monument, where three or more towers were intervisible. In addition, some towers could have been seen from sites located on mesa tops, which might in turn have been visible from other sites some distance away; a "long distance network that could have been used for defensive purposes" might have been in operation (Winter 1981: 31). Creating intervisibility and enhancing communication might be considered as one of the examples of efforts to built system of defensive sites within the community.

[10] Some free-standing towers in the lower portion of the Sand Canyon locality are very near habitation sites; the distances range from several to 30 or 40 meters to as much as 100–350 meters. I consider all of these towers to have been associated with the nearest habitation, and in most cases they were treated as such in reports from surveys conducted in the area (Adler and Metcalf 1992; Gleichman and Gleichman 1989, 1992).

## VI.2.3. Loopholes

Small, usually rectangular openings measuring about 8–10 x 12–15 cm, referred to as loopholes, were constructed in many enclosing or protecting walls and in towers at both large and small sites analyzed in this book. Their primary use seems to have been to provide a view of specific locations within the site and of surrounding areas while keeping the viewer concealed. These relatively small openings would have been of little use for shooting arrows, although projectiles might have been launched over the tops of walls.

In Balcony House loopholes are present in Nusbaum's Room 9 (1998b: 9), which is Fiero's Room 12 (Fiero 1998), and are also present above the only entrance to the alcove. This latter loophole provides a view of the access route, and might be part of a lookout platform allowing observation of anyone entering the village (Fiero 1998: 48, App. E-21). In Cliff Palace a few possible loopholes are present in a tower (Room 36), and several such features were recorded in rooms 109 and 104 on the upper ledge (Fewkes 1911: 35; Nordby 2001). The loopholes in Room 104 afford views of the Speaker Chief Complex, the northwest entry point into Cliff Palace, and Kiva W. The unusually angled loopholes in Room 109 allow observation of most of the lower part of Cliff Palace. Loopholes in Spruce Tree House are inferred to have been designed as lookout features (Fewkes 1909: 16; Nordenskiöld 1990 [1893]: 54). Mug House contains three loopholes (Rohn 1971: 54), and a possible loophole has been noted in Square Tower House. Moon House contained loopholes (Bloomer 1989: 47–48), and those in the outer wall of Site M-1 in that same complex provide a view of the main access route to the site (http://www.cs.uwaterloo.ca/~shallit/moonhouse.html). The most numerous loopholes in cliff dwellings analyzed in this book are located in walls on the two upper ledges in Long House (Cattanach 1980); several loopholes are present on the western ledge and 21 such features are located at various levels of the wall on the eastern ledge. These features provided a commanding view of various areas of the village including access points, of the slope and canyon below the alcove, of several nearby sites, and of the top of the mesa opposite the alcove.

Loopholes are also present at canyon-rim sites including at least three such features in the village-enclosing wall at Sand Canyon Pueblo. These openings are oriented at different angles probably to "enable someone from inside the site-enclosing wall to view slightly different areas of the landscape outside the wall" (Kuckelman, ed. by 2007). At Castle Rock Pueblo loopholes in a tower (Structure 404) angle north and east or southeast across an arroyo.

During my survey of Cannonball Ruin in 2009, I noted loopholes in the eastern wall of a rectangular tower in the eastern part of the pueblo that viewed toward the east and southeast at various angles; these features would have offered a good view of the surrounding mesa top and probably farm fields and water control features. Loopholes visible in the extant walls of a tower on a large boulder below the canyon rim in the northern part of the pueblo afford views toward the canyon bottom and the alcove containing the spring.

Loopholes are also present at small sites in the proposed Castle Rock community. This includes small rectangular loopholes in the tower associated with Site 5MT135; at least one of these loopholes provides a view of the only route to the tower and to Site 5MT135 in a cliff alcove. Loopholes were constructed in the southern or outer walls of rooms at Site 5MT186 and in the outer walls of at least one room at Site 5MT261. One possible loophole in a tower at Site 5MT261 affords a view northeast to the main part of the site. A loophole in the tower that is Site 5MT1842, associated with Site 5MT264, provides a view of the main part of the site in a cliff alcove 100 m from the tower.

Some loopholes were constructed in walls built along the edges of alcoves. These features vary in height above the floor of the cave but none are higher than 1 m above the floor. Site 5MT1826 contains several such loopholes; at least four are located west of the entryway, and at least six are east of the entryway. The outer wall of Site 5MT1831 contains at least 12 loopholes, and although most are angled downward, one is level, and one opening is located in the southern wall of the passageway. A possible loophole was noted in a room at Site 5MT1807. Loopholes might also have existed at other sites, especially in walls near the edges of alcoves; however, most of these walls are too poorly preserved to make an accurate assessment. Other and larger openings such as windows might have also have been used as lookouts.

## VI.2.4. Underground tunnels

Underground tunnels connected different structures within sites. Most are rectangular or square and of rather small dimensions. The tunnel in Long House that connected Kiva R and Room 50 measured about 0.4–0.6 m wide and no more than 1 m tall, which would have permitted passage only on hands and knees. Most tunnels linked kivas with rooms or towers, although some connected towers with rooms. Tunnels have been recorded at some large sites as well as at some of the small sites in the Castle Rock Community analyzed in this book. The locations of some of tunnels indicate that they were used to escape from one building to another during sudden attacks, although some tunnels might have been used in other ways, such as to facilitate the sudden and unexpected appearance of people during ceremonies conducted in kivas.

In Cliff Palace, kivas A, B and D are interconnected by tunnels, and one kiva is connected by tunnel to a room. All of these structures are associated with massive, two- or three-story buildings (Nordby 2001: 108–109). This group of structures is situated near the entrance to the pueblo at the southern end of the alcove.

The tunnels in Long House connect Kiva R and Room 50, probably Kiva T and Room 3, and Kiva N both with Kiva M and with Room 87. Kivas R and T are the first structures encountered when entering the alcove from the west or east, respectively. Some of the tunnels in Long House seem to have been designed as "emergency exits" to more secure rooms during an attack on the village. Kiva Q is connected by a tunnel with a small structure, Room 93, and indirectly with Room 60, a circular tower. A tunnel may connect kivas O and K, although this is not strongly supported by archaeological data, and Kiva K and Room 81 might also be linked by a tunnel (Cattanach 1980: 17, 86–87, 93–98, 101, 104–109, 415).

Evidence suggests the existence of a tunnel between Kiva E and Room 21 in Square Tower House (http://archive.cyark.org); however, this kiva is in the central part of the site, at the back of the alcove, and it is surrounded by the relatively high walls of rooms 15–21; thus, it is difficult to determine whether the tunnel functioned as a defensive structure or served some other purpose. One of the small sites in the Yellow Jacket Community, Site 5MT3, contained numerous tunnels that connected kivas and rooms, including a kiva that was probably one of the last kivas used at the site (Lange et al. 1986: 36). The Ismay, Watson, and Grinnell sites in the Yucca House Community contained similar features (Luebben 1982; Luebben and Nickens 1982). Underground tunnels were also present at few small sites in the Castle Rock Community, including one that connected a tower and a kiva at Site 5MT181 (Mad Dog Tower) (Kleidon 1999b), and a tunnel probably connects the kivas at Site 5MT127 (Vision House).

## VI.3. ACCESS TO WATER

The settlement pattern during the thirteenth century A.D. in the Mesa Verde region for both large sites (Varien et al. 1996; Lipe and Varien 1999; Lipe and Ortman 2000: 107) and small sites such as those in the lower portion of the Sand Canyon locality (Gleichman and Gleichman 1989: 64–65; 1992: 30) was characterized by securing water sources and constructing settlements near springs and other water sources. According to Van West and Dean (2000: 35–37), the period from about A.D. 1180 to 1250 in the Mesa Verde region was a time of favorable climate characterized by rising "regional alluvial water tables" and plentiful crop production. However, the following period, A.D. 1250 to 1300, was a time of unfavorable climatic conditions associated with the lowering of the alluvial water table and the entrenchment of stream channels, probably resulting from the Great Drought. These conditions were accompanied by a disruption of the longstanding seasonal precipitation pattern (Van West and Dean 2000: 37).

The need for drinking water, one of the most important factors in determining the location of settlements around the world and through time, is probably even more crucial during climatic perturbations and unpredictability as well as in times of threat or danger; for example, water is a crucial for victims under siege. Recent studies have revealed that most of the Early Medieval strongholds in Małopolska (Lesser Poland) (Poleski 2004), were located no farther than 100–150 m from a water source, and springs or other water sources were located within the boundaries of most sites (Poleski 2004: 93–94). A similar situation probably existed in other areas where tribal defensive settlements were built, such as in the Sudety Mountains (Jaworski 2005: 101–102). It is also necessary to remember that water sources that might have existed in the past might not be present today. An oral tradition still repeated by local people tells of water sources on the southern slope of a hill where the stronghold Naszacowice is located; these sources no longer exist (Poleski 2004: 93).

In all large canyon-rim settlements analyzed in this book, one or more springs were available within the site and flowed through the central part of the village. Some villages encompassed especially dependable water sources that were also used in historic times. The springs at Yellow Jacket Pueblo and Yucca House were important water sources for American settlers. At Cannonball Ruin, the spring and basins within the shelter below the rim of the canyon fill constantly with water so that even in the driest summers, water in the alcove is abundant (Kristin Kuckelman, personal communication 2009). These sources were probably also dependable during the Pueblo occupation in the thirteenth century A.D.

In the large cliff dwellings analyzed in this book, water sources were usually within the alcoves or nearby. The springs at Balcony House and Long House are at the back of the alcove. At Square Tower House, Spruce Tree House, and the Moon House Complex, the springs are below or on both sides of the alcove. At Cliff Palace, despite the presence of a small seep at the back of the alcove and the possibility of collecting water in small basins pecked in the bedrock, too little water would have been procured by this method to supply the entire population of the pueblo, and it would have been necessary to haul most domestic water from a distance of one to two kilometers (Fewkes 1911: 12; Torres-Reyes 1970). There is difficult to estimate if the seeps in large cliff dwellings analyzed in this book produced enough water to fully supply the pueblo, especially for long periods of time, however probably most of the springs were adequate to supply the population at almost all sites in the Great Sage Plain. In Mug House and Square Tower House, no significant amount of water was present within the alcove, although other water sources were available nearby.

The most plentiful water source in the Castle Rock Community was probably McElmo Creek, although this was not a permanent water source (also it would have been too alkaline to provide good drinking water – personal communication with Mark D. Varien, 2009), and it flowed primarily during the spring runoff and summer flashflood (and probably it was filled with water or snow during the fall or winter). Most of the habitation sites dating from the late Pueblo III period were located near seeps or springs rather than near McElmo Creek (Gleichman and Gleichman 1989: 65). The distance to the water sources varied in those sites: the water is available within the boundary of most sites or very close to them, and in several cases it is in a distance of several hundred meters of the sites.

Ancient Pueblo people in the Mesa Verde region constructed dams and reservoirs in or near some habitation sites: dams and relatively large reservoirs are near Spruce Tree House (Rohn 1977: 285–286); a reservoir, a dam and reservoir are in Square Tower House (Rohn 1977: 285); a reservoir (Site 5MV1228) is 200 m from Mug House (Wright et al. 2008); several dams and a possible reservoir are at Yellow Jacket Pueblo (Yellow Jacket Electronic Database); dams and a reservoir are at Cannonball Ruin (Lipe 1996: 3; Morley 1908: 598); a possible reservoir is in Goodman Point Pueblo (Kuckelman et al. 2004); a possible reservoir is in Yucca House (Glowacki 2001: 20); a possible reservoir is against the outer face of the village-enclosing wall at Sand Canyon Pueblo; a dam and reservoir are at a small site near Sand Canyon, Site 5MT16845 (Kuckelman, ed. by 2007; Sand Canyon Electronic Database 2004); two dams and associated reservoirs are at Castle Rock Pueblo (Kuckelman, ed. by 2000; www.crowcanyon.org); and a dam and reservoir are at Woods Canyon Pueblo, although the time of its duration and complex is questionable (Wilshusen et al. 1997: 667–675).

In the Castle Rock Community, dams are present at sites 5MT125, 5MT182, and 5MT1807. Site 5MT2001 is a small site within the Castle Rock Community where a reservoir is also present. Although other sites in the area might also contain such features, the available data are insufficient to confirm this.

# VI.4. SETTLEMENT PATTERN IN THE CASTLE ROCK COMMUNITY

The characteristic settlement pattern of the central Mesa Verde region during the thirteenth century A.D. consisted of clusters of small sites around community centers (Varien 1999; Varien et al. 2000). The proposed Balcony House Community included at least twelve sites (Ferguson 1996: 43; Fiero 1998: 17), the Cliff Palace Community included at least 33 sites (Fiero 2002; Morgan 1994: 139; Rohn 1977: 284), the Spruce Tree House Community consisted of at least 14 sites (Rohn 1977: 285), and the community or cluster of sites around Square Tower House included at least seven sites (Rohn 1977: 285). Smaller sites also clustered around canyon-rim settlements such as Goodman Point Pueblo (Kuckelman et al. 2004) and Sand Canyon Pueblo (Lipe, ed. by 1992). Some of these smaller sites were cliff dwellings, whereas others were on talus slopes, uplands, or mesa tops.

Most of smaller sites were near the community centers. In some cases routes between the community centers and nearby smaller sites is visible. Communication between Balcony House (Fiero 1998: 35) and Cliff Palace (Rohn 1977: 282) with the smaller sites in those communities was mostly along the top of the steeply sloping talus adjacent to the cliff face; this route was probably easier than climbing to the mesa top and descending back down into the canyon to each of the smaller sites. Routes also connected Square Tower House with smaller sites in that community such as Little Long House ruin (Rohn 1977). Recent research and analysis of aerial photographs have revealed ancient routes connecting sites within the Goodman Point Unit and the Goodman Point Community (Kuckelman et al. 2004).

The Castle Rock Community, in the lower portion of the Sand Canyon locality, probably consisted of around 42 sites, including the community center Castle Rock Pueblo (Site 5MT1825). The community is inferred to have covered a four- to five-kilometer radius centered on Castle Rock Pueblo (Varien 1999; Varien et al. 2000), and the boundaries of the community could have been marked by four directional shrines (Ortman 2008). All sites examined in this book that are in the lower portion of the Sand Canyon locality have been dated to the thirteenth century A.D., although it is difficult to determine if all were contemporaneous or if some sites were built before the founding of Castle Rock Pueblo in the A.D. 1250s (Kuckelman, ed. by 2000).

The sites that probably created this community were chosen for analysis in this book because of chronological criteria. The chronology was established on the basis of data collected in several surveys conducted in the lower Sand Canyon area (Adler and Metcalf 1992; Gleichman and Gleichman 1989; Varien, ed. by 1999; Electronic Database of sites from the Lower Sand Canyon area prepared by Scott Ortman, Crow Canyon Archaeological Center, Cortez, Colorado) and includes architectural styles and the types of pottery collected from the modern ground surface and from excavations. Tree-ring dates are available for only a few of these sites. These data indicate that all 42 sites examined in Castle Rock community were used in the thirteenth century A.D. (the late Pueblo III period), although it is difficult to determine whether all 42 sites were inhabited contemporaneously or if some were abandoned when others were established.

Particular sites might have been inhabited during the late A.D. 1100s or in the A.D. 1200s, and those sites are marked with question marks on the map.

However, intervisibility might be interpreted as the possibility of visual communication between sites that would have been especially useful in times of danger. Residents of particular sites might have used smoke or fire signals to warn the inhabitants of other sites of approaching attackers. This could be used as evidence that intervisible sites were contemporaneous. The phenomenon of intervisibility, and its usage during times of conflict, has been documented cross-culturally and has been recorded in other areas of the Southwest, such as on Perry Mesa in central Arizona (Ahlstrom and Roberts 1995; Spoerl 1984: 268–270; Wilcox 2001a, 2001b), in the Kayenta region in northeastern Arizona (Haas and Creamer 1993), and in recent experimental studies of intervisibility, signaling, and warning between Navajo pueblitos of the Dinétah region in the northwestern part of New Mexico (Bryan 2009; http://www.blm.gov/nm/st/en.html). Visual communication between sites that could have facilitated warning in times of danger was also noted for Early Medieval strongholds (Dulinicz 2001: 186). Ethnohistoric accounts tell of warnings of suspected attacks that allowed the escape and retreat of people, especially women and children, while men under the direction of elders stayed to defend the village (Bolton 1949: 119). This indicates that there must have been a warning system among nearby or allied sites; signals were probably received from other villages, or runners were sent in warning.

In the Mesa Verde region, theories of the possible functions of towers include their usage as communication features, especially for towers located in the line-of-sight between sites, which included towers at Hovenweep National Monument, Mesa Verde National Park, and a tower in Navajo Canyon (e.g., Ellis, ed. by 1997: 68; LeBlanc 1999: 59–61; Schulman 1950; Thompson 2004: 29). Among the sites in the Castle Rock Community I examined, six groups or clusters of sites within the community consist of four or more sites that were near each other or within visual contact. The first possible group consists of five sites: 5MT1826, 5MT1827, 5MT1828, 5MT2799, and 5MT2800. The second group consists of eight sites: 5MT264 and 5MT1842 (often considered one site); 5MT265; 5MT1831; 5MT2636; 5MT1829; 5MT13251; and 5MT14659. A third group might have been formed by sites 5MT135, 5MT133, 5MT134, 5MT132, 5MT125, 5MT126, 5MT127, 5MT129, 5MT182, and possibly 5MT186. The fourth group consists of sites 5MT181, 5MT185, 5MT186, 5MT257, 5MT261, 5MT262, 5MT263, 5MT1804, 5MT2797, 5MT2801, and 5MT10366. The fifth group is made up of five sites: 5MT1805, 5MT1806, 5MT1807, 5MT1808, 5MT1824, 5MT2644. And the sixth group consists of four sites located on Battle Rock: sites 5MT1999, 5MT2000, 5MT2001, 5MT2002; however, these might be considered one site.

Intervisibility has been confirmed in the second and fourth proposed group: Mad Dog Tower (Site 5MT181) and the tower located above Saddlehorn Hamlet (Site 5MT262) 1 km west across Sand Canyon. This intervisibility indicates that inhabitants of the two habitations could have communicated via the towers if the two habitations were contemporaneous. Other sites with towers that might have been contemporaneous with 5MT181 are Site 5MT2797, which lies 300 m to the southeast, and Site 5MT261, located 720 m to the southwest. All of these sites include a structure that may be called a tower or a "lookout" structure. From these structures, at least two, and possibly all, of the other sites were visible (Kleidon 1999b; observation made by the author). Sites 5MT185, 5MT186, and 5MT257 were in eye contact with Mad Dog Tower; the latter is located in relatively strategic high point of a talus slope on a bench overlooking McElmo Canyon.

Two intervisible sites in the first possible group listed above, Site 5MT2799, a possible tower, and Site 5MT2800, a dry-laid masonry structure, are located near each other and might have been one site. These two sites were probably not habitations, and it is possible that they were used as defensive structures or as communication features that provided intervisibility with other sites in the vicinity (Adler and Metcalf 1992: 43). They also might have functioned as communication features between the first and second groups proposed above, and perhaps with Castle Rock Pueblo as well. Site 5MT2800 was constructed on a high point overlooking the southern and northern parts of East Fork Canyon, and it is reasonable to infer that it served as an important communication feature between sites located to the south and north. The site is situated on a high, difficult-to-access point of the canyon that divides the line of possible intervisibilty between sites located to the north and south on the east side of East Fork Canyon.

Site 5MT135, in the proposed third group of sites, is visible through an existing loophole in a wall of the tower associated with that site; the site would have also been visible from the roof of that tower. Sites 5MT125, 5MT126, and 5MT127, on the eastern side of Sand Canyon, would probably have been visible from that tower as well. Castle Rock Pueblo is visible from an unnamed structure (probably tower) to the northeast perhaps indicating the importance of communication between Castle Rock Pueblo and other sites in the community.

If, within the Mesa Verde region, conflicts occurred between different Pueblo groups, whether due to environmental and climatic perturbations, competition for reduced resources or water supplies, or any other cause, these conflicts probably would have occurred between communities rather than within communities. If so, then the Castle Rock Community probably had to defend itself against other communities. The nearest communities were the Sand Canyon and the Goodman Point communities, which included two of the largest villages in the region during the second half of thirteenth century A.D. The attack on Castle Rock Pueblo that ended its occupation (Kuckelman, ed. by 2000; Kuckelman et al. 2002), might have been launched by one of these two, or possibly both, communities (Ortman 2008: 150–151) or by other communities in the Mesa Verde region (Kuckelman et al. 2002: 506).

Ethnohistoric records contain information about confederacies and alliances among Pueblo groups (Upham et al. 1994; Wilcox 1991) that has been supported in some cases by archaeological data (LeBlanc 1999: 287, 318; Spielmann 1994; Minge 1976: 49–51). Such pacts might have provided better protection for villages and lands from both Pueblo and non-Pueblo intruders; alliances between pueblos might have become more common after the mid-1600s, when Athapascan raids and attacks became more frequent (Holt 1983: 595; LeBlanc 1999: 45).

Proponents of neoevolutionionary theory such as Johnson and Earle (1987) have proposed that competition and defense are the primary factors in the development of intervillage alliances. B. Trigger (Spielmann 1994: 52 after Trigger 1976: 157–162) proposes "the model for the evolution of multiple clusters of sites in which once one settlement system had developed into a cluster, other would quickly follow suit for defensive purposes." Also, archaeological data confirm that confederacies might have been developed in conjunction with aggregation and "increasingly intense warfare, evidenced by settlement location shift from lowland areas to defensible hilltops and the palisading villages" (Spielmann 1994: 51). The examples described by Spielmann are fifteenth-century Huron villages in the Northeast and Pueblo settlements from the same time in the Rio Grande Valley.

Spielmann (1994: 51) also points out that alliances among pueblos in one cluster may have developed in part for mutual defense, whereas confederacies "may have been equally important in suppressing hostilities within local areas." Also, to defend against intruders, the ability to build alliances and take control over land is probably as important as, and in some cases even more important than, building defensive architecture and constructing sites in defensible locations (LeBlanc 1999: 287, 318; Spielmann 1994). Intervisibility between "sets" of sites and the absence of intervisibility with another "set" of sites within, for example, the Kayenta region (Haas and Creamer 1993) may be inferred as evidence of the presence or absence of political alliances, respectively (Wilcox and Haas 1994: 217).

The settlement organization of sites in the Castle Rock Community that includes sites in locations difficult to access as well as intervisible may suggest a cluster of allied sites that was integrated in one closely cooperating community. This community might have been created, and might have functioned, as a response to a threat from neighboring communities or from non-Pueblo invaders in an attempt to better defend the inhabitants of particular settlements and the entire community. It is difficult to determine if Castle Rock Pueblo was a place of refuge for the entire community in times of attack, or if particular settlements were defending themselves. Specific sites in the community, such as sites 5MT1826 and 5MT1835, which contain a wall that extends the length of the alcove and that exhibit little evidence of habitation, might have been refuges. All 15 large sites, or community centers, analyzed in this book might have been such refuges in times of danger.

## VI.5. WHO WERE THE ATTACKERS?

It is very difficult to determine the identity or cultural affiliation of the attackers against whom Pueblo groups constructed sites in defensible locations and built defensive architecture. One oft-cited possible enemy is non-Pueblo nomadic groups, mainly Numic speakers, who could have been the ancestors of historic and contemporary Ute and Paiute Indians, and who probably would have come from the Great Basin. Other possible enemies were other non-Pueblo groups such as Athapascans (Apaches and Navajos), although Athapascans probably arrived in the Southwest later, in the fifteenth or sixteenth century A.D. (Lipe and Varien 1999: 341) after the Mesa Verde region had been depopulated for at least two centuries. Conflicts could have been inter-Pueblo, involving attacks of one Pueblo habitation or community on another (see summary in Kuckelman 2002: 245–246; LeBlanc 1999; Lightfoot and Kuckelman 2001; Wilcox and Haas 1994: 214–216). One of the first archaeologists who proposed that the depopulation and migration of Pueblo societies in the Mesa Verde region was caused by nomad (Athapascan) attacks was Alfred V. Kidder (1924), and one of the first opposing theories, Pueblo-versus-Pueblo conflict, was proposed by Ralph Linton (1944).

The archaeological data for the Mesa Verde region is sparse and not sufficient to wholly support or reject any of these theories. At Castle Rock Pueblo, only a few pieces of evidence could indicate attack by a non-Pueblo group. One indication is a Bull Creek projectile point of non-local material; this type of projectile point is not typical for the area of southwestern Colorado where Castle Rock is located but is characteristic of a transition area between Pueblo and Fremont cultures in southeastern Utah (Kuckelman, ed. by 2000; Kuckelman et al. 2002: 505). Another bit of evidence includes the crania of two victims that were not flattened by cradleboarding (Kuckelman et al. 2002: 505), a practice nearly ubiquitous among Pueblo people in the Mesa Verde region during the thirteenth century A.D.

A Hopi oral tradition concerning a battle that purportedly occurred in this village links the attack to ancestral Ute Indians (Jackson 1981: 380; Lightfoot and Kuckelman 2001: 55–56). Also, many oral histories of Pueblo people refer to conflicts with other tribes such as Navajos, Apaches, Comanches, and Paiutes (Haas, Creamer 1997: 237; White 1942: 316–318; Mindeleff 1989 [1891]). In addition, oral histories of tribes such as the Navajo tell of hostile interactions with Pueblo people during some time periods (Holt 1983: 595). Hostile relations between Pueblo and non-Pueblo people, and also between different Pueblo groups, have been noted by Spaniards since the beginning of the Spanish presence in the Southwest in the first half of the sixteenth century (e.g., Bolton 1949; Hammond and Rey 1940; Winship 1904). Historic conflicts and violence between different pueblos of the same cultural affiliation are also known, such as the destruction of Sikyátki and Awatovi (Brew 1949: 20–24; Haas and Creamer 1997: 253–255; Lomatuway'ma et al. 1993: 145–147, 391–392; Malotki 1993).

Abundant archaeological and ethnographic data on defensive sites, or sites with defensive architecture, in different parts of the world indicate that such sites might have been built inside the territory of a cultural group or unit, or within the borders of a territory inhabited by a group (e.g., Keeley 1996: 56–57; Poleski 2008: 84). If we assume that defensive sites were constructed within a territory inhabited by a particular cultural group or society this may indicate that the threat from the outside, that is, from a different group or culture, was so significant that it forced the group to build most sites in a defensive manner. Alternatively, this same scenario could lead to the conclusion that the threat was from inside the territory inhabited by one "coherent" cultural group and resulted from the need for defense against nearby sites or communities. Most of the sites in the central Mesa Verde region in the thirteenth century A.D. analyzed here exhibit signs of defensive architecture or are in defensible locations, implying that the primary threat came from other communities in the same area. Conflicts between various Pueblo groups within the area might have been caused by climatic instability and competition for depleted and scarce resources in this turbulent time (e.g., Ortman 2008; Lipe and Varien 1999; Van West and Dean 2000).

# VI.6. IMPLICATIONS OF DEFENSIVE ARCHITECTURE FOR THE DEPOPULATION OF THE MESA VERDE REGION

The Pueblo Indians in the Mesa Verde region emigrated from the region near the end of the thirteenth century A.D. The region was probably depopulated by the late A.D. 1270s or early 1280s; A.D. 1280 is the latest known tree-ring date for the region (see Chapter V). This emigration has attracted the attention of scientists from different disciplines and others since the end of the nineteenth century, when the first archaeological and ethnographic research was conducted in the area. The topic is intriguing because even now, after more than 100 years of study, the reasons for this migration are not clear. The other intriguing aspect of the archaeology of the Mesa Verde region is the presence of architecture that might have been defensive. The construction of most defensive architecture dates from the thirteenth century A.D., especially in the several decades preceding the Pueblo people migration from this area to the south and southeast of the Mesa Verde region.

Several possible explanations of the migration and depopulation of the area have been proposed. Causes cited by many researchers include environmental changes like the Great Drought that occurred between A.D. 1276 and 1299, the beginning of the Little Ice Age in the northern hemisphere in the thirteenth century A.D., precipitation unpredictability in the Mesa Verde region, and a decrease in the number of permanent water sources that was probably at least partly coincident with deforestation and the depletion of natural resources (Adams and Petersen 1999; Dean and Van West 2002; Kohler et al. 2005; Lipe and Varien 1999a: 253, 265; see also Chapter II.2.a).

However, it is difficult to determine the scale of these environmental disturbances, including the Great Drought, because recent paleoenvironmental data (Van West and Dean 2000: 26–27) show that, although the climatic and environmental conditions were deteriorating, there were probably still enough good farming fields and water sources to support at least part of the population of the Mesa Verde during most of the thirteenth century A.D. These data are also supported by archaeological and environmental studies in areas such Long House Valley in the Kayenta region and by computer simulations of agent-based modeling (Kohler et al. 2005). Moreover, analyses of climatic and environmental factors led to the conclusion that "fairly productive farming could have continued in the area after A.D. 1300" (Dean and Van West 2002: 95).

However, environmental and climatic changes might have manifested differently in various areas of the central Mesa Verde region. Elevational variations affect precipitation, length of growing season, and the availability of water sources, natural resources, and wildlife. Deteriorating climatic conditions might have led first to migrations from the westernmost part and the eastern part (Totah area) of the region into the central Mesa Verde region during the first half of the thirteenth century A.D. These migrations might have continued through the A.D. 1250s and 1260s (Glowacki 2006: 139–145) and even contributed to the final migrations to the south and southeast of the Mesa Verde region into present-day Arizona and the Rio Grande Valley in New Mexico.

Environmental disturbances such as those mentioned above might have also been associated with social and demographic changes and the reorganization of Pueblo societies across the entire Mesa Verde region. The probable decrease of available farming areas and other sources of food resulting from the changing environment probably increased competition for control of the landscape, good farming fields, and other resources, and also could have caused increased mortality from malnutrition or starvation and decreased birth rates as well (Dean and Van West 2002: 97–98). These conditions could have resulted in increasing conflict and violence between Pueblo groups in the area. Individual communities were probably independent and autonomous, although inter-community alliances might have been needed because of increasing conflicts (Lipe and Varien 1999: 331–335). Conflicts could have erupted between Pueblo and non-Pueblo groups (Lipe and Varien 1999: 340–341; Kuckelman 2002; Wilcox and Haas 1994; see also Chapter IV).

Conflict and violence evidently increased in the Mesa Verde region during the A.D. 1200s (Kohler et al. 2005; Kuckelman 2002; Lightfoot and Kuckelman 2001; LeBlanc 1999; Lipe 1995; Lipe and Varien 1999; Varien et al. 1996); however, it is difficult to determine whether this increase was entirely a response to a changes in climate and environment or if it was caused by different factors. Droughts that were even more severe and worse climatic conditions occurred long before the final migration and depopulation of the area and before the Great Drought began (Dean and Van West 2002: 87; Kohler et al. 2005; Van West and Dean 2000: 26–27). A concern for defending people and food supplies is evidenced in the construction of sites in defensible locations such as cliff alcoves and in the enclosing of entire villages with relatively tall stone walls. Other evidence of violence includes human remains found at several sites that exhibit signs of violent death, burned structures associated with the final abandonment of sites, and rock art depictions of conflict (e.g., Kuckelman et al. 2002; Lightfoot and Kuckelman 2001).

Defensive architecture, defensible site locations, and sites with intervisibility within a community – to warn of approaching enemies – are characteristics of the sites examined in this book and have been noted in other parts of America as well as in prehistoric and historic societies in other parts of the world. These characteristics may indicate a response to increasing conflict and violence in the region. Although it is difficult to determine if the threat was from nomadic people from outside the region or was inter-Pueblo, the thirteenth-century A.D. architecture of the region clearly shows that the threat must have been very serious if it forced people to leave favorable living conditions on the mesa tops and relocate to cliff alcoves and steep talus slopes below canyon rims. Sites in these new locations probably also involved more effort to build and maintain, especially in terms of sites built on canyon-rims.

The data presented in this book, other data from the Mesa Verde region, data for other parts of North America and prehistoric and historic non-state societies from central-eastern and southern Europe, all suggest that a primary reason that Ancestral Pueblo people migrated from the Mesa Verde region was the increasing danger from either Pueblo or non-Pueblo hostile groups. A clear manifestation of the real and serious danger in the archaeological record is the presence of, and significant increase in, the construction defensive architecture in defensible locations in this region. This is also supported by presence of intervisibility between sites in several cluster of sites in the Castle Rock community (some of the structures like towers were probably built to enable this eye-contact).

On the basis of available archaeological data analyzed in the book supported by ethnohistoric and ethnographic records as well as the oral traditions of native societies from the Southwest it seems reasonable to say that conflict was one of the main factors (probably the main one) responsible for the decision of leaving by ancient Pueblo people their well protected, and probably populous, settlements and migrated from this area to the south and southeast near the end of the thirteenth century A.D. Conflicts and violence (as factors) were clearly related to other factors including environmental and climatic deterioration and the effects this had on food production and these two factors (conflicts and environmental disturbances) combined together were probably the main stimulators that led to the decision of leaving the central Mesa Verde region in the end of thirteenth century A.D.

It is difficult to determine whether the defensive architecture and defensible locations were not enough of an obstacle against possible attackers. Some data, such as that for Castle Rock and Sand Canyon pueblos, indicate that population aggregation, the relatively large number of inhabitants, and the presence of defensive architecture was effective protection through several decades, although near the end of the thirteenth century A.D. something changed, and the architecture, location, and village configuration were no longer effective against intruders. Perhaps the population of the region migrated gradually or some residents died from famine and diseases such that near the end of village depopulation the dwindling population was insufficient to defend against attackers. Other, probably also less important, factors that might have been partly responsible for the decisions of ancient Pueblo people to leave the Mesa Verde region include the appearance of new cults or ideologies south of the Mesa Verde region (e.g., Adams 1991; Wilcox and Haas 1994) that might have been attractive to the Pueblo societies inhabiting Mesa Verde region, especially during this turbulent time of environmental, social, and possibly religious changes.

# REFERENCES


Adams, Christopher D., Diane E. White, and David M. Johnson

2001 Apache Breastworks in Southeastern New Mexico. In *The Archaeology of Ancient Tactical Sites*, edited by John R. Welch and Todd W. Bostwick, pp. 97–110. Papers from the 1998 Fall Symposium, Arizona Archaeological Council. The Arizona Archaeologist, Number 32.

Adams, E. Charles

1991 *The Origin and Development of the Pueblo Katsina Cult*. University of Arizona Press, Tucson.

Adams, Karen R., and Kenneth L. Petersen

1999 Chapter 2: Environment. In *Colorado Prehistory: A Context for the Southern Colorado River Basin*, edited by William D. Lipe, Mark D. Varien, and Richard H. Wilshusen, pp. 14–50. Colorado Council of Professional Archaeologists, Denver.

Adams, Karen R., and Vandy E. Bowyer

2002 Sustainable Landscape: Thirteenth-Century Food and Fuel Use in the Sand Canyon Locality. In *Seeking the Center Place: Archaeology and Ancient Communities in the Mesa Verde Region*, edited by Mark D. Varien and Richard H. Wilshusen, pp. 123–142. The University of Utah Press, Salt Lake City.

Adler, Michael A.

2002 The Ancestral Pueblo Community as Structure and Strategy. In *Seeking the Center Place: Archaeology and Ancient Communities in Mesa Verde Region*, edited by Mark D. Varien and Richard H. Wilshusen, pp. 25–39. The University of Utah Press, Salt Lake City.

Adler, Michael A., and Maripat Metcalf (under the supervision of William D. Lipe, Principal Investigator)

1992 *Archaeological Survey of Lower East Rock and Sand Canyons, Montezuma County, Colorado*. Crow Canyon Archaeological Center, Cortez, Colorado. Unpublished manuscript.

Adler, Michael A., Todd Van Pool, and Robert D. Leonard

1996 Ancestral Pueblo Population Aggregation and Abandonment in the North American Southwest. *Journal of World Prehistory* 10 (3): 375–438.

Ahlstrom, Richard V.N.

1985 *The Interpretation of Archaeological Tree-Ring Dates*. Unpublished Ph.D. Dissertation, University of Arizona, Tucson, USA.

Ahlstrom, Richard V. N., and Heidi Roberts

1995 *Prehistory of Perry Mesa: The Short-Lived Settlement of a Mesa-Canyon Complex in Central Arizona, ca. A.D. 1200–1450*. The Arizona Archaeologist No. 28. Arizona Archaeological Society, Phoenix.

Alušik, Tomáš

2008 The Settlement of Cretan Mountains in the Bronze Age and the Phenomenon of Fortified Sites. In *Man and Mountains: Palaeogeographical and Archaeological Perspectives*, edited by T. Kalicki and B. Szmoniewski, pp. 75–84. Prace Instytutu Geografii Uniwersytetu Jana Kochanowskiego w Kielcach, Number 17.

Anyon, R., T.J. Ferguson, L. Jackson, and L. Lane

1997 Native American Tradition and Archaeology: Issues of Structure, Relevance and Respect. In *Native Americans and Archaeologists: Stepping Stones to Common Ground*, edited by

N. Swindler, K.E. Dongoske, R. Anyon, and A.S. Downer, pp. 77–87. AltaMira Press, Walnut Creek.

Balcony House Trail Guide
*Balcony House Trail Guide*. Mesa Verde Museum Association, Inc. Mesa Verde National Park, Colorado.

Bandelier, Adolf
1890 *Final Report of Investigation Among the Indians of the Southwestern United States, Part 1*. Papers of the Archaeological Institute of America, American Series No. 3.
1892 *Final Report of Investigation Among the Indians of the Southwestern United States, Carried on Mainly in the Years from 1880 to 1885, Part 2*. Papers of the Archaeological Institute of America, American Series No. 3.
1916 *Delight Makers*. Dodd, Mead and Company, New York.

Bedell, Melanie L.
2000 *Late Pueblo II and Pueblo III Cliff Dwellings and Community Patterns in Grand Gulch, Southeastern Utah*. Unpublished Master's thesis, Washington State University, Pullman, USA.

Bernardini, Wesley
2005 *Hopi Oral Tradition and the Archaeology of Identity*. University of Arizona Press, Tucson.

Birdsall, W.R.
1891 The Cliff Dwellings of the Cañons of the Mesa Verde. *Journal of the American Geographical Society of New York* 23: 584–620.
1898 The Cliff Palace and Its Surroundings. *The American Antiquarian and Oriental Journal*, Jan 1–Feb 25.

Blackburn, Fred M., and Ray A. Williamson
*Cowboys & Cave Dwellers: Basketmaker Archaeology in Utah's Grand Gulch*. School of American Research Press, Santa Fe.

Bloomer, William W.
1989 *Moon House: A Pueblo III Period Cliff Dwelling Complex in Southeastern Utah*. Unpublished Master's thesis, Washington State University, Pullman, USA.

Bolton, Herbert E.
*Coronado, Knight of Pueblos and Plains*. Whittlesey House (a division of McGraw-Hill Book Company, Inc. and The University of New Mexico Press), New York.

Bradley, Bruce A.
1992 Excavations at Sand Canyon Pueblo. In *The Sand Canyon Archaeological Project: A Progress Report*, edited by William D. Lipe, pp. 33–44. Occasional Papers, No. 2. Crow Canyon Archaeological Center, Cortez, Colorado.
1993 Planning, Growth, and Functional Differentiation at a Prehistoric Pueblo: A Case Study from SW Colorado. *Journal of Field Archaeology* 20: 23–42.
1996 Pitchers to Mugs: Chacoan Revival at Sand Canyon Pueblo. *Kiva. The Journal of Southwestern Anthropology and History* 3 (61): 241–255.

Bradley, Cynthia S.
2002 Human Remains. In *The Archaeology of Woods Canyon Pueblo: A Canyon-Rim Village in Southwestern Colorado* [HTML Title]. Available: http://www.crowcanyon.org/woodscanyon. Date of use: 6 December 2008.

Brew, John O.
1949 The History of Awatovi. In *Franciscan Awatovi: The Excavation and Conjectural Reconstruction of a 17th-Century Spanish Mission Established at a Hopi Indian Town in Northeastern Arizona*, by R.G. Montgomery, W. Smith, and J.O. Brew, pp. 1–43. Papers of the Peabody Museum of American Archaeology and Ethnology Vol. 36, Reports of the Awatovi Expedition Report No. 3. Harvard University, Cambridge.

Brumfiel, E.M.
2003 It's a Material World: History, Artifacts, and Anthropology. *Annual Review of Anthropology* 32(1): 205–223.

Bryan, Susan Montoya
2009 *Study looks at early Navajo use of smoke signals* [HTML Title]. Available: http://www.indiancountrytoday.com/national/45844982.html, Associated Press Write. Date of use: 8 June 2009.

Buko, Andrzej
2005 *Archeologia Polski wczesnośredniowiecznej. Odkrycia – Hipotezy – Interpretacje.* Wydawnictwo TRIO, Warszawa.

Bukowski, Zbigniew
1977 *The Scythian Influence on the Area of Lusatian Culture.* Polish Academy of Sciences, Wrocław–Warszawa–Kraków–Gdańsk.

Cameron, Catherine M.
1995 Tracing Migration Pathways from the Receiving End. *Journal of Anthropological Archaeology* 14: 203–211.
2006 Leaving Mesa Verde. In *The Mesa Verde World: Explorations in Ancestral Pueblo Archaeology*, edited by David G. Noble, pp. 139–147. School of American Research Press, Santa Fe.

Cameron, Catherine M., and Steven A. Tomka, edited by
1993 *Abandonment of Settlements and Regions: Ethnoarchaeological and Archaeological Approaches.* Cambridge University Press, Cambridge.

Carneiro, Robert
1970 A Theory of the Origin of the State. *Science* New Series 169 (3947) Aug. 21: 733–738.

Cattanach, George S. Jr.
1980 *Long House, Mesa Verde National Park, Colorado.* Publications in Archeology No. 7H. Wetherill Mesa Studies. National Park Service, Washington, D.C.

Ceram, C.W.
1977 *Pierwszy Amerykanin. Zagadka studiów prekolumbijskich.* Państwowy Instytut Wydawniczy, Warszawa.

Chacon, Richard J., and Rubén G. Mendoza (editors)
2007 North American Indigenous Warfare and Ritual Violence. The University of Arizona Press, Tucson.

Chapin, Frederick H.
1892 *In the Land of Cliff Dwellers.* Appalachian Mountain Club, Boston, MA.

Charles, Mona
2006 The Earliest Mesa Verdeans: Hunters, Foragers, and First Farmers. In *The Mesa Verde World: Explorations in Ancestral Pueblo Archaeology*, edited by David G. Noble, pp. 9–17. School of American Research Press, Santa Fe.

Chochorowski, Jan
1993 *Ekspansja kimmeryjska na tereny Europy Środkowej.* Rozprawy habilitacyjne No. 260, Uniwersytet Jagielloński, Kraków.
1999a Hiperborejczycy wieku spiżu – Epoka brązu poza zasięgiem wysokich cywilizacji w Europie. In *Encyklopedia Historyczna Świata, tom 1: Prehistoria*, edited by Janusz K. Kozłowski, pp. 202–252. Opres, Kraków.
1999b Żelazny oręż barbarzyńców – wczesna epoka żelaza poza zasięgiem cywilizacji klasycznych. In *Encyklopedia historyczna świata, tom 1: Prehistoria*, edited by Janusz K. Kozłowski, pp. 304–395. Opres, Kraków.

Churchill, Melissa J.
2002 Architecture and Site Layout. In *The Archaeology of Woods Canyon Pueblo: A Canyon-Rim Village in Southwestern Colorado,* [HTML Title]. Available: http://www.crowcanyon.org/woodscanyon. Date of use: 6 December 2008.

Churchill, Melissa J. (editor)
2002 *The Archaeology of Woods Canyon Pueblo: A Canyon-Rim Village in Southwestern Colorado,* [HTML Title]. Available: http://www.crowcanyon.org/woodscanyon. Date of use: 10 December 2008.

Churchill, Melissa J., and Scott G. Ortman
2002 Chronology. In *The Archaeology of Woods Canyon Pueblo: A Canyon-Rim Village in Southwestern Colorado,* [HTML Title]. Available: http://www.crowcanyon.org/woodscanyon. Date of use: 6 December 2008.

Cliff Palace Guide
*Cliff Palace. Mesa Verde's Largest Cliff Dwellings*. Mesa Verde National Park Guidebooks. Mesa Verde Museum Association, Colorado.

Coffey, Grant D.
2009 *Report of 2008 Goodman Point Community Testing, Montezuma County, Colorado* [HTML Title]. Available: http://crowcanyon.org/ResearchReports/GoodmanPoint/interim_reports/2008/text_2008.asp. Date of use: 10 November 2010.

Coffey, Grant D., and Kristin A. Kuckelman
2006 *Report of 2005 Research at Goodman Point Pueblo (Site 5MT604), Montezuma County, Colorado,* [HTML Title]. Available: http://www.crowcanyon.org/goodmanpoint2005. Date of use: 15 October 2007.

Colwell-Chanthaphonh, Chip, and T.J. Ferguson
2006 Rethinking Abandonment in Archaeological Contexts. *The SAA Archaeological Record – The Magazine of the Society for American Archaeology* 6 (1): 37–41.

Connolly, M.R.
1992 The Goodman Point Historic Land-Use Study. In *The Sand Canyon Archaeological Project: A Progress Report*, edited by William D. Lipe, pp. 33–44. Occasional Papers, No. 2. Crow Canyon Archaeological Center, Cortez, Colorado.

Cordell, Linda
1995 Migration and the Movement of Southwestern People. *Journal of Anthropological Archaeology* 14: 104–124.
1997 *Archaeology of the Southwest*. Academic Press, San Diego, London, Boston, New York, Sydney, Tokyo, Toronto.

Cordell, Linda S., and Don D. Fowler (editors)
2005 *Southwest Archaeology in the Twentieth Century*. The University of Utah Press, Salt Lake City.

CCAC (Crow Canyon Archaeological Center)
2000 *The Castle Rock Pueblo Electronic Database*, [HTML Title]. Available: http://www.crowcanyon.org/ResearchReports/dbw/dbw_chooser.asp?Site=5MT1825. Date of use: 10 May 2009.
2001 *The Woods Canyon Pueblo Database*, [HTML Title]. Available: http://www.crowcanyon.org/woodscanyondatabase. Date of use: 30 May 2009.
2003 *The Yellow Jacket Pueblo Database*, [HTML Title]. Available: http://www.crowcanyon.org/yellowjacketdatabase. Date of use: 23 March 2009.
2004 *The Sand Canyon Pueblo Database*, [HTML Title]. Available: http://www.crowcanyon.org/sandcanyondatabase. Date of use: 12 June 2009.

Cushing, Frank Hamilton
1981 *Zuni: Selected Writings of Frank Hamilton Cushing*. University of Nebraska Press.

Dalan, R.A., G.R. Holley, W.I. Woods, H.W. Watters, and J.A. Koepke
2003 *Envisioning Cahokia. A Landscape Perspective*. Northern Illinois University Press, DeKalb, Illinois.

Database of Tree-Ring Dates, LTRR
2007 *LTTR First Choice Data Files*. Laboratory of Tree-Ring Research, University of Arizona, Tucson. Courtesy of Jeffrey Dean.

Dean, Jeffrey S.

1969 *Chronological Analysis of Tsegi Phase Sites in Northeastern Arizona*. Papers of the Laboratory of Tree-Ring Research, Number 3. The University of Arizona Press, Tucson.

1970 Aspects of Tsegi Phase Social Organization: A Trial Reconstruction. In *Reconstructing Prehistoric Pueblo Societies*, edited by William A. Longacre, pp. 140–174. School of American Research Advanced Seminar Series. University of New Mexico Press, Albuquerque.

1996 Kayenta Anasazi Settlement Transformations in Northeastern Arizona, A.D. 1150–1350. In *The Prehistoric Pueblo World, A.D. 1150–1350*, edited by Michael A. Adler, pp. 29–47. University of Arizona Press, Tucson.

2001 *Dendrochronology of Archaeological Sites on Wetherill Mesa, Mesa Verde National Park, Colorado*. Final Report on Project 99-M1-040. Laboratory of Tree-Ring Research, University of Arizona, Tucson.

Dean, Jeffrey S., and Carla Van West

2002 Environment-Behavior Relationships in Southwestern Colorado. In *Seeking the Center Place: Archaeology and Ancient Communities in the Mesa Verde Region*, edited by Mark D. Varien and Richard H. Wilshusen, pp. 81–99. The University of Utah Press, Salt Lake City.

Deloria, V.

1992 Indians, Archaeologists, and the Future. *American Antiquity* 57: 595–598.

Donato, G.

1986 Interdyscyplinarność badań nad przeszłością. In *Teoria i praktyka badań archeologicznych*, Vol. 1, edited by W. Hensel, G. Donato, and S. Tabaczyński, pp. 29–32. PWN, Wrocław–Warszawa–Kraków–Gdańsk–Łódź.

Dongoske, K.E., M. Yeatts, R. Anyon, and T.J. Ferguson

1997 Archaeological Cultures and Cultural Affiliation: Hopi and Zuni Perspectives in the American Southwest. *American Antiquity* 64 (2): 600–608.

Downer, Alan S.

1997 Archaeologists-Native American Relations In *Native Americans and Archaeologists. Stepping Stones to Common Ground*, edited by N. Swidler, K. Dongoske, R. Anyon, and A.S. Downer, pp. 23–34. Walnut Creek–London–New Delhi.

Downum, Christian E.

1993 Southwestern Archaeology: Past Present, and Future. *Expedition* 35 (1): 4–13.

Dozier, Edward P.

1970 Making Inferences from the Present to the Past. In *Reconstructing Prehistoric Pueblo Societies*, edited by William A. Longacre, pp. 202–213. School of American Research Advanced Seminar Series. University of New Mexico Press, Albuquerque.

Driver, Jonathan C.

2002 *Faunal Variation and Change in the Northern San Juan Region*. In *Seeking the Center Place: Archaeology and Ancient Communities in the Mesa Verde Region*, edited by Mark D. Varien and Richard H. Wilshusen, pp. 143–160. The University of Utah Press, Salt Lake City.

Duff, Andrew I.

2002 *Western Pueblo Identities: Regional Interaction, Migration, and Transformation*. University of Arizona Press, Tucson.

Dulinicz, Marek

2000 Miejsca, które rodzą władzę (Najstarsze grody słowiańskie na wschód od Wisły). In *Człowiek, sacrum, środowisko. Miejsca kultu we wczesnym średniowieczu*, edited by Sławomir Moździoch, pp. 85–98. Spotkania Bytomskie IV. Instytut Archeologii i Etnologii Polskiej Akademii Nauk Oddział we Wrocławiu, Wrocław.

2001 *Kształtowanie się Słowiańszczyzny północno-zachodniej*. Instytut Archeologii i Etnologii, Polska Akademia Nauk, Warszawa.

Earle, Timothy
2002 Political Domination and Social Evolution. In *Companion Encyclopedia of Anthropology*, pp. 940–961. Routledge, London, New York.

Echo-Hawk, Roger
1997 Forging a New Ancient History for Native America. In *Native Americans and Archaeologists. Stepping Stones to Common Ground*, edited by N. Swidler, K. Dongoske, R. Anyon, and A.S. Downer, pp. 88–102. Walnut Creek–London–New Delhi.

Eggan, Fred
1950 *Social Organization of the Western Pueblos*. University of Chicago Press, Chicago.

Elliot, Michael L.
2002 Mission and Mesa: Some Thoughts on the Archaeology of Pueblo Revolt Era Sites in the Jemez Region, New Mexico. In *Archaeologies of the Pueblo Revolt: Identity, Meaning, and Renewal in the Pueblo World*, edited by Robert W. Preucel, pp. 45–60. The University of New Mexico Press, Albuquerque.

Ellis, Florence Hawley
1951 Patterns of Aggression and the War Cult in Southwestern Pueblos. *Southwestern Journal of Anthropology* 7 (2): 177–201.

Ellis, Reuben (editor)
1997 *Stories and Stone: Writing the Ancestral Pueblo Homeland*. The University of Arizona Press, Tucson.

Ember, C.R., and M. Ember
1992 Resource Unpredictability, Mistrust, and War. *Journal of Conflict Resolution* 36 (2): 242–262.

Erdman, James A., Charles L. Douglas, and John W. Marr
1969 *Environment of Mesa Verde, Colorado*. Wetherill Mesa Studies. National Park Service, Washington, D.C.

Fagan, Brian M.
2000 *Ancient North America*. London.

Farmer, Malcolm F.
1957 A Suggested Typology of Defensive Systems of the Southwest. *Southwestern Journal of Anthropology* 13 (3): 249–266.

Ferguson, T.J.
1996 *Historic Zuni Architecture: An Archaeological Application of Space Syntax*. Anthropological Papers of the University of Arizona, No. 60. University of Arizona Press, Tucson.
2002 Dowa Yalanne: The Architecture of Zuni Resistance and Social Change during the Pueblo Revolt. In *Archaeologies of the Pueblo Revolt: Identity, Meaning, and Renewal in the Pueblo World*, edited by Robert W. Preucel, pp. 33–44. The University of New Mexico Press, Albuquerque.

Ferguson, T.J., and Barbara Mills
1987 Settlement and Growth of Zuni Pueblo: An Architectural History. *Kiva. The Journal of Southwestern Anthropology and History* 4 (52): 243–266.

Ferguson, T.J. and Chip Colwell-Chanthaphonh
2006 *History Is in the Land: Multivocal Tribal Traditions in Arizona's San Pedro Valley*. The University of Arizona Press, Tucson.

Ferguson, William M., and Arthur Rohn
1987 *Anasazi Ruins of the Southwest in Color*. University of New Mexico Press, Albuquerque, New Mexico.

Fewkes, Jesse Walter

1909 *Antiquities of the Mesa Verde National Park: Spruce-Tree House*. Smithsonian Institution, Bureau of American Ethnology, Bulletin 51. Government Printing Office, Washington, D.C.

1911 *Antiquities of the Mesa Verde National Park: Cliff Palace*. Smithsonian Institution, Bureau of American Ethnology, Bulletin 51. Government Printing Office, Washington, D.C.

1919 *Prehistoric Villages, Castles, and Towers of Southwestern Colorado*. Smithsonian Institution. Bureau of American Ethnology, Bulletin 70. Government Printing Office, Washington, D.C.

1920 Field-Work on the Mesa Verde National Park: Explorations and Field-Work for 1919. *Smithsonian Miscellaneous Collections* 72 (1): 47–64, Washington. D.C.

Fewkes, Jesse Walter, with introduction by Larry V. Nordby

1999 *Mesa Verde Ancient Architecture*. Avanyu Publishing Inc.

Fiero, Kathleen

1998 *Balcony House: A History of a Cliff Dwelling, Mesa Verde National Park, Colorado*. Manuscript on file, Mesa Verde Museum Association, Inc. Mesa Verde National Park, Colorado.

2002 *Mesa Verde National Park*, [HTML Title]. Conservation of Architectural Surfaces Program for Archaeological Resources. Architectural Conservation Laboratory & Research Center, the University of Pennsylvania. Available:http://www.design.upenn.edu/hspv/mesaverde/mesa_verde.htm. Date of use: April 15 2009.

Fish, Paul R., Suzanne K. Fish, and M. Elisa Villalpando (editors)

2007 *Trincheras Sites in Time, Space, and Society*. Amerind Studies in Archaeology, Vol. 1, Series editor John Ware. The University of Arizona Press, Tucson.

Flint, Richard

2005 What They Never Told You about the Coronado Expedition. *Kiva. The Journal of Southwestern Anthropology and History* 71 (2): 203–217.

Fowler, M.L.

1997 *The Cahokia Atlas: A Historical Atlas of Cahokia Archaeology*. Revised Edition. The University of Alabama Press, Tuscaloosa, London.

Gąssowski, Jerzy

1996 *Indianie Ameryki Północnej. Od początków po wiek XIX*. Wydawnictwo TRIO, Wyższa Szkoła Humanistyczna w Pułtusku, Warszawa.

Gediga, Bogusław (editor)

1989 *Studia nad grodami epoki brązu i wczesnej epoki żelaza w Europie Środkowej*. Prace Komisji Archeologicznej Nr 7, Polska Akademia Nauk, Oddział we Wrocławiu, Wrocław–Warszawa–Kraków–Gdańsk–Łódź.

Gedl, Marek

1989 Uwagi na temat grodów ludności kultury łużyckiej. In *Studia nad grodami epoki brązu i wczesnej epoki żelaza w Europie Środkowej*, edited by B. Gediga, pp. 153–158. Prace Komisji Archeologicznej Nr 7, Polska Akademia Nauk, Oddział we Wrocławiu, Wrocław–Warszawa–Kraków–Gdańsk–Łódź.

Getty, H.T.

1935a New Dates from Mesa Verde. *Tree-Ring Bulletin* 1 (3): 21–23.

1935b New Dates for Spruce Tree House, Mesa Verde. *Tree-Ring Bulletin* 1 (4): 28–29.

Gilpin, Dennis

2001 Boundaries of Tsegi Phase Architecture in Northeastern Arizona. In *The Archaeology of Ancient Tactical Sites*, edited by John R. Welch and Todd W. Bostwick, pp. 7–19. Papers from the 1998 Fall Symposium, Arizona Archaeological Council. The Arizona Archaeologist, Number 32.

Gleichman, Carol L., and Peter J. Gleichman
1989 *An Archaeological Inventory of Lower Sand Canyon, Montezuma County, Colorado.* Submitted to Bureau of Land Management, San Juan Resource Area Office, Durango, Colorado.
1992 The Lower Sand Canyon Survey. In *The Sand Canyon Archaeological Project: A Progress Report*, edited by William D. Lipe, pp. 25–31. Occasional Papers, No. 2. Crow Canyon Archaeological Center, Cortez, Colorado.

Glowacki, Donna M.
2001 *Yucca House (5MT5006) Mapping Project Report.* Manuscript on file, Crow Canyon Archaeological Center, Cortez, Colorado.
2006 *The Social Landscape of Depopulation: The Northern San Juan, A.D. 1150–1300.* Unpublished Doctoral Dissertation, Arizona State University, Tempe, USA.

Godłowski, Kazimierz
2000 *Pierwotne siedziby Słowian.* Instytut Archeologii Uniwersytetu Jagiellońskiego, Kraków.

Griffitts, Mary O.
1990 *Guide to the Geology of Mesa Verde National Park.* Mesa Verde Museum Association, Inc. Mesa Verde National Park, Colorado. Lorraine Press, Utah.

Grossman, A.
2006 Zarys rozwoju osadnictwa kultury łużyckiej w Biskupińskim Mikroregionie Osadniczym a środowisko przyrodnicze. In *Z badań nad osadnictwem epoki brązu i wczesnej epoki żelaza w Europie Środkowej*, edited by W. Blajer, pp. 9–34. Komisja Epoki Brązu i Wczesnej Epoki Żelaza, Komitet Nauk Pra- i Protohistorycznych Polskiej Akademii Nauk, Instytut Archeologii Uniwersytetu Jagiellońskiego, Kraków.

Haas, Jonathan, and Winifred Creamer
1993 Stress and Warfare Among the Kayenta Anasazi of the Thirteenth Century A.D. *Fieldiana Anthropology*, New Series, No. 21, Publication 1450. Field Museum of Natural History, Chicago.
1996 The Role of Warfare in the Pueblo III Period. In *The Prehistoric Pueblo World A.D. 1150–1350*, edited by Michael A. Adler, pp. 205–213. The University of Arizona Press, Tucson.
1997 Warfare Among the Pueblos: Myth, History and Ethnography. *Ethnohistory* 44 (2): 235–262.

Hacker, Barton C.
1994 Military Institutions, Weapons, and Social Change: Toward a New History of Military Technology. *Technology and Culture* 35 (4): 768–834.

Hammond, George P., and Agapito Rey
1940 *Narratives of the Coronado Expedition, 1540–1542.* University of New Mexico Press, Albuquerque.
1953 *Don Juan de Oñate: Colonizer of New Mexico, 1595–1628.* University of New Mexico Press, Albuquerque.

Hanel, Joe
2007 New Insights About Water at Mesa Verde. *The Durango Herald*, July 30.

Hard, Robert J., and John R. Roney
2007 Cerros the Trincheras in Northwestern Chihuahua: The Arguments for Defense. In *Trincheras Sites in Time, Space, and Society*, edited by Suzanne K. Fish, Paul R. Fish, and M. Elisa Villalpando, pp. 11–52. Amerind Studies in Archaeology, Vol. 1, Series editor John Ware. The University of Arizona Press, Tucson.

Harding, Anthony F., and Janusz Ostoja-Zagórski
1989 Funkcja grodów typu biskupińskiego w osadnictwie halsztackim w północno-wschodniej Wielkopolsce. In *Studia nad grodami epoki brązu i wczesnej epoki żelaza w Europie Środkowej*, edited by B. Gediga, pp. 171–183. Prace Komisji Archeologicznej Nr 7,

Polska Akademia Nauk, Oddział we Wrocławiu, Wrocław–Warszawa–Kraków–Gdańsk–Łódź.

Harrill, Bruce G. and Cory D. Breternitz
1976 Chronology and Cultural Activity in Johnson Canyon Cliff Dwellings: Interpretations from Tree-Ring Data. *Journal of Field Archaeology* 3 (4): 375–390.

Hayes, Alden C.
1964 *The Archeological Survey of Wetherill Mesa, Mesa Verde National Park, Colorado.* Archaeological Research Series, No. 7A. National Park Service. Washington, D.C.

Hensel, W.
1948 *Wstęp do studiów nad osadnictwem Wielkopolski wczesnohistorycznej*, Poznań.

Hill, W.W.
1982 *The Ethnography of Santa Clara Pueblo, New Mexico.* University of New Mexico Press, Albuquerque.

Holmes, W.H.
1876 A Notice of the Ancient Remains of Southwestern Colorado Examined During the Summer of 1875. *Bulletin of the Geological and Geographical Survey of the Territories* II (I): 3–24. Washington, D.C.
1878 Report of the Ancient Ruins of Southwestern Colorado, Examined During the Summers of 1875 and 1876. In *Annual Report of the United States Geological and Geographical Survey of the Territories, Embracing Colorado and Parts of Adjacent Territories; Being a Report of Progress of the Exploration for the Year 1876*, by F.V. Hayden, pp. 381–408. Government Printing Office, Washington, D.C.

Holt, H. Barry
1983 A Cultural Resource Management Dilemma: Anasazi Ruins and the Navajos. *American Antiquity* 48 (3): 594–599.

Ingersoll, Ernest
2006 A Hopi Story About Caste Rock. In *The Mesa Verde World. Explorations in Ancestral Pueblo Archaeology*, edited by David G. Noble, pp. 137–138. School of American Research Press, Santa Fe.

Jackson, W.H.
1876a Ancient Ruins of the Southwestern Colorado. In *Annual Report of the United States Geological and Geographical Survey of the Territories, Embracing Colorado and Parts of Adjacent Territories; Being a Report of Progress of the Exploration for the Year 1874*, by F.V. Hayden, pp. 367–381. Government Printing Office, Washington, D.C.
1876b A Notice of the Ancient Ruins in Arizona and Utah Lying About the Rio San Juan. *Bulletin of the Geological and Geographical Survey of the Territories* II (I): 25–45.

Jackson, W.H., and W.H. Holmes
1981 *Hayden Survey, 1874–1876: Mesa Verde and the Four Corners.* Bear Creek Publishing, Ouray, Colorado.

Jankuhn, Herbert
2004 *Wprowadzenie do archeologii osadnictwa* [An Introduction to Settlement Archaeology]. Poznańskie Towarzystwo Przyjaciół Nauk, Wznowienia tom 20, Poznań.

Jaworski, Krzysztof
2005 *Grody w Sudetach (VIII–X w.).* Instytut Archeologii, Uniwersytet Wrocławski, Wrocław.

Johnson, C. David
2003 Mesa Verde Region Towers: A View from Above. *Kiva. The Journal of Southwestern Anthropology and History* 68 (4): 323–340.

Johnson, Allen W., and Timothy Earle
1984 *The Evolution of Human Societies: From Foraging Group to Agrarian State.* Stanford University Press, Stanford, California (second edition).

Kara, Michał, and Marek Krąpiec

2000 Możliwości datowania metodą dendrochronologiczną oraz stan badań dendrochronologicznych wczesnośredniowiecznych grodzisk z terenu Wielkopolski, Dolnego Śląska i Małopolski. In *Ziemie polskie w X wieku i ich znaczenie w kształtowaniu się nowej mapy Europy*, edited by Henryk Samsonowicz, pp. 303–327. Universitas, Kraków.

Keeley, Lawrence H.

1996 *War Before Civilization: The Myth of the Peaceful Savage*. Oxford University Press, New York.

Keeley, Lawrence H., Marisa Fontana, and Russell Quick

2007 Baffles and Bastions: The Universal Features of Fortifications. *Journal of Archaeological Research* 15: 55–95.

Kelley, Jeffery Paul

1996 *Woods Canyon Pueblo: A Late Pueblo III Period Canyon-Oriented Site in Southwest Colorado*. Unpublished Ph.D. Dissertation, Washington State University, Pullman, USA.

Kemp, Brian M.

2006 *Mesoamerica and Southwest Prehistory, and the Entrance of Humans into the Americas: Mitochondrial DNA Evidence*. Unpublished Ph.D. Dissertation, University of California, Davis, USA.

Kenzle, Susan C.

1993 *Enclosing Walls: A Study of Architectural Function in the American Southwest*. Unpublished Master's thesis, University of Calgary, Calgary, Canada.

1997 Enclosing Walls in the Northern San Juan: Sociophysical Boundaries and Defensive Fortifications in the American Southwest. *Journal of Field Archaeology*, 2 (24): 195–210.

Kidder, Alfred V.

1924 *An Introduction to the Study of Southwestern Archaeology, with a Preliminary Account of the Excavations at Pecos*. Papers of the Phillips Academy Southwestern Expedition 1. Yale University Press, New Haven.

1927 Southwestern Archaeological Conference. *Science* 66: 489–491.

Knaut, Andrew L.

1997 *The Pueblo Revolt of 1680: Conquest and Resistance in Seventeenth-Century New Mexico*. University of Oklahoma Press.

Kleidon, James H.

1999a Mad Dog Tower. In *The Sand Canyon Archaeological Project: Site Testing,* CD-ROM Vers. 1.0., edited by Mark D. Varien. Crow Canyon Archaeological Center, Cortez, Colorado.

1999b Saddlehorn Hamlet. In *The Sand Canyon Archaeological Project: Site Testing,* CD-ROM Vers. 1.0., edited by Mark D. Varien. Crow Canyon Archaeological Center, Cortez, Colorado.

Kobyliński, Z.

1988 Konstrukcje, destrukcje i rekonstrukcje: w sprawie budownictwa starszych faz wczesnego średniowiecza na ziemiach polskich. *Archeologia Polski* 33 (1): 204–210.

Kohler, Timothy A.

2000 The Final 400 Years of Prehispanic Agricultural Society in the Mesa Verde Region. *Kiva. The Journal of Southwestern Anthropology and History* 66 (1): 195–202.

Kohler, Timothy A., George J. Gumerman, and R.G. Reynoldys

1993 News from the Northern Southwest: Prehistory on the Edge of Chaos. *Journal of Archaeological Research* 4 (1): 267–321.

2005 Simulating Ancient Societies. *Scientific American* 1 (293): 76–84.

Kohler, Timothy A., and Meredith H. Matthews
1998 Long-Term Anasazi Land Use and Forest Reduction: A Case Study from Southwest Colorado. *American Antiquity* 53 (3): 537–564.

Kohler, Timothy A., Mark D. Varien, Aaron M. Wright and Kristin A. Kuckelman
2008 Mesa Verde Migrations: New Archaeological Research and Computer Simulation Suggest why Ancestral Puebloans Deserted the Northern Southwest United States. *American Scientist* 96: 146–153.

Kolb, Michael J., and James E. Snead
1997 It's a Small World after All: Comparative Analyses of Community Organization in Archaeology. *American Antiquity* 62 (4): 609–628.

Kołodziejski, Stanisław
1995 Późne średniowiecze. In *Nauka i kultura w krajobrazie Jury: pradzieje i średniowiecze*, pp. 151–162. Zarząd Zespołu Jurajskich Parków Krajobrazowych w Krakowie, Kraków.

Kozłowski, Janusz K.
1999 Archeologia i jej metody. In *Encyklopedia historyczna świata*, edited by Janusz K. Kozłowski, pp. 12–19, Vol. 1. Opres, Kraków.

Kozłowski, Janusz K., and Piotr Kaczanowski
1998 *Wielka historia Polski, tom 1: Najdawniejsze dzieje ziem polskich (do VII w.)*. Fogra, Kraków.

Kruk, Janusz
2008 *Wzory przeszłości. Studia nad neolitem środkowym i późnym*. Instytut Archeologii i Etnologii Polskiej Akademii Nauk, Kraków.

Kruse, Melissa
2007 The Agricultural Landscape of Perry Mesa: Modeling Residential Site Location in Relation to Arable Land. *Kiva. The Journal of Southwestern Anthropology and History* 73 (1): 85–102.

Kuckelman, Kristin A.
2002 Thirteenth-Century Warfare in the Central Mesa Verde Region. In *Seeking the Center Place. Archaeology and Ancient Communities in the Mesa Verde Region*, edited by Mark D. Varien and Richard H. Wilshusen, pp. 233–253. The University of Utah Press, Salt Lake City.
2003 Architecture. In *The Archaeology of Yellow Jacket Pueblo (Site 5MT5): Excavations at a Large Community Center in Southwestern Colorado,* [HTML Title]. Available at: http://www.crowcanyon.org/yellowjacket. Date of use: 12 April 2009.
2006 Ancient Violence in the Mesa Verde Region. In *The Mesa Verde World. Explorations in Ancestral Pueblo Archaeology*, edited by David G. Noble, pp. 127–135. School of American Research School Press, Santa Fe.
2008 An Agent-Centered Case Study of the Depopulation of Sand Canyon Pueblo. In *The Social Construction of Communities. Agency, Structure, and Identity in the Prehispanic Southwest*, edited by Mark D. Varien and James M. Potter, pp. 109–121. Archaeology in Society Series, Series Editor Ian Hodder and Robert W. Preucel. Altamira Press, Rowman & Littlefield Publishers, Inc. Lanham, Boulder, NewYork–Toronto–Plymouth, UK.
2010 The Depopulation of Sand Canyon Pueblo, A Large Ancestral Pueblo Village in Southwestern Colorado. *American Antiquity*, 3 (75): 497–525.

Kuckelman, Kristin A. (editor)
2000 *The Archaeology of Castle Rock Pueblo: A Thirteenth-Century Village in Southwestern Colorado,* [HTML Title]. Available: http://www.crowcanyon.org/ResearchReports/CastleRock/Text/crpw_contentsvoume.asp. Date of use: 05 May 2008.
2003 *The Archaeology of Yellow Jacket Pueblo: Excavations at a Large Community Center in Southwestern Colorado*, [HTML Title]. Available: *http://www.crowcanyon.org/*

*ResearchReports/YellowJacket/Text/yjpw_contentsvolume.asp*. Date of use: 12 May 2008.

2007 *The Archaeology of Sand Canyon Pueblo: Intensive Excavations at a Late-Thirteenth-Century Village in Southwestern Colorado* [HTML Title]. Available: http://www.crowcanyon.org/sandcanyon. Date of use: 15 June 2009.

Kuckelman, Kristin A., Ricky R. Lightfoot, and Debra L. Martin

2000 Changing Patterns of Violence in the Northern San Juan Region. *Kiva. The Journal of Southwestern Anthropology and History* 1 (66): 147–166.

Kuckelman, Kristin A., Ricky R. Lightfoot, and Debra L. Martin

2002 The Bioarchaeology and Taphonomy of Violence at Castle Rock and Sand Canyon Pueblos, Southwestern Colorado. *American Antiquity* 3 (67): 486–513.

Kuckelman, Kristin A., and Scott G. Ortman

2003 Chronology. In *The Archaeology of Yellow Jacket Pueblo: Excavations at a Large Community Center in Southwestern Colorado*, [HTML Title]. Available: http://www.crowcanyon.org/ResearchReports/YellowJacket/Text/yjpw_contentsvolume.asp. Date of use: 12 June 2008.

Kuckelman, Kristin A., Mark D. Varien, Scott G. Ortman, and Jonathan D. Till

2004 *A Proposal to Conduct Archaeological Testing at the Goodman Point Ruins Group Unit of Hovenweep National Monument*. Manuscript on file, Crow Canyon Archaeological Center, Cortez, Colorado.

Kuckelman, Kristin A., and Grant D. Coffey

2007 *Report of 2006 Research at Goodman Point Pueblo (Site 5MT604), Montezuma County, Colorado*, [HTML Title]. Available: http://www.crowcanyon.org/goodmanpoint2006. Date of use: 15 October 2007.

Kuckelman, Kristin A., Bruce A. Bradley, Melissa J. Churchill, and James H. Kleidon

2007 A Descriptive and Interpretive Summary of Excavations, by Architectural Block. In *The Archaeology of Sand Canyon Pueblo: Intensive Excavations at a Late-Thirteenth-Century Village in Southwestern Colorado* [HTML Title], edited by Kristin A. Kuckelman. Available: http://www.crowcanyon.org/sandcanyon. Date of use: 15 June 2009.

Kuckelman, Kristin A. Grant D. Coffey, and Steven R. Copeland

2009 *Interim Descriptive Report of Research at Goodman Point Pueblo (Site 5MT604), Montezuma County, Colorado, 2005–2008*. Submitted to The Southeast Utah Group National Park Service and Hovenweep National Monument. [HTML Title]. Available: http://crowcanyon.org/ResearchReports/GoodmanPoint/interim_reports/2005_2008/GPP_interim_report_2005_2008.pdf. Date of use: November 11 2010.

Kuligowski, Waldemar

2003 Kanibal, mój bliźni. *Tawacin* 64 (4): 24–30.

Kurnatowska, Zofia

1991 Tworzenie się państwa pierwszych Piastów w aspekcie archeologicznym. In *Od plemienia do państwa. Śląsk na tle wczesnośredniowiecznej Słowiańszczyzny Zachodniej*, edited by Lech Leciejewicz, pp. 77–98. Śląskie Sympozja Historyczne tom 1. Polska Akademia Nauk, Uniwersytet Wrocławski, Wrocław, Warszawa.

2000 Wielkopolska w X wieku i formowanie się państwa polskiego. In *Ziemie polskie w X wieku i ich znaczenie w kształtowaniu się nowej mapy europy*, edited by Henryk Samsonowicz, pp. 99–117. Universitas, Kraków.

2008 Początki i rozwój państwa [The Origins and Development of the State]. In *Pradzieje Wielkopolski*, edited by M. Kobusiewicz, pp. 297–395. Instytut Archeologii i Etnologii, Polska Akademia Nauk, Poznań.

Lange, Charles H.

1959 *Cochiti. A New Mexico Pueblo, Past and Present*. University of Texas Press, Austin.

Lange, F., N. Mahaney, J.B. Wheat, and M.L. Chenault
1986 *Yellow Jacket: A Four Corners Anasazi Ceremonial Center.* Johnson Books, Boulder, Colorado.

LeBlanc, Steven A.
1999 *Prehistoric Warfare in the American Southwest.* University of Utah Press, Salt Lake City.
2001 Warfare and Aggregation in the El Morro Valley, New Mexico. In *Deadly Landscapes: Case Studies in Prehistoric Southwestern Warfare*, edited by Glen E. Rice and Steven A. LeBlanc, pp. 19–49. University of Utah Press, Salt Lake City.

LeBlanc, Steven A., and Katherine E. Register
2003 *Constant Battles. The Myth of the Peaceful, Noble Savage.* St. Martin's Press, New York.

Lekson, Stephen H.
2002 War in the Southwest, War in the World. *American Antiquity* 4 (67): 607–24.
2005 Complexity. In *Southwest Archaeology in the Twentieth Century*, edited by Linda S. Cordell and Don D. Fowler, pp. 157–173. University of Utah Press, Salt Lake City.

Lekson, Stephen H., and Catherine M. Cameron
1995 The Abandonment of Chaco Canyon, the Mesa Verde Migrations, and the Reorganization of the Pueblo World. *Journal of Anthropological Archaeology* 14 (2): 143–169.

Liebmann, Matthew, T.J. Ferguson, and Robert W. Preucel
2005 Pueblo Settlement, Architecture, and Social Change in the Pueblo Revolt Era, A.D. 1680 to 1696. *Journal of Field Archaeology* 30 (1): 45–60.

Lightfoot, Ricky R., and Kristin A. Kuckelman
2001 A Case of Warfare in the Mesa Verde Region. In *Deadly Landscapes: Case Studies in Prehistoric Southwestern Warfare*, edited by Glen E. Rice and Steven A. LeBlanc, pp. 51–64. University of Utah Press, Salt Lake City.

Linton, Ralph
1944 Nomads Raids and Fortified Pueblos. *American Antiquity* 10 (1): 28–32.

Lipe, William D.
1970 Anasazi Communities in the Red Rock Plateau, Southeastern Utah. In *Reconstructing Prehistoric Pueblo Societies*, edited by William A. Longacre, pp. 84–139. Advanced Seminar Series, School of American Research Press, University of New Mexico Press, Albuquerque.
1974 A Conservation Model for American Archaeology. *Kiva. The Journal of Southwestern Anthropology and History* 39 (3–4): 213–245.
1992 Introduction. In *The Sand Canyon Archaeological Project: A Progress Report*, edited by William D. Lipe, pp. 1–10. Occasional Papers, No. 2. Crow Canyon Archaeological Center, Cortez, Colorado.
1994 Comments on Population Aggregation and Community Organization. In *The Ancient Southwestern Community: Models and Methods for the Study of Prehistoric Social Organization*, edited by W.H. Wills and Robert D. Leonard, pp. 141–143. University of New Mexico Press, Albuquerque.
1995a The Depopulation of the Northern San Juan: Conditions in the Turbulent 1200s. *Journal of Anthropological Archaeology* 14: 143–169.
1995b *National Register of Historic Places Registration Form: Woods Canyon Pueblo (5MT 11842).* United States Department of the Interior, National Park Service.
1995c *National Register of Historic Places Registration Form: Seven Towers Pueblo (Site 5MT1000).* United States Department of the Interior, National Park Service.
1996 *National Register of Historic Places Registration Form: Site 5MT 338 (Cannonball Ruins).* United States Department of the Interior, National Park Service.
1999a History of Archaeology. Chapter 3. In *Colorado Prehistory: A Context for the Southern Colorado River Basin*, edited by William D. Lipe, Mark D. Varien, and Richard H. Wilshusen, pp. 51–94. Colorado Council of Professional Archaeologists, Denver.

1999b Basketmaker II (1000 B.C.–A.D. 500). Chapter 5. In *Colorado Prehistory: A Context for the Southern Colorado River Basin*, edited by William D. Lipe, Mark D. Varien, and Richard H. Wilshusen, pp. 132–165. Colorado Council of Professional Archaeologists, Denver.

2002 Social Power in the Central Mesa Verde Region, A.D. 1150–1290. In *Seeking the Center Place: Archaeology and Ancient Communities in the Mesa Verde Region*, edited by Mark D. Varien and Richard H. Wilshusen, pp. 203–232. The University of Utah Press, Salt Lake City.

Lipe, W.D. (editor)

1992 *The Sand Canyon Archaeological Project: A Progress Report*. Occasional Papers, no. 2. Crow Canyon Archaeological Center, Cortez, Colorado.

Lipe, William D., Michelle Hegmon (editors)

1989 *The Architecture of Social Integration in Prehistoric Pueblos*. Occasional Papers of Crow Canyon Archaeological Center No. 1.

Lipe, William D., Mark D. Varien, and Richard H. Wilshusen (editors)

1999 *Colorado Prehistory: A Context for the Southern Colorado River Basin*, edited by William D. Lipe, Mark D. Varien, and Richard H. Wilshusen. Colorado Council of Professional Archaeologists, Denver.

Lipe, William D., and Mark D. Varien

1999a Pueblo II (A.D. 900–1150). Chapter 8. In *Colorado Prehistory: A Context for the Southern Colorado River Basin*, edited by William D. Lipe, Mark D. Varien, and Richard H. Wilshusen, pp. 242–289. Colorado Council of Professional Archaeologists, Denver.

1999b Pueblo III (A.D. 1150–1300). Chapter 9. In *Colorado Prehistory: A Context for the Southern Colorado River Basin*, edited by William D. Lipe, Mark D. Varien, and Richard H. Wilshusen, pp. 290–352. Colorado Council of Professional Archaeologists, Denver.

2003 *Sand Canyon Archaeological District (preferred) / 5MT.16853*. National Register of Historic Places Registration Form. National Park Service.

Lipe, William D., and Scott G. Ortman

2000 Spatial Patterning in Northern San Juan Villages, A.D. 1050–1300. *Kiva. The Journal of Southwestern Anthropology and History* 1 (66): 91–122.

Lipe, William D., and Kristin A. Kuckelman

2007 History of Investigations. In *The Archaeology of Sand Canyon Pueblo: Intensive Excavations at a Late-Thirteenth-Century Village in Southwestern Colorado* [HTML Title], edited by Kristin A. Kuckelman. Available: http://www.crowcanyon.org. Date of use: 15 June 2009.

Lomotuway'ma, Michael, Lorena Lomatuway'ma, and Sidney Namingha, Jr.

1993 *Hopi Ruin Legends*. Collected, translated and edited by Ekkehart Malotki. University of Nebraska Press, Lincoln.

Luebben, Ralph A.

1982 Two Pueblo III Kiva Complexes Associated with Subterranean Rooms, Southwestern Colorado. *Kiva. The Journal of Southwestern Anthropology and History* 1–2 (48): 63–82.

1983 The Grinnell Site: A Small Ceremonial Center Near Yucca House, Colorado. *Journal of Intermountain Archaeology* 2 (2): 1–26.

Luebben, Ralph A., and Paul R. Nickens

1982 A Mass Interment in Early Pueblo III Kiva in Southwestern Colorado. *Journal of Intermountain Archaeology* 1 (1): 66–79.

Lyons, Patrick D.

2003 *Ancestral Hopi Migrations*. Anthropological Papers of the University of Arizona, No. 68. University of Arizona Press, Tucson.

Malotki, Ekkehart

1993 The Destruction of Awat'ovi. In *Hopi Ruin Legends*, by Michael Lomotuway'ma, Lorena Lomatuway'ma, and Sidney Namingha, Jr. Collected, translated and edited by Ekkehart Malotki, pp. 275–97. University of Nebraska Press, Lincoln.

Malville, J. McKim

1991 Prehistoric Astronomy in the American Southwest. *The Astronomy Quarterly* 8: 1–36.

2006 The Cosmic and the Sacred at Yellow Jacket Pueblo and Mesa Verde. In *The Mesa Verde World: Explorations in Ancestral Pueblo Archaeology*, edited by David G. Noble, pp. 85–91. School of American Research Press, Santa Fe.

Malville, J. McKim, and Gregory E. Munson

1998 Astronomy at Balcony House. Appendix F. In *Balcony House: A History of a Cliff Dwelling, Mesa Verde National Park, Colorado*. Manuscript on file by Kathleen Fiero. Mesa Verde Museum Association, Inc., Mesa Verde National Park, Colorado.

Martin, Curtis W.

1976 *Archaeological Inventory of the Sand Canyon Cliff Dwelling Area, Montezuma County, Colorado*. Manuscript on File, Colorado Historical Society, Denver.

Matson, Richard G.

1991 *The Origins of Southwestern Agriculture*. The University of Arizona Press, Tucson.

Matson, Richard G., William D. Lipe, and W.R. Haase

1988 Adaptational Continuities and Occupational Discontinuities: The Cedar Mesa Anasazi. *Journal of Field Archaeology* 15 (3): 245–264.

McBride, Kevin A.

1990 The Historical Archaeology of the Mashantucket Pequots, 1637–1900: A Preliminary Analysis. In *The Pequots in Southern New England: The Fall and Rise of an American Indian Nation*, edited by Laurence M. Hauptman and James D. Wherry, pp. 96–116. University of Oklahoma Press, Norman.

McMahon, Todd

2000 Paradox Valley, Colorado: Cultural Interactions and Considerations for Reinterpretation. *Southwestern Lore* 66 (3): 1–29.

McMahon, Todd, and Ken Bedingfield

2001 *Reconnaissance Survey of Sites Near Paradox Valley, Montrose County, Colorado*. Prepared for The Bureau of Land Management, Uncompahgre Field Office Montrose, CO.

Metcalf, Mary Patricia

1997 *Civic Spaces: Architectural Expressions of Political Organization in the Prehistoric Northern Southwest, A.D. 1000–1300*. Unpublished Master's thesis, University of Virginia, USA.

Mindeleff, Victor

1989 [1891] *A Study of Pueblo Architecture: Tusayan and Cibola*. 8th Annual Report of the Bureau of Ethnology to the Secretary of the Smithsonian Institution, 1886–1887. Government Printing Office, Washington, D.C.

Minge, Ward Alan

1976 *Acoma: Pueblo in the Sky*. University of New Mexico Press, Albuquerque.

Mitchell, Donald H.

1968 Excavations at two trench embankments in the Gulf of Georgia region. *Syesis*, Vol. 1: 29–46.

Mobley-Tanaka, Jeanette L.

1997 The History and Prehistory of Yellow Jacket. *Southwestern Lore* 1 (63): 1–5.

2005 *Community from Within: Intracommunity Interaction and the Social Formulation of the Yellow Jacket Community, Southwest Colorado, A.D. 1200–1300*. Unpublished Ph.D. Dissertation, Arizona State University, Tempe, USA.

Morgan, William
1994 *Ancient Architecture of the Southwest*. University of Texas Press, Austin.

Morley, Sylvanus G.
1908 The Excavation of the Cannonball Ruins in Southwestern Colorado. *American Anthropologist* New Series 10 (4): 596–610.
1917 The Archaeology of McElmo Canyon, Colorado. *El Palacio* IV (4): 41–70.

Morris, Earl H.
1929 *Field Notes, Canyon del Muerto, 1929*. Western Archaeological Center, National Park Service, Tucson.

Moss, Madonna L, and Jon M. Erlandson
1992 Forts, Refuge Rocks, and Defensive Sites: The Antiquity of Warfare Along the North Pacific Coast of North America. *Arctic Anthropology* 29 (2): 73–90.

Munson, Gregory E.
2008 *Fewkes Digital Archive Project*. Paper presented in 81st Pecos Conference, Flagstaff, AZ.

Nabokov, Peter, and Robert Easton
1989 *Native American Architecture*. Oxford University Press. New York, Oxford.

Naranjo, Tessie
1995 Thoughts on Migration by Santa Clara Pueblo. *Journal of Anthropological Archaeology* 14: 247–250.
2006 "We Came from the South, We Came form the North". Some Tewa Origin Stories. In *The Mesa Verde World. Explorations in Ancestral Pueblo Archaeology*, edited by David G. Noble, pp. 49–57. School of American Research School Press, Santa Fe.

Nelson, Margaret C., and Gregson Schachner
2002 Understanding Abandonments in the North American Southwest. *Journal of Archaeological Research* 10 (2): 167–206.

Nichols, Robert F., and Thomas P. Harlan
1967 Archaeological Tree-Ring Dates from Wetherill Mesa. *Tree-Ring Bulletin* 28 (1–4): 12–40.

Nordby, Larry V.
2001 *Prelude to Tapestries in Stone: Understanding Cliff Palace Architecture*. Archeological Research Series Architectural Studies Number 4. Mesa Verde National Park Division of Research and Resource Management. Mesa Verde National Park, Colorado. With contributions by Joel M. Brisbin and Jim Mayberry.
2006 Understanding Mesa Verde's Cliff Dwelling Architecture. In *The Mesa Verde World. Explorations in Ancestral Pueblo Archaeology*, edited by David G. Noble, pp. 111–117. School of American Research School Press, Santa Fe.

Nordenskiöld, Gustaf Eric A.
1990 [1893] *The Cliff Dwellers of the Mesa Verde, Southwestern Colorado. Their Pottery and Implements*. Reprinted from original 1893 printing, translated by D. Lloyd Morgan. Mesa Verde Museum Association, Inc. Mesa Verde National Park, Colorado.

Nowicki, K.
2000 *Defensible Sites in Crete c. 1200–800 B.C. (LM IIIB/IIIC through Early Geometric)*. Aegaeum, Liège–Austin, 21.

Nusbaum, Jesse L. (Transcribed and annotated by Kathleen Fiero)
1998a Report on the Repair and Excavation of Balcony House. In *Balcony House: A History of a Cliff Dwelling, Mesa Verde National Park, Colorado*, Manuscript on file, by Kathleen Fiero, pp. 81–104. Mesa Verde Museum Association, Inc. Mesa Verde National Park, Colorado.

1998b Field Notes on Balcony House. Appendix D. In *Balcony House: A History of a Cliff Dwelling, Mesa Verde National Park, Colorado.* Manuscript on file, by Kathleen Fiero. Mesa Verde Museum Association, Inc. Mesa Verde National Park, Colorado.

O'Bryan, Deric

1950 Excavations in Mesa Verde National Park, 1947–1948. *Medallion Papers* No. 39. Gila Pueblo Foundation, Globe, Arizona.

Ortiz, Alfonso

1969 *The Tewa World. Space, Time & Becoming in a Pueblo Society*. University of Chicago Press, Chicago.

Ortman, Scott G.

2008 Action, Place, and Space in the Castle Rock Community. In *The Social Construction of Communities. Agency, Structure, and Identity in the Prehispanic Southwest*, edited by Mark D. Varien and James M. Potter, pp. 125–154. Archaeology in Society Series, Series Editor Ian Hodder and Robert W. Preucel. Altamira Press, Rowman & Littlefield Publishers, Inc. Lanham, Boulder, NewYork, Toronto, Plymouth, United Kingdom.

2009 *Genes, Language and Culture in Tewa Ethnogenesis, A.D. 1150–1400*. Unpublished Ph.D. Dissertation. Arizona State University, Tempe.

Ortman, Scott G., Donna M. Glowacki, Melissa J. Churchill, and Kristin A. Kuckelman

2000 Pattern and Variation in Northern San Juan Region. *Kiva. The Journal of Southwestern Anthropology and History* 66 (1): 123–146.

Ortman, Scott G., and Bruce A. Bradley

2002 Sand Canyon Pueblo: The Container in the Center. In *Seeking the Center Place. Archaeology and Ancient Communities in the Mesa Verde Region*, edited by Mark D. Varien and Richard H. Wilshusen, pp. 41–78. The University of Utah Press, Salt Lake City.

Osborne, Douglas (Assembled by)

1965 *Contributions of the Wetherill Mesa Archaeological Project*. Memoirs of the Society for American Archaeology No. 19. Salt Lake City. Issued as American Antiquity, Vol. 31 (2), Part 2.

Otterbein, Keith

1970 *The Evolution of War: A Cross-Cultural Study*. HRAF Press, New Haven.

Palonka, Radosław

2009 *Defensive Architecture and the Depopulation of the Mesa Verde Region, Utah-Colorado, USA in the XIII Century A.D.* Unpublished Ph.D. dissertation, Jagiellonian University, Kraków, Poland.

2010 Late Pueblo III Sites in Lower Sand Canyon Locality, Montezuma County, Colorado – Preliminary Report of the Archeological Survey of 2009. *Polish Contributions in New World Archaeology*, New Series, fasc. 2, ed. by J.K. Kozłowski and J. Źrałka, pp. 113–144.

Palonka, Radosław, and Kristin A. Kuckelman

2008 *Archaeological research at Goodman Point Pueblo and the depopulation of the Mesa Verde Region, Utah-Colorado, USA*. In Polish Contributions in New World Archaeology, New Series, Fasc. 1, edited by J.K. Kozłowski and J. Źrałka, pp. 129–168. Polska Akademia Umiejętności – Instytut Archeologii UJ, Kraków.

2009 Goodman Point Pueblo: Research on the Final Period of Settlement of the Ancestral Pueblo Indians in the Mesa Verde Region, Colorado, USA. The Preliminary Report, 2005–2006 Seasons. *Recherches Archeologiques*, Nouvelle Serie 1, ed. by W. Blajer, pp. 543–567.

Parks, James A., and Jeffrey S. Dean (With annotations by Kathleen Fiero)

1998 Tree-Ring Dating of Balcony House: A Chronological, Architectural, and Social Interpretation. Appendix B. In *Balcony House: A History of a Cliff Dwelling, Mesa Verde*

*National Park, Colorado*, Manuscript on file by Kathleen Fiero. Mesa Verde Museum Association, Inc., Mesa Verde National Park, Colorado.

Parson, Elsie Clews
1929 *The Social Organization of the Tewa of New Mexico*. American Anthropological Association, Memoirs, No. 36.

Pauketat, Timothy R.
1994 *The Ascent of Chiefs: Cahokia and Mississippian Politics in Native North America*. The University of Alabama Press, Tuscaloosa.

Peet, Stephen D.
1899 Relics of the Cliff-Dwellers. *The American Antiquarian and Oriental Journal*, March/April.

Plog, Stephen
1997 *Ancient Peoples of the American Southwest*. Thames & Hudson, London.

Poleski, Jacek
1995 Wczesne Średniowiecze. In *Nauka i kultura w krajobrazie Jury: pradzieje i średniowiecze*. Zarząd Zespołu Jurajskich Parków Krajobrazowych w Krakowie, Kraków, pp. 137–150.
2004 *Wczesnośredniowieczne grody w dorzeczu Dunajca*. Institute of Archaeology, Jagiellonian University, Kraków.
2008 Zagadka wielkich grodów Wiślan i Lędzian. *Alma Mater* 99: 78–84.

Posern-Zieliński, Aleksander
1997 Antropologia kulturowa wobec archeologicznej rekonstrukcji społeczeństw pradziejowych. In *Jakiej archeologii potrzebuje współczesna humanistyka*, edited by J. Ostoja-Zagórski, pp. 93–111. Instytut Archeologii Uniwersytetu Adama Mickiewicza (UAM), Poznań.

Posern-Zieliński, Aleksander, and Janusz Ostoja-Zagórski
1977 Etnologiczna interpretacja i analogie etnograficzne w postępowaniu badawczym archeologii i prahistorii. *Slavia Antiqua* 24: 39–71.

Powell, John Wesley
1961 [1895] *The Explorations of the Colorado River and its Canyons [Canyons of the Colorado]*. Dover Publications, Inc., New York.

Preucel, Robert W. (editor)
2002 *Archaeologies of the Pueblo Revolt: Identity, Meaning, and Renewal in the Pueblo World*. The University of New Mexico Press, Albuquerque.

Prudden, T. Mitchell
1903 The Prehistoric Ruins of the San Juan Watershed in Utah, Arizona, Colorado, and New Mexico. *American Anthropologist* New Series 5 (2): 224–288.

Rainey, Katharine D., and Sandra Jezik
2002 Archaeobotanical Remains. In *The Archaeology of Woods Canyon Pueblo: A Canyon-Rim Village in Southwestern Colorado,* [HTML Title]. Available: http://www.crowcanyon.org/woodscanyon. Date of use: 6 December 2008.

Renfrew, Colin, and Paul Bahn
2002 *Archeologia. Teoria, metody, praktyka*. Prószyński i S-ka, Warszawa.

Rice, Glen E. and Steven A. LeBlanc (editors)
2001 *Deadly Landscapes: Case Studies in Prehistoric Southwestern Warfare*. The University of Utah Press, Salt Lake City.

Riley, Carroll L.
1987 *The Frontier People: The Greater Southwest in the Protohistoric Period*. Revised and Expanded Edition, University of New Mexico Press.

Roberts, David

1993 'Reverse Archaeologists' are Tracing the Footsteps of a Cowboy-Explorer. *Smithsonian*, December, Vol. 24, Issue 9.

1999 A Social Divide Written in Stone. *Smithsonian*, February, Vol. 29, Issue 11: 118–128.

Rohn, Arthur H.

1963a An Ecological Approach to the Great Pueblo Occupation of the Mesa Verde, Colorado. *Plateau* 36 (1): 1–17.

1963b Prehistoric Soil and Water Conservation on Chapin Mesa, Southwestern Colorado. *American Antiquity* April 4 (28): 441–455.

1965 Postulation of Socio-Economic Groups from Archaeological Evidence. Contributions of the Wetherill Mesa Archaeological Project. In *Memoirs of the Society for American Archaeology*, *American Antiquity*, vol. 31, no. 2, part 2: 65–69.

1971 *Mug House, Mesa Verde National Park – Colorado*. Archaeological Research Series Number 7-D. National Park Service, Washington, D.C.

1977 *Cultural Change and Continuity on Chapin Mesa*. Regents Press of Kansas, Lawrence.

1989 Northern San Juan Prehistory. In *Dynamics of Southwest Prehistory* edited by Linda S. Cordell and George J. Gumerman, pp. 149–178. School of American Research Advanced Seminar Book. Smithsonian Institution Press, Washington, D.C.

Rohn, Arthur H., and William M. Ferguson

2006 *Puebloan Ruins of the Southwest*. University of New Mexico Press, Albuquerque.

Roney, John R.

1995 Mesa Verdean Manifestation South of the San Juan River. *Journal of Anthropological Archaeology* 14: 170–183.

Rudofsky, Bernard

2003 *Architecture Without Architects: A Short Introduction to Non-Pedigreed Architecture*. University of New Mexico Press, Albuquerque.

Rydzewski, Jacek

1995 Epoka brązu i wczesna epoka żelaza. In *Nauka i kultura w krajobrazie Jury: Pradzieje i średniowiecze*, pp. 93–112. Zarząd Zespołu Jurajskich Parków Krajobrazowych w Krakowie, Kraków.

Sand Canyon Electronic Database

2004 *The Sand Canyon Pueblo Database (Site 5MT765)*, [HTML Title]. Available: http://www.crowcanyon.org/ResearchReports/dbw/dbw_chooser.asp?Site=5MT765. Date of use: 08 June 2008.

Schaafsma, Polly

1980 *Indian Rock Art of the Southwest*. School of American Research, Santa Fe, and University of New Mexico Press, Albuquerque.

Schulman, Albert

1950 Pre-Columbian Towers in the Southwest. *American Antiquity* 15 (4): 288–297.

Schulman, Edmund

1946 Dendrochronology at Mesa Verde National Park. *Tree-Ring Bulletin* 12 (3): 18–24.

Shaw, Justine

2003 Climate Change and Deforestation: Implications for the Maya Collapse. *Ancient Mesoamerica* 14: 157–167.

Smith, Jack E.

1987 *Mesas, Cliffs, and Canyons. The University of Colorado Survey of Mesa Verde National Park 1971–1977*. Mesa Verde Research Series, Paper No. 3. Mesa Verde Museum Association, Inc., Mesa Verde National Park, Colorado.

Smith, Duane A.

2002 *Mesa Verde National Park: Shadows of the Centuries*. Revised Edition, The University Press of Colorado. Originally published in 1988 by the University Press of Kansas.

Smith, Duane A. (editor)

2005 *Mesa Verde National Park: The First 100 Years*. Mesa Verde Museum Association.

Snead, James E.

2005 *Ancestral Pueblo Warfare and Migration in the Galisteo Basin, New Mexico*. Report of the Tano Origins Project, 2005 Season.

2008 *Ancestral Landscapes of the Pueblo World*. The University of Arizona Press, Tucson.

Snow, Dean R.

2004 *The Iroquois*. Blackwell Publishing, Malden, Oxford, Carlton.

Spielmann, Katherine A.

1994 Clustered Confederacies: Sociopolitical Organization in the Protohistoric Rio Grande. In *Ancient Southwest Community: Models and Methods for the Study of Prehistoric Social Organization*, edited by H. Wills, and Robert Leonard, pp. 45–54. University of New Mexico Press, Albuquerque.

2005 Ethnographic Analogy and Ancestral Pueblo Archaeology. In *Southwest Archaeology in the Twentieth Century*, edited by Linda S. Cordell and Don D. Fowler, pp. 194–203. University of Utah Press, Salt Lake City.

Spoerl, Patricia M., and George J. Gumerman (editors)

1984 *Prehistoric Cultural Development in Central Arizona: Archaeology of the Upper New River Region*. Southern Illinois University at Carbondale Center for Archaeological Investigations Occasional Paper No. 5. Carbondale.

*Spruce Tree House Guide*.

Mesa Verde National Park Guidebooks, Mesa Verde Museum Association, Colorado.

Stanisławski, M.B.

1979 Hopi-Tewa. In *Southwest*, edited by A. Ortiz, pp. 578–602. Handbook of North American Indians, Vol. 9. W.C. Sturdevant, general editor. Smithsonian Institution, Washington, D.C.

Street, David J.

2001a *The Dendroarchaeology of Long House, an Anasazi Cliff Dwelling in Mesa Verde National Park, Colorado, USA*. Unpublished Ph.D. Dissertation, Vol. 1–2, The University of Sheffield, Great Britain.

2001b How Fast is a Kiva? The Dendroarchaeology of Long House, Mesa Verde National Park, Colorado. *Kiva. The Journal of Southwestern Anthropology and History* 67 (2): 137–165.

Śmigielski, Wojciech

1991 Grody kultury łużyckiej w Wielkopolsce. Wstęp do problematyki. In *Prahistoryczny gród w Biskupinie: Problematyka osiedli obronnych na początku epoki żelaza*, edited by Jan Jaskanis, pp. 23–35. Państwowe Muzeum Archeologiczne. Wydawnictwo Naukowe PWN, Warszawa.

Tabaczyński, S.

1998 Procesy etnogenetyczne: Doświadczenia badawcze archeologii i przyszłość. In *Słowianie w Europie wcześniejszego średniowiecza. Katalog wystawy*, pp. 79–93. Państwowe Muzeum Archeologiczne, Warszawa.

Thompson, Ian M.

2002 Native American Perspectives on Sand Canyon Pueblo and Other Ancestral Sites. In *Seeking the Center Place: Archaeology and Ancient Communities in the Mesa Verde Region*, edited by Mark D. Varien and Richard H. Wilshusen, pp. 257–262. The University of Utah Press, Salt Lake City.

2004 *The Towers of Hovenweep*. Canyonlands Natural History Association, Moab, Utah.

Thompson, Ian M., Mark Varien, Susan Kenzle, and Rina Swentzell

1997 Prehistoric Architecture with Unknown Function. In *Anasazi Architecture and American Design*, edited by Baker H. Morrow and V.B. Price, pp. 149–158. University of New Mexico Press, Albuquerque.

Tkaczuk, Diana C., and Brian C. Vivian (editors)

1989 *Cultures in Conflict: Current Archaeological Perspectives*. Proceedings of the Twentieth Annual Conference of the Archaeological Association of the University of Calgary.

Topolski, Jerzy

2000 O interpretacji i nadinterpretacji w archeologii. In *Archeologia w teorii i praktyce*, edited by A. Buko, and P. Urbańczyk, pp. 65–73. Warszawa: Naukowa Oficyna Wydawnicza Scientia.

Torres-Reyes, Ricardo

1970 *Mesa Verde National Park. An Administrative History 1906–1970*. United States Department of the Interior National Park Service Office of History and Historic Architecture Eastern Service Center, Washington, D.C.

Towner, Ronald H.

1999 Eighteenth-Century Navajo Defensive Sites in the Dintah. *Archaeology Southwest* 13 (2): 8–9.

2004 *Defending the Dintah. Pueblitos in the Ancestral Navajo Heartland*. The University of Utah Press, Salt Lake City.

Towner, Ronald H., Hugh C. Rogers, and James M. Copeland

2001 Changing Threats, Changing Responses: Tactical Aspects of the Navajo Pueblitos of Dintah. In *The Archaeology of Ancient Tactical Sites*, edited by John R. Welch and Todd W. Bostwick, pp. 111–130. Papers from the 1998 Fall Symposium, Arizona Archaeological Council. The Arizona Archaeologist number 32.

Trewartha, G.T.

1954 *An Introduction to Climate*. McGraw-Hill, New York.

Trimble, Charles E., Barbara W. Sommer, and Mary Kay Quinlan

2008 *The American Indian Oral History Manual. Making Many Voices Hear*. Left Coast Press, Inc., Walnut Creek, California.

Turner II, Christy G., and Jacqueline A. Turner

1999 *Man Corn. Cannibalism and Violence in the Prehistoric American Southwest*. The University of Utah Press, Salt Lake City.

Upham, Steadman, Patricia L. Crown, and Fred Plog

1994 Alliance Formation and Cultural Identity in the American Southwest. In *Themes in Southwest Prehistory*, edited by George J. Gumerman, pp. 183–210. School of American Research Press, Santa Fe.

Urbańczyk, Przemysław

2000 Początki państw wczesnośredniowiecznych w Europie Środkowowschodniej. In *Ziemie polskie w X wieku i ich znaczenie w kształtowaniu się nowej mapy Europy*, edited by Henryk Samsonowicz, pp. 53–70. Universitas, Kraków.

Van West, Carla R., Jeffrey S. Dean

2000 Environmental Characteristics of the A.D. 900–1300 Period in the Central Mesa Verde Region. *Kiva. The Journal of Southwestern Anthropology and History* 66 (1): 19–44.

Vansina, J.

1985 *Oral Tradition as History*. University of Wisconsin Press, Madison.

Varien, Mark D.

1999 *Sedentism and Mobility in a Social Landscape. Mesa Verde & Beyond*. The University of Arizon Press, Tucson.

2000 Introduction. *Kiva. The Journal of Southwestern Anthropology and History* 66 (1): 5–18.

2002 Persistent Communities and Mobile Households: Population Movement in the Central Mesa Verde Region, A.D. 950 to 1290. In *Seeking the Center Place: Archaeology and Ancient Communities in Mesa Verde Region*, edited by Mark D. Varien and Richard H. Wilshusen, pp. 163–184. The University of Utah Press, Salt Lake City.

2006 Turbulent Times in the Mesa Verde World. In *The Mesa Verde World. Explorations in Ancestral Pueblo Archaeology*, edited by David G. Noble, pp. 39–47. School of American Research School Press, Santa Fe.

Varien, Mark D. (editor)

1999 *The Sand Canyon Archaeological Project: Site Testing,* CD-ROM Vers. 1.0. Crow Canyon Archaeological Center, Cortez, Colorado.

Varien, Mark D., William D. Lipe, Michael A. Adler, Ian M.Thompson, and Bruce A. Bradley

1996 Southwestern Colorado and Southeastern Utah Settlement Patterns: AD 1100 to 1300. In *The Prehistoric Pueblo World, A.D. 1150–1350*, edited by Michael A. Adler, pp. 86–113. The University of Arizona Press, Tucson.

Varien, Mar D., Tito Naranjo, Marjorie R. Connolly, and William D. Lipe

1999 Native American Issues and Perspectives. In *Colorado Prehistory: A Context for the Southern Colorado River Basin*, edited by William D. Lipe, Mark D. Varien, and Richard H. Wilshusen, pp. 370–404. Colorado Council of Professional Archaeologists, Denver.

Varien, Mark D., Carla R. Van Vest, and G. S. Patterson

2000 Competition, Cooperation, and Conflict: Agricultural Production Community Catchments in the Central Mesa Verde Region. *Kiva. The Journal of Southwestern Anthropology and History* 66 (1): 45–65.

Varien, Mark D., and Richard H. Wilshusen

2002 A Partnership for Understanding the Past: Crow Canyon Research in the Central Mesa Verde Region. In *Seeking the Center Place: Archaeology and Ancient Communities in Mesa Verde Region*, edited by Mark D. Varien and Richard H. Wilshusen. The University of Utah Press, Salt Lake City, pp. 3–23.

Varien, Mark D., and Scott Ortman

2005 Accumulations Research in the Southwest United States: Middle-Range Theory for Big-Picture Problems. *World Archaeology* 37 (1), Archaeology in North America: 132–155.

Varien, Mark D., and Richard H. Wilshusen (editors)

2002 *Seeking the Center Place: Archaeology and Ancient Communities in Mesa Verde Region.* The University of Utah Press, Salt Lake City.

Varien, Mark D., Scott G. Ortman, Timothy A. Kohler, Donna M. Glowacki, and C. David Johnson

2007 Historical Ecology in the Mesa Verde Region: Results from the Village Ecodynamics Project. *American Antiquity* 72 (2): 273–299.

Varien, Mark D., and James S. Potter

2008 The Social Production of Communities: Structure, Agency, and Identity. In *The Social Construction of Communities: Agency, Structure, and Identity in the Prehispanic Southwest*, edited by Mark D. Varien and James M. Porter, pp. 1–18. Altamira Press, Lanham, Boulder, New York, Toronto, Plymouth, UK.

Watkins, Joe E.

2003 Beyond the Margin: American Indians, First Nations, and Archaeology in North America. *American Antiquity* 68 (2): 273–285.

Watson, Don

1950 *Cliff Palace. The Story of An Ancient City*. Edwards Brothers, Inc. Ann Arbor, Michigan.

1961 *Cliff Dwellings of the Mesa Verde: A Story in Pictures*. Mesa Verde Museum Association, Mesa Verde National Park, Colorado.

Wenger, Gilbert R.

1980 *The Story of Mesa Verde National Park*. Mesa Verde Museum Association, Inc. Mesa Verde National Park, Colorado.

Welch, John R., and Todd W. Bostwick (editors)

2001 *The Archaeology of Ancient Tactical Sites*. Papers from the 1998 Fall Symposium, Arizona Archaeological Council. The Arizona Archaeologist number 32.

White, Leslie A.

1935 *The Pueblo of Santo Domingo, New Mexico*. American Anthropological Association. Memoirs, No. 43.

1942 *The Pueblo of Santa Ana, New Mexico*. American Anthropological Association American Anthropologist New Series, Memoirs, No. 60.

Whitman, William

1969 [1947] *The Pueblo Indians of San Ildefonso*. No. 34 in the Columbia University Contributions to Archaeology. AMS Press, Inc., New York.

Wiese, Larry T.

2007 First Annual Centennial Strategy for Yucca House National Monument. In *The Future of America's National Parks*.

Wilcox, David R.

1991 Changing Contexts of Pueblo Adaptation. In *Farmers, Hunters, and Colonists Interactions Between the Southwest and the Southern Plains*, edited by Katherine Spielmann, pp. 128–154. University of Arizona Press, Tucson.

2005 Perry Mesa and Its World. *Plateau* vol. 2, no. 1 Spring/Summer.

Wilcox, David R., Jonathan Haas

1994 The Scream of the Butterfly. Competition and Conflict in the Prehistoric Southwest. In *Themes in Southwest Prehistory*, edited by George J. Gumerman, pp. 211–238. School of American Research Press, Santa Fe.

Wilcox, David R., Gerald Robertson Jr., and J. Scott Wood

2001a Antecedents to Perry Mesa: Early Pueblo III Defensive Refuge Systems in West-Central Arizona. In *Deadly Landscapes: Case Studies in Prehistoric Southwestern Warfare*, edited by Glen E. Rice and Steven A. LeBlanc, pp. 109–140. The University of Utah Press, Salt Lake City.

2001b Organized for War: The Perry Mesa Settlement System and Its Central Arizona Neighbors. *Deadly Landscapes: Case Studies in Prehistoric Southwestern Warfare*, edited by Glen E. Rice and Steven A. LeBlanc, pp. 141–194. The University of Utah Press, Salt Lake City.

Winship, George Parker

1904 *The Journey of Coronado, 1540–1542: From the City of Mexico to the Grand Canon of the Colorado and the Buffalo Plains of Texas, Kansas and Nebraska. As Told by Himself and His Followers*. A.S. Barnes & Company, New York.

Winter, Joseph C.

1975 *Hovenweep 1974 Archeological Report, No. 1*. San Jose State University, California.

1976 *Hovenweep 1975 Archeological Report, No. 2*. San Jose State University, California.

1977 *Hovenweep 1976 Archeological Report, No. 3*. San Jose State University, California.

Wilshusen, Richard H.

1999a Basketmaker III (A.D. 500–750). Chapter 6. In *Colorado Prehistory: a Context for the Southern Colorado River Basin*, edited by William D. Lipe, Mark D. Varien, and Richard H. Wilshusen, pp. 166–195. Colorado Council of Professional Archaeologists, Denver.

1999b Pueblo I (A.D. 750–900) Chapter 7. In *Colorado Prehistory: a Context for the Southern Colorado River Basin*, edited by William D. Lipe, Mark D. Varien, and Richard H. Wilshusen, pp. 196–241. Colorado Council of Professional Archaeologists, Denver.

2002 Estimating Population in the Central Mesa Verde Region. In *Seeking the Center Place: Archaeology and Ancient Communities in Mesa Verde Region*, edited by Mark D. Varien and Richard H. Wilshusen, pp. 101–120. The University of Utah Press, Salt Lake City.

2006 The Genesis of Pueblos. In *The Mesa Verde World. Explorations in Ancestral Pueblo Archaeology*, edited by David G. Noble, pp. 19–27. School of American Research School Press, Santa Fe.

Wilshusen, Richard H., Melissa J. Churchill, and James M. Potter
1997 Prehistoric Reservoirs and Water Basins in the Mesa Verde Region: Intensification of Water Collection Strategies during the Great Pueblo Period. *American Antiquity* 62 (4): 664–681.
Wojenka, Michał
2008 Duże i małe, czyli kilka uwag o grodziskach plemiennych. *Alma Mater* 99: 276–282.
Woodbury, Richard B.
1979 Prehistory: Introduction. In *Southwest*, edited by A. Ortiz, pp. 22–42. Handbook of North American Indians, Vol. 9. W.C. Sturdevant, general editor. Smithsonian Institution, Washington, D.C.
Woods Canyon Pueblo Database
2003 *The Woods Canyon Pueblo Database*, [HTML Title]. Available: http://www.crowcanyon.org/woodscanyondatabase. Date of use: 12 November 2008.
Wright, Kenneth R.
2006 *The Water Mysteries of Mesa Verde*. Johnson Books, Boulder, Colorado.
Wright, Kenneth R., Christopher Crowley, Geoffrey Crowley
2008 *Erosion Control at Ancient Mesa Verde*, [HTML Title]. Available: http://www.erosion-control.com/julyaugust2008/ancientmesaverde.aspx#comment_form. Date of use: 8 December 2008.
Yellow Jacket Electronic Database
2003 *The Yellow Jacket Pueblo Database*, [HTML Title]. Available: *http://www.crowcanyon.org/ResearchReports/dbw/dbw_chooser.asp?Site=5MT5*. Date of use: 12 December 2008.
Zimmerman, Larry J.
2003 *Indianie Ameryki Północnej*. Świat Książki, Warszawa.

Other unpublished sources (obtained from Crow Canyon Archaeological Center, Cortez, Colorado and Anasazi Heritage Center, Dolores, Colorado):

Archaeological Component Form
Cultural Resource Reevaluation Form
Final Nomination Form and National Register Files
Inventory Record of Site
Management Data Form
Prehistoric Archaeological Component Form
Stabilization Inventory Form

Internet Web Pages:

http://www.cs.uwaterloo.ca/~shallit/moonhouse.html
http://www.britannica.com/EBchecked/topic/214241/fortification
http://www.blm.gov/nm/st/en.html
http://archive.cyark.org
http://www.nps.gov/meve/historyculture/partnerships.htm
http://www.nps.gov/yuho
http://www.crowcanyon.org
http://www.kennewick-man.com

# PHOTOGRAPHS

Fig. 26. Cliff Palace; looking southeast (photograph by the author)

Fig. 27. Southern part of Cliff Palace (photograph by the author)

Fig. 28. Cliff Palace, looking from south (photograph by the author)

Fig. 29. View of upper ledge in Cliff Palace (photograph by the author)

Fig. 30. Upper interior part of square tower (Room 11) in Cliff Palace (photograph by the author)

Fig. 31. Part of Balcony House (photograph by the author)

Fig. 32. Spruce Tree House; looking east (photograph by the author)

Fig. 33. Central part of Spruce Tree House with rooms and a kiva (photograph by the author)

Fig. 34. Long House; looking east (photograph by the author)

Fig. 35. Central part of Long House with lower and upper ledges (photograph by the author)

Fig. 36. Part of the Long House with ladders for communication between lower and upper levels (photograph by the author)

Fig. 37. View of eastern part of the village-enclosing wall in Goodman Point Pueblo (photograph by the author)

Fig. 38. Goodman Point Pueblo: Room 205 with the *metate* bin feature in northeastern corner of the room (photograph by the author)

Fig. 39. Goodman Point Pueblo: southern part of partly excavated Kiva 307 (photograph by the author)

Fig. 40. Goodman Point Pueblo: part of the structure (probably tower) in Block 1000 (photograph by the author)

Fig. 41. Stone axe in situ in one of the structures at Goodman Point Pueblo (photograph by K. Kuckelman Courtesy of Crow Canyon Archaeological Center)

Fig. 42. Burned chunk of adobe with impressions of tree branches (part of burned roof of Kiva 501) (photograph by the author)

Fig. 43. Painted pottery sherds from Goodman Point Pueblo (photograph by K. Kuckelman, Courtesy of Crow Canyon Archaeological Center)

Fig. 44. Cannonball Ruins; looking southwest (photograph by the author)

Fig. 45. Cannonball Ruins; looking northeast (photograph by the author)

Fig. 46. Cannonball Ruins: D-shaped structure located on the canyon rim (photograph by the author)

Fig. 47. View of the surrounding area outside Cannonball Ruins from one of the loopholes in rectangular tower located in eastern edge of the site (photograph by the author)

Fig. 48. Castle Rock Pueblo; looking northeast (photograph by the author)

Fig. 49. Castle Rock Pueblo: Structure 404/409 with loophole in east wall, and north face of butte (photograph by the author)

Fig. 50. Rock art in Castle Rock Pueblo showing the fighting peoples (photograph by the author)

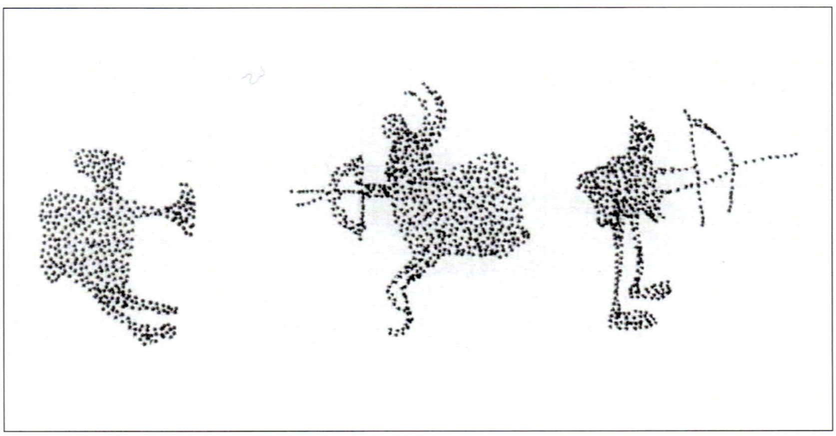

Fig. 51. Drawing of rock art in Castle Rock Pueblo (drawing by K. Kuckelman, Courtesy of Crow Canyon Archaeological Center)

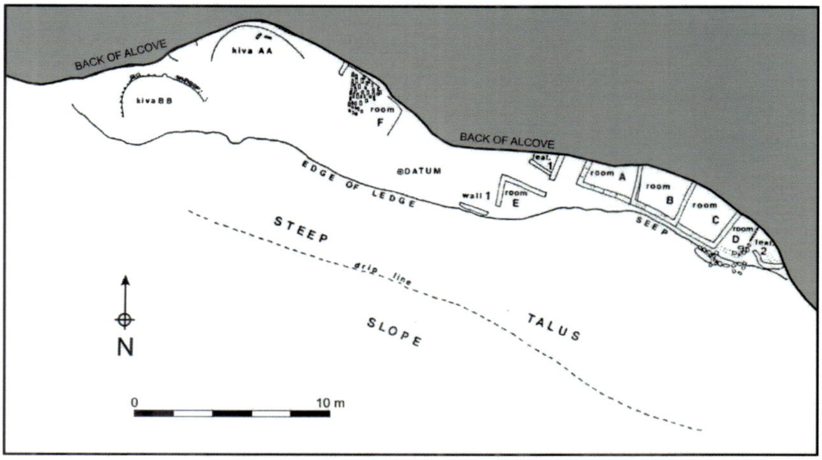


Fig. 52. Plan of the Site 5MT127, Vision House (after Gleichman and Gleichman 1989: 44, Figure 16 modified by A. Danecki)

Fig. 53. Vision House; looking northeast (photograph by the author)

Fig. 54. Part of Vision House (photograph by the author)

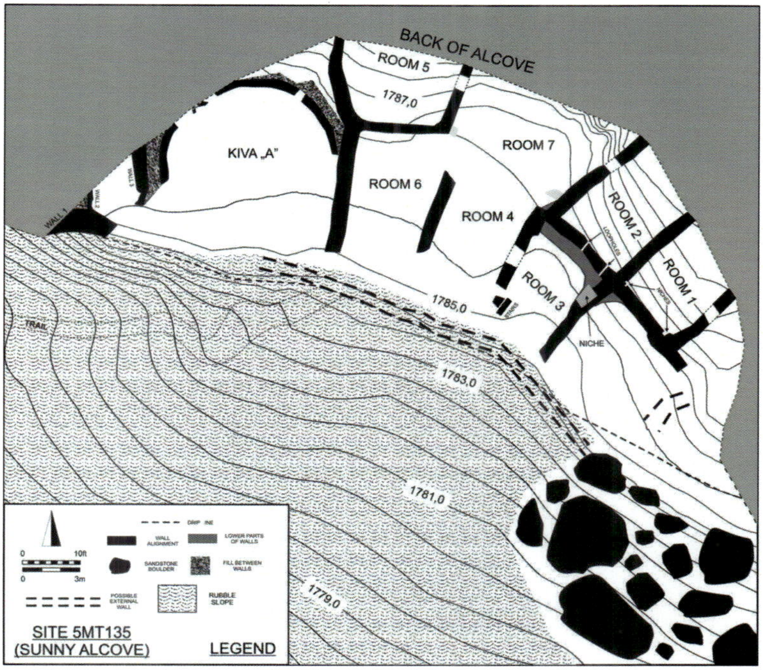


Fig. 55. Plan of the Site 5MT135, Sunny Alcove (drawing by A. Danecki, Sand Canyon-Castle Rock Community Archaeological Project)

Fig. 56. Sunny Alcove. View from the tower (Site 5MT13446) considered as a part of the site (photograph by the author)

Fig. 57. Wall S in Room 2, Sunny Alcove site with two visible loopholes (photograph by the author)

Fig. 58. Wall W of Room 3, Sunny Alcove site (photograph by the author)

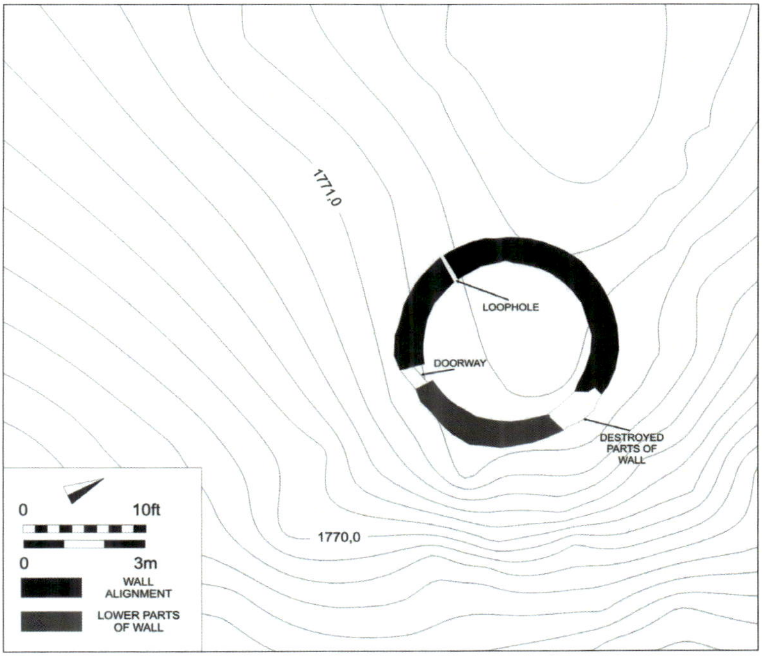


Fig. 59. Plan of tower (Site 5MT13446) located close to Sunny Alcove site (drawing by A. Danecki, Sand Canyon-Castle Rock Community Archaeological Project)

Fig. 60. Site 5MT13446, tower with visible loophole; looking from northwest (photograph by the author)

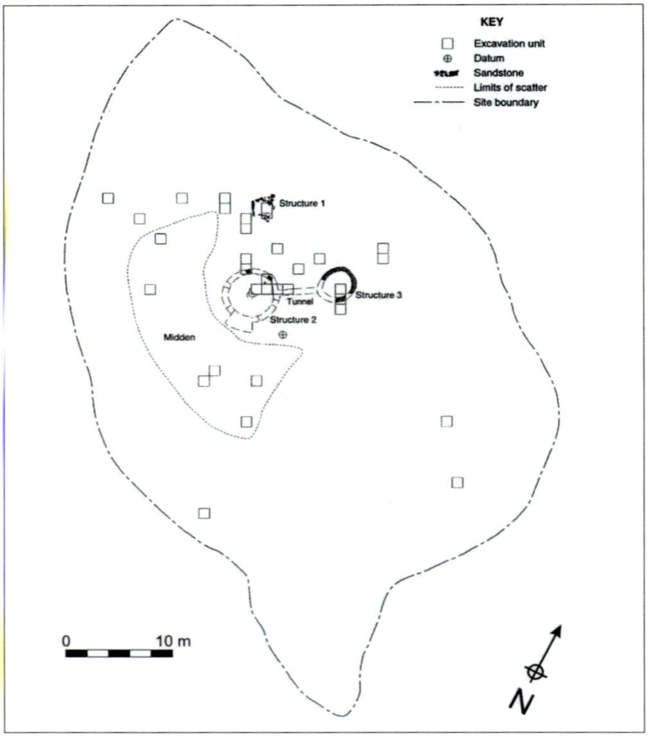


Fig. 61. Plan of the site 5MT181, Mad Dog Tower (after Lipe and Varien 2003; Figure 17 modified by A. Danecki)

Fig. 62. Mad Dog Tower (photograph by the author)

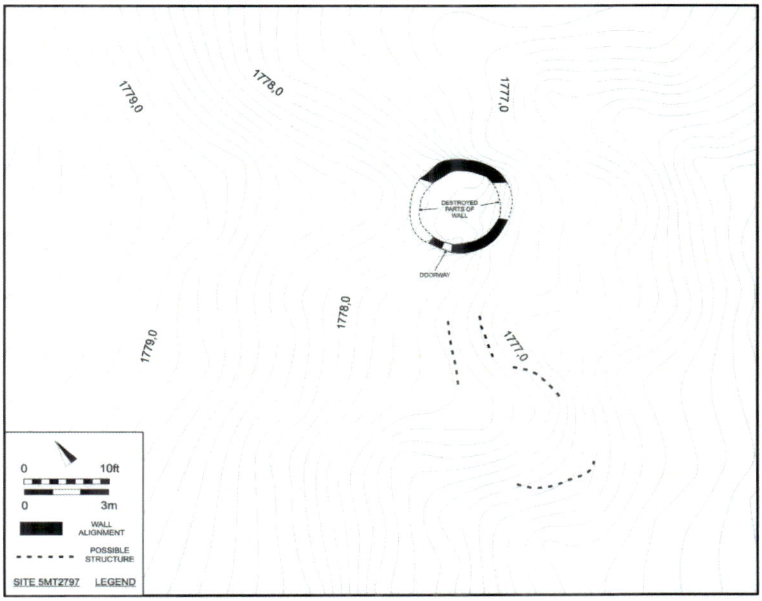


Fig. 63. Plan of tower in the Site 5MT2797 (drawing by A. Danecki, Sand Canyon-Castle Rock Community Archaeological Project)

Fig. 64. Tower in the Site 5MT2797, view from above (photograph by the author)

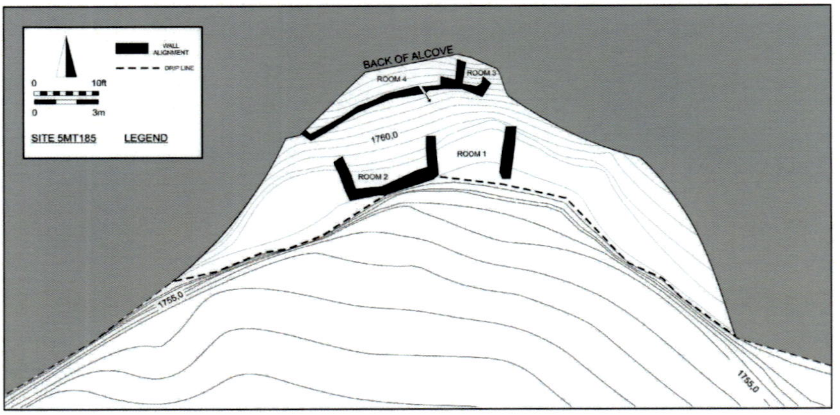


Fig. 65. Plan of the Site 5MT185 (drawing by A. Danecki, Sand Canyon-Castle Rock Community Archaeological Project)

Fig. 66. Site 5MT185 (photograph by the author)

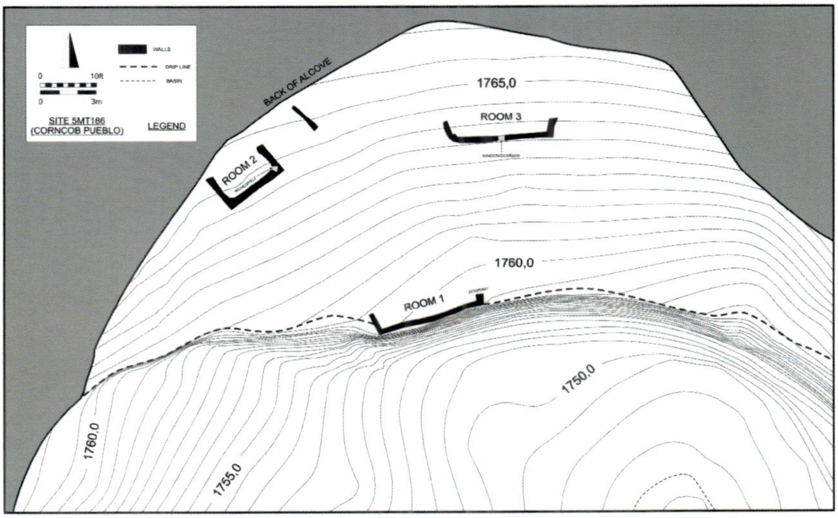


Fig. 67. Plan of the Site 5MT186, Corncob Pueblo (drawing by A. Danecki, Sand Canyon-Castle Rock Community Archaeological Project)

Fig. 68. Corncob Pueblo (photograph by the author)

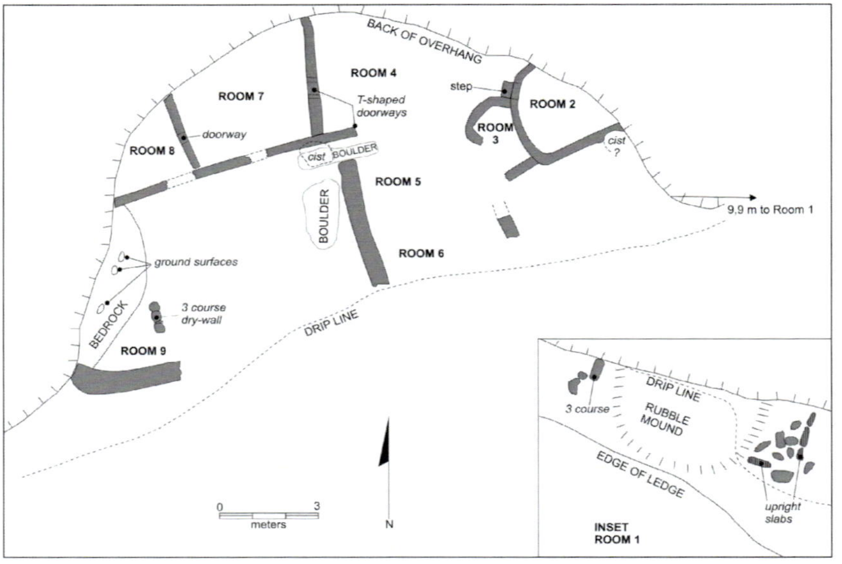


Fig. 69. Plan of the Site 5MT261 (after Ruins Stabilization Inventory Form 1975 modified by M. and. M. Przybyła)

Fig. 70. Site 5MT261 (photograph by the author)

Fig. 71. View from the Site 5MT261 to the Site 5MT257 (photograph by the author)

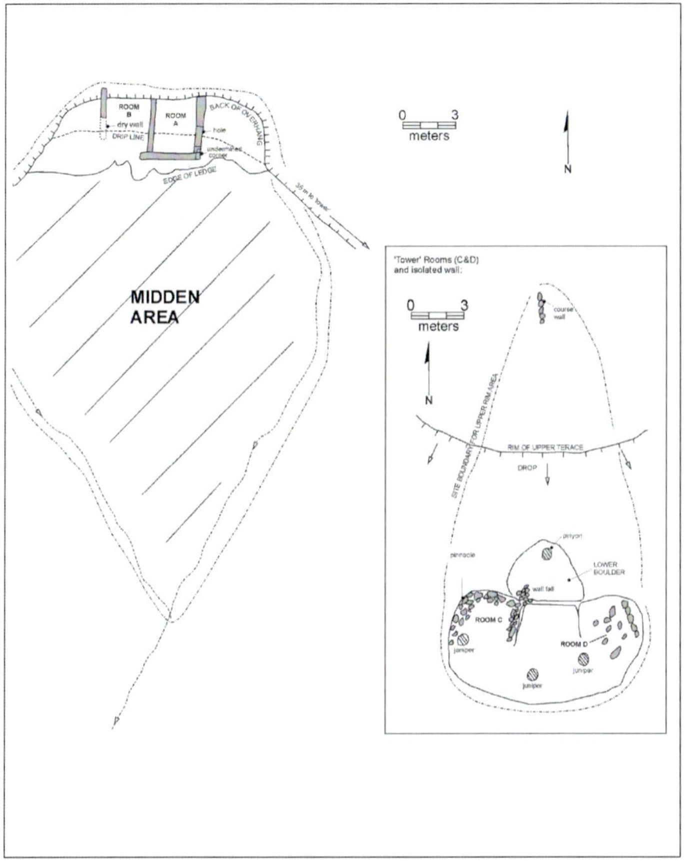


Fig. 72. Plan of the Site 5MT262, Saddlehorn Hamlet, with plan of the tower (after and Archaeological Component Form 1988 modified by M. and M. Przybyła)

Fig. 73. Saddlehorn Hamlet (photograph by the author)

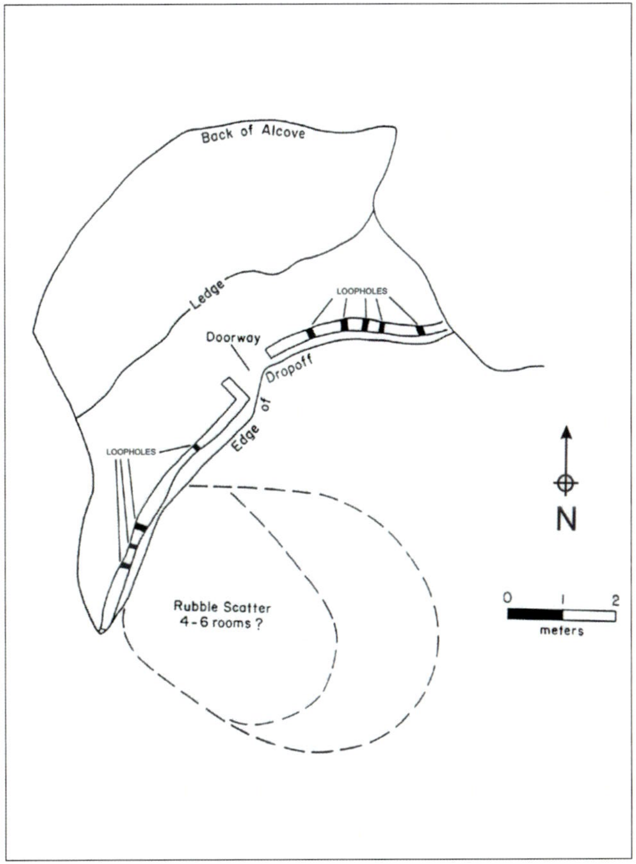


Fig. 74. Plan of the Site 5MT1826 (after Adler and Metcalf 1992: 41, Fig. 12 modified by A. Danecki)

Fig. 75. Site 5MT1826; general view (photograph by the author)

Fig. 76. Part of the Site 5MT1826 (outer wall with loopholes), (photograph by the author)

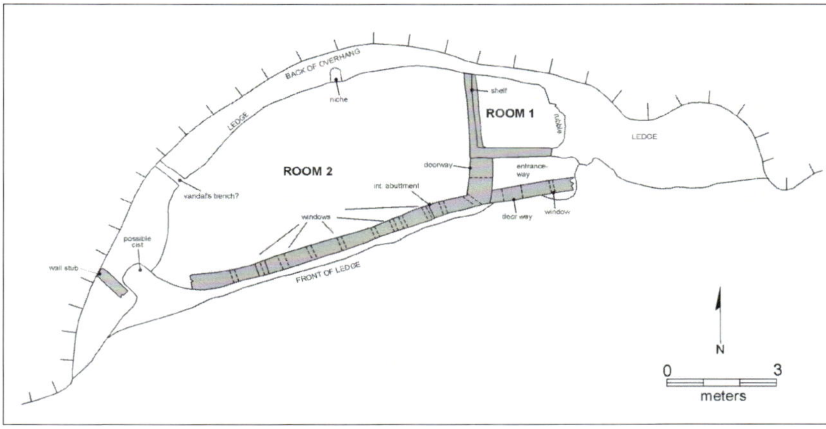


Fig. 77. Plan of the Site 5MT1831 (after Ruins Stabilization Inventory Form 1975 modified by M. and M. Przybyła)

Fig. 78. Site 5MT1831 (photograph by the author)

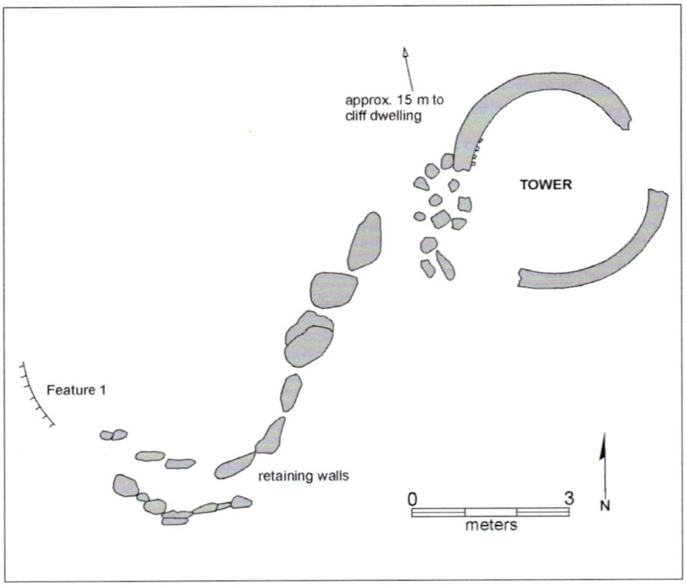


Fig. 79. Plan of tower located in the Site 5MT1831 (after Ruins Stabilization Inventory Form 1975 modified by M. and M. Przybyła)

Fig. 80. Ruins of the Site 5MT1831 tower (view from the alcove above the tower), (photograph by the author)